THE S. MARK TAPER FOUNDATION

IMPRINT IN JEWISH STUDIES

BY THIS ENDOWMENT
THE S. MARK TAPER FOUNDATION SUPPORTS
THE APPRECIATION AND UNDERSTANDING
OF THE RICHNESS AND DIVERSITY OF
JEWISH LIFE AND CULTURE

The publisher gratefully acknowledges the generous support of the Jewish Studies Endowment Fund of the University of California Press Foundation, which was established by a major gift from the S. Mark Taper Foundation.

The publisher also gratefully acknowledges the generous contribution to this book provided by the Koret Foundation.

JUDAISMS

JUDAISMS

A TWENTY-FIRST-CENTURY INTRODUCTION
TO JEWS AND JEWISH IDENTITIES

AARON J. HAHN TAPPER

For supplementary teaching tools, go to ucpress.edu/go/judaisms
and click on the Downloads tab.

UNIVERSITY OF CALIFORNIA PRESS

University of California Press, one of the most distinguished
university presses in the United States, enriches lives around
the world by advancing scholarship in the humanities, social
sciences, and natural sciences. Its activities are supported by
the UC Press Foundation and by philanthropic contributions
from individuals and institutions. For more information, visit
www.ucpress.edu.

University of California Press
Oakland, California

Library of Congress Cataloging-in-Publication Data

Names: Tapper, Aaron J. Hahn, author.
Title: Judaisms : a twenty-first-century introduction to Jews and
    Jewish identities / Aaron J. Hahn Tapper.
Description: Oakland, California : University of California Press,
    [2016]
Identifiers: LCCN 2016003686 | ISBN 9780520281349 (cloth : alk.
    paper) | ISBN 9780520281356 (pbk. : alk. paper) |
    ISBN 9780520960008 (ebook)
Subjects: LCSH: Judaism.
Classification: LCC BM562 .T37 2016 | DDC 296—dc23
LC record available at http://lccn.loc.gov/2016003686

The poem "Sinai" (p. 86) is from Merle Feld, *A Spiritual Life:
Exploring the Heart and Jewish Tradition,* rev. ed. (Albany: State
University of New York Press), © 2007 by State University of New
York. Reprinted by permission. All rights reserved.

The text "The Seeker" (p. 87) is from Andrew Ramer, *Queering the
Text: Biblical, Medieval, and Modern Jewish Stories* (Maple Shade,
NJ: White Crane Books, an imprint of Lethe Press, Inc.), © 2010
by Andrew Ramer. Reprinted by permission. All rights reserved.

Manufactured in the United States of America

25 24 23 22 21 20 19 18 17
10 9 8 7 6 5 4 3 2

The paper used in this publication meets the minimum
requirements of ANSI/NISO Z39.48-1992 (R 2002) (*Permanence
of Paper*).

To Mom and Dad
Thank you for everything

CONTENTS

Supplementary Resources (ONLINE AT UCPRESS.EDU/GO/JUDAISMS)

Key Terms

Timeline of Major Texts

Activities

Notes

PREFACE

Methods and Assumptions

Selectivity and Limits

This book aims to reflect the collective Jewish memory. Yet as renowned scholar Harold Bloom writes, "Jewish memory is a highly selective process." Although the information provided in this book was chosen with intention, of course it covers only a small slice of Jewish historical experiences. It presents pieces of the "Jewish puzzle" that together make up a multicolored, multivaried tapestry of Jewish identities. It is written as an "Introduction to Judaism" book, first and foremost for university students, and is designed to be used in a one-semester, fourteen-week course setting. That said, it can also be read like any other book of nonfiction.

An Interdisciplinary and Comparative Approach

This book is predicated on the notion that the best way to look at Judaisms and Jewish identities is through an interdisciplinary lens. It considers social identities by relying on sociology and historiography, theology and history. It utilizes anthropology, popular culture, and literature to expand the notion of religion, rather than constricting it to belief and faith alone. This necessitates the framing of Jewish-specific events using a comparative approach, contextualizing them within the larger non-Jewish milieu while also examining other religious communities' traditions in relation to Judaism.

For example, the Jewish diaspora is looked at within Diaspora Studies; the Jewish genocide (the Shoah) is discussed within Genocide Studies; Jewish nationalism is examined within the context of other communal nationalisms. And yet, as Melanie Kaye/Kantrowitz explains (herself a Jew, thus the first-person voice): "The common Jewish practice is to name our experiences differently from those with whom we might share it. Jews say antisemitism, not racism against Jews; Jews say Zion-ism, not nationalism for Jews. We cling to the name Holocaust as ours only, anxious about whether other genocides deserve the name. All this separate naming makes it harder to identify and analyze commonality and difference." The processes of familiarization and defamiliarization are fundamental to the process of deconstruction and reevaluation, especially when trying to better understand something that, from a community's own perspective, is often thought to be sui generis (one of a kind).

Focus on United States and Israel

One of the goals of this book is to reexamine dominant Jewish narratives and rituals. In order to do so, it is important to understand just what said narratives are. Only then can we look at how—and why—certain voices have been included and others excluded.

Today's dominant Jewish narratives are disproportionately rooted in the experiences of Jews living in just two countries—the United States and Israel—where roughly 80 percent of all Jews reside. Historically speaking, this phenomenon is both recent and highly unusual; within the context of a communal history that dates back more than three thousand years and stretches to almost every country in the world, this trend has only been dominant for an infinitesimal period of time.

A second reason for focusing on Jews living in these two countries is that this book is primarily written for an American audience, Jews and non-Jews alike. While chapter 1 explicitly uses dominant American narratives as a springboard into a discussion about Jewish narratives, American points of reference are relied on throughout to provide additional explanatory context.

Historical Ambiguity and Relativism

This book is less concerned with facts than with the perception of facts, referred to here as "truth" (see chapter

1). It is sometimes possible to uncover the past, to figure out what happened in a given time and place. But this book assumes that understandings of the past tell more about who is interpreting information and how it is being interpreted than about what actually happened. This applies to the performance of all identities, including Jewish ones.

For any given topic, this book's general approach is to present an assortment of currently prevalent academic theories. Sometimes these arguments are presented alongside nonacademic perspectives. In such situations, the intent is not to pass judgment on what is fact and what is not, or to weigh in on which scholars' hypotheses are more probable than others. Rather, this book contends that when speaking about history—in particular ancient history, but sometimes contemporary events as well—we are often discussing what is likely to have occurred rather than what definitively happened. The intent is to present both "facts" and "truth" together, teasing out for the reader the often nebulous line that separates the two.

Summaries and New Information

Although this book presents new ways to understand Jews and Judaisms, many sections summarize others' scholarly work. For this reason, I am entirely indebted to the countless individuals for whom uncovering this historical information has been their life's work.

Gendered, Sexed, and Sexualized Jewish Identities

Many "Introduction to Community X" books have a chapter on women or, on occasion, queer members of the group at hand. Such presentations obviously bifurcate these topics, as if women, for instance, have not always been central to the formation of said community. This book attempts to integrate subordinated gendered, sexed, and sexualized identities (e.g., women and queers) into the fabric of the overall discussion. (See special topic 0.2 in the introduction for more on the term *queer*.)

Editorial Practices

Websites and Newspapers

A number of popular websites have been used to support the information presented in the book, such as MyJew-ishLearning.com. Similarly, the book's content relies on a handful of reputable newspapers and online media, such as the *Jewish Daily Forward, Haaretz,* the *New York Times,* and *Ynetnews.* This method integrates information from outside the realm of academic scholarship, making the text more user-friendly and less dense and esoteric (i.e., less "academic").

Online Notes

To paraphrase a number of scholars, within this single book are two different books. One is for general readers: those who are in the introductory phase of learning about Jews, Judaisms, and Jewish identities, such as undergraduate university students or other nonspecialists. The second, comprising hundreds of notes, is for those who are already familiar with much of the book's content, such as graduate students and scholars, or anyone who is interested in learning more about what is mentioned in the main text, including the references on which these ideas are based. In an effort not to overburden readers, the notes only appear online (at ucpress.edu/go/judaisms) as part of the book's supplementary resources (which also include activities, key terms, and a timeline).

Transliteration and Spelling

For the most part, the book presents transliterations of non-English words, most of which are originally found in Hebrew, according to the standards of *AJS Review,* the journal of the Association for Jewish Studies. On occasion, more normative spellings are utilized in an effort to make the text more manageable and accessible (e.g., Zion instead of Ẓion or Tzion).

Translations

Unless stated otherwise, all translations from texts such as the Hebrew Bible, the Mishnah, and the Talmud are a combination of the author's and standard academic translations.

Quotations

Unless noted otherwise, any time the reader finds italicized words in a quotation, the emphasis is in the original text.

ACKNOWLEDGMENTS

This book is the result of a lifetime of living in the world as a Jew. As such, it would be impossible for me to acknowledge everyone who helped me (and this book) reach this point. In *Muslims and Jews in America: Commonalities, Contentions, and Complexities,* a book I coedited in 2011, I thanked a long list of people who played a positive role in shaping me and my work, recognizing friends and family going back as far as preschool.

Adding to that earlier acknowledgment, I'd like to begin by thanking members of the team at my publisher, the University of California Press. I have been gifted to work with editor Eric Schmidt, who has championed this project from my very first email to him, and who has since served as steward and guide from soup to nuts. Other individuals I wish to thank include Anne Canright, Maeve Cornell-Taylor, Francisco Reinking, and Rose Vekony.

In my graduate studies at Harvard Divinity School and the University of California, Santa Barbara, I first learned many of the methodologies utilized in this book. A special thanks goes to UCSB's Roger Friedland and Mark Juergensmeyer for this training. My Ph.D. advisor and mentor, Richard Hecht, will see his pedagogical fingerprints throughout these pages. Thank you, Professor Hecht, for all of your help in getting me to this point.

In terms of professional support at the University of San Francisco, where I have taught since 2007, I am indebted to Chancellor Stephen Privett, President Paul Fitzgerald, Provost Jennifer Turpin, and Deans Marcelo Camperi, Peter Novak, and Eileen Fung. I am also grateful to the College of Arts & Sciences and the critical assistance I received through the Faculty Development Fund, in particular for covering the costs of printing this book's color images. Thanks also go to my friends and colleagues in USF's Department of Theology & Religious Studies, the Swig Program in Jewish Studies and Social Justice, and the staff at USF's Gleeson Library.

For support during the process of writing this book, whether in terms of strengthening the manuscript, clarifying aspects of the book's content, or assisting the project in multiple other ways, I am grateful to the following people:

Ami Abramson, Yedidyah Glasser, Alex Greene, Ami Monson.

Talal Alyan, Camille Angel, Evelyn Baz, Sarah Bunin Benor, Menachem Creditor, Isabel de Koninck, Aaron Dorfman, Noach Dzmura, Betsy Eckstein, Karen Erlichman, Moshe Firrouz, Netanel Fisher, Claire Frost, Nancy Fuchs-Kreimer, Rahuldeep Gill, David Green, Jennifer Groen, Rachel Gross-Prinz, Andrew Hahn, Daniel Kirzane, Darren Kleinberg, Joy Ladin, Daniel Landes, Akiba Lerner, Abraham Massuda, Robin Nafshi, Elliot Neaman, Rachel Neis, Sara Paasche-Orlow, Lawrence Raphael, Ariel Rosen Ingber, Naftali Rothenberg, Jhos Singer, Tom Sosnik and family, Francesco Spagnolo, Max Strassfeld, Jen Taylor Friedman, Diane Tobin, Adam Weisberg, Lucas Welch, Stephen Whitfield, Lloyd Wolf, Jamie Wolfe, Yisroel Zaetz, Anna Zeman.

An anonymous curator at the Melbourne Museum Discovery Centre, Reza Aslan, Peter Black, Frédéric Brenner, Lee Bycel, Steven M. Cohen, Ron Coleman, J.J. Goldberg, Jill Jacobs, Oren Kroll-Zeldin, Daniel Lasker, Mayer Rabinowitz, Fred Rosenbaum, Armine Sargsyan, Benjamin Smith, Saba Soomekh, Rebecca Walker, Mark Washofsky.

Fred Astren, Jeremy Brown, Kiefer Cropper, Leonard Greenspoon (and editing team), Avi Jorisch, Nathan

Katz, Mary Kershisnik, Aziza Khazzoom, Rose Levinson, Laura Levitt, Shawn Lichaa, Charles London, Shaul Magid, Jody Myers, Shelly Phillips, Elisha Russ-Fishbane, Jacob Tapper. My sincere apologies if I have inadvertently forgotten anyone. Please know this is not a reflection of my gratitude but of a failed memory.

The late Erin Hyman, an exceptional individual whom I had the opportunity to have as this book's first editor, knowingly chose to dedicate some of her last days to improving this manuscript. For this I will be forever indebted.

The following people gave me detailed feedback on the entire manuscript, for which I offer my sincerest thanks: anonymous readers for the University of California Press, Lila Corwin-Berman, Avi Cover, Jennifer Derr, Gabe Goldman, Michael Hahn, Susan Hahn, Laurie Hahn Tapper, Micah Hyman, Ari Y. Kelman, Andrew Ramer, Andrew Sacks, Anne Tapper, and Theodore Tapper.

As this book is largely the outgrowth of teaching a variety of Jewish Studies courses at USF, including one using a title similar to that of this book, I want to thank the hundreds of students who have helped me through my teaching, in particular those with whom, along with other Jewish Studies and Social Justice program faculty, I used earlier incarnations of this manuscript.

Though it may go without saying for some, there are two customary notes to add at this point. First, the views and opinions expressed in this book, and the context in which images and quotes herein are used, do not neces-sarily reflect the views or policy of, nor imply approval or endorsement by, those individuals and/or organizations who provided permission to use them. Second, I am responsible for any errors, mistakes, or omissions found in this text.

Thank you to my immediate family—Mom, Dad, Shelly, Stone, Susan, Michael, Lisi, Jacob, Jen, Alice, Jack, Becky, Hanan, Talia, Elisheva, Debby, Andy, Sam, Nathan. Mom, thank you for being the sweet, unconditionally loving person you are. Dad, thank you for giving me your best, and for teaching me to strive to do as much as I can in the world for good. Jacob, thank you for being my brother. Laughing with you continues to be one of life's greatest treasures. Shelly, Susan, and Michael, thank you for treating me as your own flesh and blood.

Among those who have moved on to other realms, thank you Grammie and Grampie, Grandfather Abraham and Grandmother Janet, Bubbe and Zaydeh, Aunt Isabel, and David. Peace be with you all.

Finally, I am grateful to my partner, Laurie, and the love and sustenance she has given me and continues to give me, especially in terms of my efforts to grow professionally. You are my best friend, and I love you. As to my two little ones, Isaiah Everett and Delilah Yareyach, you are the lights of my life, the joys of the deepest parts of my soul, and the reason I do what I do in the world. Laurie, Isaiah, and Delilah (+ Bu and Lamington Sparkle), I love you with all my heart, soul, and being.

INTRODUCTION

Contents

Key Ideas

- Jews identify as "Jews" in terms of religion, ethnicity, culture, nation, race, and more. They are incredibly diverse and fall into multiple identification categories. For all of these reasons, the connection between two Jews, or two Jewish communities, is often replete with certainty and ambiguity, sometimes simultaneously.

- Judaism (or Judaisms) is the sum total of how Jews have historically performed and currently perform their identities in terms of thought and action, ideas and rituals. Understanding Judaisms necessitates an analysis of Jews' customs, habits, ritual practices, clothing styles, foods, and spoken languages, among other things.

- Jews make up about 0.2 percent of the world's population (one-fifth of 1 percent; see fig. 0.1 below), approximately fifteen million individuals. Eighty percent of all Jews (twelve million) currently live in two countries, Israel and the United States, in roughly equal numbers.

Twenty-First-Century Identities

Many of us have a basic human need to identify with something larger than ourselves, a need to belong. As individuals and communities, we enact constructed senses of self—identities—through our behavior and experiences, a process shaped by cultures, value systems, histories, and narratives. Our identities relate to every aspect of our lives.

Twenty-first-century identities are complex. Whether based on age, citizenship, culture, ethnicity, gender, nationality, physical ability, physical appearance, race, religion, sex, sexual orientation, socioeconomic class, or something else entirely, our social identities have a great deal of meaning for us and those around us. Much has been written about this subject, how some identities are acquired, others inborn. At times, our identities give us access to opportunities; other times, they deny us entry to jobs, homes, and even food.

All of us embody identities, which are expressed in thought and action. One way to better comprehend what it means to be a member of a group is to look at everyday aspects of the group, such as group members' customs, habits, ritual practices, clothing styles, foods, and spoken languages. We can also examine broader ideas, such as whether the group shares a collective history, an attachment to a particular place, or a common set of beliefs (e.g., a central conviction regarding the end of the world). We can explore those attributes of a group that are well established; we can also focus on a group's margins to see how less popular ideas differ from the norm.

Many identities are based on a legal or formal definition. But identities also exist in less tangible, more abstract ways. Acceptance into a group often has less to do with official credentials and more to do with whether one knows how to perform the group's identity, whether one behaves like other members of the group. Even if one is able to claim group membership because a family relative is a member, this commonly does not mean that that one will experience immediate acceptance.

The postmodern, twenty-first-century intellectual has attempted to take apart identities to the point of nonexistence. But the world in which we live currently functions as if our identities are real, as if they are material. Even though identities exist first and foremost as ideas, we largely interact with one another as if communities are defined concretely. As scholar Charles Taylor argues, contemporary identity formation is rooted in notions of authenticity existing in an individualized self.

Defying Definition? Performing Jewish Identities and Judaisms

In all of these ways, the Jewish community is like any other. Some Jews believe that there is one true form of Judaism, a single accurate worldview based on a sacred message transmitted by God to Moses on Mount Sinai some thirty-three hundred years ago, a specific way of life made up of morals and ritual laws that have been passed down from that time through today. Other Jews—arguably most—do not. Regardless of where one falls in relation to these positions, twenty-first-century Judaism is quite different from the Judaism of 1300 BCE. Of course, the identity of the Jewish community has always been changing. In fact, it is more precise to say "Jewish identities" rather than "Jewish identity," "Judaisms" rather than "Judaism."

This book is based on the idea that there have always been many different ways to perform one's Jewish identity. The category "Jew" has had countless definitions across time and space. Of course, in specific times and places there have been set notions of what being a Jew meant. But during any given period, there has been debate and disagreement over the precise parameters of who counted as a Jew. And when the community has had non-Jews define them, the consequences have sometimes been a matter of life and death.

We can speak in similarly plural terms about Christian identities and Christianities, Muslim identities and Islams, and so on. Christians and Muslims have about 2.2 billion and 1.6 billion devotees, respectively. Together, they make up more than half of the world's population. Yet members of each group have different understandings of what it means to be a Christian or a Muslim. All communities are heterogeneous to some degree, especially those with billions of constituents. Though there are often traits that individuals in a given collective share, there is also often a great deal of diversity. The larger the group and the more physically widespread it is, the more variety is present.

Because twenty-first-century Jews trace their origins back thousands of years, and because Jews have lived in widespread places throughout their history, this group is an ideal case study for the exploration of contemporary identity formation. In looking at the multiple meanings of the signifier "Jew," historically and presently, we gain a deeper understanding of how identities work: how groups' identities are fashioned and produced in general, and how this has happened among Jews in particular.

What Does Judaism Mean and What Does It Mean to Be a Jew?

For the project at hand—to get inside of what it means to be a Jew—we need to explore what it means to express one's Jewishness. Judaism, after all, is more than a belief regarding the divinity of the Hebrew Bible. Rather, it is the sum total of ways that Jews have communicated, and continue to communicate, their Jewishness, which includes the collective canon of Jewish ideas and rituals. Although, from a much narrower point of view, one is Jewish or not based simply on *halakhah* (Jewish law)—a dominant interpretation being whether one is born to a Jewish mother (i.e., "matrilineal descent")—even this has changed over the course of history (see chapters 5 and 8).

From the perspective of this book, the tapestries of the Jewish tradition—which together make up Judaisms—are vast; they are composed of a multitude of Jewish identities. They have manifested, and continue to manifest, in how Jews have lived and interacted with the world around them. They have appeared, and continue to appear, through Jewish actions and actions of Jews, Jewish clothing and ways that Jews dress. They have also appeared, and continue to appear, through identity expressions about Jews produced by non-Jews.

Another way to respond to the question at hand—what does it mean to identify as a Jew?—is to underscore that Jews are an atypical bunch. When you take into account how few Jews there are—roughly 0.2 percent of humanity, some fifteen million among the world's roughly seven billion people (fig. 0.1)—it is extraordinary that they've played such significant roles in shaping human development.

It is not uncommon to see lists of famous Jews, especially those put out by the Jewish community itself. Members of given groups often point to recognized people who are part of their community; perhaps this is a self-affirmation of a group's value. Whatever the psychoanalysis beneath the surface, from the Bible to the booming, beautiful ballads of Bette Midler and Barbra Streisand, Jews are one of the most influential minority communities in recorded history.

But compiling lists of well-known Jews doesn't really help us answer the question "who is a Jew?" Putting aside the oft-quoted notion that there are as many different definitions of what it means to be part of a community as there are members of that community, we need not begin by looking at a given collection of people and asking: Which of these people is a Jew? Instead we should

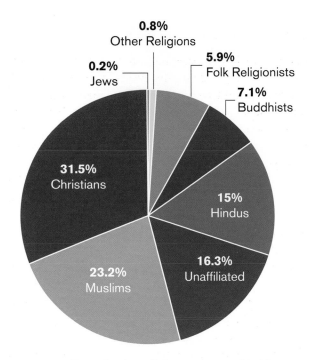

FIGURE 0.1 Sizes of major religious groups worldwide.

ask those who maintain that twenty-first-century Jews are the descendants of the biblical Hebrews: What connects these two groups? Is there any concrete evidence that connects today's Jews to Moses in a detectable, unbroken chain?

Similarly, is there anything tangible that connects the Bible's Sarah to cast members of the famous 1960s television show *Star Trek,* such as those who played Captain Kirk (William Shatner), Mr. Spock (Leonard Nimoy), and Ensign Chekov (Walter Koenig), or to cast members of the twenty-first-century Star Trek movies, such as those playing the roles of Kirk (Chris Pine), Spock's mother, Amanda Grayson (Winona Ryder), and Chekov (Anton Yelchin)? What links the biblical Miriam to United States Supreme Court justices Ruth Bader Ginsburg and Elena Kagan? What about King David's connection to singers Drake and Pink, or even Drake's connection to Pink? What links physicist Albert Einstein to Kiss's Gene Simmons? Or comedian and actor Sarah Silverman to entertainer Sammy Davis Jr. (figs. 0.2–0.5)?

How Should We Classify Jews?

Is there *any* substantial link between these people? Or is the only thing that connects these people the fact that they all identify themselves as Jewish and thus may be classified together? If so, how do we classify this com-

FIGURE 0.2. Albert Einstein, physicist.

FIGURE 0.3. Gene Simmons, bass guitarist/co–lead vocalist of the rock band Kiss.

munity? Are Jews best described as a religion, culture, ethnicity, nation, race, political orientation, or something else? And are Jews the only community that can be understood as an example of all of these categories at the same time?

Jews as a Religion

One of the most common ways to understand Jews is as adherents of the religion called Judaism. But what does "religion" mean? We can approach this question by looking at the etymology of the word. Unfortunately, its definitive roots are unknown. Some trace it to the Latin *religiō,* meaning a supernaturally imposed prohibition; others to *religāre,* that which ties believers to something (e.g., God). Moving forward, if we put aside what "religion" means within the context of an individual's life (as in, "I had a religious experience"), many use the term *religion* to describe a given group's set of beliefs. Using this criterion, it is easy to show how a core set of textually based principles have been part of the Jewish tradition for millennia.

But there are at least three basic challenges to saying that Jews are members of a religious community and end-

ing the conversation there. First, many Jews, even those who are religiously observant, argue that ritual practice is much more important to being a Jew than belief. In fact, over the millennia, a number of rabbinic authorities have stated outright that abiding by Jewish law is more central to performing one's Jewishness than is holding particular creeds.

Second, one's Jewishness cannot be judged on the basis of ritual observance alone. As one rabbi recently quipped, "Having a ham sandwich on the afternoon of Yom Kippur"—thereby breaking two separate Jewish laws (eating ham is prohibited, as is eating any type of food on the Jewish holy day of Yom Kippur)—"doesn't make you less Jewish." Within the world of religiously observant Jews, many hold that someone who chooses not to obey Jewish law is still a Jew. Breaking a group's law doesn't necessarily mean that you lose your membership in the group.

Jews as a Culture or Ethnicity

A third challenge in understanding Jews exclusively as a religious community is that many twenty-first-century American and Israeli Jews—two communities that, as of 2014, together make up more than 80 percent of the world's Jewish population—reject the notion that Judaism is their religion, preferring instead to call it their culture, ethnicity, or heritage. Two widely accepted sets

FIGURE 0.4. Sarah Silverman, comedian/actor.

FIGURE 0.5. Sammy Davis Jr., entertainer.

of data on the Jewish American community—the 2000–2001 NJPS (National Jewish Population Survey) and the 2013 Pew Center's "Portrait of Jewish Americans"—indicate that about one-quarter of Jews in the United States identify more with Judaism as their ethnicity or culture than as their religion. For those born after 1980, this number rises to 32 percent (compared to 7 percent for those Jewish Americans born before 1927). Some understand their Jewishness in this way, rather than as their religion, because they understand "religion" to be a matter of faith; roughly one in five American and Israeli Jews don't believe in God. (Based on a working definition of culture found at the beginning of chapter 7, the lines between religion and culture become further blurred.)

That said, even if someone maintains that identifying as Jewish is a reflection of one's culture or ethnicity, we must also ask: Is there really a common cultural or ethnic bond between Jews? Are the languages, rituals, and worldviews the same for, say, Alaskan Ashkenazi Jews and Ugandan Abayudaya Jews? Syrian Aleppo-identified Jews and Peruvian Incan Jews? Brazilian Amazonian Jews and Uzbekistani Bukharan Jews? It is not important whether the reader knows anything about these particular Jewish subgroups. The point is that they are very different from one another. Geography and language are only the beginning: to say that any of these pairs have the same culture or ethnicity is highly debatable.

Jews as a Nation

As for Jews being a nation rather than a religion, culture, or ethnicity, the word nation also has multiple meanings. Deriving from the Latin *nātiō,* meaning "birth," if we say that a nation is akin to a group or people, often also linked to a particular territory, this, too, can be problematic for some. More specifically, many younger (and some older) Jews do not identify as part of the Jewish nation because of the ideological baggage commonly attached to the term, whether in the sense of Jewish nationalism writ large or with reference to the State of Israel, which for many Jews embodies the "Jewish nation" above all others.

Nationality, for its part, is typically linked to one's citizenship, something that clearly cannot apply to all Jews, since they live in countries all around the world. Thus, we come back to the same basic question: Is there an essence to being a Jew? What makes someone Jewish?

Jews as a Race

In the twenty-first century, the idea that Jews constitute a race is less popular than that they are members of a religion, culture, ethnicity, or nation—at least in the United

States and Israel. One reason this notion has fallen out of favor may be that it was promoted by one of the twentieth century's most odious figures, Adolf Hitler. After Hitler's Nazi party took control of the German government, it became conventional to engage in "racial science"—measuring Jews' skull sizes and nose lengths, for example, in an effort to prove the existence of a Jewish racial type and thus document Jews' inferiority. Hitler obviously took this practice to an extreme, justifying mass genocide in the name of "racial purity."

Although race is today often considered a social construct and not a biological fact, Hitler perceived the category of race to be scientifically provable. Perhaps more interestingly, in recent years some researchers—including Jews themselves—have attempted to prove a Jewish genetic commonality.

For some, demonstrating an inherent biological correlation among Jews supports a millennia-old unbroken chain of tradition, the idea that Jews are all directly related. Responding to one such study, for example, scholar Moshe Tendler said: "I would like to think this new study is true, because it would indicate that over the course of centuries we still maintain a vast majority of loyal Jews. It is comforting because it confirms a success that no other religion can claim, that there would be inadequate intermarriage [Jews marrying non-Jews] to affect the gene pool."

Sometimes problems internal to the Jewish community arise based on racially determined definitions of what it means to be a Jew. For instance, a 2013 educational trip to Israel organized by Jews for Jewish youth, Taglit-Birthright Israel, required a nineteen-year-old Russian applicant to submit a DNA test—to prove that she was genetically Jewish—before granting her a scholarship. The girl's father, Shimon Yakerson, told reporters that it was a clear case of "racism toward Russian Jews."

Jews *Not* as a Race

Scholar Robert Pollack contends, especially given Nazi efforts to demonstrate the existence of a Jewish race, that Jews should be wary of gravitating toward any similar scientific testing. Scholar David Ellenson agrees: "It smacks of racist and racial innuendo that is suspicious for someone like me in light of the 20th century and the very negative uses to which genetic data was put."

Others, such as scholar Steven M. Cohen, argue that because of increases in intermarriage rates and American twenty-first-century cultural mores, contemporary Jews don't necessarily care about such data: "American culture has created a Jewish subgroup that is extraordinarily committed to a values conception of what it means to be Jewish, as opposed to the more collective, even tribalist conception that prevails in other countries. . . . It would be ironic and counter-intuitive for younger, postmodern Jews today to embrace evidence that appears to lend support to the idea that Jews are something like a race, or ought to be bound to each other because of some notion of common ancestry."

Even if one challenges the dominant academic idea that race is a social construct, and instead claims that Jews are linked together through biology, the fact that a non-Jew can become Jewish through the process of conversion means that Jews cannot be defined based on biology alone. Cohen, in an article written with scholar Jack Wertheimer, adds: "The openness of the Jewish people to converts makes plain that the familial bond is itself a function not solely of biology but of a shared history, a common fate, and, for much of Jewish history, closely similar religious customs and practices."

Jews as a Race *(cont.)*

There are, of course, other notions of what constitutes a race besides those rooted in biology or sociology. In December 2009, the Supreme Court of the United Kingdom weighed in on the definition of a Jew according to the British civil code. Two years prior, JFS (formerly known as the Jews' Free School)—a government-funded, Orthodox-led school in London founded in the eighteenth century—rejected a student applicant on the grounds that he wasn't Jewish. Although the Jewish identity of the boy's father was not in dispute, the school denied the Jewishness of the mother—who before the son's birth had converted to Judaism under the supervision of a Masorti (Conservative) rabbinical council rather than an Orthodox one—and, following a strict Orthodox understanding of halakhah, thus of the son.

In response, England's Supreme Court ruled that basing admission to a school receiving government funding on narrow criteria such as whether a student's mother is Jewish violated the country's Race Relations Act. The JFS decision to reject the boy was thus deemed racially and ethnically discriminatory. In other words, the court ruled that what some people—including most Orthodox Jews—would argue is a religious law, rather than a racial one, is in fact racially based.

Contemporary Expressions of Jewish Identities

One of the best ways to approach the question that lies at the core of this book—what does it mean to be a Jew?—is to look at the ways Jews express their Jewishness (special topic 0.1). This book engages this question by examining Judaism in relation to twenty-first-century Jewish communities. Yet today's Jews have built their Jewish identities on identities that emerged in years, centuries, and even millennia past. So we need to look at twenty-first-century Jewish identities in relation to expressions of Judaism that precede the present day.

Over the last half-century in particular, a number of events have expanded Jewish communal understandings of what it means to be a Jew, which has radically broadened this already vast category. For example,

• Liberal strands of the Jewish community began ordaining women as rabbis, shifting the balance of power in this centuries-old patriarchal community. (Take the story I recently heard from a rabbi in North-ern California about a boy from her congregation who visited his family on the East Coast and, upon seeing that the rabbi of his cousins' synagogue was male, said to his mother: "Mom, I didn't know that men could be rabbis!").

• Jews are marrying non-Jews at rates as high as 70 percent.

• Gay, lesbian, bisexual, transgender, intersex, and other nondominant gendered, sexed, and sexualized subgroups of Jews are reexamining traditional texts and creating new rituals and prayers (see special topic 0.2).

When contextualized within the much larger shift toward a postmodern, deconstructionist approach to human identities—where previously accepted categories related to identities have been expanded and even torn down and made uncertain—each one of these historical episodes has triggered new approaches to Jewish identities, and thus expressions of Judaisms. It is possible that there has never been a time in history that Jewish identities have been so porous.

The Structure of This Book

Chapter Themes

Each of the book's chapters revolves around a single theme that is central to the overarching exploration of the idea of Jewish identities. Although the chronology of the book vis-à-vis history is somewhat linear, each chapter, no matter what historical period is explored, is linked to the contemporary arena and can stand on its own.

NARRATIVES

After laying out the book's working definitions of "truth" and "fact," chapter 1 examines how collective memory and communal identities are constructed, both generally (for Americans, primarily) and in the Jewish community specifically, as well as some of the long-term and short-term political ramifications of this process. This discussion includes an examination of dominant and subordinated voices within individual communities. Many of the issues discussed in more detail elsewhere in the book are introduced first in chapter 1.

SINAIS

Chapter 2 focuses on the Jewish community's central text, the Torah, including an explanation of how it relates to the Bible; its perceived origins (i.e., written by God or by humans); the notion of ongoing revelation; written Torah and oral Torah; the relationship between a text and its interpretation; ritual observances and textual narratives; and some of the dominant ways Jews have interpreted the Torah in terms of God and the "Children of Israel." It also acquaints the reader with the Hebrews and Israelites, two proto-Jewish communities (groups said to be ancestors of Jews).

ZIONS

Following chapter 2's exploration of the portability of sacred ideas, chapter 3 looks at the transferability of sacred places. It complicates a dominant Jewish division of the world into "Zion" and "Diaspora" by looking at the multitude of "zions" outside of Israel. This includes a wide range of geographical and metaphorical centralized sacred sites in Jewish history, as well as the notion of exile from contemporary and comparative perspectives. Building on chapter 2, this chapter offers additional information about the proto-Jewish communities of Hebrews and Israelites, and introduces a third proto-Jewish group, the Judeans, a post-Israelite incarnation of this group.

MESSIAHS

Chapter 4 explores the ways in which sacred ideas and places have been localized in individuals—in human bodies—a phenomenon that, over time, has led to the spinning off of multiple distinct Jewish sects. It also considers the most famous Jewish messianic figure of all time, Jesus, within the larger context of other Jewish messiahs. The chapter concludes with a discussion of a messianic era, as opposed to a messianic person.

LAWS

Chapter 5 explores the significant role of legal authority in the Jewish community, also introducing a general framework for the breadth and depth of customs and rituals performed by its members. This includes a presentation of core sacred legal texts—such as the Bible, Mishnah, and Talmud—as well as foundational genres such as Midrash. It also discusses emerging voices among gendered, sexed, and sexualized Jewish subgroups (see special topic 0.2) and some of the ways that people practice Jewish law without being maximally committed to it.

MYSTICISMS

Chapter 6 focuses on the origins, emergence, and spread of Jewish mystical thought and its role in the development of new Jewish movements, such as Hasidism. It also touches on some of the diverse manifestations of mysticism among Jewish communities in the Middle East, North Africa, and Eastern Europe and ways in which, over time, elements of Jewish mysticism have become mainstream in terms of thought and practice.

CULTURES

Chapter 7 discusses some of the amazing diversity of Jewish cultures and ethnicities mentioned in previous chapters, underscoring ways in which transcultural cross-fertilization has been the norm throughout Jewish history. Looking at lesser-discussed groups of Jews—Greek, Iraqi, Kurdistani, Persian, Yemenite, Egyptian, Ethiopian, Indian, Chinese, and more—this chapter also investigates centuries-old patterns of intercommunal relations between Jews and non-Jews such as Christians and Muslims, including events central to Jewish identities such as the birth of the "Sephardi Jew."

MOVEMENTS

Chapter 8 discusses recent Jewish denominationalism, particularly in terms of the shaping and reconstruction of Jewish identities in the modern and postmodern periods. Analyzing how various movements—from ultra-Orthodoxy to Modern Orthodoxy to Conservatism, Reform, Reconstructionism, Humanism, and Renewal Judaism—have approached modernity, this chapter also offers a visual representation of some of the core differences between these movements in terms of number of affiliates, doctrine, and practice.

GENOCIDES

Chapter 9 examines the Jewish genocide, the Shoah, within the context of other twentieth- and twenty-first-century genocides, including an exploration of notions of exceptionalism and victimhood/survival. It also looks at the connection between historical episodes of anti-semitism and the Shoah, and varied intentions and consequences regarding Holocaust education. In terms of twenty-first-century Jews, the chapter unpacks the central place the Nazi-perpetrated genocide, as a collective trauma, continues to play in relation to Jewish identities today, even for those who did not experience the horrors of World War II directly.

POWERS

Chapter 10 looks at Jews' shift from positions of powerlessness to power, especially in Israel and the United States. The rise of political Zionism is discussed as well, including lesser known definitions of that ideological movement and ways in which it played a major role in establishing the first Jewish-majority modern nation-state in history, the State of Israel. In addition, the development of new Jewish identities as a result of Israel's founding is examined, including definitions of Jews in terms of civil law (i.e., "the Law of Return"), culture (i.e., the new "Israeli Jew"), and the relationship between notions of Jewishness and Arabness.

BORDERS

Chapter 11 looks at some of the de jure and de facto boundaries of Jewish identities in terms of smaller groups' affiliations with Jews officially, unofficially, practically, and legally. Following on the previous ten chapters' attempt to broaden notions of Jewish identities, this chapter challenges the argument that there are no boundaries to Jewish identities by exploring various "border communities," subgroups linked to the Jewish community in various ways: Karaites, Samaritans, African Hebrew Israelites of Jerusalem, Messianic Jews, and Kabbalah Centre devotees.

FUTURES

The book's final chapter looks at some of the core Jewish concerns regarding potential futures for the Jewish community, with a focus on the group's ultimate concern—survival: in particular, physical survival (e.g., what are the current threats to Jews? how do today's Jews produce more Jews?) and ideological survival (e.g., what are the best ways to shape Jewish identities?). It also touches on some of the important trends within the Jewish American community from the past few decades, such as the rise of environmental activism, queer activism (special topic 0.2), and multiracial and multicultural Jewish communities.

Core Ideas

Jewish Identities Are Diverse

This book unveils the multidimensional character of this ancient, ever-changing community, a group whose primary signifier has shifted multiple times (e.g., from Hebrews to Israelites to Judeans to Jews). Jewish communities are multilayered and complex; their identities are a reflection of countless factors, including the interaction of myriad cultures, ethnicities, nations, nationalities, political orientations, races, religions, and more. There are a wide range of perspectives regarding how to perform one's Jewish identities and what it means to be a Jew.

All Group Identities Are Diverse and Are Built upon Individual Identities

Although this book focuses on Jewish identities, its ultimate aim is to give readers a deeper understanding of identity formation at large, regardless of whether or not one identifies as Jewish. As the author, I have tried to address some of the ways people construct their identities, a process that I am of course deeply part of myself.

Throughout this book, I have chosen to refer to people with marginalized identities in terms of gender, sex, and sexuality—more specifically, individuals who identify as lesbian, gay, bisexual, transgender, intersex, non-gender conforming, non-sexual conforming, genderqueer, and other related terms—as queer.

Some find this term problematic, in particular those unfamiliar with the academic field of Queer Studies, pre-Millennials, and those not living in the San Francisco Bay Area and elsewhere in California, where this label is common. At the same time, it is arguably problematic to group distinct social identities under any umbrella term, whether "queer" or "LGBTQIQ" (or, for that matter, "Jew"). Some contend that no signifier-linked framework rooted in binaries can ever capture the ambiguity, fluidity, and ever-changing meanings of social identities connected to gender, sex, and sexuality.

I use the term *queer* in this book for two reasons above all others. First, this is an introductory book written primarily for academic settings, where the field of Queer Studies and ideas linked to Queer Theory are ever growing. Second, as explained in the introduction to a prayer book published by Congregation Sha'ar Zahav, *Siddur Sha'ar Zahav,* "Queer-identified is a label that many people use to describe themselves, aiming to reappropriate a term that once was used only in a derogatory fashion. We recognize that the term may elicit strong feelings. For people who suffered harassment and injury while being called 'queer,' the term may serve to bring back the pain of those times." Using the term *queer* herein intends to be positive and inclusive, and "recognize[es] that language and identity evolve over time."

To this end, I begin all twelve chapters with a personal narrative. I am aware these stories are subjective, emerging as they do out of my own life experiences and my particular social identities, many of which are privileged. Despite their subjective nature, I hope these anecdotes serve as useful entry points into the main subject of each chapter and, more importantly, help readers to remember the connection between the book's ideas and their own social identities, in terms of both overlapping patterns and unique differences. These "auto-ethnographic" vignettes are printed in a different font to distinguish them from the book's primary information on Jewish communities.

Non-Jewish and Intra-Jewish Influences

Each chapter reminds the reader of the influences that non-Jewish collectives have had on Jews. In addition, each chapter points to how Jewish subgroups have influenced one another, at times resulting in dominance and at others subordination.

Texts Built upon Texts Built upon Texts

Right from the start, this book illustrates one of the primary ways that Jews have recreated themselves over and over again, and that is through texts, especially by building new texts upon those that preceded them. The Bible's story about Cain and Abel provides an excellent example of how the original verses from the Torah have been interpreted and reinterpreted throughout Jewish history. After showing some of the different ways Genesis 4 has been translated—specifically, the verses where Cain kills his brother, Abel (chapter 2)—the book looks at how other texts approach this same biblical narrative, including the Mishnah, Talmud, ancient Midrash, contemporary Midrash (chapter 5), and the *Zohar* and Hasidic texts (chapter 6). This small exercise is intended to show how Jewish texts are shaped in relation to others, like concentric circles (see fig. 2.4).

Questions Trump Answers

Ultimately, this book seeks to question answers more than answer questions. Many "introductory" texts offer definitive understandings of a given topic (e.g., "Bible means X" vs. "there is no Bible; only bibles"). Part and parcel of a varied community such as Jews, however, is the wide range of responses possible for any given question. In using early drafts of this book with my students at the University of San Francisco, many students were confused with the book's seeming hesitation to say, for a given time and place: "*This* is what happened." Nonetheless, the book summarizes dominant scholarly perspectives on a variety of historical events in an attempt to show the variety of ways people today understand the past.

This objective echoes an idea voiced by Rabbi Shira Stutman: "Judaism is more interesting, meaningful, and authentic when it is articulated from a number of perspectives. It's boring at best, dangerous at worst, to live in a world where any story is told with only one point of view. In fact, the 21st century world, across which we can traverse in a day's time, demands [multiple voices]."

Additional Goals

Investigation of Dominant Jewish Binaries

Pedagogically, this book has a number of additional goals. For example, it looks at age-old (though overly simplistic) oppositional pairings, such as Zion vs. Diaspora, to show how, in the twenty-first century, such couplets have become, practically speaking, obsolete, despite maintaining their ideological dominance.

Imagined Communities

This book also intends to address the process in which Jews and non-Jews alike have actively shaped Jewish identities. Loosely similar to Shlomo Sand's 2010 book *The Invention of the Jewish People* (a former bestseller in the State of Israel), *Judaisms* seeks to ask to what degree Jewish histories, and identities, have a material existence. Are Jewish identities, similar to all identities, based only in thoughts and ideas, rather than in anything concrete? This question leads to other inquiries of equal importance, such as: Has Jewish history been manipulated to justify genocide against Jews? Has it, conversely, been employed to protect Jews from extermination? Do dominant Jewish narratives serve the political interests of the State of Israel?

Narratives

Contents

Key Ideas

- Communities have dominant and subordinated narratives, stories that are "true" but not necessarily "factual." These narratives are never fixed but shift over time. "Truth," an operating system of ostensibly historical facts that serves to explain a people's worldview, gives a group both legitimacy and credibility, and often describes the reasons behind a group's practices and beliefs.
- Communal "truths," or narratives, are reaffirmed through rituals.

- Dominant communal narratives—communal "truths"—often overlook subordinated ones. Just as the dominant American narrative can be said to be based in the "white" experience, the dominant Jewish narratives tend to be expressed through dominant Ashkenazi experiences. In point of fact, however, Jewish communal narratives are incredibly heterogeneous—culturally, ethnically, and racially.

Pesaḥ in Cairo

I was wearing one slightly torn, sunflower-patterned oven mitt when Cairo's March evening began to descend. In a pitiful attempt to counter the urban desert heat, a fan held together with a bent metal fork was channeling occasional waves of unbelievably hot air on me, a complement to the snail-paced breeze coming in through my windows. Before I'd moved to Egypt, the phrase "120°F in the shade" didn't mean much to me.

Now rounding out my tenth month in what locals lovingly call 'um al-dunyā (mother of the world), I had adjusted to many of the city's unique flavors. One-time oddities had become normal, such as daily walks through Cairo's now world-famous Mīdān al-Taḥrīr (Liberation Square), a metropolitan epicenter bustling with echoes of the city's twenty million-plus occupants; bumper car-esque taxi rides on highways close enough to skyscrapers that one could literally step from a car into someone's living room; a 24/7 energy and intensity that put New York City to shame.

This was a special night. Friends were on their way over to celebrate Pesaḥ (Passover), a Jewish holiday commemorating the biblical Hebrews' miraculous journey from slavery to freedom. Spending the year in Egypt, or Mitzrayim as it's known in the Hebrew Bible, I was excited to observe this holiday in the same ancient land from which, ironically, my ancestors had purportedly fled with such little time for preparation that they had no food for the road, an image seared into my brain by family and teachers alike since my earliest days of childhood. More specifically, the biblical Hebrews couldn't wait for their bread to rise, hence the flat, crunchy cracker central to the holiday called matzah.

From as far back as I could remember, celebrating Passover with a Seder meal was one of my favorite Jewish rituals. But to have the opportunity to sing songs about Pharaoh a few miles away from the pyramids; to chant poems about swarms of frogs a few feet away from the Nile River; to be living less than one hundred miles from the Red Sea, the waterway that Moses wondrously parted to allow the biblical Hebrews to escape from their slave-owners and Pharoah's soldiers: this was something the child within considered unimaginable. Even though Jews have been living in Egypt for centuries, spending Passover in the "wilderness" (one rabbinic interpretation of "Egypt") was exciting, even bizarre—all the more so for an American Jew who traces his Jewish bona fides back to Latvia, Lithuania, Poland, and Russia rather than the Middle East.

Over the next few minutes, my friends—Jewish, Christian, Muslim, and unaffiliated—arrived at my humble apartment. And after figuring out how to jam fifteen people into a room that could comfortably seat eight at most, we began the Seder's first formal ritual. Using a makeshift Haggadah (Pesaḥ prayer book; pl. Haggadot) that three of us had cobbled together, we recited a version of "Kadesh, Orḥatz . . . ," an introductory song that lays out the table of contents for the night's festivities. The epic story of slaves voyaging to freedom had begun.

The Construction of a Narrative

I begin this book with an experience involving Passover because this Jewish holiday is the quintessential embodiment of the Jewish story: it is central to the Jewish collective identity. This is one reason why the Pesaḥ Seder, the ritualized meal held the first night(s) of the holiday, is among the most widely observed traditions for Jews around the world. Every spring Jews of all stripes and colors come together to recount the "Exodus from Egypt," the account of Moses and the biblical Hebrews journeying to the Promised Land. Haggadot commonly include the phrase, "In every generation one is obligated to see oneself as if s/he went out from Egypt," reminding participants that they are not only supposed to retell the Exodus story but must also make this ancient account personal, embracing it as if it is their own journey as well.

Individual and Communal Narratives

One of the ways a community's collective memory survives—especially over the course of tens of generations—is through the telling and retelling of a master narrative (or narratives), what scholar Ilana Pardes calls a "national biography." In the case of Jews, in recounting their story this group has reinforced its self-understanding while also shaping how the 99.8 percent of the world that is not Jewish sees them.

Storytelling in and of itself is not unique. Virtually all communities engage in this practice. In fact, all of us are storytellers—narrators—in our own right. As individuals we engage in this activity through daily routines, whether at work, school, or someplace else. We do it when meeting someone for the first time, such as on a date or when applying for a job. In all of these moments we recycle stories—scripts—about who we are. Sometimes we even make things up. Through media such as Facebook and Twitter, we craft a version of our lives and our thoughts.

We do this as individuals through basic statements we

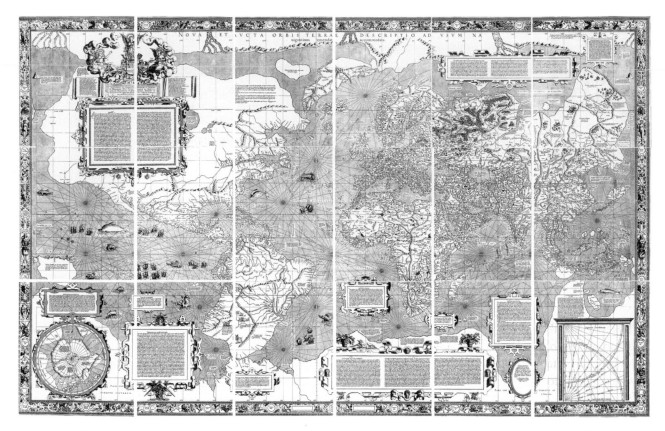

FIGURE 1.1. The Mercator Map. Most world maps found in North America and Europe are based on a sixteenth-century depiction of the world, in which Western Europe is in the center, drawn by Gerardus Mercator, a geographer and cartographer from an area now called Belgium.

make about ourselves: *I go to primary school. I am a college student. I bag groceries. I am a mechanic. I live on the street. I am an exciting person and you should spend more time with me. I am a skilled laborer and you should hire me.* We also do this as societies: *Our country fights for freedom. Our country protects us. Our country only protects some of us. Our country is built on a commitment to life, liberty, and the pursuit of happiness. Our country favors certain people over others.* Along the way, we edit these personal and communal narratives, adding pieces here, subtracting pieces there. The script is never fixed. Through this process, individual and group identities are created and re-created.

"Truth" and "Fact"

To better understand the phenomena of social identities and communal narratives, let's bring in two terms to assist us: *truth* and *fact*. Through the process of storytelling we invent "truth," which shapes a worldview or a dominant narrative. As opposed to "facts"—actual on-the-ground reality—"truth" is the construction of per-

ceptions. "Truth" can be related to facts, but more often than not it is shaped according to interpretations rather than precise historical evidence. "Truth" involves belief and trust, sometimes more than it involves concrete, scientific data.

Identities are constructs based on truth and fact. All communal identities have sets of "truth," and all communal "truths" are ever-changing. In this sense, communal "truth" is an operating system of ostensibly historical facts that serves to explain a people's worldview, thereby giving it both legitimacy and credibility. A community's "truth" often describes the reasons behind that group's practices and beliefs. It does not need to be factual, though it certainly can be. "Truths" are central to identities, whether individual or collective, because we orient toward the truth as if it is factual.

This explanation may seem counterintuitive, especially in relation to more common ways in which the term *truth* is used. Our definition of "fact," too, implies that data exist irrespective of interpretation. So let's go further.

People shape "truth"; more often than not it cannot

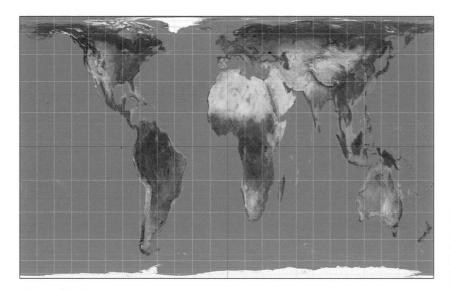

FIGURE 1.2. In contrast to the Mercator Map, the Galls-Peter projection is much closer to an equal-area map reflecting the actual sizes of the land masses found on Earth.

be proven. "Truth" is constantly created and re-created based on new information, changing perceptions, and shifts in interpretation. At any given time, a community has one or more dominant narratives, fluid stories based on the group's "truth," through which it explains and understands itself and those outside it. Communal stories can remain the same for decades, or they can change overnight. As opposed to "truth," which cannot necessarily be argued away, facts can be grappled with, debated, and fought over. Most people are unrelenting in their loyalty to their "truth," unwilling to accept other dominant ways of understanding particular events or the world at large. Many approach facts only through their understanding of "truth."

The "Truth" of the Mercator Map

Take the following example: One standard map used to teach world geography in American and many European schools is directly based on a 1569 design made by a geographer and cartographer from an area now called Belgium, Gerardus Mercator (fig. 1.1).

Though scientifically advanced for its time, and arguably not used today as it was originally intended, like all maps the Mercator projection communicates a particular perception of the world in the form of a two-dimensional image. As we now know, Mercator's portrayal of the world distorts the size of the earth's landmasses; the actual dimensions are much closer to those depicted in an equal-area map such as the Galls-Peter projection (fig. 1.2).

More importantly perhaps, according to the Mercator map Europe is the center of the world. This was Mercator's "truth," as well as Europe's. It was key to their identities. (Maps made in other parts of the world similarly place themselves in the center.) Whether or not one argues that inflating Europe's size while reducing Africa's is Eurocentric or merely nonobjective, or even that Mercator isn't to blame for the map's depiction of the earth because he intended it to be used for navigation and not geography, maps reflect value systems. They teach not just spatial relations, but political ideas as well.

Using cartography to illustrate underlying problems with narrative construction is not a trivial exercise. As scholar Marshall G. S. Hodgson argues in his renowned treatise *Rethinking World History,* maps directly reflect groups' biases. Hodgson calls the Mercator map—with its expansion of Europe and diminishment of Africa—a "Jim Crow projection," an unsympathetic comparison that links it to the legalized racism present in the United States during the nineteenth and twentieth centuries.

"Truth" and Dominant American Narratives

"Truth," 9/11, and Iraq

Let's look at a different set of examples, more overtly connected to twenty-first-century Americans. Compare, for instance, the dominant American narratives of September 10 and September 12, 2001, or the dominant Iraqi narratives of March 20 and March 23, 2003. In each case, actual events changed, suddenly and radically, the collective worldviews—and "truths"—of millions of people. In each case, too, new subnarratives simultaneously emerged that immediately reshaped the way the "other" was perceived.

Of course, there are facts on the ground regarding the individuals who died as a result of the events of September 2001 and March 2003. But these facts are often debated from the vantage point of one's "truth" and one's identity. Whereas Americans know not only the number (2,977) but also the specific names of those killed in the 9/11 attacks, in the case of the invasion of Iraq no precise number exists that accounts for the Iraqi civilians or militants who died; there are only estimates.

Further, the narratives regarding these events are different. Some think that the perpetrators of the 9/11 attacks were affiliates of Al-Qaeda, while others do not. Some think that the primary reason the United States military invaded Iraq was to indirectly weaken Al-Qaeda; others think it was to protect the American government's oil interests. There are definite facts regarding who did what in these situations. Similarly, there are definite facts regarding individuals' stated and actual intentions. But sometimes such data cannot be gathered (or are not accessible to the public). Sometimes, even when data are gathered, people are unable to accept them as fact, writing them off using the logic of conspiracies.

As these examples demonstrate, communal narratives are seemingly cohesive stories, combining interwoven strands from a number of different sources. Sometimes they are manifested orally, through scripts passed down from one generation to the next, other times visually, in the form of symbols or photos of actual people. They are based largely on perception. Such "truths" cannot be reduced to simple correctness or incorrectness. In their complexity, they are core to identities and the stories we tell ourselves, both sacred and profane. Communal "truths" regarding events as momentous as 9/11 or the invasion of Iraq have played important roles in shaping individual and group identities.

"Truth," Obama, and Racial Identities

Dominant narratives are always selective. Take President Barack Obama. Beginning in at least November 2008, subsequent to his winning the presidential election and continuing long after he was sworn in as the forty-fourth president of the United States in January 2009, the dominant American "truth" has been that in Obama the United States elected the country's first African American president. Yet as many know—as the president himself shared in speech after speech during the 2008 campaign, and as laid out in his autobiography, *Dreams from My Father* (2004)—although Obama's father was black, his mother was white. Given this fact, some have argued that he is a member as much of the white community as of the black community.

Others think that "white America" has a vested interest in seeing Obama as black because, as writer Peggy Orenstein puts it, it is "more exciting, more romantic, and more concrete [a] prospect than the 'first biracial president.'" She also probes further, asking: "Would Obama still be seen as 'black enough' if the wife by his side were white? And don't get my husband started on why Tiger Woods—whose mother is three-quarters Asian and whose father was one-quarter Chinese and half African-American—is rarely hailed as the first Asian-American golf superstar."

This isn't to say that Obama is not black. Obama, like all of us, can identify any way he chooses. Indeed, on question nine of the 2010 American census, "What is Person 1's race?," he selected a single box, "Black, African Am., Negro." He could have chosen "White," both "Black etc." *and* "White," or the last category listed on the form, "Some other race." (Whether a community with whom one identifies accepts an individual as one of its own is another issue.)

The point is, social identities are a reflection of individual and collective "truth" more than of fact, more connected to perception than to reality. If Obama had been born in the United States when the infamous "one-drop rule" was in place—which legally defined a black as an individual with "any known African black ancestry"—he would not have had a legal choice as to identifying with a particular race; the government would have made the choice for him.

It is also clear that America's history in dealing with race in centuries past continues to play a major role in identity formation today. If Obama had been born in another country, regardless of when, his racial identities would be understood differently. For instance, if he had been born in contemporary Brazil, he wouldn't simplistically be called either black or white (i.e., in terms of whiteness and blackness, there are many more racial categories in Brazil than the United States). The manner in which America has de jure and de facto understood race is subjective, as are all constructions of identity, whether racially based or not.

We can make the same points about the legal definitions of other minorities in the United States, such as Chinese Americans and Japanese Americans. Though the civil classifications for what constitutes an American as a member of one of these two categories has changed over time, as have the legal rights one has or doesn't have as a result, the fact that there have been, and continue to be, legal definitions for specific groups, defined by race or otherwise, points to the juridical qualification and quantification of identities in America.

In other words, identities are imposed from without as much as from within. And although in twenty-first-century America identity-based laws and accompanying rights are more overtly linked to constructs around gender and sex than to race and ethnicity, legal definitions for particular ethnicities and nationalities continue to exist. Native American tribes are a case in point. The statuses of one's identities are often as much related to legal parameters as to de facto social perception, although sometimes the consequences of both can be the same.

Each of us plays a role in constructing a narrative that is more "truthful" than factual. All of our social identities—whether based in ethnicity, gender, nationality, religion, sexual orientation, or something else—emerge through this process. Simply because we identify as X does not guarantee that others in society will allow us to identify this way. There are many agents involved in the construction of identities, multiple players in the shaping of our individual and collective narratives.

Other American "Truths": Ross, Parks, and Robinson

Though Obama's identities are an ongoing example, the "truth" vs. fact about other aspects of the United States' collective identity is often tied up with America's historical past. Just as Americans *know* that Obama is the first black president, Americans also *know* that Betsy Ross designed the United States' flag; *know* that Rosa Parks moved the civil rights movement forward by being the first African American woman to refuse to move to the back of a public bus after being ordered to do so; and *know* that Jackie Robinson broke the racial barrier in professional sports by becoming the first black man to play major league baseball. To some degree, it is not important that none of these three "truths" is factual.

Betsy Ross did not actually play an important role in America's independence from England, let alone any role whatsoever in creating the country's flag. Rosa Parks was not the first African American woman to refuse to move to the back of a racially segregated bus. In July 1944, eleven years and four months prior to Parks's famous stand against bigotry, Irene Morgan refused to move to the back of a racially segregated bus traveling from Virginia to Maryland. The case eventually went to the United States Supreme Court: in *Morgan v. Virginia,* the court ruled for the first time that the segregation of buses on interstate trips was unconstitutional. As for

Jackie Robinson, he certainly might be the most famous black American of the mid-twentieth century to play major league baseball. But he was not the first to break baseball's "racial barrier." Fifty years earlier, before the Negro Leagues were even established, John "Bud" Fowler and Moses Fleetwood Walker played on integrated professional baseball teams with whites, starting in 1878 and 1884, respectively.

Truth and fact also manifest in dominant American narratives in terms of every day structures. One can make this argument regarding what commercial stores (e.g., Best Buy, Kmart, Home Depot, Staples, Target, Toys-R-Us, Walmart) or fast-food restaurants (e.g., Burger King, Domino's, KFC, McDonald's, Pizza Hut, Subway, Taco Bell, Wendy's) should be built in a shopping center, or even what the "must read" books should be for high school students studying English literature (e.g., Charles Dickens, Emily Dickinson, Shakespeare, Walt Whitman). All of these are conventional parts of dominant twenty-first-century American narratives. This is not the way the United States has always been, nor will it be the probable situation for decades to come. But all are currently dominant.

American Dominants and Subordinates

The above examples deal primarily with dominant elements of American narratives. They echo what is perhaps best framed as the master American narrative. America's communal identity is rooted in the story of how, despite being a pluralistic country made up of many different subcommunities, we are all one nation. As American religions scholar Catherine Albanese writes, "[American history books] generally tell one major story, incorporating the separate stories of many peoples into a single story line arranged chronologically." This way of organizing a large communal identity communicates a common culture, a shared bond among Americans of all stripes. Such an effort can bring people together in positive ways and can help give potentially chaotic societies order.

But this method often has a sticky underbelly. For starters, groups' identities and the histories they are based on are often not neat and orderly. Most of the time, says Albanese, events, and the impact they have on shaping identities, "unfold gradually, over centuries." Crafting simple "connect-the-dots" stories about complex histories is disingenuous. It discounts the ways in which communities recreate themselves time and time again, often not in isolation but through contact with the "other." As historian Lawrence Levine puts it, "To teach a history that excludes large areas of American culture and ignores the experiences of significant segments of the American people is to teach a history that fails to touch us, that fails to explain America to us or to anyone else."

More challenging is that a community's dominant narratives marginalize other narratives, sometimes even relegating or disregarding these minority subnarratives to the point of rendering them invisible. This is one reason why dominant narratives—and identities—are directly linked to power (see chapter 10). The voices of those with less power are typically pushed to the periphery or ignored; their identities and accompanying stories become much less important. Take the notion that the United States of America is the most multicultural and multiethnic nation in history, which reflects the country's deep tolerance for the "other." Such a "truth" exists hand in hand with the disregarding, and even conceal-ment, of subnarratives, in particular as related to histori-cal atrocities that took place in this land even before the United States was officially established.

Specifically, not until the 1960s did state-sanctioned high-school textbooks begin mentioning the horrors of American slavery or the genocide of Native Americans, and then it was in only the most cursory of ways. Prior to this time, mainstream American history textbooks either discounted or justified these monumental compo-nents of America's past. Some argue that American text-books continue to shape inaccurate communal narra-tives, one that persists in marginalizing minorities and their stories in an effort to sanitize American identities.

Others say that the exclusion of current events, including genocides taking place internationally, simi-larly cleanse the American government's role in history, often focusing instead on lauding the United States for fighting on behalf of the underdog, despite evidence to the contrary. This isn't to say that present-day histori-cal revisionists trump historians who preceded them. Rather, there are multiple ways to construct communal narratives, countless ways to dissect communal identi-ties. Most commonly, communities—including national entities such as the United States—paint themselves in a positive light, choosing to leave the parts of the story they are not necessarily proud of on the cutting room floor.

Marginalizing specific subnarratives also creates the problematic binary of "normative" vs. "fringe." Those subnarratives put into the basket of "normalcy" are given more credence and credibility. They effectively become endorsed, which leads them to be concretized further. The opposite takes place for those subnarratives thrown into the "fringe" basket. They are scoffed at, discussed as if they are fictitious and maybe even deceitful, leading to further ostracization. As historian Thomas Tweed puts it, "Historical narratives . . . are never 'just' history. There is always a great deal at stake for narrators and readers, always much to gain and lose in power and meaning."

"Truth" and Dominant Jewish Narratives

Like dominant American narratives—or dominant Ger-man narratives or dominant Chinese narratives, etc., which are all exceptionalized versions of history—domi-nant Jewish narratives are ethnocentric: they reflect self-interest. Similarly, dominant Jewish narratives—again, like any other communal narrative—reflect the Jewish people's "truths" and are not always factual.

A Common Jewish Narrative

One common Jewish narrative—one that is often taught in Jewish parochial schools, supplementary Jewish edu-cational programs (i.e., "Hebrew schools"), Jewish adult education and conversion classes, and elsewhere—goes something like this:

> Contemporary Jews are descendants of the biblical Hebrews, who, starting with Abraham, were the first people to accept monotheism, the belief in a single God. Tracing their lineage through the Bible, from Abraham to Isaac to Jacob (later named Israel) and his twelve sons (a.k.a. the Children of Israel), and continuing on through Moses and Joshua, the Hebrew and Israelite slaves escaped to freedom, going on to wander in the desert wilderness for forty years. This epic tale involves an evil emperor (Pharoah), a miraculous escape (through a major body of water that splits into two, creating a pathway), a revelation from God (Mount Sinai), receipt of a set of moral codes (the Ten Commandments or Directives), and passage to a land promised to them by God, a geographi-cal area loosely correlated with the current borders of the State of Israel.

> Throughout history Jews have been persecuted, oppressed, and murdered simply for being Jewish. Exiled from their homeland, the Holy Land, a number of times—most significantly in 586 BCE and 70 CE, when their First and Second Temples were destroyed—this resilient com-munity has persevered and survived over and over again, against all odds. Though there have been many attempts to annihilate them, most notably the Holocaust or Shoah—the European Jewish genocide of World War II—they wondrously returned to their birthplace, the Land of Israel, in the twentieth century and, in 1948, established a new country, a Jewish state, where they continue to fight for their existence today.

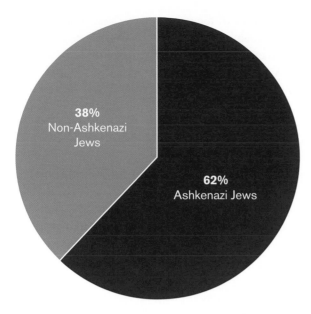

FIGURE 1.3. Worldwide population of twenty-first-century Ashkenazi and non-Ashkenazi Jews (the latter group includes African American, Chinese, Ethiopian, Indian, Mizrahi, and Sephardi Jews). In approximately 1500 CE, the proportions were reversed.

Many Jews are familiar with this story; it is core to their Jewish identities. Even Jews who shun Jewish ritual of all kind typically *know* about the Exodus from Egypt. Even Jews who do not believe that there ever was a group of Hebrew slaves accept this account as their narrative. It is their "truth."

Ashkenazi Jewish Ascendancy

The Jewish community is no different than any other group so far as shaping its own "truth" goes. Just as dominant historical American narratives largely reflect the experiences of whites (though this is in the process of changing as we speak), today's dominant Jewish communal narratives largely reflect the experience of one particular subgroup: Ashkenazi Jews in Israel and the United States, those Jews who trace their lineage back to Eastern European and Russian, Christian-majority places. Of course, the Ashkenazi subgroup can be broken down into smaller subdivisions, just as we can do with "white America."

Putting a significant point to the side for a moment—i.e., male, heterosexual supremacy, a form of domination that abounds in communal narratives well beyond those of the Jewish community—there are a number of possible explanations for the rise of Ashkenazi hegemony within dominant Jewish narratives, four of which are addressed below. Though none of them validates the lack of focus on non-Ashkenazi Jews, each serves as a window into better understanding this trend, both within the Jewish community in particular and in other communities more generally. Such understandings are also important because Ashkenazi dominance is only a current trend in the Jewish community; it is not the way it has been throughout this centuries-old community's history, and may not be the future trend among Jews either.

It is important to add that hegemony—the dominance of one social group over others—does not necessarily imply malevolent intentions. Nor does it mean that one group undoubtedly concocts a master plan to dominant all other subgroups within a given community. Although this may be the case in some situations, it is certainly not always the case. Exclusionary practices related to the construction of narratives are often unplanned. Nonetheless, for subordinated groups, they are commonly perceived to be problematic at best and immoral and violent at worst. In such cases, dominant groups' intentions lose their importance.

MOST JEWS TODAY ARE ASHKENAZI

Although being a majority member of a community neither ensures dominance nor pardons the discounting of minorities, sometimes there is a relation between mass and power, population numbers and authority. In this case, a considerable number of twenty-first-century Jews worldwide identify as Ashkenazi. Of the world's roughly fifteen million Jews (0.2 percent of the world's population), about 40 percent (6 million) live in the United States, 40 percent live in Israel, 10 percent (1.5 million) live in Europe, and 10 percent live elsewhere. Given that approximately 80 percent of American Jews (4.8 million), 50 percent of Israeli Jews (3 million), and most European Jews self-identify as Ashkenazi, we can safely say that a majority of Jews worldwide are Ashkenazi (about 9.3 out of 15 million, or 62 percent; see fig. 1.3—though some estimate that as many as 80 percent of all Jews are Ashkenazi.)

In 1500 CE, however, Ashkenazi Jews made up only 33 percent of the world's Jewish population, a number that increased to 40 percent by 1800 and 90 percent by the turn of the twentieth century. (This rapid population increase is commonly attributed to higher birth rates and lower death rates, especially in comparison to non-Ashkenazi Jewish communities.) Their numbers then decreased as a result of the Shoah (Holocaust). Some contend that in 1070, Ashkenazi Jews made up only 7 percent of the world's Jewish population. In short, whether or not current dominant Jewish narratives are rooted in Ashkenazi experiences because Ashkenazi Jews are the largest single subgroup of the Jewish community, for most of the last thousand years Jewish narratives were not dominated by Ashkenazi Jews, nor were most Jews Ashkenazi.

INTRA-ASHKENAZI HOMOGENIZATION IN THE UNITED STATES

Over the last century, in particular the last fifty years, the Ashkenazi population has become more homogeneous. In this process disparate Ashkenazi subgroups have blended together to form a much larger group. In the nineteenth and twentieth centuries, most Ashkenazi Jews relocated to the United States and Israel (prior to 1948 more commonly called Ottoman Palestine and then British-occupied or British Mandate Palestine). Although Ashkenazi standardization was gradual, as of the twenty-first century very few Ashkenazi Jewish Americans under forty can discern any differences between Ashkenazi subgroups.

For example, if two random twenty-something Ashkenazi Jewish Americans found out that their respective family backgrounds were German and Russian, chances are they would not be able to point to key differences in their familial customs or histories, especially if they were third- or fourth-generation Americans. In contrast, in the nineteenth and twentieth centuries and well before, in Europe, what is now Israel, and the United States, such differences among Ashkenazi Jews were incredibly important. Even differences within a single group, such as German Jews—for example, speaking German versus Yiddish (a Jewish dialect that combines elements of German and Hebrew) as their first language—were central to one's Jewish identity. It was also not uncommon for such subgroups to consider marriage between them to be a form of intermarriage (as opposed to intra-group marriage).

Take a minor controversy involving the first synagogue established in the Western United States. To this day, two different synagogues stake this claim: Congregation Emanu-El and Congregation Sherith Israel, both located in San Francisco, about 1.5 miles from one another. What we know definitively is that these two synagogues were founded around April 1851. At this time, at least two subgroups of Ashkenazi Jews began to meet regularly for prayer, one that identified as Bavarian (later called German) and another that identified as Prussian Poles (later called Poles). Although both communities spoke German, there were multiple subcultural differences between them. For decades thereafter, these two Ashkenazi subcommunities remained at odds because of their ethnic differences. Today, there are no tensions between members of these two synagogue communities; and even if there were, they would not be due to any intra-Ashkenazi differences.

By approximately 1920, two dominant groups emerged from American Ashkenazi Jewish communities nationwide: "Germans" and "Russians." (I use quotation marks because many of those with German citizenship were ethnically Polish and many of those with Polish citizenship were ethnically Russian, etc.) Within these subcommunities, some individuals affiliated with different religious denominations—such as Reform, Orthodox, and somewhere in between—and some did not, often affiliating instead with socialist groups (e.g., Jewish Labor Bundists). Ashkenazi Jews were quite active in an array of politically identified Jewish organizations; by one count, in New York City alone more than 3,600 such affiliations existed in the early 1920s. In other words, aside from differences in Ashkenazi Jewish Americans' cultural backgrounds, they were also heterogeneous in multiple other ways.

However—and this is the most important point for the topic at hand—by the second half of the twentieth century a shift was already under way, such that now, in the twenty-first century, Ashkenazi Jews under forty whose families have been in the United States for three or more generations, can rarely differentiate themselves from other Ashkenazi Jews in terms of intra-Ashkenazi ancestry. There might be differences in terms of affiliation with distinctive denominations, political orientations, or socioeconomic status; but whether or not one is of German, Polish, or Russian descent, for example, is largely irrelevant. Instead, the dominant binary in the U.S. is Ashkenazi/non-Ashkenazi (see below).

THE SHOAH, THE STATE OF ISRAEL, AND ASHKENAZI JEWS

A third phenomenon that helps explain the current situation of Ashkenazi hegemony is that, for many Jews, the two most significant Jewish events of the twentieth century were the Shoah (Holocaust) and the establishment of the State of Israel, both of which are intrinsically linked to the Ashkenazi communal experience. World War II's genocide of six million Jews (two out of every three Jews in Europe and one out of every three in the world) predominantly affected Ashkenazi Jews.

As for the founding of the Jewish State, most late-nineteenth- and early-twentieth-century Zionists were Ashkenazi, especially those who took key military and administrative positions in the years leading up to and immediately following Israel's establishment as a new country. The Ashkenazi imprint on Israel—a country based on a particular social identity (i.e., the self-proclaimed Jewish State)—has predominated ever since.

ASHKENAZI JEWS AND WHITENESS IN THE UNITED STATES

A fourth trend in the growth of Ashkenazi hegemony, especially as it now exists in the United States (and parts of Europe), is that, over the course of the twentieth-century, Ashkenazi Jews "became white." Like many other minority groups, Ashkenazi Jews were not born into whiteness but gradually transitioned into this position as their Americanness (and Europeanness) became increasingly accepted. Earlier in Jewish American history—as recently as the late nineteenth century—Jews were considered by some to be black, both metaphorically and literally. Because whites, as a collective, have more power and privilege than any other group in the United States, once Ashkenazi Jews were perceived to be white, their power increased in turn, particularly in the spheres of academia, government, media, and popular culture (i.e., movies, music, and television; see chapter 10). Much of the time non-Ashkenazi Jews, in contrast, have been perceived as nonwhite or "people of color" (see special topic 1.1).

Ashkenazi/Non-Ashkenazi: The Dichotomization of Jews

Ashkenazi ascendancy in Israel and the United States occurred in different historical contexts, especially in terms of whiteness, blackness, and racial construction. But in both countries, since at least the 1950s, there have been dominant and subordinated Jewish identities, and in both countries Ashkenazi Jews have been dominant. Perhaps as a result, the most common Jewish Israeli and Jewish American ethnic self-understanding has revolved around the binary of Ashkenazi/non-Ashkenazi, with those in the latter category usually referred to as Sephardi or Mizraḥi (lit., Easterner), even though these two latter terms actually mean different things (see below).

If we look at Israel in particular, in the years immediately after its establishment in 1948 these two overarching identity categories emerged to represent myriad heterogeneous groups of Jewish immigrants. As in the United States, those generally from Christian-majority communities in Europe and Russia were called Ashkenazi. But there was also an influx of hundreds of thousands of Jews from Muslim- and Arab-majority countries

SPECIAL TOPIC 1.1
ASHKENAZI-NESS AND BEING WHITE

In twentieth- and twenty-first-century America, whiteness is a privileged social identity. Much more than a biological fact, it is a construct, an idea that, at least in the American context, has largely been understood in terms of blackness: i.e., what it is *not*. Whiteness, like all racial constructs, exists relationally—in relation to other racial constructs—and can manifest differently across time and place. This is similar to the idea that no group can be understood without respect to an "other."

Similarly, Ashkenazi Jews exist in terms of what they are not; they are *not* "Jews of color." Further, just as the superficial term "people of color" is problematic in its homogenizing of all nonwhites, categorizing non-Ashkenazi Jews as a single group is equally problematic. Of course, the term *white* homogenizes distinct groups under a single name as well, but because "whites" have a disproportionate amount of societal power, especially in the United States and Israel, this conflation is arguably less problematic.

in the Middle East and North Africa, many of whom were arriving at the same time (specifically in the 1950s). The latter, representing diverse communities, were usually grouped together as Sephardi or Mizraḥi, or, in some situations, under one of more than twenty other terms, such as Arab, Levantine, Middle Easterner, or Oriental.

What Is Dichotomization?

Scholar Aziza Khazzoom calls this type of ethnic formation "dichotimization." She explains that in Israel, initial economic disparities linked to ethnic identities became embedded in the fabric of society such that they still exist today, more than sixty years after the country was established. Although the country's founders may not have intentionally created social inequalities based on immigrants' countries of origin, she says, they clearly marginalized non-Ashkenazi Jews, starting with the use of overt labeling. Those more severe in their analysis of this issue, however, argue that the process of "othering" happened quite purposefully (see chapter 10), and call it just as inaccurate and unjust as the American white/black duality.

Sephardi Jews

Intentionality and agency aside, Khazzoom notes that dichotomization has been problematic on other levels, including the fact that, like the expression "people of color," neither the term Sephardi nor Mizraḥi has a clear definition. For starters, Jews immigrating to Israel from the Middle East and North Africa—coming from such diverse places as Algeria, Egypt, Iran, Iraq, Lebanon, Libya, Morocco, Syria, Tunisia, and Yemen—had much less in common, in terms of tradition and ritual, than did Ashkenazi Jews arriving from Poland, Russia, or elsewhere in Europe, due in part to their relative lack of physical interaction. There were also many differences between subcommunities of Jews arriving in Israel from the same country (see chapter 7).

Further, rather than claiming the ethno-cultural heritage of the country they had left, some non-Ashkenazi Jews, including some of those immigrating to Israel from Europe, chose to identify with the place their ancestors had been expelled from as far back as the fifteenth century, Spain and Portugal. These Jews called themselves Sephardi, tracing their family lineage to *Sepharad,* the modern Hebrew word for Spain.

During the Spanish and Portuguese Inquisitions of the late 1400s and prior, on a number of occasions Jews in the Iberian Peninsula were given three explicit choices by their Christian rulers: death, expulsion, or conversion to Christianity. Among those who chose conversion, a small number of families identified as Catholic publicly but continued to practice Jewish rituals in private. (An even smaller number went this route but returned to Judaism publicly a few generations later.) Such Jews have been called by various names, including Conversos, Crypto-Jews, and Marranos.

As for those who were expelled, many ended up in countries bordering the Mediterranean Sea. Their descendants have generally identified as Sephardi ever since, despite the disconnect from fifteenth-century Spain and Portugal. Due to the diversity of communities self-identified as Sephardi, when contemporary Jews in Israel or America claim this identity, it commonly tells less about an individual's background than does claiming to be Ashkenazi.

Case Example: Moroccan Jews

For example, take the case of Moroccan Jewry. Some fifteenth-century Jews fled from Spain and Portugal to nearby Morocco. But not all of today's Moroccan Jews identify as Sephardi. In fact, Moroccan Jews can be divided into a number of subgroups. Some trace their lineage in Morocco to before the first century CE, including some—particularly Moroccan Berbers—who maintain that their proto-Jewish ancestors migrated from Jerusalem following the Babylonian Exile of 586 BCE (see chapter 3). Others migrated to Morocco after the Arab Muslim conquest of North Africa in the seventh and eighth centuries.

Still others are descendants of Conversos who fled to Morocco from the Iberian Peninsula in the seventeenth and eighteenth centuries, having spent several centuries practicing Judaism in secret. Some arrived in Morocco after fleeing Russian pogroms in the nineteenth century. Some came from France during the nineteenth and twentieth centuries, when Morocco was under French colonial rule. A small number reside in Ceuta and Melilla, Spanish-controlled cities located in mainland Africa (in what looks to be part of Morocco from a bird's eye view), and travel to and from Morocco on a regular basis for business. In short, even if you learn that an individual identifies as a Moroccan Jew, a great deal of ambiguity remains as to what this actually means.

Further, if we look at just one subgroup of Moroccan Jews, those identifying as Sephardi whose ancestors fled the Iberian Peninsula during the Inquisitions of the 1490s, there is a considerable lack of homogeneity. Indeed, evidence suggests that fifteenth-century Iberian Jews had multiple subidentities. A number of scholars, in fact, argue that the term Sephardi wasn't used until centuries *after* the Inquisitions, adopted to describe previous generations. According to this argument, the "original" Sephardi Jews—i.e., from whom today's Sephardi Jews descended—would not have applied that term to themselves. (Initial uses of this moniker may have pointed to a geographical designation and not a particular culture.)

Sephardi, Mizraḥi, or Non-Ashkenazi?

It has been historically problematic to homogenize Jews immigrating to Israel or the United States (or wherever) from the same country, let alone multiple countries. Nonetheless, masses of non-Ashkenazi Jews arriving in Israel in the 1950s and 1960s were usually labeled simply Sephardi. Scholar Ella Shohat says that if we are to understand this phenomenon, we must look at agency—that is, the subgroup influencing the discourse. According to Shohat, non-Ashkenazi communities did not choose the terms to describe themselves; Ashkenazi Jews named them on their behalf.

As for what word should be used for Jews of Middle Eastern and North African descent if not Sephardi or Mizraḥi, Khazzoom contends that it is not that important what non-Ashkenazi Jews are called, whether it is either of these names or something else entirely, such as *Edot ha-Mizraḥ* (Communities of the East). Much more important is how one particular Jewish subgroup, Ashkenazi Jews (in her research, specifically in Israel) has dominated others, a phenomenon connected to the nonfactual, but "true," dichotomy of Ashkenazi/non-Ashkenazi Jews.

Pesaḥ in Cairo

Upon reaching the core eating part of the Passover Seder, I went to the kitchen to bring out the night's first course, matzah ball soup. For some American Jews, this dish is as central to a Jewish holiday like Pesaḥ as fireworks are to an American Fourth of July celebration. But it is more precise to say that this is "Ashkenazi Jewish food" (or even "Ashkenazi American Jewish food") as opposed to saying it is a "Jewish food." Those 1.2 million American Jews and 3 million Israeli Jews who don't identify as Ashkenazi may not want to be told this is *their* food. The same can be said for bagels, *bab-kah,* borscht, gefilte fish, ḥallah, and kugel—all foods commonly used to symbolize Jewish food in American pop culture at large, despite being historically Ashkenazi.

At my Seder, as soon as the soup came out some of my guests smiled and said: "Of course! What else would you serve on a *Jewish* holiday!" Countless Jews and non-Jews alike *know* that matzah ball soup is quintessentially Jewish—even non-Jews living in Egypt. This is a "truth." Similarly, many people—especially Americans—are familiar with words such as *chutzpah, glitch, mensch, schlep, schmooze,* and *schmuck,* even if they don't know that these words were Yiddish before they also became part of American parlance. One would be hard pressed to find a word derived from a non-Ashkenazi Jewish community that has worked its way into modern American English in a similar fashion.

Narratives and Rituals

For me, eating matzah ball soup is a basic Jewish ritual. In my family, which is Ashkenazi, one would not think of serving anything else on Passover or Rosh Hashanah, the Jewish New Year. Ritual customs are one way that communities reinforce and pass on their narratives, especially to future generations.

Dominant Narratives and Dominant Rituals

To an outsider, such ceremonial observances may seem strange. To an insider, they are likely to be seen as normal. Such practices can take the form of placing one's right hand over one's left breast and pledging allegiance to a country or sitting cross-legged in meditative thought while quietly saying a single word or phrase repeatedly.

Similarly, Jews have an annual ritual involving the drinking of four cups of wine while chronicling their communal journey from imprisonment to liberation. Each spring Jews commonly come together with family and friends to retell the majestic and powerful saga of hundreds of thousands of people fleeing slavery, who are just about to be recaptured and returned to captivity by battalions of angry soldiers when their humble leader, a man of so few words that his brother must speak on his behalf, raises his shepherd's crook high in the air and divides a vast sea into two, thereby creating a path that the slaves can cross through. Ergo, the Pesaḥ Seder.

There isn't anything intrinsically problematic about me, an Ashkenazi Jew, serving an Ashkenazi dish on a Jewish holiday, nor would there be anything wrong with a non-Ashkenazi Jew (or non-Jew) doing so (or an Ashkenazi Jew serving a non-Ashkenazi dish, for that matter). A more fundamental challenge emerges, however, when a single subgroup's identity—in this case, Ashkenazi expressions of Jewish identities, manifesting here in matzah ball soup—becomes symbolic of the larger group's identities. Among Jews specifically, this process moves non-Ashkenazi rituals and rites to the side, which not only conceals them but in fact replaces them with something else. Like most forms of dominance, this is more problematic for non-Ashkenazi Jews than Ashkenazi ones. As is the case with most subordinated groups, these non-Ashkenazi subcommunities already know the dominants' narratives; the opposite is rarely the case.

Lesser-Known Narratives and Lesser-Known Rituals

As with most Jewish practices, a variety of customs are brought into play in the ritual performance of the Passover Seder (figs. 1.4 and 1.5). For example:

- Afghani and Persian Jews have a tradition of gently whipping one another with long scallions during a celebrated Passover song ("Dayenu'), symbolizing the Egyptian slave masters' treatment of the biblical Hebrew slaves.
- Ethiopian Jews have a tradition of breaking all of their household's earthenware dishes and making new ones during their pre-Passover preparations, a practice based on biblical verses instructing the Hebrews to remove (as in "not possess") and not eat any non-kosher-for-Pesaḥ food during the holiday.
- Jews from Cochin, India, have a custom stricter than that of the Ethiopians, whereby they keep a room in

FIGURE 1.4. Bnai Israel Indian Jews preparing homemade *matzah* (flat, crunchy cracker) for *Pesaḥ* (Passover).

FIGURE 1.5. A Yemenite Jewish family, originating from the city of Habban in eastern Yemen, celebrating a Passover Seder in their new home in Tel Aviv (c. 1946), then occupied by British military forces.

their home—year round—solely for Pesaḥ utensils, ensuring these eating tools don't come into contact with non-kosher-for-Pesaḥ food. (Fig. 1.4 illustrates another Indian Jewish tradition).

- Some Jews from Gibraltar, Greece, and Italy mix clay dust into their ḥaroset, a dish commonly served on Pesaḥ, symbolizing the mortar biblical Israelite slaves used when building. A group of Jewish Union soldiers in the American Civil War reappropriated this ritual by putting an actual brick on their Seder table because they did not have the ingredients to make ḥaroset.
- Hungarian Jews have a tradition of decorating their Seder table with the most expensive gold and silver that they own, symbolizing the jewels the biblical Hebrews asked their Egyptian neighbors for before fleeing.
- Moroccan Jews have a tradition of eating a sheep's head the first night of Pesaḥ, symbolizing the

ancient lamb sacrifice that the biblical Hebrews were instructed to perform.

- Some Yemenite Jews keep their door open throughout the Seder in anticipation of the Messiah's return. In contrast, Jews from Tunisia (specifically, Djerba) and Libya have a custom of prohibiting "strangers" from entering their homes or benefiting from their belongings during the first two days of Pesaḥ. (Fig. 1.5 shows a Yemenite Passover Seder.)
- As for more dramatic theatrics, in a number of Jewish communities (including Iraqi, Kurdish, Libyan, Moroccan, Syrian, Tunisian [Djerban], and Yemenite) attendees put on costumes or use props, either during or right before the Seder, and reenact the Exodus narrative, playing specific biblical characters.
- One ultra-Orthodox sect, the Gerrers, who trace themselves back to the pre–World War II Polish town of Góra Kalwaria, have a tradition of pouring a barrel of

water on the ground and crossing over it, symbolizing Moses's parting of the Red Sea as described in the Torah. (This ritual takes place on the seventh day of Pesaḥ and not during the Seder itself.) Other communities have similar variations of this ritual.

Although there are countless Pesaḥ rituals, the Passover Seder—in the United States, at least—has become quite Ashkenazi-fied. For example, in television shows such as *Curb Your Enthusiasm, Family Guy, Gossip Girl, The Nanny, The Rachel Zoe Project,* and *Rugrats,* or movies such as *Family Business, It Runs in the Family, Marjorie Morningstar,* and *When Do We Eat?,* characters perform Seders using Ashkenazi-specific customs, reflected in the songs and melodies that are integrated into the evening and the types of food eaten, among other things.

This doesn't mean that communities such as Afghani and Persian Jews aren't free to practice their own Passover rituals on this holiday. Even so, while the consequences of cultural dominance are potentially less damaging than legal dominance, to those subordinated the end result is still problematic. Cultural influences often shape a community's worldview. Dominant ideas, whether originating within a cultural context or not, are often internalized, a process that habitually becomes externalized and further normalized, especially in today's interconnected world. Such ideas are also frequently used to justify legal practices. Through this process, dominance can lead to the withering and expunging of subordinate identities and practices.

An Orange on the Seder Plate

Of course, Ashkenazi hegemony isn't the only form of intra-Jewish dominance that plays out through the Passover Seder—as an interesting contemporary example illustrates. A core Pesaḥ ritual is to place a dish on one's Seder table that is filled with various ritual foods, a custom dating back to the first few centuries CE (fig. 1.6).

In the early 1980s, scholar Susannah Heschel suggested adding an orange to the Seder plate as a symbol of the fruitfulness gained when Jewish lesbians and gay men are active in Jewish life. By spitting out seeds from the orange, one could ritualize the rejection of homophobia within the Jewish community.

Sometime thereafter, however, she learned that the meaning behind the ritual she created had been rewritten. "Somehow . . . the typical patriarchal maneuver occurred: my idea of an orange and my intention of affirming lesbians and gay men were transformed. Now

FIGURE 1.6. A Seder plate containing both centuries-old symbols, such as *ḥaroset, maror,* and *karpas* (explained in note), and more recent ones, such as an orange; a ceramic egg (traditionally, an actual egg is used), symbolizing spring as well as new life; olives, symbolizing peace in Israel and Palestine or an end to the Israeli occupation of the West Bank and Gaza; and *zeroa,* or beetroot (traditionally, a roasted shankbone), symbolizing the sacrifice of a Paschal lamb. Substituting a ceramic egg, seeds or flowers, and beetroot allows people to observe both traditional customs and vegan or vegetarian practices.

the story circulates that a man said to me that a woman belongs on the *bimah* [the stage found at the front of some synagogue prayer halls] as an orange on the seder plate. A woman's words are attributed to a man, and the affirmation of lesbians and gay men is erased. Isn't that precisely what's happened over the centuries to women's ideas?"

The Tribe vs. *Diaspora*

THE TRIBE

Depictions of Jewish rituals—and Jews—that represent an Ashkenazi identity as *the* Jewish identity, as opposed to presenting an Ashkenazi identity as *an* Ashkenazi identity (or *a* Jewish identity), are found in other parts of American popular culture, including those explicitly created by Jews. Take, for example, the difference between two visually based art forms produced in the early twenty-first century. The first is the acclaimed 2005 short film made by artist Tiffany Shlain, *The Tribe,* self-described as addressing what it means "to be an American Jew today."

Weaving together archival footage, animation, and

graphics, the film, though interesting, engaging, and well crafted, is resoundingly Ashkenazi-centric. For example:

- the background music is largely Klezmer, a type of music imported to the United States in the late nineteenth century by Yiddish-speaking Ashkenazi immigrants;
- American Jewish history is limited to immigrants who came from Eastern Europe and Russia;
- almost all of the photos of Jews from outside the United States are similarly Euro-centric;
- a list of historically violent episodes carried out against Jews focuses mainly on European and Russian Jewish communities (a few ancient Middle Eastern events being the exception).

Even the way that biblical characters are presented—in the form of Barbie dolls (Barbie's history is central to the movie as well)—is akin to portraying Jesus as a white European male.

This is not to say that 20 percent of the film's footage should have focused on the 20 percent of American Jews who are not Ashkenazi. Indeed, the film includes several minor pieces of information that are not rooted in Ashkenazi experiences. However, in its portrayal of American Jews, Israeli Jews, and even biblical Hebrews, *The Tribe* embodies Ashkenazi subnarratives and not the larger Jewish communities' narratives, thus reinforcing Ashkenazi—and white—dominance in an effort, ironically enough, whose ostensible goal is to illustrate how diverse the Jewish community is. The movie even says that the quintessential American doll, Barbie, with her blonde hair and blue eyes, doesn't "look Jewish" (in the film's own words: "All [Jewish] subtribes can agree Barbie doesn't look Jewish")—a problematic claim in its own right. In other words, *The Tribe* reinforces the very message it is attempting to critique, contending that there are set ways that Jews should and should not look at the same time it is supposedly shattering this formula.

DIASPORA

Not all artists focusing on the Jewish community stereotype Ashkenazi Jews as *the* Jews. Photographer Frédéric Brenner, for example, explicitly shapes a far different perspective. One of his most famous projects, *Diaspora,* took him around the world for twenty-four years to photograph Jews from tens of countries. When asked about his goals, he said: "I would say that if there is one thing that I would like to achieve, it is first and foremost to break an emblematic representation of the Jew." He wanted to bring the margins to the center in order to show the reality of Jewish diversity, adding that although he started his quest believing in the "oneness" of Jews, he now believes in the "many-ness."

His project leaves the audience with a lingering question: If Jews are so different from one another, if they are *not* all Ashkenazi but in fact much more diverse than even the multilayered photographs of *Diaspora* suggest, what actually connects such diversity? To quote Brenner:

> What do all these people that I have photographed have in common, if not their differences? When you take out ideology, religion, all those scaffolds that we have imported in our life, what remains? One of the sentences that is going to be one of the excerpts of my book is this sentence of Kafka in his *Diaries* where he says, "What do I have in common with the Jews? I have so little in common with myself." And the very idea of discontinuity is at the heart of my project. I would say that the three key words are really paradox, ambivalence, and discontinuity, and to say that this very discontinuity starts within ourselves.

By presenting us with images of Jews from Argentina, China, Ethiopia, India, Morocco, Portugal, South Africa, Yemen, and beyond, *Diaspora* rejects the idea that Ashkenazi narratives aptly represent *the* Jewish narrative. In so doing, it complicates dominant Jewish narratives, destabilizing such "truths." Other photography projects, such as Scattered Among the Nations' *Jews of Color: In Color,* similarly challenge the dominance of the Ashkenazi Jewish archetype in focusing on relatively unknown, non-Ashkenazi Jewish communities.

Yet such projects are the exception to the rule. Even when Jewish community centers have exhibits focusing on non-Ashkenazi groups, they commonly present these groups as strange, further distancing them from more dominant forms of Jewish "authenticity." "Truth"-wise, they are exotic; factually, they are not.

Pesaḥ in Cairo

Our Cairene Pesaḥ Seder lasted about ninety minutes, much shorter than at home with my family. But considering that most of the guests were first-timers, I considered it a success. The topics of discussion ranged from the freedom narrative of Passover to modern-day struggles for human rights, such as the American civil rights movement of the 1960s. We also spoke about social justice issues closer to where we were sitting, such as those related to the Israeli-Palestinian conflict.

As the evening concluded, I reflected on how meaningful it was for me to experience this Jewish tradition with other Jews and with non-Jews. But I also noted some of the minor discomfort I felt over how a few specific passages in the *Haggadah* might be understood by my guests, most of whom knew very little about Jewish ritual practices of any kind.

The narrative of the Passover Seder reinforces itself. It is a ritual in which *the* Jewish narrative—for those identifying as Ashkenazi, Mizraḥi, Sephardi, or another Jewish subgroup altogether—is explicitly retold, year after year, in countless different ways. With each retelling, Jews' dominant stories gain strength, creating internal, Jewish-centric storylines that play in a loop.

Despite my momentary pangs of unease, I also knew that it is almost impossible to find a community that does not teach its narrative ethnocentrically. Perhaps that very tension—acknowledging dominant Jewish narratives while also holding onto the wider, richer corpus of Jewish narratives writ large; staying loyal to one's particular identities while never straying from a steadfast commitment to the universality of humanity—is the challenge.

Even though many Jews act as if there is a single way to practice Judaism, there has never been one Judaism, only Judaisms; never one type of Jew or Jewish identity, only Jews and Jewish identities.

Sinais

Contents

Key Ideas

- The Torah, or Five Books of Moses, is a core "totem" of the world Jewish community, representing a set of moral and ethical codes and sacred stories. Like all sacred texts, the Torah only exists in relationship to its interpretations. Some Jews consider the continued interpretation of the Five Books of Moses to be an ongoing form of revelation.

- The Hebrew Bible is a collection of sacred texts written (from approximately the tenth to second centuries BCE) and compiled (from around the fifth century bce to the second century CE) over the course of hundreds of years. Some Jews believe in the Bible's divinity, whereas many others maintain it was written by humans.
- God is described in the Torah as male, which has had a major impact on Jewish social discourses, theological beliefs, and ritual practices.
- The Bible follows the lineage of one particular group, which has led to the development of the notion of Jewish chosenness. Some Jews understand chosenness to describe an inherent superiority, whereas others reject this idea, instead focusing on possible intentions behind the Torah's focus on the Jewish people.

Dawn on Mount Sinai

My friend and I started climbing the 7,497-foot mountain in the dark, hoping to reach the peak before sunrise. The hike was much more strenuous than we had anticipated, to say nothing of the fact that we weren't wearing proper footwear for an ascent of this sort. Three or so hours after we began the silent trek, we arrived at the top, or at least the highest point on the mountain to which one is permitted to climb.

The place had a certain peaceful air to it, and the view was astounding. It helped that we were alone, aside from the residents of St. Catherine's Monastery, located at the mountain's base, and, surprisingly enough, a man we met at the summit who was selling soda and snacks to hikers such as ourselves. After washing down a few too many packages of Oreo cookies with Coke—something not so strange for my twenty-two-year-old self—my friend and I sat down on some flat-topped boulders and shared a few moments in silence. Dawn on Mount Sinai.

Often called Jabal Mūsā, the mountain of Moses, by Muslims, and Mount Ḥoreb by Jews and Christians, this mountain is said to be *the* majestic site that Moses climbed in order to receive the Ten Commandments (or Directives), the only place described in the Torah where a mass number of people encountered God "face to face." People have been making pilgrimages to this site, located in the Sinai Peninsula in Egypt, for hundreds of years—by some accounts, since as far back as the third century CE.

For my friend and me, it didn't really matter whether this was *the* Mount Sinai. Neither of us necessarily believed that this place was the famous biblical site. I had my doubts about the Torah's description of the majestic

event as well, a dramatic episode involving thunder, lightning, fire, smoke, and a quaking mountain where more than 600,000 individuals witnessed God's "voice." But I did consider the Torah text to represent the "truth."

At an early age, I learned all about Moses and the burning bush, the Israelites' exodus from Egypt, and the forty years of wandering in the desert. This is true of many Jews, for whom the stories laid out in the Five Books of Moses are part of dominant Jewish narratives. Whether it's the tale of Moses or the Garden of Eden or Noah and the flood, these accounts are emblazoned into the mind of the Jewish collective, even if in only a vague sense.

Many, if not most, Jews today don't believe that the Torah is a historical record of events; they don't believe it is factual. But they do hold these ancient stories to be "true," even if they reject most of the ritual practices based in the Bible's first five books. And each year on Pesaḥ they celebrate one of the core narratives in the Torah, the Israelites' exodus from slavery to freedom.

Sacred Place: Mount Sinai

Whereas most Jews probably aren't even aware that there is a specific mountain in the Sinai Desert that people today say is *the* Mount Sinai, of those Jews who do, most have certainly never traveled there. Yet Mount Sinai serves as both a literal and metaphorical "totem" for the entire Jewish community. In *The Elementary Forms of Religious Life,* sociologist Emile Durkheim explains that communities commonly adhere to a "totemic principle," an idea embodied in a physical object that represents a set of moral and ethical codes for a given group of people. "The images of the totem," says Durkheim, "are more sacred than the totemic being itself."

For Jews, the importance of Mount Sinai lies in its symbolism, the idea that in this place Moses proverbially touched the hand of God. This is where God delivered a set of laws to the biblical Israelites. Neither the Israelites nor their descendants, however, developed a cultic practice centered on this mountain or any other physical location connected to the transmission of the Torah. Rather, the totem of Mount Sinai is found in the Torah scroll, which tells the community's ancient narrative.

Using a Durkheimian framework, we can say that Mount Sinai is the "tangible form in which the intangible substance is represented in the communal imagination," having existed as a central totemic "symbol" of the Jewish people for millennia, perhaps since the episode described in Exodus. Jews do not habitually return to Mount Sinai in order to reconnect with God; rather, it lives in the Jewish communal imagination, embodied in Torah yet existing beyond the text, firmly ensconced in the Jewish collective's dominant narratives.

Sacred Text: Torah and the "Apple"

The Torah's "truth," alive in the collective mind of Jews worldwide, is shaped by interpretation. Take the story of the Garden of Eden, for example. In Genesis, before creating Eve, God tells Adam, the first and only human in existence, that he can eat from any tree in the garden except the Tree of Knowledge of Good and Evil. Nonetheless, Adam and his new partner, Eve, disobey God and partake of the tree's fruits. And what was the forbidden fruit that they ate? Everyone *knows* that it was an apple. But was it? The Hebrew text only uses the word *pri,* "fruit."

To some degree it doesn't matter why an apple became the de facto designation of the unknown fruit. We do know that a fifth-century Latin translation of the Hebrew Bible rendered the word *pri* as *mālum,* or apple, linguistically linking it to *malum,* evil, a Latin term used a few verses prior to describe the snake that enticed Adam and Eve to eat from the tree. Other early biblical interpreters saw a connection between the pain experienced by Adam and Eve after being banished from Eden and the love-sickness that plagued the author of the Song of Songs (both in relation to God), whose description of despair employs the imagery of an apple. More recently, the apple was popularized by the seventeenth-century *Paradise Lost,* in which the English writer John Milton describes the fruit as such. But the explanation may be something else entirely.

The factuality of the matter was replaced by "truth" long ago. In popular culture, the fruit is an apple. This isn't much different than depicting the Torah's Moses or the Christian Bible's Jesus as a white man, as seen in paintings, books, and movies. Over time these representations—these interpretations of sacred texts—have become true, shaping the perspectives of the books' readers for centuries thereafter. In the sixteenth-century painting *Adam and Eve,* for example, the Italian artist Titian depicts the fruits hanging from the forbidden tree in the Garden of Eden as apples (fig. 2.1).

This same process applies when considering fact vs. "truth" regarding Mount Sinai. Whether or not St. Catherine's Monastery is located at the base of *the* Mount Sinai, and whether or not Mount Ḥoreb and Mount Sinai are even the same mountain, most Jews don't worry about such questions. As scholar Jon Levenson explains in *Sinai and Zion,* "The historical question about Sinai,

FIGURE 2.1. In this painting, *Adam and Eve* by Titian (c. 1550), the serpent, depicted as half snake and half human child, gives Eve the forbidden apple.

as important as it is in some contexts, misses the point about the significance of this material in the religion of Israel. . . . History in the modern sense is not the goal of the Sinai narratives. . . . Sinai was a kind of archetype, a mold into which new experiences could be fit, hundreds of years after the original event, if such there was."

This explains why Jews from across the faith spectrum—from secular humanists to ultra-Orthodox—know the name Mount Sinai. Whether or not they believe the biblical description surrounding the giving of the Torah at Mount Sinai, or even know the details regarding the larger narrative of the Hebrew Bible, what happened on Mount Sinai is "true" for all of them, believer and nonbeliever alike.

The Bible

Bibles

The Bible is among the oldest and most popular books of all time. But *which* Bible? What do we mean when someone says *the* Bible or when they refer to Scripture? When twenty-first-century Americans use the term *Bible* they commonly assume others know what they're talking about. But there is no definitive book called the Bible; there are only versions. In fact, all Bibles are collections of individual books, anthologies of sorts (as reflected in the Greek root of the word, *biblia,* meaning books).

Hebrew Bible

Most relevant for us is the "Hebrew Bible." Though also called the Old Testament, for many Jews this name is a theological statement because it reinforces a core Christian belief: with Jesus came a new divine revelation, a New Testament, which replaced the one before (an idea some understand as supersessionist). To avoid the implication of such a position, we won't be using the term Old Testament. In fact, unless otherwise noted, from this point forward, when the term *Bible* is used, it refers to the Hebrew Bible, which is made up of the Torah (Five Books of Moses), the Prophets, and the Writings. When the term *Christian Bible* is used, it refers to the Old Testament and the New Testament together. When most mention the Hebrew Bible, however, they are referring to a particular version (special topic 2.1).

What Is a (Biblical) Canon?

Before getting into the specifics of when these books were collected into a single volume, we need to consider what a canon is: a core set of communal texts arranged into a list or collection of books and given an authoritative status. In other words, such compilations are themselves the product of particular interpretations.

Nevertheless, more often than not they are perceived as immutable and absolute. As mentioned in the previous chapter, another way to understand a canon is as a dominant narrative, no matter whether it manifests as books attributed to the creator of the universe or must-read texts for high school English literature students. For centuries, communities that accepted the Bible have believed that their particular collection of texts was woven together into a single, cohesive, divinely sanctioned book; that the way it is, is the way it is supposed to be. Many believe their version to be the only true version. The fact that many books from the ancient Middle East didn't make their way into any biblical canon, and those that did were likely organized based on the determination of a small group, has been, at best, a marginal idea over the last two millennia.

When Was the Bible Canonized?

Since scholars began applying a critical lens to the endeavor of Bible study, some have asserted that the biblical canon was compiled in stages, sometime around 400 BCE for the Torah, 200 BCE for the Prophets, and 90–100 CE for the Writings. Others have held that all three sections were compiled between the second century BCE and the first century CE or during the first two centuries CE. Some notable scholars, such as Saul Lieberman, contend that even in the first century CE modifications were still being made to the Torah's text. Scholar Shaye Cohen concurs with Lieberman, suggesting that there were a number of different biblical canons in the first century CE.

Who Canonized It?

We don't know who canonized the Bible. For example, we lack evidence that a centralized Israelite or Judean (see chapter 3) authority imposed a unified biblical canon on their community. That said, Judean subcommunities argued more over biblical interpretation than over which books were to be considered part of the Hebrew Bible. Whatever the case, there is less consensus today among academics regarding when the Bible was canonized than in previous times.

Does the Bible Include All Ancient Middle Eastern Texts?

To make matters more complicated, discoveries of other ancient texts—such as the Dead Sea Scrolls (also called the Qumran scrolls), a collection of texts sometimes cate-gorized as part of the apocrypha (Latin for "secret," referring to noncanonical sacred texts from the same era) and other times as pseudepigrapha (Greek for "false name," referring to sacred texts attributed to authors who did not actually write them)—have played an important role in destabilizing previously accepted "publishing dates."

The unearthing of such texts, however fragmentary, has reinforced, if not altogether confirmed, the argument that many sacred texts were present in the ancient Middle East aside from those included in the Bible. It also has shed light on the existence of different versions of the Bible. Some, for example, were written entirely in Aramaic, rather than Hebrew. Ultimately, we do not know precisely when the Bible and the books collected therein were canonized, nor what authoritative body carried out this task. Some point to particular biblical prophets, such as Ezra and Nehemiah; others to "the rabbis" of the Mishnah and Talmud (discussed below and in chapter 5). But the bottom line is, we don't know.

When Were the Books of the Bible Written?

Not only do we not know when the books in the Bible were collected into a single volume (i.e., canonized), but we also don't know when the individual texts were written. One dominant position holds that the Torah can be traced to between the thirteenth and eighth centuries BCE, the Prophets to the eighth through sixth centuries BCE, and the Writings to the sixth through third centuries BCE.

Does the Bible Depict Historical Events?

In an attempt to reconcile biblical stories with historical evidence, some have attempted to locate supporting archeological data. Yet excavations in modern Israel, among other places, have led scholars to starkly different positions. In one case, a scholar interpreted an inscription found on an ancient, newly unearthed container to be proof of the historicity (historical actuality) of King David and King Solomon—two figures written about in the Bible, each of whom ruled united monarchies in the ancient areas of Israel and Judea (parts of modern-day Israel and the occupied West Bank, the latter also commonly called Palestine). Another scholar, however, opined that the theory regarding the ancient vessel's connection to the Bible was methodologically flawed.

In the end, as with many other questions—When was the Bible written? Who canonized it, and when?—the answer is that we don't know. Some, such as the great twentieth-century philosopher and rabbi Abraham

Joshua Heschel, have noted that the historical nature of the Torah is much less relevant than the laws contained within it. Others have added to this perspective, calling the Torah the collective response to the revelation on Mount Sinai.

Who Wrote the Bible?

Perhaps the biggest question of all is, who wrote—or perhaps better said, who composed—the Bible? To better understand the different ways people answer this question, it is useful to think of a spectrum. At one end are those who believe the Bible is purely the word of God; at the other are those who contend it is entirely the work of humans. According to Bible scholar James Kugel, these two ends of the spectrum are irreconcilable.

God as Author

Among those who believe the Bible is the word of God, there are disparate views as to how God communicated it to humans. Some believe that while God gave the Torah to Moses on Mount Sinai, word for word, God took a different approach with the Prophets and Writings: there, God revealed particular messages directly to individual prophets, which they transformed into written prose, and inspired the authors of the Writings such that those texts can be said to be authored by both God and humans (though some Talmudic authorities note that particular books in the Writings are actually fictional).

For those who believe in the Torah's divine nature, perceived inconsistencies in the text are not a problem with the Torah but arise from our lack of understanding. If, for example, God is referred to by different Hebrew names, these names must refer to something deeper, such as God's distinct attributes. Why, you may ask, are certain stories and laws repeated multiple times? The answer: to teach something important or to underscore the significance of a particular verse. Devotees who take this vantage point believe that the Torah is a perfect, infallible text (similar to the Qur'an for Muslims). It contains no contradictions or mistakes. Any suspected errors are rooted in inaccurate perceptions, which reflect human imperfection.

Humans as Authors

Those who maintain that the Bible was written by humans (and only humans) provide different answers to these same questions.

Today's biblical scholars often echo a theory solidified in nineteenth-century Europe called the Documentary Hypothesis. This argument contends that the Torah (to say nothing of the Prophets and Writings) is a compilation of texts written by different human authors (and/or communities or schools) and put together into a single collection by various editors, or perhaps a single editor. This early form of biblical criticism designates general groups of authors as J, E, P, and D: J for the Jahwists or Yahwists, those texts using the name *YHWH* for God; E for those texts where God goes by the name *Elohim;* P for texts focusing on Priestly rites; and D for the author(s) of the fifth book of the Torah, Deuteronomy.

This challenge to the divine perfection of the Bible goes back at least to eleventh-century Europe, when a few figures publicly noted what they considered to be historical inconsistencies, for example that some of the Edomite kings in the Torah who are presented as having lived at the same time as Moses actually lived much later. Other individuals came along in the fourteenth and sixteenth centuries to raise similar points.

Perhaps the two most noteworthy Europeans who challenged the Torah's divinity prior to the eighteenth century were the philosophers Thomas Hobbes and Baruch Spinoza, both of whom wrote books suggesting outright that (a) human beings wrote the Bible and (b) Moses wasn't even involved in the process. Unsurprisingly, Jewish and Christian practitioners were not comfortable with such theological challenges. Spinoza was excommunicated by the Jewish community of Amsterdam altogether.

Putting aside lone voices such as Hobbes and Spinoza, most of the first generation of scholars engaging in modern biblical criticism had a different objective than contemporary ones. As Kugel explains, "The whole point of modern scholarship was to sweep aside everything people had always thought of the Bible—the debris of the traditional interpretations of the multitudinous schools and sects—in order to discover pure, unadulterated Scripture, the 'real Bible.'"

In other words, modern biblical criticism began as an effort to retrieve the "real" divine text, which was hidden within the Bible, perhaps due to human error during the transmission process. In contrast, twenty-first-century biblical scholars begin with the fundamental assumption that the Torah was created by humans; they don't assume that there is an original "unadulterated" form of the text distorted by humans, which can be uncovered.

Although they may dismiss the specifics of the Documentary Hypothesis (i.e., with authors J, E, P, and D), the core idea on which it is based—that humans wrote the Bible—continues to drive biblical criticism today.

Another way to frame this discussion is by saying that the Documentary Hypothesis and other such theories approach the Five Books of Moses via literary criticism, as if one should analyze this text using the same tools one would for any other ancient text. When questions about the Torah are raised from within this school of thought—e.g., Why is God called by different names? Why are certain stories and laws repeated multiple times? Why are there overt nonsequiturs in the text? Why do other ancient Middle Eastern and African communities have similar stories to those found in the Torah?—the standard answer is the same: because the Torah is made up of texts written by different human authors. To put it somewhat flippantly, the grand editor(s) didn't have a computer to work with; there was no "spellcheck" program that could point out textual inconsistencies and redundancies.

Although the editing process was clearly not as polished as today, the Bible, as Richard Elliot Friedman, the author of *Who Wrote the Bible?,* contends, was the first comprehensive text of "national history," at least among the communities of the ancient Middle East. Rather than aiming to produce a well-written literary masterpiece, the editor/s (or redactor/s) had the goal of reconciling opposing sacred sources, including ones that some might have simply left on the cutting-room floor. Whether an individual or a group, the editor, Friedman points out, was an artist of sorts, someone who was wise, erudite, literarily sensitive, and committed to embracing seemingly disparate stories and fashioning them into a single, cohesive narrative. In other words, the primary goal was to make the Five Books of Moses more understandable to those living at that time.

Two Torahs: Written Torah and Oral Torah

The Relationship between the Written and Oral Torahs

The Documentary Hypothesis and other theories of this kind challenge the general way that Jews (and non-Jews) have oriented themselves to the Torah—used here in its narrowest sense, to mean the Five Books of Moses—for millennia: as if it were the word of God. For the rabbis of the Mishnah and Talmud, sacred texts commonly dated to the first through third centuries CE and the third through eighth centuries CE, respectively (see chapter 5), the Torah was given by God to Moses on Mount Sinai—not just the "Written Torah" (i.e., the Five Books) but the "Oral Torah" as well, the explanation of the Pentateuch's written word. (Many Jews today add that the Oral Torah is embodied in sacred texts of postbiblical generations—such as the Mishnah, Talmud, etc.—including a number of different written commentaries that began as oral traditions.)

The distinction between the Written Torah and Oral Torah and "evidence" for the existence and necessity of both are reflected in various texts. For instance, in the Written Torah it says, "Come to Me on the mountain and wait there, and I will give you the stone tablets and the Torah and the Commandment what I have inscribed to instruct them" (Exod. 24:12). Expanding on this verse, one postbiblical tradition—i.e., found in the Oral Torah—says, "When God had finished [teaching the Torah to Moses], God said, 'Go and teach it to My children. . . . Give them the Bible in writing and the Mishnah, Agaddah, and Torah orally, for it is the latter which separate Israel from the Gentiles.'"

Some maintain that the Oral Torah had to have been given at the same time as the Written Torah, that without it Moses would never have been able to explain the written tradition (special topic 2.2). Others hold different understandings, such as one attributed to an eighteenth-century figure, Rabbi Menachem Mendel of Rymanov, who explained that all God said at Sinai was "Aleph," the first letter of the Hebrew alphabet; through that one letter all Written and Oral Torah has been derived.

From the Revelation at Sinai to Ongoing Revelation?

Most non-Orthodox Jews and, arguably, a minority of Modern Orthodox Jews do not believe the Oral Torah (e.g., the Mishnah and Talmud) was communicated by God to Moses in the same fashion as the Written Torah, but instead believe that it developed over the course of history based on the authority of the rabbis. The Mishnah, thought to be one of the first sets of books elucidating the Torah's laws, itself does not say that it was given to Moses on Mount Sinai, and thus may support this view. Only texts that appeared after the Mishnah was completed, including the Talmud, make such claims. (Chapter 5 discusses "the rabbis" and these texts in detail.)

The Talmudic rabbis believed that God's revelation on

Mount Sinai continued through them and their interpretations of the Written Torah. This isn't to say that they believed their words had the status of the Prophets or Writings. Rather, they considered their interpretations an ongoing form of revelation, a continuation of Sinai in terms of their authority as the legitimate interpreters of God's law.

Scholar Michael Fishbane explains this as follows: "[Mishnaic and Talmudic] Judaism tried to minimize the gap between a divine Torah and ongoing human interpretation by projecting the origins of authoritative exegesis to Sinai itself. But even this mythification of a chain of legitimate interpreters did not so much obscure the distinction between revelation and interpretation as underscore it." Many Jews today, Orthodox and non-Orthodox alike, agree with this perspective, holding that God's revelation at Mount Sinai did not end the process of revelation. Rather, in and through God's continued relationship with humans, revelation remains ongoing.

This is a dominant idea in the Reform movement, the largest religious denomination among American Jews (see chapter 8). In 1999, they formally reaffirmed that "revelation is a continuous process, confined to no one group and to no one age." This idea was stated both by their leadership in 1937 as well in the early twentieth century by Solomon Schechter, one of the founders of today's second-largest denomination of American Jewry, the Conservative movement. Though coming from a slightly different angle, key nineteenth- and early-twentieth-century Jewish philosophers, such as Martin Buber and Franz Rosenzweig, reached similar conclusions.

Written Torah: What's in the Five Books of Moses?

Basic Storyline

Whatever position one takes regarding the Bible's origins, according to the Five Books of Moses the experience that took place between God and the Israelites at Mount Sinai was a continuation of something that began years prior, a covenant first made between God and a Hebrew man named Abraham, that continued with Abraham's son Isaac, grandson Jacob, and great-grandchildren—

FIGURE 2.2. Created by Jen Taylor Friedman, the *Minyan of Tefillin Barbie* depicts a *minyan* (an edict in the Talmud requiring a quorum of ten adult males, or, in many contemporary communities, males and females) of Jewish Barbie dolls praying together. Each is wearing a set of *tefillin* and a *tallit* (prayer shawl); collectively, they are reading from a Torah scroll, laid out on a waist-high platform. While it is not uncommon to see women wearing *tefillin* in Reform, Conservative, and other liberal Jewish movements, one would be hard-pressed to find women engaging in this ritual in an Orthodox setting, despite the existence of premodern Jewish legal texts permitting women to do so.

specifically Jacob's sons, also known as the Children of Israel. While the stories about Adam and Eve through Jacob and his thirteen children form the prelude to the Torah (Genesis), the remaining four books focus on the story of Moses and the Israelites, tribes that eventually make their way to the Land of Israel, which begins a new "chapter" of the narrative, described in the book of Joshua, the first book of the Prophets.

As for the second and third sections of the Bible, the Prophets and Writings, these texts can be categorized into four general areas:

- those chronicling the Israelite narrative of conquest, kingdom, and exile, organized and named according to the authorities of the day;
- those attributed to particular prophets, which contain many different messages, communication styles, and literary techniques, while voicing both judgment of and compassion for the Israelite community;
- wisdom texts;
- and poems, prayers, and songs.

Another way to organize the range of biblical texts, whether the Written Torah or the Prophets and Writings, is to group them as laws or narratives, ritual observances or stories.

Law and Ritual Observance: 613 Directives?

Two of the many ways that Jews enact their identities are by observing *halakhah* (Jewish law, discussed further in

chapter 5) and studying Torah. For those intent on following halakhah, according to the Mishnaic and Talmudic rabbis, there are 613 *mitzvot* (biblical directives) in the Five Books of Moses that Jews are obligated to follow. (Some contend that all Jewish law can be traced back to these mitzvot.) This, however, is but one position, one "truth."

The Talmud cites only one individual who actually calculated the number of directives as 613; in a few other places the text simply presents the number as 613, as if it was already common knowledge. But aside from noting that there are 248 positive and 365 negative directives (i.e., something one must do versus something one should refrain from doing), the individual who stated that there are 613 mitzvot did not specify what they are.

In fact, the same passage from the Talmud that refers to 613 mitzvot says that King David reduced the number of directives from 613 to 11, the prophet Isaiah from 613 to 6, and the prophet Micah from 613 to 3. The most famous of these lists of mitzvot is undoubtedly the Ten Commandments (or Ten Directives). However, authorities in the Mishnah and Talmud also say that there are many more than 613 rules in the Torah because each one of the 613 mitzvot has multiple subrules.

Over time Jewish authorities have categorized and counted the Torah's laws in many other ways. Some maintain that it wasn't until the medieval period, with the acceptance of the legal interpretations of Rabbi Moshe ben Maimon, or Maimonides (see chapter 5), that the number 613 became part of dominant narratives of halakhah. Regardless, because many of the mitzvot deal with rituals one can only perform in the Temple of Jerusalem (chapter 3), which was destroyed close to two thousand years ago, and others specifically deal with agricultural practices and thus are more suitable to agrarian communities, it is impossible to observe all 613 mitzvot today.

Narrative and Torah Study

For Jews, the Torah is the core of the Hebrew Bible. It is much more important than the Prophets or Writings. In fact, the Five Books of Moses form the core of *all* Jewish texts; whether directly or indirectly, all Jewish writings refer back to the Torah, even the Prophets and Writings. (Some passages from the Prophets and Writings are best understood as the first interpretations of the Torah, with particular segments addressing seeming ambiguities in the Torah text.)

Some Jews even maintain that the Torah was created before the world, that it served as the blueprint for creation. For most others, especially Jews who believe in the Torah's divine nature, it is an amazingly deep text that has multiple layers. Some strata are more literal, some more metaphorical, and some more mystical. As one famous Mishnaic rabbi says, "Turn the Torah over and over because everything is in it."

Many Jews across the globe commonly read sections, or *parshiyot,* of the Torah each week; after a full calendar year they have read through the entire text, at which time they start again from the beginning. In synagogues, the Five Books of Moses are commonly read from a Torah scroll (fig. 2.2)—a parchment made from the tanned skin of kosher animals, such as cows, written on with black ink partially made from gallnut powder and other natural ingredients, by a trained scribe (fig. 2.3)—a ritual object treated as sacred by all denominations, regardless of their stance regarding the text's origins.

Jewish law states that a Torah scribe *(sofer* or [female] *soferet)* can only create a new Torah by copying the text from another Torah. For some, this is the ultimate proof that the scroll's divine words have remained unchanged since they were first given by God on Mount Sinai to Moses, who, according to one textual tradition, passed them on to Joshua, who passed them on to the Elders, who passed them on to the Prophets, who passed them on to the Men of the Great Assembly (i.e., the Mishnaic and Talmudic rabbis), and so forth to today.

If one's first visit to a synagogue is on a day that includes a Torah service (when members of the commu-

FIGURE 2.3. *Soferet* (female scribe) Julie Seltzer, working on a Torah scroll at the Contemporary Jewish Museum in San Francisco. The first woman known to have scribed an entire *Sefer Torah* (Torah Scroll) is Jen Taylor Friedman, a task completed in 2007.

nity read from a Torah scroll), at first glance it may seem as if the attendees are worshipping the Torah itself—as if, ironically, it is an idol. (Ironic insofar as the third of the Ten Commandments/Directives prohibits idol worship.) After it is taken out of a special area of the synagogue—where it is commonly stored in a sacred bureau called an ark *(aron)* or sanctuary *(heikhal or eikhal)*—in a detailed ceremony involving a number of prayers, the Torah is often carried around the synagogue. Everyone in the room stands and faces the Torah, wherever it is at the time. When it is brought nearby, practitioners have the opportunity to kiss the scroll, whether by putting their face on the outer casing (made of solid wood, metal, or fabric) or by touching one's prayer book or the corner of one's *tallit* (prayer shawl) to it and then kissing the part of the book or shawl that came into contact with the sacred object.

This is but one example of how the Torah embodies revelation. It is the central access point—the axis mundi—of the Jewish community in terms of connecting with the creator of the universe. Torah is *the* sacred intersection between God and humanity, not in terms of place, but in terms of ideas. To use a Greek term, it is the *logos* (word) of God. Torah is not confined to a particular location; there is not one physical Torah, nor is there one single place where it resides. Rather, Torah is the concretized word of God, the documented revelation that took place on Mount Sinai, something that is accessible to all those who are part of the community. It contains the "truth" for Jews of all stripes.

Cyclical Rituals and Cyclical Narratives

Another way to understand the observance of the weekly Torah reading is as a cyclical ritual based in a cyclical narrative. The Torah says that the holidays described therein need to be observed annually, a ritual practice that scholar of religions Mircea Eliade refers to as a "repetition of cosmogonic time" (a narrative focused on the origin of the world). In abiding by the laws and customs linked to each holiday, Jews reenact moments of "truth," times when the world's chaos shifts toward order in and through God and God's word. In observing these holidays, Jews repeatedly reactualize God's cosmic plan, regenerating it over and over again.

Eliade understands this phenomenon (which is core to many religious traditions, Christianity, Hinduism, and Islam among them, and not specific to Judaism) to be ahistorical. By engaging in annual ritual observances, a community steps out of its historical timeline, where time moves forward from a starting point toward an end, and enters into a circle with no beginning or end. When rituals are linked to time in this way (or, more accurately, unlinked), the cycle of time serves as an "eternal return," a never-ending revisiting of a community's original sacred act.

Annually reenacting events in the Torah in the form of specific holiday observances not only explains the reasoning behind each holiday, but it also allows practitioners a way to return to the original events themselves, which likewise reunites them with God. For example, through the observance of Pesaḥ, Jews retell and reexperience the act of God leading the Israelites out of slavery and into freedom; through the observance of Shavuot, Jews reenact the receiving of the Torah on Mount Sinai.

Interpreting the Torah

Text and Interpretation

Another key component of the Torah's narratives is the way human-to-human interactions are described and, perhaps more important, the way they are interpreted (e.g., interpreting the "fruit" in the Eden narrative as an apple). In other words, there are two elements to each of the Torah's archetypes: the text and the interpretation of the text (akin, for some, to the Written Torah and the Oral Torah).

Regarding the text, the Torah presents each narrative as a matter of fact. Events are described as if they happened, which for many is the unfolding of God's master plan. Yet the Torah exists only insofar as it is interpreted, as is the case with all sacred texts, whether the Torah, Gospels, Qur'an, etc. The moment a verse is encountered, the process of interpretation begins. The Torah does not exist in a vacuum; it cannot be separated from its interpretation.

The Torah's dominant narrative is male-centric, whether approached broadly (i.e., virtually only males serve in positions of communal authority and leadership) or narrowly (in particular situations of marriage, for example, where polygyny is common while polyandry doesn't exist). Likewise, only heterosexual human relationships are sanctioned. (This bias is explored in a number of important books, all of which were written over the last half century; only since the 1990s did a group of scholars begin addressing such issues with regularity.)

It is well accepted, and largely indisputable, that the primary authorities interpreting the Torah—for centuries—have been solely male. As scholar Tamar Ross notes, "Irrespective of how we choose to interpret the metaphysical grounding of male hegemony in the Torah, there is no denying that a rigid view of gender and distinct gender roles became further entrenched with the development of the rabbinic tradition," seen in such texts as the Mishnah and Talmud (chapter 5).

Of course, male dominance is not unique to sacred texts such as the Torah. Though the stakes are incredibly high for books attributed to God, dominant archetypes—whether male-centric, hetero-centric, or representing any other form of bias—are omnipresent, found even in such seemingly mundane things as children's books. One study of books for American second to fourth graders found that only two, or less than 1 percent, featured a Latino/a—and not white—main character. Another found that just 3 percent were written by or about Latinos. Marginalizing specific voices is so common that we often don't notice it at all.

Texts Built upon Texts upon Texts

A great deal of Jewish life revolves around texts, one of many reasons Jews are sometimes called People of the Book. But all Jewish texts, to one degree or another, are based on those that came before. At the core of this system—perhaps best understood in terms of concentric circles—is the Torah (fig. 2.4). It is difficult, if not altogether impossible, to fully grasp the meaning of the Prophets or Writings without first having read the Five Books of Moses; their very existence depends on the presence of the Torah. There are dozens of instances of the prophets referencing characters found in the Torah (e.g., the prophet Isaiah refers to the Torah figures Abraham, Sarah, and Jacob). In addition, when prophets such as Isaiah rail against the masses for not following God "ways," the rabbinic authorities of the Mishnah and Talmud believed Isaiah was referring precisely to the mitzvot described in the Torah.

An Example of Interpreting Torah: Gen. 4

Special topic 2.3 contains three different translations of a short passage from Genesis about Adam and Eve's first two children, Cain and Abel. The translation on the left is from the Jewish Publication Society (JPS), the one in the middle is from the HarperCollins Study Bible, and the one on the right is from Everett Fox. Although the three texts are similar, they are not the same.

While some might say that the differences are minor, when we consider that for many people we aren't talking about a translation of something as mundane as a magazine article but are speaking about the word of God, these nuances are gravely important. If you believe that the creator of the universe is the original author of this text, the issue of whether a single word is translated one way or another is no small matter. Comparing translations—or more accurately, comparing interpretations—underscores the fact that no sacred text exists irrespective of an interpreter.

Methods of Interpretation: PaRDeS

Over the years, Jews have developed a number of methods for interpreting their core sacred text, the Torah. Four of the most widely known ones today are often referred

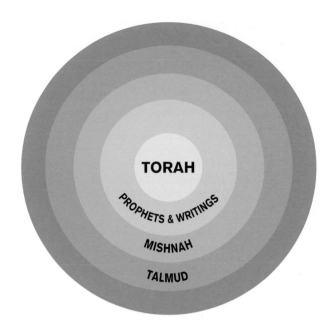

FIGURE 2.4. How Jewish sacred texts build upon one another.

to by the mnemonic PaRDeS, standing for the words *pshat, remez, drash,* and *sōd,* understood respectively as the simple or plain, allusive or allegorical, homiletical, and secret or mystical meaning(s) of a given word or passage from the Torah. Although these four approaches certainly do not encapsulate the vast breadth of ways that Torah has been interpreted in the Jewish tradition, they are dominant approaches today and thus worth looking at more closely.

Applying these methods to verses one and two of Genesis 4 (special topic 2.3), a pshat reading of the text is that Cain and Abel were brothers. However, a remez interpretation—something hinted at in the text and pointing to a potential deeper meaning—is that they were twins. In coming to this conclusion, commentators have noted that the passage does not mention individual instances of conception, but only a single conception.

As for a drash understanding, according to one source, Cain had a twin, who, however, was not Abel: this twin was a sister. As for Abel, this same drash notes that he was born at a separate time, along with two sisters; thus, Abel was born a triplet. A drash is akin to a twenty-first-century sermon; one approach to this "homiletic" form of interpretation is to examine a particular word or phrase using other biblical verses. (Interpreting the "fruit" in the Eden narrative as an apple is also an example of a drash.)

SPECIAL TOPIC 2.3
GEN. 4:1–10

	Jewish Publication Society	Harper Collins Study Bible	Everett Fox
1	Now the man knew his wife Eve, and she conceived and bore Cain, saying, "I have gained a male child with the help of the Lord."	Now the man knew his wife Eve, and she conceived and bore Cain, saying "I have produced a man with the help of the Lord"	The human knew Havva his wife, she became pregnant and bore Kayin. She said: Kaniti/I-have-gotten a man, as has YHWH!
2	She then bore his brother Abel. Abel became a keeper of sheep, and Cain became a tiller of soil.	Next she bore his brother Abel. Now Abel was a keeper of sheep, and Cain a tiller of the ground.	She continued bearing—his brother, Hevel. Now Hevel became a shepherd of flocks, and Kayin became a worker of the soil.
3	In the course of time, Cain brought an offering to the Lord from the fruit of the soil;	In the course of time Cain brought to the Lord an offering of the fruit of the ground,	It was, after the passing of days that Kayin brought, from the fruit of the soil, a gift to YHWH,
4	and Abel, for his part, brought the choicest of the firstlings of his flock. The Lord paid heed to Abel and his offering,	and Abel for his part brought of the firstlings of his flock, their fat portions. And the Lord had regard for Abel and his offering,	and as for Hevel, he too brought—from the firstborn of his flock, from their fat-parts. YHWH had regard for Hevel and his gift,
5	but to Cain and his offering He paid no heed. Cain was much distressed and his face fell.	but for Cain and his offering he had no regard. So Cain was very angry, and his countenance fell.	for Kayin and his gift he had no regard. Kayin became exceedingly upset and his face fell.
6	And the Lord said to Cain, "Why are you distressed, and why is your face fallen?	The Lord said to Cain, "Why are you angry, and why has your countenance fallen?	YHWH said to Kayin: Why are you so upset? Why has your face fallen?
7	Surely, if you do right, there is uplift. But if you do not do right sin couches at the door; its urge is toward you, yet you can be its master."	If you do well, will you not be accepted? And if you do not do well, sin is lurking at the door; its desire is for you, but you must master it."	Is not thus: If you intend good, bear-it-aloft, but if you do not intend good, at the entrance is sin, a crouching-demon, toward you his lust—but you can rule over him.
8	Cain said to his brother Abel . . . and when they were in the field, Cain set upon his brother Abel and killed him.	Cain said to his brother Abel, "Let us go out to the field." And when they were in the field, Cain rose up against his brother Abel, and killed him.	Kayin said to Hevel his brother . . . But then it was, when they were out in the field that Kayin rose up against Hevel his brother and he killed him.
9	The Lord said to Cain, "Where is your brother Abel?" And he said, "I do not know. Am I my brother's keeper?"	Then the Lord said to Cain, "Where is your brother Abel?" He said, "I do not know: am I my brother's keeper?"	YHWH said to Kayin: Where is Hevel your brother? He said: I do not know. Am I the watcher of my brother?
10	Then He said, "What have you done? Hark, your brother's blood cries out to Me from the ground!"	And the Lord said, "What have you done? Listen; your brother's blood is crying out to me from the ground!"	Now he said, What have you done! A sound—your brother's blood cries out to me from the soil!

As for an interpretive approach based in sōd, this is by far the most difficult way to understand the Torah for all but Jewish mystics. Largely found in Kabbalistic texts such as the thirteenth-century *Zohar* (see chapter 6), a sōd interpretation of the birth of Cain and Abel might address metaphysical ideas, such as pure and impure aspects of God. For example, according to the *Zohar,* the serpent in the Garden of Eden embodies an impure aspect of God. He even seduces and has sex with Eve, passing his "demonic filth" on to her, who subsequently passes it on to Adam and, later, to Cain and Abel. This "filth" affects Cain much more than Abel, and eventually plays a role in his murdering his younger brother.

It is common for remez and drash interpretations to be driven by a seeming ambiguity in the text. For example, in this story we are never explicitly told Cain's motive for murdering his brother. In fact, the JPS and Everett Fox translations of verse eight use ellipses, a series of dots that usually indicate an omission of a word, phrase, sentence, or paragraph to bring attention to a gap in a story's plot. In this case, the translators wanted to point out that it is unclear what Cain said to Abel immediately before he murdered him (or perhaps they are bringing attention to missing words in the text). But this punctuation mark isn't found in biblical Hebrew, either in the earliest forms of this verse found to date or anywhere else in the Bible.

For a translator, no matter whether this seeming ambiguity is approached from the perspective of one who believes the Torah is the word of God, the text leaves the reader with questions. Although both JPS and Fox try to address this mystery using ellipses, HarperCollins translates verse eight a different way entirely, putting words into Cain's mouth that don't actually appear in the biblical Hebrew. This is their way of solving the ambiguity of what Cain said to his brother prior to murdering him (see chapter 5 for other ways people have interpreted this uncertainty).

Interpreting the Torah: The Depiction of God

Perhaps the most important persona in the Torah is the creator of the universe, God. Literally speaking, God is a biblical character, most often described anthropomorphically, utilizing explanatory terms commonly applied to humans. Not only is God depicted in the Five Books of Moses as having feelings (e.g., getting angry, having compassion), but God also is described in human bodily terms. During the Exodus from Egypt, for instance, God is said to have a "mighty arm"; a few times when angry, God has a fuming "nose." Human characters in the Torah have conversations with God, just as one would with another person. All of these descriptions can loosely be described as theistic understandings of God, ones in which God, the all-powerful creator of the world, has one-on-one relationships with humans, cares about the world, and is integrally involved and active in day-to-day events. This is a pshat (simple or plain) reading of God as depicted in the Torah.

Another way to understand God is through a monistic lens, an interpretation rooted in sōd. Monistic belief maintains that there is no personal aspect to God; God exists outside of words, beyond any modicum of human comprehension. This approach, largely incorporated into Jewish mystical thought (see chapter 6), holds that attaching characteristics to God essentializes God, something humans cannot accurately do, as we do not know anything definitive about God's nature (other than, perhaps, knowing what God is *not*).

Many people, Jews and otherwise, have a theistic understanding of God, based in a pshat reading of the text. Most people reading the Torah use the gendered pronoun for God that is found in the text's biblical Hebrew, which is male *(he, him, his)*. This has led to the assumption that God is male, which has a number of important implications, partially because it says in Genesis that humans are created in God's image (Gen. 1:27).

As scholar Judith Plaskow notes, "If God is male, and we are [created] in God's image, how can maleness *not* be the norm of Jewish humanity? If maleness is normative, how can women not be Other?" Put another way, to quote philosopher and theologian Mary Daly: "If God is male, then male is God." The Torah's referring to God using male terms has shaped the sociopolitical culture of its readers for millennia. It has also helped produce male-dominant ideologies both linked to and irrespective of the Torah. In languages such as Hebrew, Arabic, and English, for example, masculine terms function as the norm or generic language for humanity as a whole, whereby feminine terms connote only femaleness.

In other words, the fact that the Torah refers to God using masculine pronouns directly affects how it is interpreted. Through both fact and "truth," God is male in dominant Jewish narratives. Like other religious traditions, including Christianity, this has played a historically significant role in shaping social discourse, theological belief, and ritual practice. Its importance cannot be overstated (despite the brief discussion here). In an effort to confront this problem, Plaskow contends: "Feminism demands a new understanding of God that reflects and supports the redefinition of Jewish humanity."

In contrast, scholar Rachel Adler admits that anthropomorphism may be necessary because it is the constructed mechanism Jews use to discuss God. But, she adds, if the language chosen is male-centric, it needs to be acknowledged that this decision affects the entire context in which Jews speak about God. Further, "any discussion of feminine God-language is invariably haunted by the fear of inauthenticity."

Interpreting the Torah: "Israel" and Chosenness

Aside from God, the Torah focuses on the lineage of one particular strand of humanity, starting with Adam and Eve and ending with Moses and the Israelites. This might be best understood as a pshat (simple) reading of the Five Books of Moses. Although Genesis pays particular attention to Adam and Eve's first two children, the family tree followed throughout the rest of the Torah actually extends through their third son, Seth. Thereafter, there are ten generations from Adam to Noah and another ten to Abraham.

In the narrative about Jacob, one of Abraham's grandchildren, he is instructed to change his name to Israel *(Yisrael).* Thereafter, his twelve sons are called by the name the Children of Israel *(Bnei Yisrael).* (Jacob's sole daughter, Dinah, does not have the same status as her brothers. In particular, no "tribe of Dinah" is mentioned in relation to the other Israelite tribes.) From the first book of the Prophets, Joshua, onward, after the land of Canaan is conquered the tribal divisions among the biblical Israelites—divided up based on their descendancy from Jacob's twelve sons, or in the case of Ephraim and Menasheh, Jacob's grandsons (fig. 3.3)—become the primary way to identify someone. (Interestingly, by the Torah's own account, the masses fleeing ancient Egypt in the story of the Exodus were a "mixed multitude," and not homogeneously Israelites.)

Chosenness as Superiority

One way to understand how a small part of humanity becomes the heart of the Torah is to see this branch of the family as special or chosen. Historically, Jews and non-Jews alike have perpetuated this idea, echoing the mantra that Jews are *the* chosen people. (For example, a 2012 study found that 70 percent of Israeli Jews believe that Jews are the "Chosen People," as in chosen-by-God

because of their inherent extraordinary nature.) In many instances in history, this idea played a role in Christians oppressing and persecuting Jews.

Putting aside the prevalence of the chauvinistic notion—found in nations throughout history, from ancient Greece and Rome to contemporary Great Britain and the United States—of *any* community having a privileged purpose in history, chosen by God or otherwise, there are many different understandings of chosenness within the Jewish community, going back at least two millennia. On one end of the spectrum are those who believe that God chose the Hebrews (later known as Israelites, Judeans, and Jews) because of their inherent superiority in relation to others.

It is easy to grasp where this perspective comes from, simple to see the Torah as a sacred text in which God selectively and intentionally privileges one part of the human family above all others. In fact, this is a straightforward interpretation (pshat). After all, according to Genesis, God did just that, choosing Abraham and telling him that God would bless him and make his descendants into a great nation (Gen. 11). This *is* quite a promise, especially from the creator of the universe.

The idea of the Israelites' uniqueness as the reason for God to have chosen them over other nations is supported by other biblical passages, such as Deuteronomy 7:6–8, where God says to the Israelites: "Adonai, your God, chose you to be a treasured people from all other nations on earth. It is not because you are the most numerous of peoples that God set God's heart on you and chose you—indeed, you are the smallest of all nations. But it was because God favored you and kept the oath that God made to your forefathers." This notion is repeated elsewhere in the Torah.

One of many rabbinic texts that echo this same understanding is the following: "Rabbi Simeon ben Yohai began his discourse with the verse 'He stood and measured the earth' (Hab. 3:6). That is, the Holy One took the measure of all peoples and found no people other than Israel worthy of receiving the Torah." Another common rabbinical text, also based on an interpretation of Torah passages, is found in the prayer over wine *(Kiddush),* made on the Sabbath and other important holidays, which includes the phrase: "who has chosen us and sanctified us above all other nations." Similar passages can be found in many *siddurim* (Jewish prayer books), included in prayers recited on other special holidays in the Jewish calendar.

The eleventh- and twelfth-century philosopher and poet Yehuda Halevi is perhaps best known for expanding the notion of the Jewish community's inherent chosenness—the "'choicest' of all [hu]mankind," a different "species" of human that is "angelic in nature"—to include the prophetic ability to communicate with God. If not for their common interaction with other nations, he notes, they would not have softened or become "tainted" with impurity. (A subcategory of ethnocentric texts supporting this general idea focuses on the unique humility of the Jews as opposed to less modest qualities.) Other medieval scholars, such as Saadiah Gaon, Abraham ibn Daud, and Moshe ben Maimon (Maimonides) echoed similar ideas. Other Jewish mystics from this same era also commonly made claims of superiority.

Rejecting Chosenness as Superiority

In contrast, a number of contemporary Jews have shunned such ideas, even rejecting the notion of chosenness outright. Most of these individuals identify with Judaism's more liberal streams. For instance, Mordecai Kaplan, whose ideas form the core of Reconstructionist Judaism (see chapter 8), called chosenness an "anachronistic" idea; it was expunged from the first Reconstructionist prayer book altogether. Unsurprisingly, many of those who reject this idea do so, partially at least, because of the inherent racial supremacy that such a doctrine invokes. (Sixteenth-century philosopher Baruch Spinoza also rejected the notion of an innate Jewish superiority.)

The following statement, made by scholar Jon Levenson in *Sinai and Zion,* reflects a point of contention among the various sides of this debate, resonating more with those critical of this doctrine: "The Near Eastern approach has developed parallels to almost every aspect of Israel's culture. Her laws resemble Mesopotamian law; her Temple is typically Canaanite; even her monotheism. . . . My experience has been that the desire to uphold a belief in the uniqueness of Israel is strongest among Jews."

Chosenness as Choosing Different Things

All of this said, such voices are not simply a reflection of twentieth- and twenty-first-century thought. For centuries, scholars have supported ideas that gravitate toward anti-ethnocentrism. One tradition in this school suggests that it was not God who chose Abraham, but Abraham who chose God. According to one text, after giving it a great deal of thought, Abraham (then called Abram) concluded that there was only one God in the world, not many. In other words, rather than being recognized by

God for his genius, which he subsequently passed down to his descendants, Abraham came to a belief in monotheism based on rational thought. Although this still reflects positively on Abraham, it bases his uniqueness in thoughtful analysis rather than a superhero-like nature.

Another thread in this school is that God chose this community as a last resort: God went to every nation on earth, and no people other than the Israelites would accept the burden of keeping the biblical directives. Some who think along these lines have gone in a slightly different direction, arguing that in choosing to accept the directives, the Israelites took the strict moral code upon themselves; *they* made the choice, not God. (This tradition has been used to support ethnocentrism as well, as if the Israelites made this choice only because of their inherent superiority.)

According to yet another trend that steers clear of Jewish superiority, the Israelites had no choice in the matter. A passage in the Talmud says that when the Israelites were in the Sinai desert, God picked up Mount Sinai, held it over their heads, and told them that if they did not accept the Torah God would drop the mountain on top of them. At the end of the day, then, the Jewish community maintains a range of understandings of chosenness.

Sinai and the Twenty-first Century

All of these positions are founded in part in passages from the Jewish tradition that suggest that the souls of all Jews—who have lived at any time, in any place, and including even those not yet born—were present at Mount Sinai. This idea is found in a number of places, such as in rabbinic interpretations of verses describing when Moses reminds the Israelites about the revelation at Sinai, framing the encounter as a moment when God delivered a "great voice that never stopped" (Deut. 5:19); or when Moses reminds the Israelites that God's revelation is "forever," or eternal, lasting for all future generations (Deut. 29:28).

Perhaps the greatest challenge to more recent interpretations of Judaism is the idea that already-present Jewish traditions cannot simply be overturned or erased. Even though new ways of understanding Torah are constantly emerging in the Jewish community, there is tension between an unchanging text and ever-changing interpretations. Such endeavors are more difficult when one identifies with a less dominant community—such as women or queers (see special topic 0.2)—whose voices have been overwhelmingly omitted from the canon for centuries.

Ironically perhaps, the Talmudic patriarchs whose understandings of the Torah have been used to justify narrowing the interpretive lens actually helped create the very framework that now permits new interpretations to enter into communal conversations. At the same time that male- and non-queer-centric perspectives of Torah were concretized within the Mishnaic and Talmudic canons, these same rabbis included traditions that encouraged a broader sense of inclusion—a backdoor, if you will, for female and queer voices to enter into the discourse (see chapter 5).

Over the last fifteen years, less ascendant groups within the Jewish collective have begun to add their voices to the larger community's discussions regarding the interpretation of Torah. Whereas women's voices began to gain prominence in the American Jewish community in the 1970s and 1980s, at the same time that the Reform and Conservative movements began ordaining women as rabbis, queer Jews have become much more outspoken in shaping their own Jewish identities since about 2000.

By reading themselves into the texts, by uncovering their voices from underneath the mountain's rocks, today's marginalized Jews are discovering that they have always been "Standing at Sinai," spiritually and metaphorically. All Jews were *there*. According to that belief, in hiking Mount Sinai my friend and I were returning to a place our souls had already been.

Zions

Contents

Key Ideas

• Two basic ways humans organize sacredness, in places and objects, are by orienting toward something as sacred and/or believing it is metaphysically different from other places or objects of its kind. For Jews, Zion is a sacred space.

• A community can have different types of structures of power. One model is having a single, centralized location, embodied in a spider; a second is having multiple locations at the same time, embodied in a starfish. This directly relates to how Jews can understand a single Zion or multiple Zions.

- Although the binary of Zion/Diaspora continues to be core to Jewish communities, with Zion most commonly understood as the Land or State of Israel and Diaspora as everywhere else, historically speaking Jews have had multiple Zions simultaneously. For many, these ideas are experienced much more metaphorically or spiritually than physically. Even today, most choose to live outside the Land of Israel (understood as Zion by some).

- Before they were called Jews, it is widely thought that this community was called Hebrews, then Israelites, and then Judeans. Throughout these communal "incarnations," the group was quite heterogeneous. Whatever the name, this community was forcibly exiled, or dispersed, from the Land of Israel a number of times.

The United States of Zion

I was in one of the oldest synagogues in California, Congregation Sherith Israel, with sixteen students from the University of San Francisco, the Jesuit Catholic university where I teach. Each week, the class met at a different site of importance to Bay Area Jewish communities, places such as a Jewish Community Center, a Jewish parochial school, and the Contemporary Jewish Museum. Today we were at one of the area's many Reform-affiliated synagogues, originally founded by Orthodox Jews.

One of the core ideas of the course is that communal identities are performed, a phenomenon that manifests in a number of different ways. For the Jewish community—because people consider their Jewish identities to be a reflection of their culture, ethnicity, nationality, political orientation, race, religion, and more—there are, perhaps, more ways to enact their identities, their Jewishness—more ways *to be* a Jew—than there are for other groups.

One way that Jews have been able to exist, and even thrive, is through their "portable identity." The community has had the ability to reconstruct itself time and again, to habitually acclimate from place to place. More nomadic than most, Jews have had a transmutable notion of the revelation at Mount Sinai. Their collective understanding of this event has shifted from one form to others, from an extraordinary, cosmic experience with God on Mount Sinai to the words found on a Torah scroll.

Another way lies in their long-standing adaptation of the idea of Zion, also known as the "Promised Land." The mutability of this concept is exemplified in Sherith Israel by a stained glass picture on the upper wall of the synagogue's main sanctuary. Originally unveiled in 1905, it depicts Moses and the biblical Israelites standing at the foot of a mountain. Moses has the Ten Commandments in hand, while the Israelite leaders are carrying flags, representing, one assumes, the twelve tribes of Israel.

But on closer inspection, one sees that the flags do not depict ancient Israelite symbols (indeed, the colors and designs were made up); perhaps the most obvious non-biblical flag is that of the United States of America. Nor are Moses and the Israelites standing at the foot of Mount Sinai. Instead, their backdrop is the Sierra Nevada mountain range, with two of Yosemite National Park's most iconic peaks, Half Dome and El Capitan, rising over each one of Moses's shoulders (fig. 3.1). The people in this powerful image are not in the Middle East but Northern California; Moses is facing away from Yosemite and the physical city of Jerusalem far to the east, and toward San Francisco, a new Promised Land.

In this stained glass picture, Zion has been re-created yet again, this time in the Golden State, a location many synagogue founders would have no doubt referred to by the Yiddish term *di Goldene Medina* (the Golden Land). This Yiddish phrase has been applied to countless places, often to denote a place where one can find freedom, justice, and opportunity. For the early members of this synagogue, California—not New York, not the United States, and not the Land of Israel—was the Promised Land, San Francisco the new Jerusalem.

Where Is Zion?

Although the concept of Zion has its origins in the Middle East, the Jewish community has exported it to other locations innumerable times. Congregation Sherith Israel's particular version may be unique, but the phenomenon itself is not. (Non-Jews have also imagined Zion in many different places, including the United States. For example, the early Puritan colonialists commonly called their new land "the New Zion." Thomas Jefferson even suggested putting the word *Israel* on the new country's official seal.) But while Jerusalem may be considered the site of the first Zion, the Jewish community has not always had a single center. Some would argue they never did.

One dominant Jewish narrative today—perhaps *the* current dominant narrative—divides the world into two zones, Zion and Diaspora, embodied respectively in the biblical Land of Israel (or, for some, the State of Israel) and everywhere else. But this is not the only way Jews have organized, and continue to organize, geographical or ideological space. The majority of Jews who maintain

FIGURE 3.1. Moses holding the Ten Commandments . . . in Yosemite National Park. This stained glass window is found in the main sanctuary of Congregation Sherith Israel in San Francisco.

this dichotomy, in particular those who live outside the Land of Israel, also think of their own country as their home and their center. This phenomenon helps explain how Jews have, at times, had multiple religio-political centers—or multiple Zions—at once. Similar to Sinai in terms of the transferability of revelation, in Zion we see the unfixed nature of Jewish space, both sacred and political. Just as Sinai is understood as the nexus of God and humanity, so, too, has Zion played this role.

Diaspora and Zion: The Starfish and the Spider

In *The Starfish and the Spider* (2006), Ori Brafman and Rod Beckstrom look at two basic organizational systems. The first, represented by a spider, is centralized. If you remove a leg from a spider, it becomes impaired but doesn't die. However, if you remove its head, it dies. The second type

of system, akin to a starfish, is decentralized and much more difficult for most of us to comprehend. Unlike other animals, a starfish doesn't have a head or even a center. You cannot attack its core because it doesn't have one. In Brafman and Beckstrom's own words, "[A starfish's] central body isn't even in charge. In fact, the major organs are replicated throughout each and every arm. If you cut the starfish in half, you'll be in for a surprise: the animal won't die, and pretty soon you'll have two starfish to deal with. Starfish have an incredible quality to them: If you cut an arm off, most of these animals grow a new arm. And with some varieties . . . the animal can replicate itself from just a single piece of an arm . . . each one will regenerate into a whole new starfish."

Most twenty-first-century communities are built around a single center; they are like spiders and are centralized. But it is possible, in both the animal world and in human societies, for a given entity to have multiple epicenters rather than one. In contemporary American and Israeli Jewry, dominant narratives are that Jews had, and have always had, one sacred center: Zion. Everything else has been the Diaspora. It is even common for well-known American media outlets, such as the *New York Times,* for instance, to refer to non-Israeli Jews, no matter their country of origin or residence, as "diasporic Jews." But even though one dominant Jewish communal "truth" divides the world into two (Zion and Diaspora), historically Jews have had many different centers, including multiple places referred to as Zion. In other words, Jewish communities have adhered to the notion of the spider and the starfish at the same time.

Take, for example, some of the evidence found in Charles London's book *Far from Zion* (2009). London traveled to Jewish communities around the world to explore their understanding of the notion of homeland. In Bosnia-Herzegovina, he encountered Jews who utilize Jerusalem—a common synonym for Zion—as a "blank space in which to write the place they longed for most, the place they felt most at home." He describes one member of this community as living "the ideal of a spiritual homeland detached from a physical homeland, or perhaps attached to too many physical homelands. . . . There would always be a hole in his heart in the shape of Israel, and if he moved there, there would be another hole in the shape of Bosnia. . . . Everyone has a place they never want to forget." For such Jews, both Israel and Bosnia-Herzegovina are Zion.

London observed this same phenomenon among Jews in Uganda, Iran, and Cuba, all of whom refer to both their own countries and the State of Israel as Jerusalem, Zion, and the Promised Land. As London puts it, these Jews orient themselves toward multiple Zions, many sacred spaces, at once. This doesn't mean that they replaced the biblical Zion with Bosnia-Herzegovina, Uganda, Iran, or Cuba. Rather, for them, these sites overlap and coexist. It is as if they have (at least) two centers, two homelands, two places—metaphorically and literally—that act as foci for spiritual orientation and self-definition.

Of course, these countries are not the only places where Jews have lived that exemplify this phenomenon. Frédéric Brenner, the artist mentioned in chapter 1 who spent a quarter century traveling around the world to visually document the complex notion of the Jewish diaspora, came across this trend in a number of other places. For instance, there is a saying in the Jewish community of Akhaltsikhe, Georgia, that "from Akhaltsikhe *yetzeh torah* [the Torah emerged]"; Salonika, Greece, has been known as "Jerusalem of the Balkans"; and Quba,

Azerbaijan, has been called "Jerusalem of the Caucuses." Jews in Uzbekistan have a custom of purchasing two burial plots in preparation for death, one in their local cemetery and a second in Jerusalem. Perhaps this phenomenon is also embodied in the traditional custom of saying "Next Year in Jerusalem" at the end of the Passover Seder, even if one is performing the ritual in Jerusalem itself.

As London explains, "While [the biblical] Zion itself remains essential to a Jewish identity, these other places that these Jews ha[ve] imbued with Jewish meaning are equally important. . . . These Jews would also not be their full Jewish selves without a connection to, say, Nabugoye Hill in Uganda, or the community center in Sarajevo [in addition to Israel]. For them—and me—the narrative of Jewish space does not stop with Israel. Israel is a beginning but not an ending. It's a long story we have to tell and we're not done telling it."

London's book reinforces the notion of Israel as Zion even as he shows how Jews also consider Zion to lie outside the Land of Israel. In this sense, he both stabilizes and destabilizes the Zion/Diaspora binary. Put another way, yes, in dominant Jewish narratives, the Middle East's Jerusalem is Zion and the center of the world. And yes, at the same time, there are multiple centers. As London explains, "Jerusalem is an anchor, but it is not the ship"; and the ship—the Jewish community, or more accurately, Jewish communities—is never at a full stop.

How Does Something Become Sacred?

When discussing Zion, it is worth noting two basic ways to understand sacredness. One is that a place or object in the material world is sacred because it is inherently special. The second is that it becomes sacred once it is labeled as such. Calling a place sacred distinguishes it from that which is profane, sometimes considered the norm.

One of the most common ways for a location to become sacred is in conjunction with a ritual that is practiced there. In the words of historian of religions Jonathan Z. Smith, "Ritual is, above all else, an assertion of difference . . . a means of performing the way things ought to be in conscious tension to the way things are. Ritual relies for its power on the fact that it is concerned with quite ordinary activities placed within an extraordinary setting, that what it describes and displays is, in principle, possible for every occurrence of these acts."

As an example of how an object becomes sacred, let's take holy water, an idea familiar to many (including a large number of students at the Jesuit Catholic university where I teach). If two glasses of water are taken from the same source, one of which qualifies as holy water and one that does not, most would contend that there is no molecular difference between the two. The only difference is that the holy water has been blessed by a religious leader (e.g., a priest). In other words, according to Smith, the distinction between the two glasses of water has to do only with how people orient to them.

Origins of "Zion"

Zion, Jerusalem, and the Temple

For the Jewish community, Zion is a sacred center, whether ideological or spiritual. But what is Zion and where did the idea come from? Though the prebiblical origins of this term are uncertain, the first time the word appears is in the book of Samuel, in the Hebrew Bible, when it is used to refer to a newly conquered stronghold in Jerusalem that King David captures from the Jebusites, an event some date to roughly 1000 BCE. The text tells us that after capturing this location, David relocates his power base there from Hebron. In other words, Jerusalem was never the community's only center, or even the first one, though it has been a central space for most of Jewish history. (As to the historicity of the Bible, refer to chapter 2.)

From this point forward, Zion, the City of David, and Jerusalem become synonymous (sometimes implicitly) when referring to the Temple or Temple Mount, which is built (and later rebuilt) in Jerusalem, or when referring to Zion as the "dwelling place of God" or "mountain of God." Later in the Bible, Zion comes to represent the Land of Israel at large, in particular after the Israelite tribes are exiled by the Assyrians, during the eighth century BCE (an event discussed later in this chapter). Thereafter it also comes to symbolize the Israelites, as in Isaiah, when God's people and Zion are spoken of as if they are one and the same, as well as in other ancient texts, such as the Apocrypha or apocalyptic literature, when the Israelites are referred to as the "Daughter of Zion," with the city of Jerusalem representing their mother.

In other words, at least during their early history, from the moment they capture Zion it becomes an epicenter of power for the Israelites, consistently intertwined with monarchical rule. Zion also quickly becomes understood as an elected place where a God named Yahweh has chosen to "dwell." In a certain way, Zion replaces Sinai as the cosmic nexus between God and the Israelites. God is no longer understood in relation to Mount Sinai (as "the one on Sinai"), but instead in relation to Zion (as the one "who dwells on Mount Zion").

Not only is David the first individual of Israelite descent to conquer Zion, the mountain, but because he is responsible for bringing this place into the proto-Jewish fold (at this stage the communities at the heart of this book are best understood by the name of their Israelite subtribe and not as "Jews") he is also charged with building God a "house to dwell in," something God instructs him to do through the prophet Natan. Nonetheless, it is generally accepted that, according to the Bible, David's successor and son, Solomon, actually builds the first Temple (fig. 3.2) in Jerusalem (though one psalm specifies that God, and not Solomon, was the actual builder). Prior to this point, the Tabernacle and Ark are said to have been housed in another city altogether, Shiloh, where a separate temple existed, perhaps more than a generation before David. (It is also possible that David built a temple in Jerusalem prior to Solomon's birth.)

Although neither David nor Solomon was instructed to build the Temple on Zion specifically, according to postbiblical authorities (in particular the Mishnaic and Talmudic rabbis; see chapter 5), that is where it was built, on a site also called Mount Moriah. By the time of the Talmud, sometime between the third and eighth centuries CE, Zion's status had expanded. Some passages go to the extreme of contending that the entire world was created from Zion. Others say that the foundation stone located on Mount Zion was the epicenter of creation, Zion the world's belly button.

Zion and the Israelite Division of the Land of Israel

To backtrack for a moment, according to the Torah, God makes a promise to Abraham, a Hebrew, that he and his descendants will receive land. This promise is renewed with one of Abraham's sons, Isaac, and again with a grandson, Jacob, whose name is later changed to Israel. Years later, when the Israelites, or the sons of Israel and their accompanying tribes, arrive at the eastern border of the "Promised Land," the Bible says that before entering the territory they divided it up among the male members of their tribes, with a minor concession given to a small group of women from the tribe of Menasheh. Figure 3.3 portrays a family tree connecting Abraham to the individuals after whom the twelve Israelite tribes are named, Jacob's twelve sons. (One basic challenge to this narrative is that specifications of the "Promised Land's" borders are described differently in a number of biblical passages.)

FIGURE 3.2. What the First Temple in Jerusalem may have looked like.

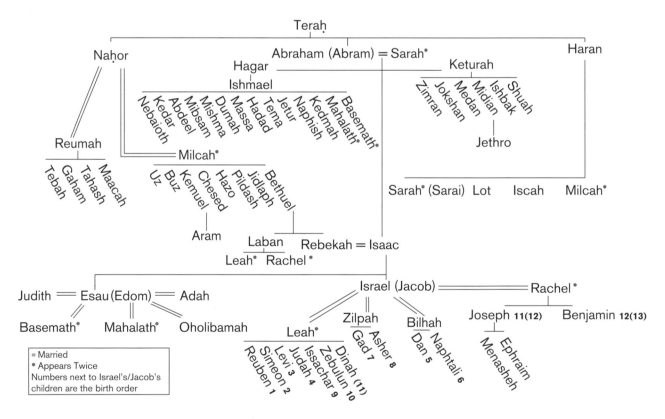

FIGURE 3.3. Biblical family tree. After Moses dies (Deuteronomy) and Joshua leads the Israelites against the people living in the Land of Israel (book of Joshua), the land is divided up among the twelve tribes of Israel, each of which was named after one of Jacob's (i.e., Israel's) sons (or, in the case of Ephraim and Menasheh, grandsons). This family tree thus shows the familial connection between Abraham and his great-grandsons, the Children of Israel. Note: Although Dinah is technically the eleventh child born to Jacob/Israel, in terms of the "12 Tribes of Israel," Dinah was marginalized; Joseph was considered the eleventh (male) child and Benjamin the twelfth.

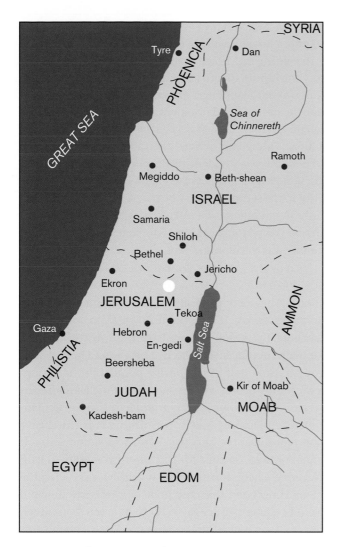

FIGURE 3.4. The Kingdoms of Israel and Judah (c. ninth century BCE).

For centuries, both prior to David's reign and after Solomon's, the Israelite-controlled land was divided and redivided, despite a number of attempts to unify it, such as those of Hezekiah, a Judean king who lived in the seventh century BCE. Only under David and Solomon were the Israelite kingdoms actually united. According to the book of Kings, immediately after Solomon's death, the northern tribes—sometimes described as the tribe of Ephraim and other times as made up of various Israelite tribes, perhaps ten of the original twelve—split apart from the southern ones, usually known by the name of the largest tribe among them, Judah, which maintained Jerusalem as their capital (fig. 3.4). Some consider the northern tribes that relocated as the "lost tribes."

From Zion to "Zions" in the Land of Israel

According to a number of ancient nonbiblical sources, over the next few centuries the northern Israelite kingdom's capital shifted from Shechem (also known by its Roman name, Nablus, southeast of Samaria) to Tirzah (between Samaria and Beth-shean) to Samaria. The northern kingdom also developed new sacred centers in the cities of Dan and Bethel. In other words, as of the ninth century BCE, the biblical Israelites had multiple hubs. Some argue that the authors of later biblical texts, such as 1 and 2 Chronicles, were responsible for pushing the narrative of the Jerusalem Temple as the supreme place to connect with God, retroactively creating what became a dominant way of understanding sacred space for centuries to come.

A great deal of theory (or educated speculation) guides us through this ancient period. According to one study, during the second century BCE the proto-Jewish Israelite community living in this area experienced ebbs and flows in terms of the importance of the land generally as opposed to the Temple in Jerusalem specifically. This understanding is further complicated when seen in light of the growing proto-Jewish communities outside the Land of Israel at this time, as well as the existence of at least four other temples (see "Temple or Temples?" below). Such shifts in Jewish communal narratives are reflected in nonbiblical texts, which often depict the latest site as having been important post-factum for much longer than actually may have been the case.

Who Was Living in the Land of Israel (a.k.a. Zion)?

Who Were the "Israelites"?

Putting aside multiple different population centers in the Land of Israel, the Israelites were likewise not homogeneous. Even during the short periods when the Israelite kingdom is thought to have been united, excavations have led to a number of academic theories regarding its make-up, specifically in terms of people who might best be described as having been Canaanite, Israelite, and/or Philistine (all communities referenced in the Bible). Some scholars argue that these groups may have lived alongside one another for centuries, as opposed to only beginning in around the year 1250 BCE, when the Israelites first entered the land and conquered it (as described in the book of Joshua). Others suggest that the first Israelites, maybe more accurately called proto-Israelites, were actually Canaanites. In fact, one scholar argues that we probably wouldn't be able to distinguish between a Canaanite, a Philistine, and an Israelite if we met one on the road. It is quite possible that many of these peoples had a "composite culture."

Others disagree with these claims, arguing instead that there were clear lines both between and sometimes within these three groups. There is evidence to suggest, for example, that Israelite subcommunities worshiped different deities—not just a single God called Yahweh but also a second deity, El, and a third deity, Asherah, a goddess who may have been the consort of Yahweh or El. At the same time, specific passages in the Torah prohibit Israelites from marrying Canaanites, among other non-Israelite groups. This points to the possibility that Israelite intermarriage (Israelites marrying non-Israelites) may not have been uncommon, a situation that may have frequently led to intercultural cross-fertilization (why else would there have been a prohibition?).

These data point to a number of possibilities that challenge today's dominant Jewish narratives portraying the Israelites as uniform. Among the assertions we may confidently make are these:

- The Israelites were made up of different subgroups.
- The Israelites absorbed other tribes, similar to the Canaanites.
- Distinct communities claimed the Land of Israel (later called by some Zion) as theirs; it was not exclusive to the Israelites.
- Israelite subcommunities didn't worship the same God.

In other words, from the earliest moments of Israelite history, this group was diverse. Israelite identities were never fully standardized and unvaried.

How and When Did the "Israelites" Become "Jews"?

At the time when the northern and southern kingdoms were united, the tribe of Judah, referred to in Greek as *Ioudaios* and in Hebrew (and Arabic) as *yehūdi,* was the largest of the Israelite tribes. We find the word *yehūdi,* the modern Hebrew word for Jew, in a number of both biblical books and noncanonical texts from the same era. Scholars generally believe, however, that the meaning of this ancient term is not equivalent to today's word *Jew,* but rather indicates a member of the Judean tribe. Perhaps the most common theory is that the shift in terminology from "Israelite" to "Jew" took place after the

northern kingdom (i.e., "Israelites") were exiled and the southern kingdom ("Judeans") stayed put.

According to scholar Shaye Cohen, at this time in history the Judean identity was an ethnic-geographical signifier, akin to labeling a group today as Edomite, Egyptian, or Syrian; it did not identify a member of a specific religious group that practiced Judaism or worshiped Yahweh. Moreover, within the Judean collective there were numerous subidentities, especially after the Assyrian conquest (eighth century BCE; see below). In short, prior to the second century BCE (a period discussed more fully in chapter 5), it is likely that although the term *Hebrew* was no longer used to refer to these communities, neither was the moniker, *Jew.*

Even by the period of Roman rule, in the first century BCE, when the term *Jew* became part of conventional discourse (as evidenced in texts from the time), Jews and Romans were often indistinguishable from one another "corporeally, visually, linguistically, and socially." As for male circumcision, which at best would have distinguished only half of the Jewish population from non-Jews, in the second century BCE, under the Hasmoneans (a semi-autonomous Judean group living in the Roman-controlled Land of Israel), performing this ritual gave non-Judeans entry into this Judean subcommunity. It took at least a century for this physical marker to gain currency. Then, during the first century CE—when the Romans declared that any male who was circumcised would be assumed (negatively) to be a Jew—circumcision took on a new symbolic significance (though this may have only been the practice in the city of Rome).

The First and Second Exiles—Were They Exiled from Zion?

Assyrian Exile

In the eighth century, commonly dated to 722 BCE, the Assyrian Empire destroyed the northern kingdom of Israel. Many Israelites were sent into exile, especially those of higher socioeconomic classes, and foreign groups were brought in to colonize those Israelites who were permitted to stay, both common Assyrian practices. (It is reasonable to assume that a subgroup from the northern kingdom also fled to Judah, directly to the south.) Some maintain that it is at this point that the Israelites, or at least some of them, were first exiled or dispersed (a word that, like *diaspora,* comes from the Greek: *dia* 'over, across' + *speirein* 'to sow, scatter'). If we date the first Jewish diaspora to 722 BCE (or thereabouts), it is clear that the central location from which the Israelites were dispersing was not Jerusalem—not Zion—but another city to the north, probably Samaria.

In the decades after the Assyrian conquest, the southern kingdom, Judah, likely became a semi-independent or client state of the Assyrians, eventually embracing cultural practices of the Assyrians and Canaanites, including those of worship—even enacting such rituals in the Temple itself. Some, however, hold a contradictory view, suggesting that during this time there was a revival of national customs among the Judeans, especially in the areas under the new authority.

Babylonian Exile

Approximately 125 years later, in the sixth century BCE, the Babylonians overtook the southern kingdom. Most date the Babylonian conquest, usually called the "Babylonian Exile," to 586 BCE. Yet some say that the Babylonians actually conquered Jerusalem as early as 597 BCE, the same year they began to deport and exile Judeans away from the immediate area.

Perhaps the preeminence of the year 586 BCE in the historical record, especially as taught within Jewish environments today, is due to this being when the Babylonians definitively destroyed Jerusalem and the Temple, as well as a number of other important Israelite and Judean cities. Some suggest that this mass wreckage was partly a reaction to an unsuccessful Judean rebellion against the Babylonians, which ended with the starvation of many of Jerusalem's inhabitants and a mass exile of as many as 20,000 Judeans. Others maintain that the poorest Judeans were permitted to stay, though most of them soon left for Egypt. Still others claim that there is no evidence to support the idea that a majority of Judeans were exiled. As with so much about this era, we're simply not sure.

Returning under the Persians

A little less than fifty years after the Temple was destroyed, in about 539 BCE, Persia conquered Babylon. According to one tradition, their king, Cyrus, carrying out a directive from the god Marduk, decreed that worshipers of other gods could resettle in their sacred cities (i.e., those from which the Babylonians had exiled them) and that all sacred sites that had been destroyed could be repaired. Other scholars are not so sure, arguing that Cyrus was not so much religiously tolerant as indifferent to locals' beliefs. In any event, whether or not he permitted the rebuilding of the Temple, no movement was made for another eighteen years (c. 521 BCE), two emperors later, once King Darius took over.

According to the Bible, during this same time the prophet Ezra returned to Judah, claiming the authority to impart and enforce "the teaching of God," which many interpret to mean the Five Books of Moses or a version thereof. In other words, the Torah, or parts of it, had been lost (literally or in terms of practice). Together with a local governor named Nehemiah, Ezra is said to have reestablished the observance of Torah-based laws among Jerusalemites, thereby recentralizing power in Zion.

Once the Temple was rebuilt under the authority of Ezra and Nehemiah, a period began when previously unpracticed (and perhaps not yet expressed) rituals were integrated into the Temple services. During this time, the site came to be understood as the meeting place for God and humans, an earthly nexus. This spot even came to embody worldly perfection, with the linkage of the Temple to the Garden of Eden. But the historical existence of the figure Ezra is far from clear. Some consider him to be a biblical fabrication.

Did Everyone "Return" Post-Exile?

Whatever actually happened, most scholars maintain that neither before the Babylonian Exile of 586 BCE nor after Torah-based laws were arguably reestablished in Jerusalem following the 530s BCE did all Israelites, Judeans, and members of related groups choose to live in the vicinity of Jerusalem. Many from this macroclan chose to live outside or far away from Zion (i.e., Jerusalem), even after they were given permission to return. Egyptian Judeans, for instance, largely stayed put throughout this time. In fact, there is no evidence that Egyptian Judeans considered moving "back" to Zion, even after the conquest of Egypt by Persia's King Cambyses in 525 BCE, which made such a trip easier (his rule followed Cyrus's). Many Judeans in areas we now call Iraq and Syria also chose to stay where they were, often playing important roles in the development of their more recently established Judean communities.

Some Babylonian Judeans went further and justified remaining in Babylon by denying the supremacy of the Land of Israel as *the* sacred center. For example, though written much later (and perhaps read back into history, retroactively), the Babylonian Talmud (one of two Talmuds, this one dated to the third through eighth centuries CE; described in detail in chapter 5) contains contrasting opinions: while some rabbinic voices say that living in the Land of Israel is a biblical directive, others

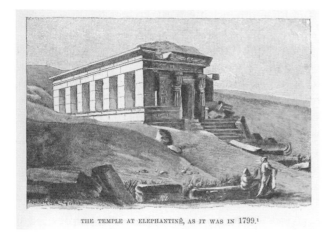

THE TEMPLE AT ELEPHANTINÊ, AS IT WAS IN 1799.[1]

FIGURES 3.5A–B. The Elephantine Temple, in southern Egypt: a drawing of how it may have appeared c. 1799 *(left)* and its remains in 2011 *(right)*. Notice the similarities between this temple and the one depicted in figure 3.2.

proclaim that returning to the Land of Israel is a transgression. One Talmudic rabbi even asserts that living in Babylon is itself akin to living in the Land of Israel, citing a passage from the biblical book of Zechariah (dated to around the sixth century BCE) to support his claim.

If the books of Ezra and Nehemiah are any indication, life was not easy for those who remained in Zion. Further, new schisms arose between those Judeans and Israelites who stayed and those who returned following Cyrus's proclamation. Among other disputes, the most prominent had to do with whether or not the Temple should be rebuilt. Those that did not want it rebuilt ostensibly did not place a greater significance on its pre-exile site (Zion) relative to other places.

Temple or Temples?

Many maintain that before the Second Temple was destroyed in 70 CE, Jewish worship was centered on *the* Temple in Jerusalem. Yet between the Babylonian Exile (sixth century BCE) and the first century CE, in the period between the first and second time the Temple was destroyed, proto-Jewish temples were built on at least four other sites. The presence of these places suggests that ritual worship during this period was less centralized than many contemporary Jews believe.

The first two temples were in Egypt: one in Elephantine, on the Upper Nile, and the second in Leontopolis, on the Lower Nile, called the temple of Onias. The third was the Tobiad sanctuary at Araq el-Emir, located in modern Jordan. The fourth was the Samaritan temple built on Mount Gerizim, found just outside Nablus in

today's northern region of the occupied West Bank, the latter area also commonly called Palestine.

Nonetheless, a dominant trend in scholarship is that none but the Jerusalem Temple was prominent during this 500- to 600-year period.

The Elephantine Temple

The historical community on Elephantine Island in Upper Egypt, near today's southern Egyptian city of Aswan, dates back to the seventh century BCE. Although we do not know when the first of this site's four or so sacred structures (fig. 3.5) was built, among 400 to 500 documents excavated from the Elephantine location, dated to the fifth century BCE, are some that say they were destroyed toward the end of the same century. Other important artifacts are letters between priests in Jerusalem and Elephantine that indicate the latter group worshiped a God named Yahweh (or Yaho), as well as other gods (perhaps just multifaceted elements of Yahweh); there is also evidence that the Elephantine community observed Passover. Many agree that animal sacrifices were performed in this temple, as at the Temple in Jerusalem.

The Oniad Temple

According to the first-century CE historian Josephus, the temple of Onias in Leontopolis, northeast of the capital of modern Egypt, Cairo, though much more modest, was modeled after the Jerusalem Temple, and even lasted a few years longer, through 74 CE. Although we don't know whether it was built under the authority of

Onias III or Onias IV, both of whom came from a lineage of high priests, or someone else entirely, according to the Mishnah and Talmud (see chapter 5) rabbinic authorities sanctioned the Leontopolis temple as a place where sacrifices were permitted. Oniad Levites and priests performed these rituals, just as in Jerusalem. (In ancient times, you could only be a priest—in Hebrew, *kohayn*—if you were male and your father was also a priest; priests were a subset of the tribe of Levi.)

The difficulty of establishing the significance of this site—aside from the dearth of sources and the ambiguity of those that we have—is compounded by the fact that Egyptian Jews from this era, such as Philo of Alexandria (first century BCE to first century CE), never mention a temple other than the one in Jerusalem. Still, some scholars maintain that the existence of two temples in Egypt illustrates the strength of Egyptian Jewish communities and the necessity of a local temple in their ritual life.

The Tobiad and Samaritan Temples

Third is the Tobiad temple at Araq el-Emir, some ten miles west of today's Jordanian capital, Amman. Despite debates as to when this temple was built—as early as the sixth century BCE or as late as the second century BCE—and arguments over whether the man after whom it is named, Tobiah, was a "Judaizing Ammonite" or a "Yahwist Jew," many scholars consider this to have been a legitimate Judean temple. As for the Samaritan temple on Mount Gerizim, immediately north of Shechem (or Nablus), the Samaritans living in the area today claim that their ancestors refused to move the sacred center to Zion centuries ago because the Torah only mentions Mount Gerizim's importance, never Zion's. (This last temple is discussed further in chapter 11.)

Living under the Romans . . . and Post-70 CE

By the time the Romans defeated the Greeks in the first century BCE, a process that began more than a century prior, Jews had multiple epicenters of life, including Alexandria, Babylonia (particularly the city of Babylon), and Jerusalem. Most Middle Eastern scholarship regarding this time, however, focuses on Jews who lived in Greek and Roman Palestine. Even so, it is widely held that by the time the Temple was destroyed in 70 CE, most Jews in the world did not live in Jerusalem; rather, the most Jewishly populated Middle Eastern city at the time may have been Alexandria.

In the first century CE, many outside of Palestine had the freedom to return to Jerusalem but chose not to, in part because there was no major call for them to make the journey. Using contemporary terms to reconstruct the various identities of these Jewish communities, we might say that at this time there were Alexandrian Jews, Arab Jews, Babylonian Jews, Cairene (Cairo) Jews, Egyptian Jews, Ethiopian Jews, Jerusalem Jews, Indian Jews, Persian Jews, and so forth. Whether or not all of these microcommunities identified as being part of a single macrocommunity is unclear.

Setting aside the lack of uniformity among Jews, both in Jerusalem and elsewhere, a number of concrete changes took place in Palestine-based Jewish communities following the destruction of the Second Temple, including the end of ritual animal sacrifice. It is likely that this was the central change in Jewish practice related to post-Temple Jewish life, something replaced by the recitation of verbal prayers. Of course, before the Temple was destroyed other forms of worship were practiced in this sacred site, including nonsacrificial verbal prayer and the playing of music.

Some believe that only after the destruction of the Second Temple did synagogues—communal gathering places for the explicit purpose of reciting verbal prayer— become central to Jewish worship. In fact, this was the dominant academic position for most of the twentieth century. However, more recent archeological findings dispute this theory. Synagogues predating 70 CE are found in multiple Middle Eastern sites, some going as far back as the third century BCE. Although it is possible that synagogues proliferated post-70 CE, it is clear they were not all birthed as a result of this major historical event.

Just how one defines a synagogue comes into play here, of course. Ultimately, we don't know when these gathering places became normalized. (The contemporary custom of calling synagogues "temples" is usually explained in relation to the way temples replaced *the* Temple.) We do know, however, that for centuries synagogues have been designed to reflect the architecture of the Temple, a practice that continues today. This has led some to contend that synagogues became the symbolic embodiment of and replacement for the Temple.

Another important shift in post-70 CE Jewish practice, at least in terms of the attempt to reconstruct Jewish history in relation to today's trends, was toward the study of Torah as a form of ritual worship. According to one story commonly taught in Jewish communities in Israel and the United States, in the days leading up to the final siege of Jerusalem, a few years prior to 70 CE, a prominent rabbi, Yochanan ben Zakkai, snuck out of the walled city in a coffin with the intention of establishing a new center for the Jewish community, as Jerusalem was soon to be destroyed. The rabbi charmed a Roman general to grant him permission to start a new school in a place called Yavneh.

Because in contemporary scholarship the Pharisees, a sect discussed in chapter 8, are often linked to the rabbis of the Mishnah and Talmud and are commonly credited with being the ancestors of today's Jews, this story is frequently used to bolster the idea that the Pharisees "saved" Judaism by reshaping it as a text-based—rather than Temple-based—devotional community. Scholars, however, argue not only that this story is a fabrication, but also that many other things aside from putting an end to animal sacrifices occurred at this time that led to ascendant forms of Jewish expression, including the end of severe Jewish factionalism (which, according to this argument, actually pre-dates 70 CE).

Zion and Diaspora

Zion/Exile or Zion/Diaspora?

The destruction of the Second Temple led to another Jewish diaspora, or *galut,* a Hebrew word that means exile. Though often used interchangeably, *diaspora* and *exile* have distinct meanings. Existential understandings aside, the latter term implies an imposed or forced move from one place to another, usually involving a collective trauma. In contrast, the former term connotes something much softer, a scattering or dispersion of a group from one place to another. Although the Jewish diaspora has historically been used as a primary example of the general phenomenon of diaspora, with the deepening of the contemporary field of Diaspora Studies, which employs a comparative perspective, it is now widely held that multiple groups are diasporic, including Armenians, Chinese, Greeks, Lebanese, Nigerians, Palestinians, and Tibetans, to name but a few.

When a group is forced to disperse from a particular place, the process of dispersal becomes an important part of their communal identity; more often than not it engenders a sense of powerlessness. Perhaps for this reason, many groups are firm and consistent in their use of the term *exile* over *diaspora* to underscore the violent nature of having been forced to relocate. Interestingly, the contemporary Jewish community tends to use the terms synonymously.

Among other fundamental ideas to emerge out of the field of Diaspora Studies is that a diasporic people need not have one epicenter—a single homeland—in order to fall into this category. The interactions of diasporic groups with various "hostlands" (as opposed to "homelands") are often more telling than any absolutist notion that they should be constantly striving to return to a single place.

In the case of the Jewish community, despite the "truth" that the Land of Israel, Zion, continues to serve as *the* homeland today, factually speaking "diaspora Jews" (i.e., Jews that live in one of the almost two hundred countries around the world that are not Israel) exist independent of both Jewish Israelis and the State of Israel. Given the fear some Jews have that the State of Israel might not exist in the near future (see chapters 9 and 10), it can be argued that the presence of Jews around the world (i.e., everywhere except Israel) offers a greater potential for the survival of Jews and Judaisms than does the sanctuary of the Jewish State.

Indeed, historical examples abound of Jews longing to return to a Zion that is unconnected to Israel. For example, Jews expelled from fifteenth-century Spain and Portugal longed to return to the Iberian Peninsula and not the Middle East. Nineteenth- and twentieth-century Jewish immigrants to the United States often wished to return to Poland or Russia. This latter group, according to historian Rebecca Kobrin, "shared a collective memory of their former home, created newspapers to articulate and carry on its traditions, and collected and distributed vast sums to rebuild its institutions."

As scholar Arnold Eisen aptly argues, even the Torah contains multiple examples of exile, or homelessness, with no explicit connection to Zion, starting with Adam and Eve's expulsion from the Garden of Eden. Although some might read Genesis from a simple, or *pshat,* perspective (see chapter 2), it seems the Torah also approaches exile both metaphorically and metaphysically.

Take, for example, a rabbinic interpretation of the rock Jacob laid his head on before falling asleep, ascending on high via a ladder, and wrestling with an angel (Gen. 28). One idea is that Jacob's "pillow" is a synonym for the Land of Israel—not the geographical but the metaphysical Land of Israel, that is, the Torah itself. In the nineteenth and early twentieth centuries, ideologues reaffirmed this existential notion of Zion. Twentieth-century philosopher Martin Buber, for example, writes that a Jew could be in exile even while in the Land of Israel. Buber's contemporary, Franz Rosenzweig, notes that "to the eternal people, home never is home in the sense of land."

This idea is also described in intricate detail in Jewish mystical texts dated to the thirteenth and fourteenth centuries. In the foundational Kabbalistic text, the *Zohar* (see chapter 6), the Jewish people (described as "Israel") are understood to be living in exile from God. Some mystics attribute this state of being to a process that began with Adam and Eve. Others see it as an illustration of how, in humanity's exile, God is exiled from Godself because human beings are created in God's image (Gen. 1:27).

Privileging Zion over Diaspora

Because Diaspora and Zion have become so entangled over the centuries, for most Jews it is practically impossible to separate them. Some even feel that since the founding of a new Jewish-identified country in 1948, diasporic Jews have been devalued, especially by Jewish Israelis, despite the fact that for most of Jewish history 99.9 percent of Jews were *only* diasporic (in terms of living outside the Land of Israel). For many such Jews, Zion continues to be more a metaphor than anything else. But with each devaluation of Jews living outside the Jewish State the notion of Zion or the State of Israel as *the* epicenter of Jewish life is reinforced.

Jewish Israelis in particular have played a major role in this process, primarily through ideological Zionist-based messaging. As scholar Dina Porat notes, "The origins of Zionist identity are based in the need to draw a clear distinction between Zionism and earlier forms of diasporic existence: Zionist identity was forged and fostered vis-à-vis the Jewish diaspora. The Zionist movement was created as a way to solve the miseries of the Jewish situation in the diaspora by returning to the Land of Israel and thus opening a new page in history. This process necessitated severing all ties to the past, denigrating the diasporic Jews and their characteristics, and glorifying the bravery of the new Jews." Along these lines, some argue that the government of the State of Israel and Zionists have had a disproportionate influence on dominant Jewish narratives over the last half-century.

Many American Jews have been disturbed by the perceived Israeli usurping of the world's multiple Zions. Reacting to a censure leveled at American Jewry by Israeli prime minister David Ben-Gurion in 1950, one prominent Jewish American, philanthropist Jacob Blaustein, said, "We must sound a note of caution to Israel and its leaders . . . the matter of good-will between its citizens and those of other countries is a two-way street: . . . Israel has a responsibility in this situation—a responsibility in terms of not affecting adversely the sensibilities of Jews who are citizens of other states by what it says or does.

In this connection, you are realists and want facts, and I would be less than frank if I did not point out to you that American Jews vigorously repudiate any suggestion or implication that they are in exile. . . . To American Jews, America is home."

Despite such protests, the Zion/Diaspora binary voiced by Ben-Gurion, among others, remains dominant. Consider the way many write about Jewish geographical space, using such terms as *homeland* for Israel and *hostland* (or Diaspora) for everywhere else. In contrast, scholars (and brothers) Daniel and Jonathan Boyarin boldly suggest that the diaspora "may be the most important contribution that Judaism has to make to the world."

Of course, the Jewish genocide or Shoah of World War II challenged the ability of Jews to live among non-Jews (primarily in Europe), even confirming for some that the so-called diaspora world is not safe, whereas Zion is (see chapters 9 and 10). As scholar Sidra Ezrahi notes, "The Holocaust may have turned the European exile from a place in which Home was imagined to a 'real' home that can only be recalled from somewhere else and reconstructed from its shards; retrospectively, that is, the destruction seems to have territorialized exile as a lost home." Ezrahi also points out that throughout Jewish literature one finds depictions of Zion "in its most radical form . . . an imaginative license that has no geographical coordinates." Zion, in other words, exists irrespective of physical place, let alone the Israeli nation-state.

In response to this idea, novelist and philosopher Rebecca Goldstein presents a fictional character named Jascha challenging a "rabid Zionist Zev Ben-Something-or-Other": "Homeland? . . . I suppose by this you mean some wilderness on the other side of the globe, on which I have never laid eyes, and which I don't even know how to picture, but which, from its description, even by those who profess themselves its eternal lovers, can promise me *nothing*. And yet, if I am to believe the arguments of people like you, it is that place, and not here in the Europe of my birth, and of my father's birth, and of my father's father's father's birth, that I am to think of as my authentic homeland."

The End of the Dominant Zion/Diaspora Binary?

Although there are many more Jews living in the State of Israel now than there were prior to 1948, when the country was established, most of today's Jews—60 percent— do not live there, and there is no indication that this will change in any major sense in the near future. In fact, as mentioned in chapter 1, although roughly 40 percent of the world's Jews live in Israel, just as many live in the United States.

In addition, when comparing American and Israeli Jewry specifically, we find more Jewish Israelis leaving Israel than American Jews moving there. Between 1948 and 1993, in fact, five times as many Jews moved from Israel to the United States than vice versa. Similarly, despite the massive immigration of Russians to Israel following the collapse of the Soviet Union, in 2003 more Jews moved to Moscow from Israel than the other way around. This is not to say that because 80 percent of the world's Jews live in only two countries it is accurate to reformulate the Zion/Diaspora duality to include Israel and the United States as representing Zion and everywhere else counting as the Diaspora. As stated above, Zion has existed outside of place and time for most of Jewish history.

Nonetheless, the Zion/Diaspora dyad remains a dominant idea among Jews. Most Jewish prayer services, Orthodox, Conservative, Reform, or otherwise (see chapter 8), include prayers asking God to hasten the "ingathering of the exiles"—a reference to passages in the Bible describing the Hebrews' and Israelites' scattering across the world before returning to the Promised Land. And yet most non-Israeli Jews who recite these prayers do not mean them literally. Many have the ability to move to the State of Israel but will never do so. In other words, when Jews make this prayer many, if not most, intend a metaphorical return, not a literal one. This does not mean that the "Return to Zion" idea is dead. Rather, both notions—Zion as homeland and other countries as homeland—exist in tandem.

The Diaspora Museum or the Museum of the Jewish People

Part of the problem with the Zion/Diaspora framework is connected to the notion of hegemony, not just ideological but also cultural or ethnic. This is embodied in the following example: One of the places many Jewish tourists, especially Americans, include on trips to the State of Israel is Tel Aviv's *Beit Hatfutsot*. Founded in 1978 with the English name Nahum Goldmann Museum of the Jewish Diaspora, this renowned site houses numerous exhibitions on Jewish life outside the Land of Israel. In 2005, the Israeli Parliament (Knesset) voted to support the expansion and upgrade of the museum using government funds; in the process it was renamed The Museum of the Jewish People.

A few points are worth mentioning here. First, when renaming the museum's English name in 2005, their leadership expressly decided to remove the term *diaspora*

from the museum's English name, thus making it more inclusive, while maintaining the Hebrew name, Beit Hatfutsot, which means "Diaspora House," thereby further concretizing the Zion/Diaspora worldview (i.e., the museum has an official Hebrew name and an official English name). As most of the world's Jews do not understand Hebrew, those visiting the museum are unlikely to realize the two names are are not translations of one another. In other words, perhaps in an effort to acknowledge Jews who do not live in Israel, the museum's leadership chose to maintain the hierarchical division between Zion and everywhere else, but did so somewhat surreptitiously.

When explaining these changes, the museum's leadership stated that one of the goals of the reconstruction was to make the facility much less Ashkenazi- and male-centric. This clearly reflected an awareness of how the museum reinforces the intra-Jewish dominance of specific identities. Ironically, the Babylonian Jewry Heritage Center, located twenty minutes south of Beit Hatfutsot, in the nearby city of Holon, has always focused on non-Ashkenazi history, but continues to be virtually unknown among Jewish tourists.

Beit Hatfutsot's leadership decided to acknowledge the problematic nature of the Zion/Diaspora binary by both destabilizing and reinforcing it, conceding their Ashkenazi-centrism while continuing to marginalize the nearby Babylonian Center. This illustrates the current crossroads that Jews have reached: despite an opportunity to reexamine a dominant Jewish narrative, this has not led to a concrete embracing of a whole-heartedly new self-understanding.

Home Is Zion, Zion Is Home

If you go to Jerusalem today and decide to visit Mount Zion, you will most likely be taken to a place that has inaccurately been called by this name for centuries. Today's "Mount Zion" is actually southwest of the ancient site of Zion. In this sense, even Zion isn't Zion.

And yet Zion does exist. Whether one lives in the State of Israel, the United States, or anywhere else under the sun, not being in Zion is to live in existential exile. This is different from saying either that Zion is Israel or that there is no Zion.

Even Jews who immigrate to Israel don't necessarily feel it is their home. Take the following description of a group of Iranian Jews living in Israel, quoting an article titled "Longing for a Lost Country": "*Ha'aretz* correspondent David Oren . . . reported on a cultural event that took place in Bat Yam (a small coastal town adjacent to Tel Aviv), which was attended by some 500 Iranian immigrants *(olim)*. Oren could not quite grasp why the participants 'were all united in their longing for days bygone; for the days and nights in [the Iranian cities of] Teheran, Shiraz, Isfahan, Hamdan and Abadan before the ousting of the Shah. . . . At first glance,' as Oren said, 'the event reminded me of a group of exiles in a foreign land.'" Similar feelings of "exile in Zion" have been expressed by Iraqi Jews living in Israel, among other groups.

No matter where a Jew lives, he or she can still feel the pain of being in exile. In the words of legal scholar Milton Konvitz,

> We American Jews are living in exile, in *Galuth*. . . . Jews in Israel are in no different condition. For the condition of the Jew, every Jew, in or out of Israel, is to live in Galuth, in exile. . . . Every Jew, in his character as Jew, is both at home and homeless. The American Jew is at home in the United States, as is every American; he is, at the same time, in exile, as is every Jew. And the Israeli Jew is at home in the State of Israel, as is every Israeli; he is, at the same time, in exile, as is every Jew. Homelessness does not end with the attainment of freedom and equality in a free democratic country; nor does it end with the attainment of national independence and statehood in Israel. Like Jacob, he [the Jew] is eternally the sojourner.

Zion, like any homeland, is a complex idea. Even if someone travels to his or her own Zion, new attachments are then constructed. As scholars Alex Weingrod and André Levy put it, "Return is not the end of the story, but rather another beginning that develops new contents and new directions."

As for whether Zion is ever literal, perhaps it comes down to how one orients toward the Exodus from Egypt as explained in the Torah (chapter 1). Egypt, *Mitzrayim,* is a real place. But it is also a metaphor for exile, for diaspora. So, too, the Land of Israel in the Bible is a geographical place, as well as an ideal that humanity has not yet attained but which it has been promised. Indeed, the Torah, the core text of the Jewish community, ends with the Israelites outside of and looking into the Land of Israel (or Zion). Even the generation of Hebrews and Israelites that wandered together in the desert for decades are unable to reach the Land of Israel by the end of the Torah's narrative. Yes, the Israelite saga continues in the book of Joshua and thereafter, but if the deepest levels of Torah are not literal, than the fact that "Israel" is unattainable cannot be overlooked.

So . . . What Is Zion?

In the twenty-first century, the lines between Zion and Diaspora, home and exile, have become intertwined and can no longer be separated. But this has not always been the case. As scholar Erich Gruen notes, the obsession with the notion of Zion vs. Diaspora is modern, a reading back into history as if that is how Jews have always understood their Jewish identities. Perhaps one's struggle (or not) with these ideas reflects one's Jewish identity, and how one understands oneself relative to one's obligations as a Jew.

Maybe the paradoxes related to the pairings of Zion/ Diaspora, home/exile, are best explained by photographer Frédéric Brenner. As he puts it, "Exile? Home? What do these words mean when the dimension of exile is omnipresent in the land of Israel? This was what I wanted to investigate: If, for two thousand years, the issue was how to remain Jewish among strangers, in Israel the issue has become how to keep one's identity among Jews. Jews had to settle in Israel in order to become Yemenite, German, Ethiopian, to understand that they had actually been at home, in exile."

In other words, Jews' identities are inherently portable, no matter where they live. This is one of the paradoxical threads that tie Jews together. Similarly, philosopher Isaiah Berlin rhetorically asks: "What does every Jew have in common, whether he hails from Riga or from Aden, from Berlin or from Marrakesh or Glasgow?" He answers his own question: "A sense of unease in society. Nowhere do almost all Jews feel entirely at home."

Today, Zion and galut, home and homelessness, are perhaps more important to Jews as metaphors, descriptive terms, than anything else. Yet this binary remains, both literally and metaphorically, territorially and spiritually. Ben-Gurion's claim that American Jews live in exile is still true for American Jews; at the same time, American Jews believe the United States is their home. Jews continue to live in Zion and galut no matter where they are.

FOUR

Messiahs

Contents

Key Ideas

- During the development of Judaisms, Jews have expressed the notion of the portability of God or the divine within sacred words (Sinai), places (Zion), and people (messiah, tzadik)
- Notions about the term messiah have changed over time, including whether it means an individual messiah or a messianic age. Even within the Bible and the Talmud there are multiple understandings of messiah.
- Over the last two millennia there have been tens of individuals who Jews have believed were the messiah, including as recently as the 1990s.

The Messiah Is Dead, Long Live the Messiah!

In December 1994, midway through a cross-country trip from Baltimore to Los Angeles, a friend and I spent the weekend in New Orleans. The day before we got there we called the Chabad Center of Tulane University to see if they could arrange for us to be hosted at someone's house for a Friday evening Sabbath, or *Shabbat,* meal. One of the world's largest and most widespread Jewish organizations, Chabad emerged out of the Lubavitch sect of ultra-Orthodox Judaism. One of their many programs offers Jews free, home-cooked Shabbat and holiday meals, something our twenty-one-year-old selves took advantage of whenever possible.

After we arrived at our host's home, a short walk from the Tulane campus, we asked him some questions about Chabad, starting with how he became involved in this unique institution and movement. Eventually, the clueless college student within asked him the question I was most interested in—the one question I no doubt should not have asked, and one that left him somewhat speechless: "What is Chabad going to do now that the Rebbe's no longer alive? Is someone going to take his place as your movement's new leader?"

A little more than six months earlier, on June 12, 1994, a ninety-two-year-old Russian American rabbi named Menachem Mendel Schneerson died. Known to devotees and nondevotees alike simply as "the Rebbe," Schneerson was no ordinary Jewish religious leader. For years, some Jews—albeit almost exclusively Lubavitch Jews—had believed he was the messiah, someone who would carry out biblical prophecies related to the end of times and bring about the redemption of the world.

That same summer, I had been studying Jewish texts in an Orthodox *yeshivah* (seminary) in the Jewish Quarter of the Old City of Jerusalem. During one of my first weeks there, while walking from my dormitory building to the cafeteria, I noticed that something was different about the people I passed in my neighborhood's narrow alleyways. They seemed distressed about something. Given the everyday realities of this part of the world, I knew that the possibilities for their abnormal behavior were pretty much endless. Most likely, I thought, something had happened overnight related to the ongoing conflict between Jewish Israelis and Palestinians.

But then I learned that the Rebbe had died. Although the *yeshivah* I was studying in did not proclaim allegiance to the Rebbe and was not part of the Lubavitch community who venerated him, many of the students and teachers at my school had a deep respect for Schneerson. Some may even have believed he was the messiah.

I had first heard about Schneerson years before, when visiting New York City. In the early 1990s, Chabad began plastering posters of the Rebbe around parts of Brooklyn (largely in an area called Crown Heights, where Chabad has its main headquarters) as well as in the State of Israel (fig. 4.1). The placards and billboards seemed omnipresent, and they weren't subtle in terms of connecting Schneerson to the messiah. They usually had a large picture of the Rebbe, his right hand held up as if taking an oath or in mid-wave, with a statement underneath or alongside that read "The King, the Messiah," or "Long live our Master, our Teacher, our Rabbi, the King, the Messiah Forever."

For me, the most striking thing was that members of the

FIGURE 4.1. Rabbi Schneerson ("the Rebbe") alongside the Hebrew words for "Long live our master, our teacher, our rabbi, the King Messiah, forever."

Jewish community were loudly and proudly claiming that a living human being was the messiah. Some Lubavitch Jews were so convinced that Schneerson was going to reveal himself as the messiah that in the days leading up to his death, and in particular between his death and his funeral, held less than a day after he expired, they danced in the streets of Brooklyn. A small group continued celebrating even after he was buried, as they were expecting him to be resurrected. Some Lubavitch Jews continue to maintain that Schneerson still *is* the messiah, now more than twenty years after his death.

After I first learned about Schneerson, I asked Jewish teachers of mine about this phenomenon and what it meant in terms of Judaism. "I thought Jews didn't believe in the messiah. Isn't that a Christian thing?" I was far from the only Jew to have these thoughts.

Despite having many positive things to say about the Rebbe and his followers, and despite believing in the coming of the messiah himself, one prominent American Orthodox rabbi, Norman Lamm, commented on the Lubavitch community's veneration of Schneerson by saying, "Why in heaven's name do they have to get latched onto this dreadful messianic business? There's an element of idolatry there that scares me very much."

Back in New Orleans, once my host overcame his inclination to start sobbing following my reminder of the hole in his community's proverbial heart, he told me that Schneerson could never be replaced; no one could ever step into his shoes. Fortunately, my insensitive question regarding the Rebbe was put to the side as we moved onto other matters.

Meanwhile, however, history has taught us something very different: The Rebbe-cum-messiah can—and perhaps will—be replaced. If indeed history repeats itself in this particular situation, there should be another Jewish messiah in the near future.

The Messiah: A Centuries-old Idea

Putting aside some contemporary Jewish discomfort with it, the messianic idea goes back millennia. It is deeply embedded in the Jewish tradition. Historically speaking, the Chabad movement's belief that their former leader was the messiah was not unique. By some counts, since the first century CE there have been more than fifty Jewish messiahs, Schneerson among them (see special topic 4.1). What has changed along the way, however, is the meaning of the messianic idea, for it has had a number of incarnations. Over time, this phenomenon has also led to the proliferation of new Jewish sects, some of which became new religions in their own right—Christianity, of course, the best known.

Along with the belief in the messiah yet another new concept developed within the Jewish community: the portability of God (or the divine), not just within sacred words (Sinai) or spaces (Zion), but within people—and not simply insofar as everyone is created in the image of God (Gen. 1:27), but within particular individuals being perceived as having extraordinary characters, including divinely given, supernatural abilities. In other words, messianic figures, and to a lesser extent Jewish leaders perceived as saints or holy men, began serving as *axes mundi*—centers of the world—for their respective communities.

Some might argue that the messianic idea is not relevant to most Jews' lives today, but I would disagree. Aside from the roughly 10 percent of Jews worldwide who identify as Orthodox (and thus, in principle, pray for the coming of the messiah a minimum of three times each day), many Jews believe in the possibility of an ideal world, a utopia of some sort, as well as in a responsibility to move the world toward this goal. In this sense, belief in a messianic age continues to be actively present in many Jews' lives. Some might simply call this hope.

Messiah—"Anointed One"

Most commonly translated as "messiah," the Hebrew word *mashiah*—*christos* in Greek—literally means "one who is anointed." One of the earliest Middle Eastern references we have to the anointing of a person, as opposed to a ritual object, is found in the second book of the Torah, Exodus. In the passage in question, God instructs Moses to anoint Aaron, the Israelite community's first high priest, along with his two sons, thereby consecrating them with a new stature in the community. Later on in the Torah there are other laws regarding ways to anoint priests.

After the Five Books of Moses, the next time we see the word *mashiah,* or any derivation thereof, in the Bible isn't until the book of Samuel (that is, quite some time later), when God tells the prophet Samuel that Saul and David need to be anointed prior to their becoming kings. Thereafter, it appears in the Bible only a handful of other times. Not one of these biblical examples explicitly describes the transformation of an individual from an ordinary human into one who is divine or godly, one of the primary ways this word has been understood since at least the first century CE. Rather, in each instance it seems the ritual of anointing someone with oil signifies a shift into a new role, whether high priest, king, or prophet, both for the individual and for the community at large.

Other ancient Middle Eastern texts also touch on the messianic idea from as early as the second century BCE, whether in terms of a messiah figure or a messianic time. Some maintain that the idea of the messiah entered Israelite society from another ancient community, such as the Canaanites or Egyptians. For example, the Sibylline Oracles, a collection of Egyptian-based texts dated to between the second century BCE and the second century CE, discuss a "blessed man" delivered by God to wage violence on the wicked and build a temple for the righteous. Others hold that the concept has Assyrian, Babylonian, or Persian origins. Still others, such as the twentieth-century philosopher Martin Buber, are adamant that it is Judaism's "most profoundly original idea," ridding us of any theory that it originated outside the Jewish community.

Ways to Become Anointed

As for different ways to become anointed, biblical prophets sometimes claim to have been consecrated directly by God, as opposed to having been rubbed with oil by another human. (One example of an exception to this pattern is when God instructs Elijah to anoint his successor, Elisha.) Once anointed, a prophet is able to anoint someone else, such as when transitioning another into the priesthood, as the prophet Moses does with his brother Aaron, or into the crown, as Samuel does with Kings Saul and David. Although the ritual of anointing does not transform Aaron, Saul, or David into a superhuman, it gives them a recognized status whereby they are set apart from others. It symbolizes their new, explicit connection to and protection by God.

What It Means to Have Been Anointed, for the Individual and Community

The communal functions these anointed figures serve are different, despite their commonality in terms of the ritual by which they achieve their status. Among their shared qualities, two of the most often cited are (1) the genealogical connection between the messiah and King David—as it says in the second book of Samuel, which predates Isaiah: someone from the "seed" of David will "build a house" in God's name, and in turn, God will establish a kingdom for him forever; and (2) the linkage between the messiah and an era of utopian peace, as in this passage from Isaiah 11:6: "And the wolf shall dwell with the lamb, and the leopard shall lie down with the kid; and the calf and the young lion and the fatling together; and a little child shall lead them." Along with passages found in Zechariah, Isaiah 11 is one of the core sections of the Bible that people today turn toward when exploring the messianic idea. Other qualities commonly linked to the messiah and/or messianic age include the resurrection of the dead, a period of great destruction, and a return to the "laws of Moses."

Additional books of prophets, though much less overt, are commonly used as "proof" for particular perspectives on the messiah or a messianic age. For example, in the book of Haggai, the prophet says that God told him about an imminent era of peace. Because Haggai also speaks about a Judean named Zerubbabel in these same passages, some maintain that Haggai believed Zerubbabel was the messiah. This text's connection to the idea of a messiah is ambiguous if for no other reason than that neither the word *mashiah* nor any derivation thereof appears

in even a single verse of this book. The book of Zechariah makes similar implicit linkages between Zerubbabel (as well as the high priest) and the messiah, and includes an overt prophecy that Zerubbabel will be the one to finish building God's house. Perhaps more to the point, neither book explicitly describes the messiah as a figure who will personally bring about a time of peace.

Changing Notions of the Messiah in the Bible

A number of scholars argue that within the Bible itself the notion of the messiah changes. In other words, the progression of the messianic idea is not a strictly postbiblical phenomenon. As the more than twenty texts of the prophets are commonly understood to have been written over the course of centuries, this assertion makes sense, especially since many traditions relied more on oral transmissions than on written ones. Scholar Joseph Klausner, for instance, argues that only after it was rooted in the Israelite community did the messianic idea come to represent a future utopian age, thereby distinguishing it from the messianic understanding held by Greeks and Romans, which often focused on a glorious past.

The Postbiblical Messiah

Over time the messianic idea changed further. Although some say it wasn't until the first or second century CE that the idea the messiah would be an individual with supernatural abilities became part of messianic discourse, scholar Jacob Neusner puts the date of this development later. He contends that the normative understanding of the messiah as found in core Jewish texts such as the Mishnah (written sometime between the first and third centuries CE) includes no supernatural abilities whatsoever, in contrast to passages from the Jerusalem and Babylonian Talmuds (written sometime between the third and eighth centuries CE). (Chapter 5 discusses the Mishnah and Talmud in detail.)

Prior to the Talmud, says Neusner, "messiahs were merely a species of priest, falling into one classification rather than another." Others support this argument, saying that the Mishnah has only two explicit references to the messiah, outside of those describing the anointing of a priest or a vague future age—but not *the* ultimate end of the world—both of which are tangential. For example, scholar Richard Horsley says, "We have little or no literary evidence *that,* let alone *how,* Palestinian Jews at the time of Jesus were thinking with regard to some sort of 'anointed' figure."

As for why the meaning of the messiah might have morphed during the first few centuries CE in particular, some maintain it was a result of another widely held perception, one much closer to tangible reality: the Jews of Palestine were about to be wiped out by the Romans. Along these lines, the idea of a superhuman messiah may have come about because this was a period of increased external and internal conflict. Others refute such theories, pointing out that if this were indeed the case other messianic figures would have emerged at other times of desperation in Jewish history.

Whatever the reasons, this period saw a new understanding of the messiah. The following interpretation became the new norm during the first few centuries CE: "Messianism is the expectation of an individual human and yet transcendent saviour. He is to come in a final eschatological [end of days] period and will establish God's Kingdom on earth. In a more strict sense, messianism is the expectation of a royal Davidic savior at the end time." Prior to this time, the word *messiah* did not mean a supernatural figure.

Messianic Variations (e.g., in the Talmud)

A number of texts from the Talmud and other rabbinic sources from this era include the requirement that the messiah should be, to use contemporary terminology, some sort of superhero. On the whole, however, these texts exhibit little consistency. Some Talmudic voices say that the messianic age was at hand then and there (between the third and eighth centuries CE). Some maintain that the messiah would rebuild the Temple. Some say he would be a king, others a rabbi. Some Talmudic figures relate tales of meeting the messiah, while others—such as the Talmudic sage Hillel—expressed disbelief that the messiah will ever come. Some said the messiah will come but that they don't want to see him. Some say that the messiah will come five thousand years after creation, while others say six or seven thousand.

Some say that the messiah's coming depends entirely on whether people have morally proven themselves to deserve it. Some give precise directives as to how Jews need to act in order to hasten the messiah's coming. Some say that the world needs to be in a state of utter lawlessness for the messiah to emerge, whereas others hold the opposite view, saying instead that the world needs to be in a state of utopian peace. Some say the messiah will bring all of the Jews worldwide "back" to the Land of Israel, the "ingathering of the exiles." In addition, there are disagreements over the messiah's name, which is said

FIGURE 4.2. In the final years of the Jewish revolt against the Romans led by Bar Kokhba (c. 132–135 CE), the rebels made their own coins by overwriting images found on Roman coins with Paleo-Hebrew letters. Etched on these pieces of metal were phrases such as "year one of the Redemption of Israel," "year two of the Freedom of Israel," and "for the Freedom of Jerusalem." The image above left is thought to be a depiction of the Temple. Some argue that the star above the Temple alludes to the belief that Bar Kokhba was the messiah, a position maintained by the Talmudic sage Rabbi Akiba. Others say this was a normal aesthetic symbol of the time and has no meaning in terms of messianism. The image above right is thought to be a *lulav,* a ritual object used during the Jewish holiday Sukkot, also known as the Feast of Tabernacles, which is made up of branches from a palm, a willow, and a myrtle, as well as a lemonlike fruit called an *etrog.* Some say the image of the *lulav* illustrates Bar Kokhba's commitment to Jewish law and ritual.

to be, for example, Haninah, Menahem the son of Hezekiah, Shiloh, Yinnon, the "leper scholar," or Peace. Estimations of how long the messiah will reign range from forty to four hundred years.

One of the individuals that Talmudic rabbis claim God chose to be the messiah was Hezekiah, a king of Judah during the seventh or eighth century BCE (long before these rabbinic figures were alive). This king was never able to actualize his messianic potential, however; one opinion is that he didn't praise God with hymns, something done by traditional greats such as King David.

Also mentioned in the Talmud is the belief of Rabbi Akiba—one of the most important Palestinian leaders of his day—that his contemporary, the second-century CE Jewish leader Bar Kosiba, also called Bar Kokhba, was the messiah. Bar Kokhba is probably best known for leading the final rebellion against the Romans, which ended in 135 CE (fig. 4.2.) Yet Akiba may have been alone in thinking Bar Kokhba was the messiah.

More to the point, Akiba was wrong. Bar Kokhba was killed and did not fulfill any messianic prophecies. Interestingly, in one passage we are told that contemporaries of Akiba killed Bar Kokhba after he was unable to prove that he could judge people based on their scent, one of countless traits the messiah was supposed to have. (One renowned Talmudic rabbi, who may have been a contemporary of Akiba's but surely was not alive during the era of Bar Kokhba, Yochanan ben Zakkai, is credited with saying: "If you have a sapling in your hand and they say to you that the messiah has come, go and finish planting the sapling, and then go out to receive the messiah," illustrating a practical approach to evaluating whether or not someone is the messiah.)

Around this same time a new layer was added to the understanding of the Jewish messiah. As expounded upon in the Talmud, alongside the messiah son of David, a second messiah—the messiah son of Joseph— was to arise, only to die shortly thereafter, thereby paving the road for the messiah son of David. Some scholars argue that this tradition emerged only after Bar Kokhba's death—as an attempt to justify Rabbi Akiba's mistaken belief that the anti-Roman warrior was *a,* but not *the,* messiah. Others argue that it emerged in an effort to acknowledge, though not accept, Jesus, whose human father was named Joseph (i.e., the messiah son of Joseph). During the medieval period, between the eighth and thirteenth centuries CE, this tradition developed further.

Jesus, a Jewish Messiah (and "Christian Jews")

Of those who either claimed to be the messiah or had others impose this title upon them, the most renowned, of course, is Jesus, whose narrative developed alongside that of Bar Kokhba (though they did not live at the same time). Passages from the Talmud are dismissive of both figures. In Christian-majority societies, non-Jews understood texts that rejected Jesus's messianic status as heretical, if not criminal, and sometimes used them to justify persecuting Jews. (Some twenty-first-century antisemites continue this practice today.)

The belief that Jesus was the messiah brought with it a number of new ideas, most of which developed during the second and third centuries CE, or later. For starters, Jesus was probably the first individual people believed was the messiah postmortem—more specifically, after he died and, according to Christian doctrine, was resurrected. But this idea didn't emerge in a vacuum. Early Christian Jews (see below), like other Jewish sects from first-century Palestine, rooted their particular interpretations of the messiah in biblical passages that may not be obvious to a contemporary reader, many of which are found in the Talmud and early Christian Jewish sources.

It is critical to point out that Christian Jews and non-Christian Jews were all part of the Jewish milieu—from the dominant perspectives of Jews of the time—until the third or even fourth century CE, an argument most prominently offered by Daniel Boyarin (though many scholars challenge it). As Boyarin explains,

Jesus, when he came, came in a form that many, many were expecting: a second divine figure incarnated as a human. The question was not "Is a divine Messiah coming?" but only "Is this carpenter from Nazareth the One we are expecting?" Not surprisingly, some Jews said yes and some said no. Today we call the first group Christians and the second group Jews, but it was not like that then, not at all. Everybody living in Palestine during this era, aside from Romans—both those who accepted Jesus and those who didn't—was Jewish (or Israelite, the actual ancient terminology).

By the fourth century CE there were many more categories of Jews than merely those who believed in Jesus and those who did not. (The Pharisees and other Jewish sects from this era are discussed in chapter 8.)

In other words, in relation to Jesus the boundaries between Christian Jews and non-Christian Jews were ambiguous for centuries. Only in the fourth century CE, says Boyarin, did the borders start to solidify, but even then only gradually. To complicate matters, other groups existed during this time that are linked to both Christian Jews and non-Christian Jews, such as those called "proselytes, God-fearers, and *gerim.*"

Boyarin also argues that the belief that Jesus was the messiah was not necessarily the primary difference between Christian Jews and non-Christian Jews. One of the new additions to the messianic idea—that the messiah needed to die and be resurrected—was a *Jewish* belief through and through; only over the course of time was it retroactively applied to a group later called non-Jews. This, however, is not a fact, but open to a great deal of debate.

One thing we can say, as Jacob Neusner argues, is that it was precisely during the Talmudic era that the concept of the messiah "came to literary expression [and] was then shaped to serve the larger purposes of the nascent canonical system as a whole," a phenomenon seen in the development of the Christian community as well.

Many More Jewish Messiahs

In addition to Jesus, the ancient historian Josephus named a number of other people whom his contempo-

SPECIAL TOPIC 4.1
A PARTIAL LIST OF JEWISH MESSIAHS

Fifth century
Crete: A man claiming to be the reincarnation of the biblical Moses

Seventh century
Syria: Unnamed man

Eighth century
Syria: Serenus or Sari'a

Persia: Abu Isa or Ovadia of Ifsahan; Yudghan or Yehuda of Hamadan; Mushka

Eleventh century
France: Unnamed man

Spain: Ibn Arye

Morocco: Moshe Al-Dar'i (originally from Yemen)

Somewhere between Syria and Egypt: Shlomo

Twelfth century
Baghdad (in today's Iraq): Daughter of Joseph the physician

Morocco: Unnamed man

Spain: Ibn Aryeh

Kurdistan (and/or today's Iraq): David Alroy or David al-Ro'i

Thirteenth century
Greece, Italy, Spain, and the Land of Israel: Abraham Abulafia

Fifteenth century
Yemen: The messiah of Bayhan

Sixteenth century
Austria: Asher Lemlein

Land of Israel/Ottoman Palestine: Isaac ben Solomon Luria Ashkenazi

Spain and Portugal: Ludovico Diaz; Ines of Herrera; David Reuveni or David Ha-Re'uveni; Shlomo Molkho (the latter two individuals also traveled elsewhere in the Mediterranean)

Sixteenth and seventeenth centuries
Land of Israel/Ottoman Palestine: Haim ben Joseph Vital Calabrese

Seventeenth century
Turkey: Sabbatai Tzvi

Yemen: Suleiman Jamal al-Aqt'a

Eighteenth century
Ukraine and Russia: Israel ben Eliezer or the Baal Shem Tov, a.k.a. the Besht

Turkey and Poland: Jacob Frank

Eighteenth and nineteenth centuries
Poland: Ewa Frank

Russia: Israel of Ruzhin

Ukraine: Rabbi Nahman of Bratslav

Nineteenth century
Ukraine: Israel of Ruzhin; the Komarno Rebbe, a.k.a. Eizikel or Yitzchak Eizik Yehuda Yehiel Safrin

Yemen: Shukr Kuḥayl; Shukr Kuḥayl II or Yehuda bar Shalom (the latter figure claimed to be the former reincarnated)

Nineteenth and twentieth centuries
Yemen: Yusuf Abdallah or Yosef Eved-El

Western Europe: Theodor Herzl

Western Europe, Israel, and Palestine: Gershom Scholem

Twentieth century
United States and Israel: Menachem Mendel Schneerson

---

raries considered to be messiahs, including Jesus ben Hananiah, Judas of Galilee, Menachem, Samaias, Theudas, "the Egyptian," and even the non-Jewish Roman leader Vespasian. However many messianic figures there actually were in first-century Palestine, any evidence of an eschatological (the doctrine of the end of the world) understanding of the messiah prior to Jesus of Nazareth is virtually nonexistent.

Further, dozens of Jewish communities have believed the messiah was in their midst, as recently as the end of the twentieth century. Some of these figures are listed in special topic 4.1. As you can see, most of them have emerged in Western and Eastern Europe, countries bordering the Mediterranean Sea, and the Middle East, and have appeared in almost every century since the first century CE.

Some of these figures were said to have performed miracles, foretold future events, called for a cessation of particular ritual laws (e.g., those forbidding the eating of meat, drinking of wine, engaging in sexual intercourse, wearing of leather, and many of the other dictates linked to the observance of the Jewish Sabbath, *Shabbat*), and added prayers to those already part of standardized religious practices in their community. Some challenged local non-Jewish authorities, while others focused their efforts on transforming the entire world. Some claimed to be a descendant of King David.

Some of these figures were accompanied by a second individual, who proclaimed the first person to be the messiah and understood himself to be akin to a prophetic herald or the messiah son of Joseph and the other figure the messiah son of David. Some changed their name after assuming the mantel of the messiah. And some had devotees in multiple countries, Sabbatai Tzvi's followers being perhaps the most geographically widespread. Jacob Neusner sums up this variety by saying, "[The messiah] is an all but blank screen onto which a given community would project its concerns. . . . He was depicted as whatever people most wanted—king, savior, wonderworker, perfect priest, invincible general, or teacher—but also as the figure of the end and conclusion of history."

Some challenge the idea of putting all these individuals into the same category. For example, in comparing messianic figures from the first century CE with the rise of Jesus as messiah in the second and third centuries CE, scholar Richard Horsley says that "it would be nothing but pure speculation to draw any connection [between these distinct movements]." Nonetheless, a great deal of messiah scholarship engages in comparative analysis, looking at the similarities and differences between these figures within the context of the phenomenology of the messiah.

Certain academics maintain that it was between roughly the fifth and fifteenth centuries that stages to the messianic process broadened. Aside from the notion of the messiah son of Joseph and messiah son of David, a new question emerged as to how the messiah son of David would die and then be resurrected. Another idea, underscored by the twelfth-century scholar Maimonides, is that the figure embodying all the required characteristics of the messiah—including the rebuilding of the Temple and gathering of the "exiles"—would be a human being rather than some sort of superhero. Others, however, argue that during this time the array of traditions regarding the messiah became not broader, but narrower.

The Messiah and the "World to Come" (Heaven and Hell?)

An important idea that emerged during the first through third centuries CE and became integrally linked to the messiah is the concept of the afterlife, most commonly referred to in Hebrew as *olam haba* (the world to come) and often juxtaposed to *olam hazeh* (this world). Yet the phrase *olam haba* is nowhere to be found in the Bible.

The closest thing there is to an idea of life after death in the Bible is a reference to something called "Sheol," an ambiguous place that might be akin to a netherworld or subterranean realm.

Aside from sacred yet noncanonical texts written during the postbiblical era (roughly the third century BCE to the second century CE), the core postbiblical Jewish texts expressing ideas about the afterlife are the Mishnah and Talmud. Yet just as there is a wide range of ideas regarding the messiah, so too these books present a number of disparate notions of what happens to people after they die. Most passages examine the way in which one's behavior in this world affects what happens in the world to come, while some discuss the process of how humans will be judged upon death.

Some of these Mishnaic and Talmudic discussions use the term *olam haba* to refer to the world's collective future during its next phase, rather than to an individual's postlife existence. In such instances, the term *yimei hamashiaḥ* (the days of the messiah) and *olam haba* are often used interchangeably. Other terms are also found in the Mishnah and Talmud, such as *Gehenna* and *Gehennom,* most often understood as a place where wicked people go after they die (i.e., "hell"), and *Gan Eden,* or the Garden of Eden, analogous to some sort of utopia.

From the Talmudic era through the twenty-first century, the meaning of these terms has changed countless times. As for why they began to emerge in Middle Eastern Jewish communities between the second century BCE and third century CE, many scholars contend that, like the messianic concept itself, these ideas came about as a result of Jewish communities' interaction with non-Jews, whether Persians, Greeks, Romans, or another group entirely.

Today, the majority (according to one poll, 61 percent) of Jews in the United States don't believe in an afterlife, while among Israeli Jews that number is 44 percent. In fact, it is not uncommon for Jews to say, erroneously, that there is no such tradition within Judaism. At the same time, as discussed later in this chapter, many Jews believe in a messianic age while not believing in an afterlife. Although traditional texts seem to often employ the words *yimei hamashiaḥ* and *olam haba* synonymously, twenty-first-century Jews who reject the notion of a world to come don't seem to make this connection.

Mysticisms and Messiahs

In the medieval period, the messianic idea became intertwined with Jewish mystical thought. Most Jewish mystical schools (see chapter 6) include the ideas that (1) the cosmos is moving toward an end, purpose, or goal—a *telos*—and (2) there is a direct relationship between the holy and mundane, the sacred and the everyday, the human collective and the individual.

One of the earliest medieval mystics to explicitly deepen the connection between messianism and mysticism—which focuses much more on God proper than on the manifestation of God in a messiah—was Abraham Abulafia, a thirteenth-century Jew who lived in Greece, Italy, Spain, and the Land of Israel. Although Abulafia's ideas later became central to Jewish mystical thought, during his lifetime he did not gain a following as a messiah. Indeed, aside from his own proclamations, it isn't clear that anyone else considered him to have had messianic potential.

In contrast, the sixteenth-century mystic Isaac Luria had a notable following, largely after he moved to Safed, in the Land of Israel, where he remained for the last few years of his life (see chapter 6). Luria is credited with being one of the primary Jewish figures to shift the messianic discussion from a focus on a supernatural individual who would reveal himself to the masses to the idea that the collective might be able to hasten the messianic age together. Toward the end of his life Luria claimed to be the messiah son of Joseph, while one of his students, Haim Vital, was deemed his potential heir (i.e., the messiah son of David).

Sabbatai Tzvi—A Mystical Messiah

According to the renowned twentieth-century scholar of Jewish mysticism Gershom Scholem, one of the qualities that caused Luria's understanding of the messianic idea to proliferate at this time, even among those living outside the Land of Israel, was its unique integration of mysticism and messianism. Scholem says that these ideas became particularly dominant among Jews living in the region of present-day Turkey. One potential reason is that one century prior, in the fifteenth century, a rabbi named Isaac Abarbanel helped spread the belief that the Inquisitions were a precursor to the age of the messiah. Because many Jews who embraced this idea were descendants of Sephardi Jews who fled the Iberian Peninsula during the Spanish and Portuguese Inquisitions, this collective had a propensity for a conviction in the messiah.

In seventeenth-century Smyrna (also known as Izmir), a Jew named Sabbatai Tzvi revealed that he was the messiah (fig. 4.3), a claim that was publicly supported by an Egyptian Jew, Rabbi Nathan of Gaza. As had been the case with messianic figures before him, such as Jesus and

SABETHA SEBI
Vermeynden Meſſias Der Ioden

FIGURE 4.3. According to renowned scholar of Jewish mysticism Gershom Scholem, this is the only known portrait of Sabbatai Tzvi, sketched by one of his contemporaries (c. 1665).

Bar Kokhba, many Jews rejected Tzvi's bold proclamation; he was soon excommunicated for making such a brazen assertion. But being shunned by Jewish authorities did not deter him, and his following gradually grew larger and larger, in particular in regions encompassed by today's Turkey (where Tzvi's movement began), the Balkans, Italy, and Lithuania.

Most Jewish authorities rejected Tzvi because some of his declarations ran counter to local traditional practice. For example, he said that in the time of the messiah all biblical directives *(mitzvot)* were no longer compulsory, an idea some refer to as "redemption through sin." He also performed public spectacles, such as one instance where he "married" a Torah scroll. Like many controversial figures in history, he gained both additional naysayers and devotees through these acts.

In 1666, however, things changed substantially. In an effort to curb his popularity, the Ottoman sultan—the ruling political authority of the region—gave Tzvi a choice: either renounce himself as messiah and convert to Islam or be put to death. Shocking his followers, Tzvi chose the former option. A number of his devotees maintained that he was only pretending to be Muslim in public while continuing to be Jewish in private, an act with historical precedent (similar to the Conversos of fifteenth- and sixteenth-century Spain and Portugal, discussed in chapter 1). Thereafter, a number of new Sabbatian subsects emerged, some moderate and others extreme. To this day, a semi-clandestine community of Tzvi devotees exists in Turkey and other places, sometimes referred to as the Dönme or "Crypto-Jews." Twenty-first-century members of this community trace their lineage directly back to the seventeenth century, immediately following Tzvi's public conversion to Islam.

The eighteenth-century figure Jacob Frank might also be included in the subcategory of Jewish messiahs who integrated core components of Jewish mysticism into their worldview. In fact, Frank claimed to be the reincarnation of Sabbatai Tzvi (and like the latter, he, too, converted, but in his case to Christianity). He also believed in the Lurianic notion of *tikkun olam,* the concept that each one of us has a responsibility to assist in God's transformation and ultimate redemption of the world (see chapter 6). Some of his followers were referred to as "Zoharites," alluding to the core mystical text that emerged some centuries prior, the *Zohar.* A number of Hasidic leaders—beginning with the founder of Hasidism, the Baal Shem Tov, and continuing with the Rebbe—fall into this lineage as well.

Hasidism—Mysticisms and Messiahs

Beginning in the eighteenth century, Hasidism emerged as an influential new movement within the Jewish collective. According to some scholars, because this innovative variation of Judaism followed the upheaval caused by the conversions and deaths of two prominent messianic figures, Sabbatai Tzvi and Jacob Frank, Hasidism played a role in maintaining the messianic notion that one individual could be the key to the world's redemption. Others see this idea, which is core to the Hasidic movement, as a sublimation or reaction to Sabbatianism and Frankianism, an overt attempt to gain distance from these failed messianic movements. More likely, as individual Hasidic sects developed, different theological and ideological strands developed in turn. There is no "one size, fits all."

Messianism aside, most agree that, from its inception, Hasidic thought has been steeped in many of the schools of Jewish mysticism that preceded it. For example, central to Hasidism is the idea of the *tzadik,* or righteous leader, one of whom has existed at the heart of each Hasidic community (i.e., there could be many different *tzadikim* living at the same time in different communities). This idea was also core to the mystical schools that emerged in sixteenth-century Safed, in the Land of Israel, as is discussed in chapter 6.

The veneration of Hasidic rabbis, akin to that of saints in other religious traditions, centralizes power within individual persons while creating multiple avenues for the masses to have contact with such figures. This phenomenon allowed each Jewish community in Russia, the Ukraine (where Hasidism emerged), and Poland (one of the primary places to which it spread) to have both their own potential messiah (embodied in their *tzadik*) and their own Zion (concretized in their village).

The Persistence of the Messianic Idea among Contemporary Jews

One may hold that the messianic idea is peripheral to Judaism or, at a minimum, marginal to core Jewish texts. Indeed, it can be reasonably argued that the notion of a messiah is, word-count-wise, not central to the Bible, Mishnah, or Talmud. But since the first few centuries CE, if not prior, this idea has had significant importance for Jews.

This is evident, for starters, in the persistent recurrence of messiahs in a range of Jewish communities for over two millennia (see special topic 4.1). Moreover, calculations for when the messiah can be expected to appear are found in hundreds of Jewish texts, from earlier times through today. A third common manifestation of this centuries-old idea is found in the *Amidah,* one of the traditional prayers halakhically prescribed to be said three times a day (dated to between the third and fifth centuries CE); it asks God to "rebuild" the "throne of David" in Jerusalem and to hasten the "offspring of David" to come (or reveal himself) to humanity, both clear references to the messiah or a messianic age.

A fourth indicator exists well beyond the Jewish community. During the twentieth century, the messianic idea of a utopian era was reincarnated within a number of ideologies worldwide that many would even refer to as "secular" or "nonreligious." Communism, nationalism, and socialism, to name but three, are all rooted in the notion that a society based in particular ideals will move people toward utopia. Regardless of these modes' differences in terms of actually structuring societies, the rhetoric within each draws upon the notion of a messianic age.

Fifth, many Jews, whether identifying as "religious," "secular," or something else entirely, have gravitated toward a more fervent belief in a messianic age since the establishment of the State of Israel in 1948 and, perhaps even more so, following Israel's military victories in the war of June 1967, which some call a "miracle" (see chapter 10). A connected idea is that the immigration of Jews to the Jewish State is a fulfillment of the prophecy of the "ingathering of exiled" Jews who are "returning" to the Land of Israel, something even some self-proclaimed "secular" Jews believe is happening. (Some incorporate "end of days" thinking into their belief system, with the Shoah representing the ultimate catastrophe to befall the Jewish people and the establishment of the State of Israel as the ultimate sign of redemption.)

To put it simply, many Jews today still gravitate toward the notion of an individual messiah or a messianic age (the two are not mutually exclusive, of course). Regarding the former, Chabad-affiliated Jews specifically and Orthodox-identified Jews generally are not the only ones who believe a messiah will appear. In Israel, whose population encompasses 40 percent of the world's Jews, roughly 50 percent maintain this belief, and have done so consistently for at least the last fifteen years.

The Messianic Age

As for belief in a messianic age as opposed to a personal messiah, many Jews believe in the potential to transform "the world as is" into "what the world can be." Although threads of the belief in a messianic age go back to the first few centuries CE, the modern Reform movement can take partial credit for the more recent spread of the messianic era. During the nineteenth century, the newly established Reform movement declared that they believed in a future messianic age of perfection even as they rejected the coming of a messianic individual. They also removed the explicit connection between the messianic age and the need for all Jews to "return" to the Land of Israel or the need to rebuild the Temple. Instead, they proclaimed that Jews have the opportunity to share the ethical and universal dimensions of the Bible with everyone—thus helping move the world toward the messianic age.

These doctrines were reiterated in one of the American Reform movement's most important documents, "The Pittsburgh Platform" of 1885, which still has a great deal of meaning for today's progressive movement, and

FIGURE 4.4. During the 2008 presidential campaign, many Americans projected a messianic belief (or hope) onto then-candidate Barack Obama.

in many of their official platforms since, such as one that was adopted at their annual conference in 1999. (The various Jewish movements are discussed in chapter 8.)

Behind the conjecture that many American Jews today believe in the potential of a messianic age we find evidence in at least two areas that may, on first glance, not seem directly related: "Israel advocacy" and "service." With both, Jews are engaged in action that they see as moving the world toward its potential. For instance, most Jews in the United States and Israel believe in supporting the government of the State of Israel, referred to by conventional Jewish institutions as "Israel advocacy" or "pro-Israel support." For many, advocating on behalf of the Jewish State is a form of activism that embodies the idea of being a "light unto the nations." Even with declines in this arena across generations, the data confirm that the overwhelming number of Jews still maintain an allegiance to Israel. (The ambiguity of expressions such as "support for Israel" is considered in chapter 10.)

In regard to "service," or social justice volunteerism, Jews often call such endeavors acts of tikkun olam, which in turn are linked to the belief in one's responsibility to help move the world toward its potential. The end toward which acts of tikkun olam are moving is a contemporary understanding of the messianic age, a time of greater societal equity. Countless studies have been conducted regarding how younger American Jews perform their Jewish identities through service, including volunteerism that doesn't explicitly help other Jews. Similarly, for decades Jews have written about how striving to make the world a better place is a core Jewish value.

The messianic idea has fueled hope and progress for both Jews and non-Jews for centuries. During the 2008 United States presidential election, many Americans projected what might now be seen as unrealistic hopes onto then-candidate Barack Obama. Even a small sampling of well-known media sources since that time illustrates the use of the term *messiah* in American popular culture (fig. 4.4).

The Messiah Will Come (but That's Not Him!)

According to scholar Kenneth Seeskin, "The simple truth is that [Jews] can't live without the idea that the future does not have to repeat the mistakes of the past." Hope—embodied in a messianic age—must remain on the horizon. Whether or not such an idea is linked to a messianic figure is a different matter. Historically, given how many figures in the Jewish community have claimed to be the messiah, doubts regarding any such assertions are perhaps best understood in the words of the twentieth-century Jewish Israeli ideologue Yeshayahu Leibowitz: "The Messiah who comes, the Messiah of the present, is invariably the false messiah."

Some speculate that one reason these figures have gained followings was because of their charisma, a somewhat intangible attractive personality and presence that led people to gravitate toward them. Though there is no proof that all of the messianic figures mentioned in this chapter were charismatic, twentieth-century leaders of religious communities, whether new religious movements or otherwise, are often said to have this characteristic. Yet as scholar Bryan Wilson aptly puts it, "Charisma is not a personality attribute, but a successful claim to power by virtue of supernatural ordination. If a man runs down the street proclaiming that he alone can save others from impending doom, and if he immediately wins a following, then he is a charismatic leader: a social relationship has come into being. If he does not win a following, he is simply a lunatic." Of course, history has also shown us that a messianic figure can have a following (and so be considered charismatic) at the same time that others think him or her to be a lunatic, as evidenced by Sabbatai Tzvi, among others.

As with the case of Tzvi, the messianic idea is best understood in the context of specific times and places. To paraphrase scholar William Scott Green, the term *messiah* "is all signifier with no signified; the term is notable primarily for its indeterminacy." Green adds that despite its rare appearance in ancient texts, the primary reason scholars and nonscholars alike have attached such importance to this idea is that the main title applied to Jesus in the Christian Bible is the Greek word for messiah, *Christos*. Given that one of every three people on the planet identifies as Christian, this importance, he says, speaks for itself.

Within the Jewish community, a current dominant "truth" regarding the messiah can be summarized thus: the date of the messiah's coming is now (or any day now), and the agenda is "complete change." To quote Jewish Israeli writer Amos Oz, "In Judaism, the messianic idea is only relevant in the future tense . . . that's where he should always be. It doesn't mean not to do much and everything will be taken care of. In the Jewish tradition we have to act, every day, every hour. We have to make moral decisions, almost every minute. Sitting idly waiting for the Messiah is a sin." At the same time, while some Jews reject the idea that an individual messiah will bring about a new era, many believe in the potential of the era itself, a new period of time that will embody our ideals—or, for some, our worst fears.

FIVE

Laws

Contents

FIGURES 5.1A–B. Two *mikva'ot* (sing. *mikveh*). *Left:* This ancient mikveh, located in Jerusalem, is no longer used. *Right:* A contemporary mikveh in San Francisco. The cover is placed over the water when the mikveh is not in use to ensure the water's cleanliness and to deter evaporation.

Key Ideas

- Halakhah (Jewish law) plays a central role in the Jewish community, even for those who don't consider it obligatory. Halakhot are most often crafted by individuals who have been given the authority to do so, such as the Talmudic rabbis. But halakhah is not just shaped by legal jurists. The greater Jewish collective also plays a role in how it has developed.
- The Mishnah is a collection of laws that explain the mitzvot (biblical directives) found in the Torah. Similarly, the Talmud contains rabbinic interpretations of the Mishnah.
- During the medieval period, there was a general shift within halakhah from a system based on a plurality of opinions to uniformity.
- Until the twentieth century, Jewish law was defined almost exclusively by males, a gender-based bias present in the Jewish community for millennia. Some feminists understand halakhah's "Invisible Gorilla" as a system that merely presents different roles for males and females; some think the Talmudic rabbis were relatively progressive for their time (i.e., in terms of shaping the legal responsibilities for Jewish women); and some think that the entire halakhic system, rooted in the Torah, reflects male and masculine dominance, at the expense of females.

Are You *Sure* You're Jewish?

About six weeks into my summer studies at an Orthodox *yeshivah* (seminary) in the Old City of Jerusalem, I was asked to go to the office of the school's *mara de-atra,* the individual who made decisions regarding Jewish law *(halakhah).* As he was revered in the yeshivah, I was nervous. Because I had no idea why I was being summoned, I was also curious.

I knocked on the office door and heard a gentle voice say, "The door's open. Come in." Bearded and clothed in his community's semi-official uniform—a black sport coat and pants, a white button-down dress shirt, and a pointy black *kippah* (head covering; plural *kippot*) that sat on his head like a pyramid—the rabbi waved his arm in the direction of an empty chair. As soon as I sat down, he said, "I notice on your application to study at our school that your father was born Jewish but your mother converted. You wrote down that her conversion was completed prior to your being born and that it was conducted under the auspices of the Conservative movement. Did I get that right?"

"Yes," I politely answered.

"Well," he softly responded, "it seems that you may not be Jewish. Conversions performed by Conservative rabbis are sometimes *kosher* (halakhically valid) and sometimes not." In what I believe was an attempt to diffuse any tension, he smiled and said, "Lucky for you it wasn't performed by the Reform."

He went on to explain that, for the time being, I could continue my studies at the yeshivah with the caveat that I was to conduct research into the conversion (alongside his own). When was the conversion done? Where was it done? Was the *mikveh* (ritual bath) my mother used kosher (fig. 5.1)? Who were the witnesses? Were they kosher? Were they men? And so forth. He told me that the stakes were very high. Existentially speaking, he said, whether or not my mother's conversion was kosher would determine whether or not I had a Jewish soul.

As I left his office, my initial reaction was a mix of confusion and resentment. Questions flew through my head like a CNN news ticker on overdrive. How could my mom not be Jewish? Could her Jewish identity be nullified on a technicality? And what about me? How could the amount of water in my mom's mikveh, some thirty years ago—years before I was even born—change *my* identity?

Did it not matter that I went to a Jewish parochial school for thirteen years? Was it beside the point that I spent ten summers at a religious summer overnight camp affiliated with the Conservative movement, where we prayed every day, observed the Jewish Sabbath and *kashrut,* as well as many other halakhic rituals? What about my Bar Mitzvah? Regularly attending synagogue on Shabbat and other Jewish holidays? My numerous trips to the Holy Land? My active involvement in my university campus's Jewish students' center?

That night, while going over the day's events, I realized something obvious yet profound. My problem wasn't with the rabbi whatsoever. In fact, any negative feelings I had projected onto him had dissipated. My issue was with halakhah, the system of Jewish law. Yes, of course the rabbi had a stricter interpretation of Jewish law than many, including other Orthodox rabbis. But ultimately the question of whether my Jewish identity could be turned on its head was not something he invented. The parameters regarding the ritual bath in which my mom had submerged some three decades prior were based in a system of law that dated back centuries.

The next day I visited the home of my own rabbi, more liberal than those at the yeshivah yet nonetheless wedded to halakhah. He agreed with the premise of what I had been told. There are precise rituals that one must complete in order to become a Jew. As we are both Americans, he made the analogy to becoming a citizen of the United States, contending that during the naturalization process one must pass a set of tests, which, among other things, demonstrate a "knowledge and understanding of the history and principles and form of government of the United States." If successful, after a formal interview, one then takes an Oath of Allegiance at a naturalization ceremony, a ritual that officially means one has become a United States citizen. My rabbi, who considered halakhah to be obligatory, pointed out that all legal systems have rules, especially those governing who can and cannot join a community.

At the time I disagreed, responding that one's Jewish identity is much different than citizenship. *Identity is internal as much as external,* I remember saying. *My Judaism, my Jewishness, is my religion as much as it is my culture, ethnicity, or something else entirely. It's not the same thing as having rights as a citizen of a country. One can take on an identity without having to take a test.*

Putting our immediate discussion to the side, my rabbi walked over to a bookcase in his library, where he quickly located a number of *teshuvot*—halakhic responses, or responsa, to particular questions of Jewish law—on the issue at hand, all written by Orthodox and Conservative legal experts. Over the next few weeks, after making a few phone calls regarding the mikveh my mom had used in her conversion and applying this information to these teshuvot, the halakhic specifics of my mom's conversion were clarified; it had been kosher, which meant that my Jewishness—my identity—was not in doubt. Nonetheless, the experience left me with deep questions regarding social identities and the seeming ease with which some can become undone.

Is Identity Strictly a Legal Matter?

Since that time, over twenty years ago, I have given a great deal of thought to this experience. Can someone's identities be deleted overnight on a technicality? Or in this particular case, if there was one cup too little of natural water in the mikveh my mom converted in, would that make me an outsider to the only ethnic and religious community I had ever known? If the filter connecting one basin of water to another were too congealed, would that invalidate my identity? Does Jewishness really depend solely on ritual and legal requirements? Or are Jewish identities more malleable than that?

What about halakhah? Like all legal systems, halakhah is ever-changing. Like all legal systems, Jewish law creates boundaries that put people, and their actions, into categories. But who gets to decide halakhic issues? Whose halakhah is it? And based on what authority? What about those Jews—which includes most Jews worldwide—who don't believe that Jewish law is obligatory? Who adjudicates for them? Anyone? Or do they live outside the law? Is law an all-or-nothing process? And have halakhic practices ever been agreed upon by all Jews?

Talmud and Mishnah

As discussed in previous chapters, the core legal text of all of Judaism is the Bible—more specifically, its first five books, the Torah. But scholars today commonly argue that in terms of ritual customs and practices, for Jews in the twenty-first century, the Talmud is more relevant than the Torah. (This holds true even if only a small number of Jews are familiar with the Talmud.) When Jews perform halakhic or meta-halakhic (discussed toward the end of this chapter) acts, the rituals they observe are much closer to the prescriptions in the Talmud than the Torah. Further, when legal jurists decide how to interpret halakhah today, they use rules found in the Talmud and, almost unanimously, rarely go back to the Torah for assistance in making their decisions.

And so: what is the Talmud?

The Talmud is a compilation of texts attributed to "the rabbis," a group of men who lived from roughly the first through eighth centuries CE. Often printed in twenty-volume sets, the Talmud is long. If someone studied one page of Talmud each day, it would take about seven and a half years to finish an entire set. But people rarely read or study the Talmud from beginning to end; rather, they approach it piece by piece, usually completely out of order.

The oldest parts of a page of Talmud are composed of two sections: a portion from the Mishnah, followed by the Gemara. The Mishnah is a set of books many refer to as legal that are generally dated to the first through third centuries CE (though this is not definitive); the Gemara is rabbinic commentary and interpretation of the Mishnah, written from approximately the third through eighth centuries CE. A slice of Talmud begins with a short text from the Mishnah; the Gemara then usually runs on for a number of pages before another piece of the Mishnah is presented (see fig. 5.2).

The Mishnah also exists independent of the Talmud and can be studied as such. (Unlike the Talmud, some contend that there is an internal consistency to the Mishnah.) It is divided into six sections, which are in turn subdivided into sixty-three subsections. The six major sections cover topics pertaining to agriculture, holidays, women, civil and criminal law, the Temple, and purity. As a collection of laws, the Mishnah is a type of digest, similar to books of Roman law published around the same time. More than half of the Mishnah's content focuses on rituals directly related to the Temple, which means that no one has been able to perform such *halakhot* (plural of *halakhah*) since the first century CE. While the Mishnah is written in a particular form of Hebrew, the Gemara is written in Hebrew and the related language of Aramaic.

There are actually two sets of Talmud, one called the Jerusalem or Palestinian Talmud, dated to the third through fifth centuries and attributed to those living in the Land of Israel, and a second called the Babylonian Talmud, roughly twice the size of the former and dated to sometime between the fifth through eighth centuries. The Babylonian Talmud is studied more than the Jerusalem one for a number of reasons: its size (i.e., it is more comprehensive); it was edited and redacted two to four centuries later, so it is more recent; and few manuscripts of the Jerusalem Talmud survived into modernity, and those that did are chock full of repetitive passages and textual errors.

Interaction between Palestine-based rabbis and Babylonia-based rabbis, mentioned in both Talmuds, is thought to have gained traction only after the destruction of the Second Temple (70 CE). Some scholars think that the Babylonian Talmud was written in relation to the Jerusalem Talmud, as if the rabbinic voices in the texts were in dialogue with one another, despite living in different regions. Yet we don't know, nor do we know how the Talmud was collected into a single volume, integrating rabbinic voices that ranged across centuries, or who edited it. If you study Talmud today, no doubt you will use the so-called Vilna edition, one particular manuscript of the Babylonian Talmud that has become dominant above all others, yet one that differs from previous versions and, in the words of scholar Tal Ilan, "hardly represents an authentic tradition."

Priests vs. Rabbis

Priests

During the proto-Jewish era—the period when members of this community were not yet called Jews, but rather Israelites or Judeans, before about the fifth century BCE—one of the identity-based hierarchies of power was rooted in one's status as a priest, a Levite (from the tribe of Levi), or a generic Israelite. (Priests were originally a subset of the Levites.) This social structure was important when the First and Second Temples were standing. In fact, various priestly lineages were constantly wrangling over power. Other notable communal authorities were judges, prophets, and kings, all of whom are referenced in the Bible.

Rabbis

In the first century, particularly after the Second Temple was destroyed and in spite of priests' efforts to maintain their power thereafter, another collective of Jews began to emerge: "the rabbis." (The root of the Hebrew word for rabbi, *rav,* means great, but the most common translation of the term is "teacher.") The rabbis of the Mishnah are also called the *Tanna'im*—from the Aramaic *tanna,* meaning one who repeats—referring to how they communicated the Mishnah to one another orally. The rabbis who came thereafter, and whose voices are found in the Gemara, are called the *Amora'im*—from the Aramaic *amora,* meaning one who discusses—because of their lengthy deliberation of legal intricacies. With rare exceptions, until the twentieth century all of these communal authorities were men.

Some say that the rabbinic collective existed as early as the fifth through third centuries BCE, though going by a different name: sages, or *ḥakhamim.* But evidence about this is ambiguous at best. Nor is it clear that prior to the second century CE (let alone thereafter) there was a common understanding of halakhic issues in Jewish communities living in the Middle East and North Africa, whether based in the Mishnah or otherwise. In fact, we don't really know when the Mishnah or Talmud became the core of dominant communal understandings of halakhah. Many argue that this process took centuries. The main source attesting to the Talmud's centrality to the Jewish community as well as the rabbis' eclipsing of the priests (largely due to the destruction of the Temple) is the Talmud itself. For these reasons, it has been challenged as the authoritative halakhic text for centuries (albeit largely by marginal Jewish groups).

Rabbis Today

The title *rabbi* has a much different meaning today than it did during Talmudic times. Twenty-first-century rabbis routinely fulfill a number of communal roles that Talmudic rabbis did not. Today's rabbis, only some of whom serve as professional leaders in synagogues (sometimes called "pulpit rabbis"), serve as relationship therapists and family counselors as much as anything else, supporting people through times of both tragedy and joy. Many teach in schools and universities. But during Talmudic times these individuals were, on the whole, halakhic arbiters who had "day jobs" that often had nothing to do with their rabbinical responsibilities (e.g., some were blacksmiths, others brewed and sold beer). In fact, there is sound evidence not only that "rabbis" in the first few centuries CE in Palestine had virtually no connection to synagogues, but some even disapproved of them.

If you want to become a rabbi today, depending on what denomination or movement you affiliate with, the process is akin to getting a graduate degree, in terms of having to take certain courses and pass specific tests.

Back in the day, however, one could only be ordained as a rabbi if another rabbi granted you this title. For almost all of Jewish history, only men were allowed to be rabbis. The first woman to officially become a rabbi, Regina Jonas, wasn't ordained until 1935, in Berlin, under the auspices of the Reform movement. American movements only began institutionalizing this trend in the 1970s (see chapter 8).

The Mishnah and Self-Proclaimed Authority

As scholar Jacob Neusner writes, the Mishnah was initially accepted as the definitive interpretation of the Torah because Judah the Prince (Yehudah Ha-Nasi), the political authority of the second- and third-century Palestinian Jewish community living under the Romans, declared it to be. (He is commonly credited as the Mishnah's editor, though this is not conclusive.) Thereafter, the Mishnah reinforced this authority by proclaiming itself to be the written form of the Oral Torah. A few times, the text even asserts an unbroken chain connecting it directly to the revelation Moses received on Mount Sinai. In fact, there is no other textual evidence that gives the Mishnah this authority aside from the Mishnah.

An earlier Jewish tradition held that one was halakhically prohibited from writing down the Oral Torah. This law was eventually broken, and the Oral Torah was written down in the form of the Mishnah—or so says this tradition—ostensibly in order to preserve a potentially lost oral tradition. Further, as Neusner notes: "the framers of the Mishnah never tell us why we should do what the Mishnah instructs, let alone explain what will happen if we do" (or do not) follow its codes.

The Talmud, which builds upon the Mishnah, reiterates the claim that the rabbis had a direct connection back to Sinai. It also delves deeper into the Mishnah, presenting a system of logical argument to support the Mishnah's explanation of law, thereby reinforcing the authority of both. Yet the Talmud does not expound upon the entire Mishnah, but only small selections thereof, sometimes just a few sentences from a single chapter. More often than not, the Talmud explains the connection of a particular Mishnaic discussion to the Torah. Usually the Mishnah assumes the reader knows which *mitzvah* (biblical directive) it is explaining.

To complicate matters, according to the renowned twentieth-century scholar Saul Lieberman, no single version of the Mishnah ever existed upon which all others were based; there were only versions. Other texts may have existed that had the same authority as the Mishnah (during the same time period, at least); the Mishnaic and Talmudic rabbis were clearly familiar with these writings, which never made it into the Mishnah itself, though some are found in a collection called the Tosefta, while others simply appear in the Talmud in the context of particular arguments. Some scholars have hypothesized that parts of the Mishnah are written in response to the Tosefta, while others argue the opposite.

Halakhah and Agaddah

Both Mishnaic and Talmudic texts can be placed into two general categories: *halakhah* and *agaddah,* the latter understood as stories. Sometimes we see a third category, a hybrid of the two, called *midrash halakhah;* in such situations, a text presents an agaddic passage within the context of a halakhic ruling. For example, in the first section of the first chapter of the Mishnah, a text commonly taught to students who are learning Mishnah for the first time, we see the passage found in special topic 5.1.

One can learn a number of things from this mishnah that are unrelated to the content itself. (Note: *Mishnah,* with a capital M, usually means the entire set of books collected together and called by this name. Lower-case *mishnah* [pl. *mishnayot*], in contrast, usually means a single, particular teaching from the Mishnah. In other words, the Mishnah is made up of many mishnayot.) For starters, the oldest versions of the Mishnah and Talmud, like the Torah, lack punctuation, which leaves the door open for multiple interpretations of a given passage. This mishnah (like all mishnayot) also assumes that the reader is familiar with certain words, such as:

Shma: Composed of several biblical texts, this is a core prayer—recited in many Jewish communities—and affirms one's belief in a single god. For some it is the heart of every prayer service, and many recite it before going to sleep at night. This mishnah is exploring the issue of what time of day no longer constitutes the night as one of the mitzvot is to recite the Shma when one goes to sleep (i.e., at night) and when one wakes up (i.e., during the day).

trumah: This is a designated part of a sacrifice (usually a vegetable or fruit rather than an animal) that only the priests and their families were allowed to eat.

first watch: The sages divided the night into three periods or watches. The first watch (i.e., the first third of the night) begins, according to some, not at sundown but only after three stars have appeared in the sky.

SPECIAL TOPIC 5.1
THE *SHMA* PRAYER (MISHNAH)

After what time can one recite the *Shma* in the evening? From the moment the Priests enter [their homes] to eat their *trumah* through the first watch. This is the opinion of Rabbi Eliezer, but the Sages say "until midnight." Rabban Gamliel says "until *'amud hashaḥar.*" It happened once that his sons came from a house of drinking and said to him, "We haven't recited the *Shma* yet." He told them, "If *'amud hashaḥar* hasn't arrived than you are still obligated to recite it." And not just in this case, but anytime the Sages say "until midnight," the *mitzvah* can be completed up until the *'amud hashaḥar.*

SPECIAL TOPIC 5.2
BECOMING A *NAZIR* (MISHNAH)

[If someone says,] "I will become a *Nazir* when a son is born to me" and a son is born to him, he becomes a *Nazir.* If a daughter, a *tumtum,* or an *androgynous* is born to him, he does not become a *Nazir.* But if he said, "When I see that a child is born to me [I will become a *Nazir*]," even if a daughter, a *tumtum,* or an *androgynous* is born to him, he becomes a *Nazir.*

'amud hashaḥar: Literally "the pillar of the dawn," this refers to the period of time immediately before sunrise, a part of the day when there is daylight though the sun has not yet risen.

mitzvah: A biblical directive (see chapter 2).

house of drinking: One might translate this term as a place where one goes to drink, particularly alcohol (i.e., "a bar"), but some interpret it to mean a wedding or festival celebration.

The mishnah found in special topic 5.2, which presents halakhah only (rather than halakhah with agaddah), assumes familiarity with a number of terms as well:

Nazir: An individual who has taken a specific set of vows, usually involving not consuming particular foods (e.g., grapes) or liquids (e.g., wine) and not cutting one's hair. Also translated as Nazirite.

tumtum: An individual born with genitalia not clearly meeting conventional, binary-based norms, who is often assigned a sex at some point; sometimes understood today as intersex. As it says in another mishnah, "a *tumtum* [is] sometimes a man and sometimes a woman."

androgynous: An individual identified as intersex, perhaps having elements of both male and female genitalia. As explained in another mishnah, "An *androgynous* is in some respects [legally] equivalent to men, and in some respects [legally] equivalent to women, in some respects [legally] equivalent to men and women, and in some respects [legally] equivalent to neither men nor women. . . . Rabbi Yosi says, 'As for an *androgynous,* this is a unique being of her own. The sages were unable to decide if [an *androgynous*] is a man or a woman.'"

Both of these mishnayot present multiple answers to a legal question, a structure that is not the exception but the rule in the Mishnah. We also learn that particular opinions are included; therefore, we can assume others are excluded. Sometimes, as in the first mishnah with Rabban Gamliel and his sons (special topic 5.1), a de facto decision becomes de jure. On occasion it is simple to categorize a text as either halakhic or agaddic, but very often the two categories cannot be separated.

We also know that only certain topics are covered in the Mishnah and Talmud. Despite the lengthy conversations among the Talmudic rabbis, subjects are chosen selectively. For instance, a disproportionate number of Mishnaic texts focus on laws concerning women, who are largely portrayed, in Neusner's words, as "abnormal, anomalous, dangerous, dirty, and polluting." Examining what is included and excluded gives us insight into dominant rabbinical worldviews. Further, studying these volumes in relation to the Torah illustrates just how different the Mishnaic legal codes are from biblical texts, including discussions of legal matters that never receive any explicit mention in the Five Books of Moses whatsoever.

The Talmud: Looking for Answers vs. Looking for Questions

The Talmud focuses considerable attention on halakhic directives regarding how to engage in religious rituals and practices. Another primary concern is to convey ethics and values. Indeed, one of the most famous passages in the Talmud is the story of a non-Jew who comes to Rabbi Hillel and asks the rabbi to teach him the entire Torah while standing on one foot. The legendary rabbi replies: "What is hateful to you, do not do unto another. The rest is commentary. Go and learn."

But the Talmud can also be studied with a different intent: to discover questions rather than answers. One of the most interesting things about Talmudic discussions is how the rabbis tackle a topic, often looking for previously unmentioned approaches to an issue rather than merely seeking to concretize answers. In fact, although much of halakhah divides the world into two categories (e.g., pure/impure, kosher/nonkosher), frequently the rabbis analyze things that don't fit into a simplistic binary, such as the division of the day and night into a number of sections (see, e.g., special topic 5.1).

The following story gives a taste of one of the dominant approaches the Talmudic rabbis take when exploring a situation:

> A student approaches a Talmud teacher and asks to be taught the Talmud. The teacher rejects the student, saying that he is not yet ready because he lacks an understanding of Talmudic logic. The student insists, and the teacher eventually relents, giving the student the following scenario: Two men go down a chimney. When they reach the bottom, one has a dirty face and the other has a clean face. She then asks the student: "Which one washes his face?" Without hesitating, the student says: "The one with the dirty face!" The teacher says: "No. The one with the clean face looks at the other one, sees a dirty face, and thinks that his face must also be dirty; he then goes off to clean his (already clean) face." The student says: "I understand. Please give me another question."
>
> The teacher then repeats the same scenario and question. Surprised, the student tells the teacher he already knows the answer and repeats what the teacher said previously: "The one with the clean face washes." "Wrong," says the teacher. "The one with the dirty face sees his clean-faced companion look at him and immediately goes to clean his own face. Why? He thinks that his face must be dirty because of the way his clean-faced companion looked at him." "I understand," says the student. "There can be more than one answer to a question. Please give me one last try."
>
> The teacher says: "This is your last question. Here is the scenario." She then proceeds to give the same exact scenario and question a third time. Utterly perplexed, the student says that he has already learned both answers to the question and repeats them. The teacher then responds: "Wrong. If two men go down a chimney, how can only one end up with a dirty face? Before answering the question you needed to ask another question. This is what the Talmud does."

Whereas for some, answering a question with another question is counterintuitive, for the rabbis of the Talmud it is a valid, and even encouraged, way to engage in dis-

Torah

Genesis 4:10

Then God said, "What have you done? Your brother's blood[s] cries out to Me from the ground!"

Mishnah

Mishnah Sanhedrin 4:5

... Capital cases are not like cases concerning property. In cases concerning property an individual can pay money and reconcile with another, but in capital cases the [victim's] blood and the blood of his descendants are on [the guilty] one's hands for eternity. As it says [in Gen. 4:10], "*your brother's blood[s] cries out.*" It doesn't say *brother's blood* but *brother's bloods*, referring to all of his future descendants as well. Another interpretation of *brother's bloods* is that his blood splattered all over the [nearby] trees and rocks. Therefore [we know that] a single human was created to teach that if one destroys a single soul, Scripture charges him as though he destroyed an entire world, and if one saves a single soul, Scripture charges him as if he saved an entire world. [A single human was created] for the sake of peace between all creatures, so that no one can say to another, "My ancestor is greater than your ancestor ... "

Talmud

BT Sanhedrin 37b–38a

Note: The text in small capital letters is from the Mishnah.

Rav Judah the son of Rabbi Hiyya said, "[The plural term *bloods*] teaches that Cain inflicted many bruises and wounds upon his brother because he didn't know how a soul departs [from a body; so he stabbed his brother] until he reached [his throat]." ... Rav Judah the son of Rabbi Hiyya also said, "Since the day the earth opened its mouth and [ate] Abel's blood it has never opened [its mouth] again, as it is written, 'From the edge of the earth have we heard songs, glory to the righteous' [Is. 24:16]—from the 'edge of the earth have we heard songs, glory to the righteous,' [meaning] from the edge of the earth but not from the mouth of the earth" ...

THEREFORE [MAN WAS CREATED ALONE]—Our rabbis taught, "Man was created alone." Why? So the heretics won't say, "There are many [different ruling] powers in heaven [and each created its own human]." Another explanation is [that man was created alone] for the sake of the righteous and the wicked, so the righteous might not say, "We are the descendants of the righteous," and the wicked [will not] say, "We are the descendants of the wicked." Another explanation is for the sake of [different] families, so they wouldn't fight with one another ... "

cussion. In fact, some characterize this as the primary method of discourse in the Talmud.

From Torah to Mishnah and Mishnah to Talmud

One way to understand the relationship between the Torah, Mishnah, and Talmud is to look at the passages found in special topic 5.3. Here you find a verse from the Torah (left), a snippet from the Mishnah (middle), and a short section from the Talmud (right). In chapter 2 (special topic 2.3) we looked at three English translations of the biblical story of Cain and Abel, of which the sentence from the Torah in special topic 5.3 is a part. Let's see how the rabbis interpret this section of Torah.

In this mishnah, the rabbis focus on one letter from one verse of Torah, a letter that is attached to the Hebrew word that means "your blood" (and thus makes this singular word plural, as in "your bloods"). For the rabbis, the Torah doesn't have any mistakes. The text is divine, word for word and letter for letter. As such, in their perspective the extra letter in this word must be there for a reason: God wanted the rabbis to dig deeper into the Torah's hidden meaning.

In this effort, the rabbis explain that the Torah says "bloods" rather than "blood" to teach that when Abel was murdered it wasn't just him who died; all of his future descendants were killed as well. In fact, given that he was one of the first human beings in existence, it is as if Cain didn't just murder his brother; he murdered an entire world of people. The Mishnaic rabbis connect this to their discussion of capital crimes (found immediately prior, in M. Sanhedrin 4:1–4) to teach that it is of utmost importance whether or not witnesses bear false testimony in capital cases, because each life is sacred. Every one of us is akin to the entire human collective.

Like the mishnah on the Shma prayer (special topic 5.1), this mishnah (special topic 5.3) incorporates both halakhah and agaddah. So, too, does the accompanying Talmudic section. But what is perhaps most important is to recognize that whereas the Mishnah is an explanation of the Torah, the Gemara is an explanation of the Mishnah. (In this case, the Gemara is everything but the text written in small capital letters, which is from the mishnah.) Further, if you look at a page of Talmud today (fig. 5.2), you find a number of additional commentaries—primarily focused on resolving ambiguities found in the Gemara—written over the course of many centuries.

Put another way, a page of Talmud is made up of explanations upon explanations upon explanations. Not only does a page of Talmud incorporate interpretations written over millenia, but twentieth- and twenty-first-century editions include contemporary understandings as well. All of these discussions, whether related to halakhah or agaddah or both, are rooted in verses from the Torah, Prophets, and/or Writings. This is one reason why modern students studying Talmud commonly have a number of other books on their desks at the same time, including one or more Bibles.

Another interesting thing about the Talmud is that it is not uncommon for the text to present a conversation between rabbis who lived in different times, resembling the following imagined discussion between three United States presidents:

> Thomas Jefferson told Abraham Lincoln: "I do not think that the framers of the Constitution had it in mind to prohibit slavery." To which Lincoln answered: "I cannot conceive that they did not!" John Kennedy interrupted: "Mr. Jefferson, you are correct in theory. And Mr. Lincoln, you are correct in practice."

This creative technique allows for detailed and deep conversations between halakhic figures who could never have had actual discussions historically.

Laws and Definitions: Defining a Christmas Tree

Another way to understand law, Jewish or otherwise, is to see it as a system that defines things. For instance, when I recently took my university students to our local Jewish Community Center, we took a trip to the building's roof to see their *sukkah,* a temporary hut, largely made of natural materials, built for the holiday Sukkot (the plural of *Sukkah*) and within which Jews sit, eat, and even sleep during the weeklong celebration. Once we reached the roof, our host asked the students how one could evaluate whether or not this was a kosher sukkah. In other words, he said, can any structure be a sukkah? Or does it need to have a set number of walls, be made out of particular material, and so forth?

After learning that none of the students had ever seen a sukkah before, our host used the following example by way of explanation, which my students easily related to: You have just started college and are living with someone in your school's dormitories who is not familiar with Christmas. At the beginning of December you decide to put a small Christmas tree in your relatively tiny room. But how would you *define* the tree? How would somebody *know* it's a Christmas tree and not something else? How tall would the tree have to be? Is there a minimum height? And what would the tree need to be made of? Is plastic okay, or would it have to be natural? Does it have to be decorated with a certain number of ornaments? Does it need to have a star at the tippy top? Can anything be a Christmas tree simply if someone designates it as such?

The point is that at some stage, a thing can become another thing: At what point does a tree become a Christmas tree? Only after you assign it that label? After you dress it in decorations? Moreover, at what point does a tree stop being just a regular, ordinary tree? After it is chopped down? What about after the tree's wood is turned into pulp? What about after the pulp is made into paper?

Many things can change into other things. Definitions help us grasp what things are and help us communicate with others (how do we talk about X if we both don't have a similar definition of X?). Putting aside the obvious—that there are all too many things that simply cannot be organized or categorized in a nice and tidy way—halakhah is structured as if everything of necessity *can* be categorized. Once defined, rabbinical authorities can offer responses as to what particular things one is permitted to do or is prohibited from doing in relation to the defined idea. For the Talmudic rabbis, the Torah is the word of God. If there is a biblical directive (which there is), for example, that a "rebellious son" must be put to death, there must be a legal definition for a "rebellious son." Without such a definition, such a mitzvah could not be observed. Once defined, the rabbis subsequently decide on other details related to this idea.

What Does "It" or "Them" Mean?

In my university classes, another way I try to illustrate to students the connection between the Torah and the Tal-

שנים

רבינו חננאל

גליון הש״ס

FIGURE 5.2. The first page of the Babylonian Talmud (Vilna ed.), including a section of the mishnah that discusses the *Shma* prayer (see special topic 5.1). The middle column contains a few lines from the Mishnah, followed by the Gemara. The writings surrounding the middle column on all sides are explanations of the Gemara, written over centuries. The first word of this section, or tractate, of Talmud is larger than the rest and set off by a border for aesthetic reasons only.

FIGURE 5.3. A group of women wearing *tefillin* in New York City.

mud—in the eyes of the Mishnaic and Talmudic rabbis, at least—is by asking students to interpret the following verse, which is repeated in the Torah four times (and is actually part of the Shma; see special topic 5.1): "Bind them as a sign on your hand and let them serve as a frontlet between your eyes." Whether the verses refer to the object as "it" or "them"—as the pronoun differs among the four verses—just what the verse is referring to is not explicitly clear. After we study these four verses, I put a set of *tefillin* on my arm and head, like the people in figure 5.3. I then ask the students whether they think the small black boxes attached to my arm and head with leather straps are what is meant by "it" and "them" as written in the Torah verses.

As I mentioned in chapter 2 (special topic 2.2), I was taught in yeshivah (seminary) that we *know* Moses received both the Written and Oral Torah on Mount Sinai. ("Would God have given Moses a set of biblical directives without explaining them first?"). Thus, for some, the Mishnah and Talmud contain information received directly from God. For others, arguably including some of the rabbis, the Mishnah is understood as an interpretation, rather than an explanation, of the Torah.

For our purposes, it is most critical to underscore that the rabbis could perform linguistic gymnastics with regard to any passage from the Torah. (Some, such as the case of the "rebellious son," seem more of an interpretive leap than others.) As Orthodox feminist writer Blu Greenberg famously writes, "Where there is a rabbinic will, there is a halakhic way." Put differently, in the words of scholar Joel Roth: "As the sole normative interpreters of the meaning of the Torah, Torah means whatever the rabbis say it means."

The Talmud and Self-Proclaimed Authority

The rabbis were clearly aware of their self-authorized power, as a number of passages in the Talmud illustrate. One of the most famous *agaddot* (plural of *agaddah*) from the Talmud that illustrates this, summarized in special topic 5.4, begins with a discussion about the laws of purity, specifically regarding an oven. Thereafter, we learn that there is a disagreement over legal interpretation between one rabbi and all of the other members of the court. (Some say there were seventy members of the *Sanhedrin,* the Talmudic "Supreme Court." Others say that there were 125. That said, we aren't entirely sure if there actually was a court at all.)

For many introduced to this Talmudic passage for the first time, what Rabbi Joshua says and does—with the implied consent of his rabbinical colleagues—is heretical. Most of my university students don't understand how a human could ever tell God to, proverbially, mind God's own business.

In fact, most ask how God could give a group of people a sacred text and then allow them to interpret it any way they like, even contrary to God's original intention. Some today say that the rabbis' interpretation of the Torah phrase "It is not in heaven," which Rabbi Joshua uses to rebut the author of the Torah, God, is taken out of context. However, the rabbis maintain that the Torah itself gives them the authority to interpret the Torah.

Their logic is often understood as follows: The Torah teaches that after Moses received the sacred texts from God, he was instructed to gather together seventy Israelite elders to assist him in "bearing the burden" of leading the million-plus nomadic desert community. The Mishnah teaches that the seventy elders then gave their author-

A rabbi named Eliezer is arguing against everyone else in the ancient Talmudic "Supreme Court" regarding a matter of halakhah. After exhausting every possible logical argument, Rabbi Eliezer loses his temper and tells his colleagues that if he is correct, the carob tree nearby will fly up out of the ground. Amazingly, it does. The other rabbis say that they don't care because the tree has nothing to do with the argument at hand.

Rabbi Eliezer then says that if he is right the stream of water nearby will flow in the opposite direction. Although the stream does as he suggests, he is once again told by his colleagues that the stream has nothing to do with the argument. By this point, Eliezer has clearly lost his patience. He then says that if he's right, the walls of the building they are in will crash down, at which time the walls start to crumble. But then Rabbi Joshua, thought to have been second in command at the court, scolds the walls, telling them that they should stay out of the argument. The walls stop halfway, respecting the requests of both Eliezer and Joshua somewhat equally.

Finally, at wits' end, Eliezer uses the last card up his sleeve. He says that if he is correct, God will say so, at which point God (i.e., the "heavenly voice") says that not only is Eliezer correct in interpreting this particular halakhah, but he is always correct. Joshua leaps to his feet and, citing part of a verse from the Torah, declares, "It is not in heaven!," essentially scolding God for weighing in on the matter. Citing another rabbi (Jeremiah), the unnamed narrator of the story tells us that what Joshua meant by this is that the rabbis have the final authority to interpret the Torah, not God.

The epilogue to the story is that God smiles and says, "My sons have defeated me. My sons have defeated me."

Moses goes up to God's realm and sees God putting detailed marks on the letters of the Torah (i.e., special calligraphic elaborations that are added to particular Hebrew letters). A bit perplexed, he asks God what God is doing. God tells Moses that in the future there will be a man named Akiba ben Joseph who will interpret a number of halakhic laws from the seemingly inconsequential marks. Intrigued by this future person, Moses asks God if he can see Akiba. God tells Moses to turn around.

The next thing Moses knows, he is in the back row of a classroom listening to a lesson on law taught by none other than Akiba. Unfortunately for Moses, he doesn't understand what Akiba is saying because the halakhic logic is over his head. Finally, one of Akiba's students asks Akiba how he knows that what he is telling his students is correct. Akiba responds by saying that God told these same things to Moses when Moses received the Torah, and Moses subsequently passed it down, generation to generation, all the way down to Akiba himself. Despite his own confusion, and even though from Moses's vantage point God never told him what Akiba says God told him, Moses is not angry upon hearing Akiba's response. Instead, he is comforted.

To sum up the relationship between the Talmud and the Mishnah, it is useful to return to the notion of a spectrum used in chapter 2. On one end are those who consider halakhah—including the Mishnah, Talmud, and all law developed since—to be the strict product of human, and not divine, interpretation. Most academic scholars gravitate toward this end. On the other end are those who believe that all halakhah was given at Mount Sinai, both the Oral and Written Law (also called the Oral and Written Torah; see chapter 2). Another way to see this latter end of the spectrum is, in the words of scholar Elizabeth Shanks Alexander, as the "actualization of interpretive possibilities already embedded within the text of the Written Torah." Although one doesn't see such a range of explanations in the Mishnah, from the Talmud onward countless texts offer such perspectives.

Midrash

Around the same time that the Mishnah and Talmud materialized, another important genre emerged called Midrash. Though different from halakhic parts of the

ity to the next generation of elders, and so on, all the way down to the current generation. This is one of the dominant traditions found in the Talmud as well.

For the rabbis, there is no irony in the autological reasoning that the very authority Rabbi Joshua says God gives them is rooted in verses of the Torah that he and his colleagues interpret. Other dominant traditions in the Talmud point to the unique position that the rabbis had in creating law. In one passage, summarized in special topic 5.5, we are told a fascinating story involving God, Moses, and the second-century Talmudic sage Rabbi Akiba.

Mishnah and Talmud, this category of sacred writings is similar to agaddot. From the Hebrew word *drash* (to demand, seek, search, or re-search), Midrash is a significant method of interpreting the Bible that portrays the Bible through particular worldviews. In the words of scholar James Kugel, it is "an overwhelmingly broad field of inquiry . . . the foundation-stone of rabbinic Judaism."

Also focusing on biblical verses rather than entire books, Midrash approaches phrases and even sentence fragments as part of a much larger, unified text (i.e., a single text called the Bible). In other words, the "documentary hypothesis," which holds that humans—and not God—decided which books became part of the biblical canon and which did not (chapter 2), is anathema to the authors of rabbinic *midrashim*. (As with the terms Mishnah and mishnah, Midrash is the entire genre, while midrashim are individual examples from the genre.) For the rabbis, the Bible, in its entirety, is a single, perfect text. Any verse from the Torah can have as much in common with a verse from the Prophets or the Writings as it can with another verse from the Torah.

By way of example, let's return to the passage from Genesis in which Cain murders Abel. In special topic 2.3, both the JPS and Everett Fox translations interpret the first part of verse eight as "Cain/Kayin said to his brother Abel/Hevel . . . " Both translations use ellipses, even though this series of three dots is not found in the original biblical text. (As mentioned in chapter 2, perhaps these two translations assume a few words are missing.) Indeed, Torah scrolls found today, like the oldest ones in existence, lack punctuation entirely.

For the rabbis, this gap in the sentence's syntax could not be attributed to a mistake in transcription. This is how the original text must have always read. If there is something unclear, the problem cannot lie with the text; it must be rooted in the process of human interpretation. (This approach holds for many Christians in relation to the Christian Bible and Muslims in relation to the Qur'an, as well.) It is into such situations that midrashic authors entered, offering a number of possibilities to "fill in the blank," even as they understood these seeming gaps to be intentional.

In one of the earliest collections of midrashim on the narrative about Cain and Abel in the book of Genesis, rabbis approach verse eight's ambiguity in a number of interesting ways, probably drawing on a variety of oral traditions that aimed to "fill in the blank." It is likely that the three paragraphs reproduced in special topic 5.6 comprise more than a handful of rabbinic interpretations, perhaps put together by one or more editors.

SPECIAL TOPIC 5.6
"YOUR BROTHER'S BLOODS" (MIDRASH)

Note: The text in small capital letters is from the Torah.

AND CAIN SPOKE UNTO ABEL HIS BROTHER. What did they quarrel about? "Come," they said [to each other]. "Let's divide the world up." One took all of the land and the other all of the world's movable objects. The former said, "The land you're standing on is mine; get off!" The latter responded, "What you are wearing is mine. Strip!"

Out of this quarrel, CAIN ROSE UP AGAINST HIS BROTHER ABEL. Rabbi Joshua of Siknin said in Rabbi Levi's name that both of them took land and both of them took movable objects. So what did they quarrel about? One said, "The Temple must be built in my area," and the other replied, "It should be built in mine." [Where did they learn this from?] It is written [in Genesis], AND IT CAME TO PASS WHEN THEY WERE IN THE FIELD—*field* refers to the Temple, as in the passage "Zion shall be plowed as a field" (Mic. 3:12) [Zion is sometimes used as a synonym for the Temple; see chapter 3].

CAIN ROSE UP AGAINST HIS BROTHER ABEL. Judah the son of Rabbi said that their quarrel was about the first Eve. Rabbi Aibu said that the first Eve had returned to dust [before they were born, so they couldn't have argued about her]. So then what did they argue about? Rabbi Huna said [Cain and Abel were not twins but] that a twin [girl] was born with Abel, and each claimed her [to be theirs]. One said, "I will have her because I am the firstborn," and the second said, "I will have her because she was born with me."

Similar to the arguments found in the Talmud (and not Mishnah), midrashim are commonly based on interpretations of other biblical texts. For instance, in the second midrash in special topic 5.6, the interpretation of the verse from Genesis is supported by a verse from the book of Micah, one of the prophets. As always, the author is verse-centric; the verse from Genesis is what is being explained, not the verse from Micah. In fact, it is not uncommon for the other biblical verses cited in support of the verse at hand to seem to a modern reader as if they have been taken out of context.

Some ancient midrashim may have served a purpose akin to a modern-day sermon, used to teach an audience a particular lesson. Others, especially many of the earliest ones, were probably attempts to heal apparent dissonance within seemingly inconsistent biblical passages—

FIGURE 5.4. A depiction of Cain and Abel by Oswalt Kreusel from c. 1591.

to illustrate the Bible's textual unity. And some early midrashim do not fit into either of these two categories, but instead are more similar to stories or legends about particular characters from the Bible or Talmud. One of the most famous examples of Midrash, a text that incorporates several different kinds of midrashim, is the Passover *Haggadah,* the core text used during a Passover Seder (see chapter 1).

Contemporary Midrash

Initially, midrashim were narrative only. Over time, they also began to appear in other forms, such as paintings and poetry. For example, figure 5.4 is a sixteenth-century image of what might be called a midrash regarding Cain and Abel. Whether or not this artwork can be understood as a midrash on Genesis 4:8 specifically or whether

The men rushed ahead,
They always do—
in battle to defend us,
in eagerness, to get the best view,
to be there with each other
as a community.

We followed later—
some of us waited
till we were done nursing,
others waited to go together
with those who were still nursing.
Most of us were herding several children,
carrying a heavy two year old
on one hip
(it's hard to move forward quickly
with a heavy two year old on one hip).
Last came the very pregnant ones—
when you're that far along
it's your instinct to be afraid of crowds,
afraid of being jostled,
you hang back,
you feel safer being last.

Anyway, I was one of the ones
with a heavy two year old on one hip—
such a sweet body he had,
warm soft delicious flesh.
He was afraid of the noise,
he clung to me so tightly,

his fingers in my neck,
his face buried in my neck.
I showered him with little kisses,
not so much to comfort him
as out of habit
and my pleasure

The earth shook, it vibrated,
and so did I,
my chest, my legs
all vibrating.
I sank to my knees
all the while with this little boy attached to me,
trying to merge himself back into me.

I closed my eyes
to be there more intensely,
it all washed over me—
wave upon wave upon wave . . .

And afterwards, the stillness
of a nation, a people
who had been flattened, forever imprinted,
slowly raising themselves, rising again from the earth.

How to hold onto that moment
washed clean
reborn
holy silence . . .

the artist even intended it to be categorized as a midrash, it answers a number of seemingly ambiguous details not explicitly found in the biblical narrative.

An artist can also create a work of art *as* a midrash, such as contemporary examples found in special topics 5.7 and 5.8. The first is a powerful poem by Merle Feld called "Sinai" that expands upon Exodus 19–20, when Moses and the Israelites receive the Ten Commandments at Mount Sinai. Specifically, her fourth stanza picks up on Exodus 19:16, where it says: "And on the third day, in the morning, there was thunder and lightning and a dense cloud on the mountain, and the voice of an exceedingly loud horn. And all the people that were in the camp trembled."

Perhaps most important is the subnarrative that Feld opens up to us—what it might have been like for an Israelite woman, such as a mother holding a toddler, to expe- rience the revelation at Sinai. This also gives insight into what it would have been like to be an Israelite female wandering in the desert with her community. As men- tioned in chapter 2, according to the Torah there were more than 600,000 adult males among the Israelite tribes. If we include women and children, the population probably exceeded one million bodies.

But because the Torah text is male-centric (e.g., women and children aren't included in the census), based on the text alone we have little sense of what it was like to be a woman at this time, especially one with a child. Feld's piece is that much more insightful, therefore, given the pshat of Exodus 19:15, the verse immediately before the thunder and lightning appear, when Moses tells the Isra- elites that men must stay away from women in order to be ritually prepared to receive God's revelation.

In special topic 5.8, an insightful passage by Andrew

Ramer called "The Seeker," we find another midrash that gives voice to the voiceless. Contrary to the heteronormative script of the Torah, Ramer creates a reflection of what it may have been like to be homosexual during the era of the Genesis narratives, indicating that people with varied identities in terms of gender and sexuality have been around since the beginning of humankind (i.e., since the era of Eve and Adam).

Midrashim such as special topics 5.7 and 5.8 open the tent to include marginalized points of view. But what is perhaps most telling about them is that they use the rules of Midrash itself to widen the communal lens. Rather than add verses to the Torah text, they unearth what some consider to have already been there, a path first laid out by the male-centric rabbis themselves.

Gender and Feminisms: The "Invisible Gorilla" in Jewish Law

For millennia, Jewish practice has been developed almost exclusively by men. Although some contend that an authority figure (e.g., a judge) can evaluate a situation regardless of his own social identities, including his gender, many disagree. In the late 1990s, two Harvard University professors, Christopher Chabris and Daniel Simons, launched a fascinating experiment that illustrated the subjectivity of perception; specifically, how people often see only what they expect to see.

These researchers told the subjects in their experiment that they were going to be shown a thirty-second video with a group of people repeatedly passing basketballs to one another. The subjects' task was to count the total number of times the balls were passed from one person to another based on what color shirt the people in the video were wearing. The subjects weren't told ahead of time that, about halfway through the video, a person dressed as a gorilla would walk into the middle of the action, look at the camera, thump her chest, and walk out, spending about nine seconds total on camera (fig. 5.5).

After watching the video, subjects were asked how many passes had been made. Then they were asked an open-ended question: Did you notice anything unusual in the video? The experiment was conducted with people of different ages, in different contexts, in different countries around the world, but the results were always the same: roughly 50 percent of viewers did not notice the gorilla. (If you watch the video with the foresight that you already know what's going to happen, it is shocking to see how obvious it is that a gorilla walks into the center of the screen.)

Chabris and Simons refer to this phenomenon as "inat-

SPECIAL TOPIC 5.8
"THE SEEKER" (MIDRASH)

And the days of Adam after he begat Seth were eight hundred years; and he begat sons and daughters. And all the days that Adam lived were nine hundred and thirty years; and he died. —(GEN. 5:4–5)

Jerah was the youngest son of Eve and Adam. Even as a boy he knew that he was different from his many brothers and their sons and from the sons of his many sisters. When he was older he set out to find someone else who was like him. He walked and wandered from village to village and town to town, to all the places where they had settled, but nowhere did he meet anyone who was like him. Weary, after months of wandering, he came to the village of his favorite sister, Hodesh.

Now Hodesh had a son named Naam, and Naam was the same age as Jerah. When Jerah and Naam looked at each other for the first time, their hearts like birds flew out of their breasts toward each other. And their lips called out the other's true name. And their bodies opened, one to the other, so that their souls could dance joyfully together on the earth.

Jerah and Naam built for themselves a house of stone in the village established by Hodesh. They lived there happily for seven hundred and twenty-eight years, in the midst of their family. And they were buried side by side in the cave where they first had buried Hodesh.

FIGURE 5.5. A frame from the "Invisible Gorilla" experiment.

tentional blindness," people's inability to see things that are directly in front of them (through no fault of visual impairment). They explain further: "When people devote their attention to a particular area or aspect of their visual world, they tend not to notice unexpected objects, even when those unexpected objects are salient, potentially important, and appear right where they are looking."

To take this one step further, when we explore systems of thought, such as those related to society and culture—structures that are around us at all times—we are often unaware of the foundational assumptions upon which they are based. We can call this lack of awareness structural blindness or, depending on the value judgment placed on what is being ignored, structural violence. And even though social identities aren't the only contributors to the development of legal thought, identities always play a part in the interpretive process. Simply put, in the words of scholar Tal Ilan: "Much of what has been written as history *per se* is in fact the chronicle of men's lives."

The following passage, from an essay by writer Cynthia Ozick, underscores the seeming lack of consciousness within the Jewish community about the default of what Ozick calls "masculine universalism":

> When Adin Steinsaltz, the eminent contemporary scholar and interpreter of the Talmud, writes that the Talmud is "the collective endeavor of the entire Jewish people," he is either telling an active conscious falsehood; or he has forgotten the truth; or he has failed to notice the truth. The truth is that the Talmud is the collective endeavor not of the entire Jewish people, but only of its male half. Jewish women have been omitted—by purposeful excision—from this "collective endeavor of the Jewish people," which has "continued throughout the centuries to be part of a constant creative process." A loss numerically greater than a hundred pogroms; yet Jewish literature and history report not one wail, not one tear.

What may have been a slip of the tongue illustrates the norm in the Jewish community, not just now, but for centuries past. Surely, many say, women didn't come up with the biblical practice permitting polygyny while prohibiting polyandry, or Talmudic statements such as "Though a woman is like a pot of filth whose mouth is full of blood, all chase after her" or "Women are a separate people." The contrast becomes starker when we consider that such generalizations are never made by the rabbis about men. As for the framers of the Mishnah and Talmud, what is most important to them, says scholar Rachel Adler, "is the orderly transfer of women and property from one patriarchal domain to another . . . women are themselves ineligible to be normative members of the community." Rather, they are often controlled by males halakhically.

Acknowledgment that there is a gorilla in our midst is not something that can be taken for granted. Nor is it necessarily something that has taken place in terms of major structural improvement, even in the most liberal of contemporary Jewish communities. Perhaps the situation is explained best by scholar Anne Lapidus Lerner, who writes: "In the grand long view of Jewish history, change has taken place at breakneck speed; measured by the pace of change in today's fast-evolving world, it is rather slow." This is one reason that modes of thought focusing on gender equality, especially those written by women, are commonly referred to as "feminist theology," whereas everything else is referred to simply as "theology."

Let me be clear here. In this book, "feminism" is not defined as an ideology calling for the equality of women at the expense of men; rather, it relates to equality for all, regardless of one's gender. This is the most common academic understanding of feminism today. As Adler notes, "The impact of gender on Judaism . . . is not a women's issue; it is an issue for everyone who seeks to understand Judaism."

Defending the Invisible Gorilla

Many of those defending halakhah maintain that it is not a system of inequalities but of differences: men and women simply have divergent roles. Such arguments often end up focusing on the various obligations male and female Jews have as laid out in the Talmud, which states that women are not subject to any "time-bound" mitzvot, positive biblical directives that must be performed at a set time. Rather, women are required to observe only negative mitzvot—things to abstain from doing.

In other words, someone looking into this particular understanding of halakhah—the predominant one for centuries, and the one still maintained in most Orthodox communities—may conclude that men have more important roles to play than women simply because they have more religious obligations to perform than women. Adler has referred to this as the performance of negation, where "the characteristic posture of [women's] Judaism is negation rather than affirmation."

Revealing the Invisible Gorilla

There have been a number of stages in the increasing sensitivity of Jewish communities to perceived structural inequality between males and females (to say nothing of other inequalities, such as sex and sexual orientation, which, for the rabbis, are closely related to gender-related issues). For example, in the initial phases of the American Jewish feminist movement, in the early 1970s—which mirrored that of the American feminist movement at large in basic ways—attention was paid almost exclusively to the subjugated role women had vis-à-vis halakhah (and perhaps as an outgrowth, the reduced role women had within Jewish social institutions).

Simply put, whether one focuses on texts from the Mishnah and Talmud or passages from the Torah, halakhah is gendered. Countless laws relating to the different ritual obligations that one has are dependent on whether one is deemed to be halakhically male or female (or another category; see special topic 5.2). Perhaps this is why early critiques of inequality among Jews focused on working within the confines of halakhah to reorder the system. For example, rather than reject halakhah altogether, some writers, almost entirely women, brought halakhic issues such as those related to divorce and adultery to the fore, calling for change in specific laws.

A second approach that has emerged out of Jewish feminism focuses on known examples of important female figures in history, such as the Talmud's discussions of a highly intelligent woman named Beruriah, or unearths previously marginalized or unknown examples of women who have played central roles in Jewish communities. The following examples are instructive:

• A passage from the Tosefta (Meg. 3:11) states that anyone could be included in the minyan of seven needed to be able to read from the Torah during Shabbat morning prayers, even a woman or child;
• Twenty-five women (compared to 605 men) are mentioned in the Talmud, one of whom (Beruriah) is connected to scholarly discussions;
• There is evidence that women had prominent positions in some ancient Palestinian synagogues, including serving as a community's chief authority;
• Seventeenth-century Kurdistani Jews had a female leader called "rabbi";
• There was a seventeenth- and eighteenth-century German Jewish female leader and scholar named Glückel of Hameln;
• There was a nineteenth-century Hasidic female spiritual leader named Hannah Rachel Verbermacher, also known as the Maid of Ludmir;
• During the seventeenth through nineteenth centuries, a genre of Jewish prayers written by women (in Yiddish) emerged in parts of Europe and Russia.

Scholar Judith Plaskow says of such research, "Reconstructing women's history enables [people] to see that 'Judaism' has always been richer, more complex, and more diverse than either 'normative' sources or most branches of modern Judaism would admit. It permits [people] to see that Torah embraces many patterns and variations of religious experience, that its boundaries are far broader than traditionally allowed." Yet others critique these efforts, saying it should not be necessary to produce "evidence" to justify the equal treatment of women within halakhah. Still others say there are simply too few past instances to support historical gender-based equality.

Some scholars have taken a third approach, pointing out how the Talmudic rabbis created a more progressive halakhic system than existed previously. For example, Judith Hauptman, perhaps the best-known scholar advocating this perspective, contends:

> The rabbis upheld patriarchy as the preordained mode of social organization, as dictated by the Torah. They thus perpetuate women's second-class, subordinate status. They neither achieved equality for women nor even sought it. But of critical importance, they began to introduce numerous, significant, and occasionally bold corrective measures to ameliorate the lot of women. In some cases, they eliminated abusive behaviors that had developed over time. In others, they broke new ground, granting women benefits that they never had before, even at men's expense. From their own perspective, the rabbis were seeking to close the gap that had developed over time between more enlightened social thinking and women's more subordinate status as defined by the received texts, biblical and rabbinic, without openly opposing such texts.

Hauptman considers her scholarship "contextualized feminism," though critics argue otherwise, some even calling her work "apologetic."

In the final analysis, it would be presumptuous to take the Talmudic descriptions of men and women and their respective social status to be a close approximation of historical fact. Most likely, say many scholars, depictions of women in the Talmud (e.g., Beruriah) bear little relation to actual events. Further, these representations, says scholar Judith Baskin, are "frequently at odds with the Jewish cultures that existed in different times and places during which the literature of rabbinic Judaism was produced."

"Radical" Jewish Feminism

Critics of attempts to recalibrate halakhah based on contemporary understandings of equality note that such efforts have only reinforced the notion that men are the norm and women the exception. In calling for changes to specific laws or arguing that women should be able to perform any ritual that men do, feminists sometimes base their argument, perhaps inadvertently, on the assumption that equality means women want and should get to do what men do. Orthodox feminist writer Blu Greenberg, for example, frames her position with statements such as "women have the same innate potential, capability, and needs as men," thereby holding up men as the yardstick by which women should measure themselves. Rachel Adler underscores this problem in explaining that without changes to the halakhic system, women will remain "peripheral Jews" in the eyes of halakhah, from the perspective of these legal codes constantly striving to be "honorary men."

In contrast, a more critical approach contends that, as has been often quoted in Jewish feminist circles, the formula to simply "add women and stir" cannot change an entire system, especially one that is more than two millennia old. Such feminists argue that because halakhah is rooted in the notion that there is a stark difference between men and women—a difference presented as the natural order of things rather than a construct developed specifically by the Mishnaic and Talmudic rabbis and connected to the Bible and generally to societies at large—the entire system needs to be changed.

Such voices have asserted that the dominant gender binary (i.e., the division of people into two basic categories, males and females) presented by halakhah is not so different from the idea expressed by Simone de Beauvoir in her influential mid-twentieth-century book *The Second Sex,* where she argues that men have constructed societies that exclude women, thereby marking them as "Other"—indeed, *the* Other. Thus, men are the norm and women the exception.

Along similar lines, Judith Plaskow contends that "the Jewish women's movement of the last decade . . . has been less concerned with analysis of the origins and bases of women's oppression that render change necessary. It has focused on getting women a piece of the Jewish pie; it has not wanted to bake a new one! . . . These writers seem not to have fully understood the implications of their own categories, however, for they tend to assume that the Otherness of women will disappear if only the community is flexible enough to rectify halakhic injustices. . . . Our legal disabilities are a *symptom* of a pattern of projection that lies deep in Jewish thinking." Some have called approaches such as Plaskow's "radical feminism," versus simply "feminism." Such notions are part of more recent waves in Jewish feminist circles.

In the words of Adler, "The *critical task* is to demonstrate that historical understandings of gender affect all Jewish texts and contexts and hence require the attention of all Jews." It isn't enough to point to one or two halakhic laws that illustrate gender-based inequality, as the issue is systemic. Elaborating on legal scholar Robert Cover's famous essay "Nomos and Narrative," Adler writes that the entire context in which the rabbis approached the world was male-centric.

Since Jewish history has been transmitted by men, so goes the argument, Jewish tradition doesn't reflect women's realities. Such claims are even supported by non-feminist-identifying scholars such as Shaye Cohen, who in one essay writes that based on the Bible, Mishnah, and Talmud, it is clear that the rabbis had an ambiguous stance, at best, on whether women are 100 percent part of the Jewish people's covenant with God.

The Most Recent Wave in Jewish Feminism

The latest wave in Jewish feminist thought, similarly reflecting trends in American feminist and queer theory at large, reexamines all previous efforts on the basis that they reflect the traditional notion of gender and sex, which divides humanity into two possibilities only. Despite passages from the Mishnah pointing to the existence of people identified with a gender or sex outside the dominant binaries, such as the tumtum or androgynous (special topic 5.2), and even though there are midrashim explaining that Adam was an androgynous and Abraham and Sarah were *tumtumim* (plural of *tumtum*), feminist scholarship prior to the beginning of the twenty-first century chiefly excluded differentiated notions of gender, arguing for feminist equality while assuming that the two categories of male and female exhaust human variation. In contrast, recent scholarship falling into the genre of Jewish feminist and Jewish queer thought begins by assuming that neither gender nor sex can be accurately bifurcated; instead, each of these concepts is multivaried. It is with this presumption in mind that such scholarship reapproaches Torah and other sacred Jewish texts.

The Narrowing of Halakhah: Post-Talmudic Law

The word *halakhah* literally means the path or the way. For the Talmudic rabbis there were multiple paths, and consequently a diverse range of rabbinic opinion on any given halakhic issue. A famous passage from the Talmud says, "These and these are [both] the words of the living God, and the halakhah follows the School of Hillel." The first half of the statement points to the value the rabbis place on the plurality of opinion, an ethos not shared by all Jewish sects prior to 70 CE (see chapter 8). In fact, many mishnayot, such as the one on the Shma prayer we saw in special topic 5.1, don't state which rabbinic opinion is the one to follow; instead, they leave it to the reader to choose from various possibilities. However, from approximately the tenth century CE onward, the bottom line for a given halakhic issue became more restricted.

One reason for the narrowing of halakhic opinion was that from the seventh century forward there was no longer a rabbinical high court. Even among those who maintain that no court called the Sanhedrin (preceded by the *Anshei Knesset Hagedolah,* literally the Men of the Great Assembly) ever existed, all can agree that by this time there was no centralized, large group of rabbis making decisions together. Instead, designated rabbis provided answers to specific halakhic questions using the Talmud as a basic source. A system thus emerged wherein one went to a local rabbinic authority *(mara de-atra)* to figure out the halakhah on an issue.

Jewish authorities beyond the Land of Israel and Babylonia, including North Africa and Spain, began to take root, as did new schools of halakhic thought. (This is to say nothing about Jews living in places such as China, Ethiopia, and India—see chapter 7—who often worked outside of the Middle East-based halakhic frameworks altogether.) Now halakhah began to become more codified, with texts emerging that gave definitive answers on halakhic issues, where previously there was a more multiopinioned approach. Some of these codes were collected in manuscripts, with each halakhic question followed up by a single answer or *teshuvah* (pl. *teshuvot*).

The *Mishneh Torah* of Maimonides

Sages such as Saadia ben Joseph Alfayumi (better known as Saadia Gaon), the ninth- and tenth-century head of the rabbinic academy at Sura, in modern-day Iraq—credited with making Arabic the *lingua franca* of Middle Eastern Jews for centuries thereafter and who even translated the Torah into Arabic—was one such regional halakhic arbiter. But other rabbis were even more geographically authoritative, presenting halakhic bottom lines not just for their own local Jewish community, but for all Jews.

By the eleventh century, a small number of rabbis had begun to publish these opinions. On any given issue, such as "Until when can one recite the Shma?," rather than repeating the various perspectives found in the Mishnah and Talmud, they instead presented a single answer to a halakhic question. One of the most famous of these individuals, the twelfth- and thirteenth-century figure Moses ben Maimon (also known as Maimonides or Rambam), in his arguably grandiosely titled *Mishneh Torah,* didn't even reference sources. Instead, he presented his teshuvot as definitive.

Although, as scholar Stephen Passamaneck states, no post-Talmudic legal authority—including Maimonides—ever "superseded earlier [halakhic] works entirely or substantially," such as their primary reference point, the Babylonian Talmud, it is clear that Maimonides and other rabbis from this era, by whittling several opinions down to one, radically shifted the halakhic landscape. This is especially true in light of assertions such as the one Maimonides made in the introduction to the Book of Commandments, which helped him prepare the *Mishneh Torah,* that "outside of this work there was to be no need for another book to learn anything whatsoever that is required in the whole Torah, whether it be a law of the Scriptures or of the Rabbis."

During Maimonides's lifetime some of his critics went so far as to burn his books (particularly those dealing with philosophy and not law). But over time, his *Mishneh Torah* became one of the most important legal texts for Jews living in the Mediterranean region, and eventually most of the world. Although he wrote this book in Hebrew, his primary scholarly language was Arabic, or more precisely a dialect referred to as Judeo-Arabic, not uncommon for Jewish scholars from the eighth through thirteenth centuries who lived in the region of the Mediterranean Sea. Maimonides lived in Spain, Morocco, and Egypt, all Muslim-majority locations at the time. (The Islamic Empire had spread rapidly from the Arabian Peninsula, both north and west, beginning in the seventh century.) By at least the twelfth century, Arabic, including its multiple dialects, had become the primary language in North Africa for Muslims and non-Muslims alike.

Medieval Rabbis under Muslim and Christian Rule

It is important to briefly mention a few other historical influences that led to various shifts in Jewish understanding of halakhah. First, rabbinic leaders living under Muslim rule, such as Maimonides, needed to take Islamic law, *shari'a,* into account when adjudicating on halakhah. (Even though some Jewish communities were protected by Muslims as a result of shari'a, Muslim practices were not homogeneous; see chapter 7.) By the tenth century, when internal schisms split the Muslim empire into autonomous regions, Jewish communities were likewise divided into almost the same regions. Halakhic practices then became linked to these geographic areas.

Likewise, many of the Ashkenazi rabbinic authorities living under Christian rule—in communities located in northern France, England, Germany, Poland, and elsewhere in the more northerly reaches of Europe— were influenced by Christian laws. For instance, in one important halakhic ruling from the eleventh century, Gershom ben Judah, a German rabbi of some renown, banned polygyny (for one thousand years). Based in customs explicitly found in the Torah, however, the practice of taking multiple wives was permitted in Jewish communities living under Muslim rule, in part because Muslim law also allowed this practice. Of course, the question as to whether Rabbi Gershom made this ruling to conform to the Christian-dominant culture is a matter of debate among scholars.

A third situation during this era that is worth noting is that in the eighth or ninth century, a New Middle Eastern Jewish community, the Karaites (see chapter 11), emerged in opposition to the rabbis. The Karaites had different understandings of the rules regarding halakhic interpretation than the rabbis. Most importantly, this meant that Karaite and non-Karaite communities of Jews sometimes butted heads due to their differing perspectives. Because the Karaite community in the Middle East grew quite large at the time (as opposed to currently, in the twenty-first century, where they make up about three-tenths of one percent of the worldwide Jewish community), historically it is important to note this schism.

The *Shulḥan Arukh*

In the mid–sixteenth century, a code of law called the *Shulḥan Arukh* (lit., *A Set Table*) by Joseph Karo gained acceptance among Jews as a practical summary of halakhah. Karo was born at the end of the fifteenth century in Spain; after being expelled during the Spanish Inquisition, his family resettled in Turkey. As an adult, he made his way to Safed in the Land of Israel, where he wrote the *Shulḥan Arukh*. Though based on other legal compendia, including Maimonides's *Mishneh Torah,* Karo's work was easier to read than those of his predecessors and quickly gained mass appeal. Although it was also criticized by scholars of its day precisely for its relative simplicity, by the seventeenth century even some of the most respected rabbinic intellectuals used it as the basis for their own commentaries. (Karo originally wrote the *Shulḥan Arukh* for Sephardi Jews in particular, but Ashkenazi authorities, such as Moses Isserles, added explanations for non-Sephardic communities.)

Legal codes like the *Shulḥan Arukh* define ritual practices from the moment one wakes up in the morning to the moment one goes to sleep. It mandates the way one gets out of bed, how far away a wash basin should be from where one sleeps (to ensure the washing of hands and face before anything else), and even how to properly put on one's shoes (including how to tie them, if need be). (The closest non-Jewish legal system to halakhah in terms of being all-encompassing is shariʿa, which also presents a maximalist approach to one's life, covering aspects of life from A to Z.) Of course, in the past as today, not all Jews observed halakhah. Also, some laws de facto became more important than others, as is true of every legal system.

The significance of the shift from Talmudic plurality to halakhic singularity cannot be overstated, nor can the uniqueness of the earlier multivocal approach. According to scholar Hanina Ben-Menahem, the Talmudic model of accepting multiple legal opinions is completely absent in American and European law, where only bottom lines apply on any given issue. In the United States and Europe, one would never find an idea such as the following, taken from the Talmud: "Rabbi Hama said, 'Now since the law has not been stated either in accordance with the view of Rab and Samuel or in accordance with the view of Rabbi Eleazar, if a judge decides as Rab and Samuel it is legal. If he decides as Rabbi Eleazar it is legal.'" Despite the centuries-long prominence of the Talmud for Jews who abided by halakhah, the rabbinic responses of later Jewish authorities, including contemporaries, have become much more important (with only marginal exceptions).

Belief vs. Practice

Halakhah focuses almost exclusively on what laws Jews need to follow, not on what ideas Jews need to believe. This is an important distinction, especially in light of the emphasis that Christianity, with more adherents than any other religion, places on faith over religious practice. While both the Mishnah and Talmud mention different Jewish beliefs—the divinity of the Torah, resurrection of the dead, the messiah, the world-to-come—neither text mandates that Jews must hold these beliefs, nor does either list all of these things.

At the same time, it would be inaccurate to portray

Jewish ritual practice as if it existed outside belief altogether. Many beliefs, though not necessarily required, are assumed. For example, it is nowhere stated that Jews must believe in a male-centric God. Yet implicitly this has been the norm from the very inception of the Torah, which overwhelmingly reflects a male God cloaked in stereotypically male imagery. (Perhaps as a logical outgrowth, as mentioned until recently Jewish law was written exclusively by men.) In other words, while Jewish ritual practice is more important than belief in terms of overt theological statements, the entire corpus of Jewish life has been implicitly predicated on the notion that publicly proclaiming a belief in a female God is heretical.

Modern Jewish Customs, Laws, and Meta-Halakhah

The nineteenth-century emergence of the Reform or Liberal movement in Germany brought stark changes. Many religious practices that accentuated differences between Jews and non-Jews were marginalized, if not altogether expunged. In the United States, for example, some Reform Jews, including their rabbis, began openly eating nonkosher food, something unheard of among American Jews from the time of colonialism through the 1800s, despite the great difficulties in keeping kosher at the time.

Yet for customary practices to become de facto law was not a new phenomenon. As far back as the Talmud, the idea of a custom becoming permanent law—regardless of the legal process of rabbis arguing over a law's meaning—gained a great deal of traction. This led to a number of new laws over the centuries, such as Ashkenazi Jews' custom-that-became-law of not eating legumes (e.g., beans and lentils) during Passover, despite their distinction from the grains customarily prohibited during this holiday. In fact, during the twentieth century some notable halakhic authorities ruled that prevailing customs observed by the masses (such as smoking cigarettes), though breaking aspects of halakhah (i.e., humans are created in the image of God and are responsible for taking care of their bodies, which are a reflection of the divine; yet smoking is clearly bad for one's health), were permissible because if they were prohibited, people would continue doing them anyway.

Put differently, customs are linked to dominant narratives. What becomes a community norm often subsequently becomes codified as law, sometimes replacing other laws in the process. Among twentieth- and twenty-first-century American Jews, a number of customs have developed that this book calls meta-halakhic. In other words, although from a traditional point of view these practices are not halakhic, because they have a clear logic, and because they are commonplace among American Jewry, they have taken on a status akin to practical law. For many, such practices help to separate the sacred and profane. Two of the clearest examples deal with kashrut, the laws regarding what is and is not halakhically permissible in relation to eating, and Shabbat.

Meta-Halakhah and Kashrut

From a traditional halakhic, or de jure, point of view, the food one eats is either kosher or not. De facto, however, contemporary American Jews who "keep kosher" adhere to one of several general customs. For instance:

- Some keep their home kosher, bringing only kosher food into it, yet eat nonkosher food outside their home.
- For those who eat out at non-hekschered (non–rabbinically supervised) restaurants, some eat only uncooked vegetables (i.e., and nothing else, but especially nothing cooked).
- Some hold that you can't eat any food from a non-hekschered restaurant, especially one that serves unkosher meat.

In other words, from a meta-halakhic perspective there are various degrees of keeping kosher. Such a hierarchy is not written down anywhere; it exists only on a collectively imagined continuum. (Some would not agree that these *are* the unwritten standards.) If such Jews affiliated with a movement, they would probably identify as Conservative or Reform, or perhaps as "lapsed Orthodox Jews," somewhat akin to self-identified lapsed Catholics at my university, who, though once committed to strict Catholic ritual, have gone in another direction while still maintaining an affiliation with Catholicism.

From a meta-halakhic point of view, the worst thing someone could eat at McDonald's is an item with ham or bacon (or any other part of a pig). The second worst would be an item with beef and cheese, such as a cheeseburger (mixing "meat" with "milk" is prohibited according to the rules of kashrut, so this would be a double whammy). The next worst would be eating chicken and cheese, followed by a hamburger without cheese, and finally chicken without cheese. It would be better to eat something that didn't have either beef or chicken, such as a fish filet. Better still would be to eat only french fries (assuming they weren't fried in lard). But the very best thing to eat at McDonald's, from a meta-halakhic point of view, would be something like a salad or ice cream, a food item that isn't cooked whatsoever.

Meta-Halakhah and Shabbat

Another good example of meta-halakhic practices is found in ways to observe Shabbat. Although, traditionally speaking, one either follows the halakhic laws of Shabbat or does not, many American Jews have their own meta-halakhic customs for the period of time between Friday night and Saturday night. For example, as explained in a piece by writer Ari Goldman, "Many Ways to Celebrate Shabbat," here are some of the ways people observe Shabbat meta-halakhically:

- David uses the telephone to make outgoing calls but doesn't take incoming calls. Syd receives calls but doesn't make them.
- Although Gloria doesn't follow most halakhot pertaining to Shabbat, she does refrain from doing one particular activity that is banned on the Sabbath: knitting.
- Sandy drives his car, which is halakhically prohibited to do on Shabbat, but he does not drive it on the highway.
- Leslie drives but doesn't carry money, the latter another Shabbat prohibition. (This became a problem one Saturday when she encountered a tollbooth on her way to visit her mother. She began to explain to the toll taker that she is a Sabbath observer and doesn't carry money, but he quickly cut her off: "Lady, then why are you driving?" She convinced the toll taker to let her through anyway.)
- Ilan has sexual relations with his girlfriend on Friday nights, halakhically prohibited unless the couple is married, but tears open his condom package earlier in the day so that he does not violate Shabbat by tearing unnecessarily.
- Fred, a school teacher, observes Shabbat halakhically all year except for the summer, which he "takes off" so he can drive to and from the beach each weekend.
- Jerome smokes a Cuban cigar once a week, on Shabbat, despite a halakhic prohibition against lighting a fire on the Sabbath.
- In his youth, Lenny, a "Deadhead" (a devotee of the rock band the Grateful Dead), smoked marijuana at concerts except when they landed on Shabbat. On those occasions he baked hash brownies before Shabbat began.

In most of these cases, the individuals described are not following the traditional halakhic laws of Shabbat. From a strict halakhic perspective, unless there is a life or death situation—in which case any Shabbat law can be broken—on Shabbat one is not allowed to make phone calls, knit, drive a car, carry money, have premarital sexual intercourse (although this holds true for any day of the week), or smoke, whether cigars or marijuana. But from a meta-halakhic perspective the boundaries around these actions are varied, the main point being that these people are marking Shabbat as a different day from the rest of the week.

Who Is a Jew: Law or Laws?

The conversion question raised at the beginning of this chapter is not particularly unique insofar as rates of Jews marrying non-Jews—in everywhere but the State of Israel—have skyrocketed over the past fifty years (a topic that is discussed further in later chapters), which has played a role in a greater emphasis on the halakhic specifics of a given conversion. In fact, the debate over who is a Jew goes back as far as the beginning of the Jewish community itself (and before that, back to the Judean, Israelite, and Hebrew communities).

Yet some maintain that only since the nineteenth century has this become a significant issue, due to the emergence of the Reform movement, which declared ritual aspects of many Jewish laws, for all intents and purposes, null and void. As of 2013, there is only one thing that all organized Jewish movements—Conservative, Orthodox, Reform, Reconstructionist, Renewal, and Secular Humanist—agree on regarding who is (or is not) a Jew: Messianic Jews (e.g., Jews for Jesus; see chapters 8 and 11) are not "real Jews." Aside from that, there is no single transdenominational edict offering a definitive explanation of Jewishness.

One of the many things that laws construct are borders, defining who is in and who is out; adjudicating what behavior is permitted and what behavior is prohibited. Given the current state of Jewish practice worldwide, it is challenging to see commonalities between various subcommunities, especially when there is no agreement as to what makes someone a Jew. But this is actually not a recent trend. There has never been a single set of halakhic rules that all Jewish communities worldwide adhered to. There have only been sets of laws.

Mysticisms

Contents

Key Ideas

- Jewish mystical thought and practices aim at communicating with God experientially, rather than only intellectually. Mystics commonly aspire to understand God in as deep a way as possible; believe that God resides in all things, both living and nonliving; and commonly practice regimented and detailed rituals, including various forms of prayer.

- Jewish mysticisms today are a compilation of a number of different forms of mystical thought and prac-

tices that emerged over the course of centuries in locations around the world. Likewise, Jewish mysticisms have been influenced by non-Jews (e.g., Christians, Gnostics, Greeks, Hindus, Muslims, and Zoroastrians).

- In sixteenth-century Safed and eighteenth-, nineteenth-, and twentieth-century Russia and Eastern Europe, Jewish mysticisms were embraced and popularized among non-elite Jewish communities. Two of the most important figures from these eras, respectively, are Isaac Luria and the Baal Shem Tov. Although Jewish mysticisms are primarily practiced by a select few Jews today, a number of ideas and rituals that originated in Jewish mystical communities are now part of mainstream Jewish practices.

Visiting a Holy Saint in Morocco

After meeting up at the Casablanca airport, my friend and I headed over to the rental car office, drove into the Moroccan capital for a quick bite, and then hit the road to the south. After a few days in Marrakesh, we began to make our way toward the western edge of the Sahara Desert. En route, we had one stop to make: the tomb of a holy man known to Moroccans—Jews and Muslims alike—as Rabbi David U-Moshe or Ḥakham Dawid U-Mussi.

Several weeks before, another friend of mine had visited me in Fes, where I was spending the summer studying. During his travels around the country, he had chanced upon the rabbi's shrine; it had been one of the highlights of his trip. But he didn't give me much to go on. All I knew was that from the main highway we would pass through a town, Agouim, located at the foot of the Atlas Mountain range, where we would need to stop and ask the locals to point us toward the dirt road to the pilgrimage site. Since it was unmarked, neither of us spoke French, and my Arabic was not yet up to snuff, the odds were stacked against us.

Throwing caution to the wind comes with the territory for a traveler in his twenties, though. After asking what seemed like every person in town, we pieced together a vague idea of where we needed to go, jumped in our car, and headed back toward Marrakesh; fortunately, we only had to backtrack a few miles. After trying three or four different dirt roads, we found the right one and, somewhat miraculously, eventually reached the rabbi's resting place.

Before we had even gotten out of the car, a local caretaker appeared out of nowhere on the hill above us and waved his hands in a motion that seemed to say, "Follow me." We obliged, of course, not having any clue what else to do, and scampered up the incline. We eagerly watched him unlock a metal door to one of the site's many white buildings with a key that seemed as large as one of those foot-long fake keys-to-the-city that United States mayors give to visiting celebrities. The area was very quiet, mysteriously so. There seemed to be no one around for miles, aside from the Berber caretaker and his family.

We entered the building and realized that not only were we in a synagogue, but we had also reached the rabbi's shrine (fig. 6.1). Oddly enough, there was an almond tree *inside* the building, jutting out toward the entrance from a rock under which David U-Moshe was buried. The tree seemed to overlook, or perhaps protect, the great saint's grave.

Between what I had been told and what we gleaned from the locals, we knew that both Jews and Muslims considered the rabbi a saint and his burial place a holy pilgrimage site. According to one tradition, David U-Moshe originally made his way to Morocco's Atlas Mountains from sixteenth-century Palestine. Tasked with raising money to support the Jewish community's "return" to the Holy Land, after arriving in Morocco he died saving a local group of Jews and Muslims from a plague. Ever since, Moroccans of all faiths have visited the rabbi's resting place to pray and ask for blessings.

Later we also learned that thousands of Moroccan Jewish Israelis visit the site annually, usually in autumn, staying for days or as long as a month, a ritual referred to as a *hillula*. Once the twenty or so empty buildings reach capacity, the remaining visitors set up tents and a communal campfire. To this day, the ritual observances include visits to David U-Moshe's grave, lighting candles, round-the-clock prayers, and sometimes feasts of freshly slaughtered goat meat, shared with Muslim locals as a form of *tzedakah* (charity).

Saints, *Tzadikim,* and Mystics

One reason people visit mystics' graves is that these saints are commonly believed to have—and to continue to have, even in death—extraordinarily close relationships with God. In fact, visits to David U-Moshe's grave do not reflect a new practice for Jews; evidence of such graveside pilgrimages date back as far as the biblical books of Joshua and Jeremiah, which depict events dated to the twelfth through sixth centuries BCE.

Many Jews refer to these deceased saints as *tzadikim* or *tzadikot* (for males and females, respectively), "righteous ones," a term that goes back to the Talmud, if not before. Commonly, saints attain this status after performing one or more miracles—such as walking on water (e.g., Rabbi Yaakob Abihatsira) or curing the sick (e.g., Rabbis Moshe Haliwa and Raphael Anqawa)—while living a particularly devout life, often involving ascetic devotional practices. Many saints also experience some sort of revelatory dream about future events. In Morocco, there are even instances of Jewish saints revealing themselves to Muslims (but not Jews), individuals whom Muslims continue to venerate today. It is also not uncommon for sainthood

FIGURE 6.1. Shrine of David U-Moshe. This sacred tomb, adjacent to and accessible through a synagogue, is believed to have been built directly above the site where David U-Moshe was buried. In this photo it is difficult to make out the almond tree, located in the alcove next to the shrine.

to exist within familial dynasties, usually passed from father to son.

There are differences between the ways Muslims and Jews worship saints in Morocco, but there are also quite a few similarities. For one thing, Moroccan Jews have historically been influenced by Sufis (Muslim mystics). In addition, many of the oral traditions of Moroccan Jews that connect biblical events with Morocco—Noah's Ark, the prophet Daniel, and three of King Solomon's sons are all said to be buried there—are also maintained by Muslims.

Although Jewish mystics also lived elsewhere, we know more about Jewish mystics living in Muslim-majority places such as Morocco because, simply put, more research has been conducted on them. The region of David U-Moshe's tomb, in the Moroccan Atlas Mountains, was home to a number of other mystics dated to the sixteenth century. According to scholar Issachar Ben-Ami, there are more than 650 sites of Jewish saints in Morocco, twenty-five of them women, though David U-Moshe is one of the most famous.

Like fellow mystics in eleventh- through fourteenth-century Spain and fifteenth- and sixteenth-century Safed, in the Galilee region of the Land of Israel, many of these Moroccan saints were allegedly visited by the prophet Elijah, had divinely revealed dreams, and produced Jewish mystical writings. Some of the Moroccan Jewish mystics moved to Safed at the same time that David U-Moshe traveled to Morocco, illustrating a connection between these two remote, mountainous regions.

In Morocco and elsewhere, ritual pilgrimage to the burial places of tzadikim is one of countless mystical practices in Judaism, one of the ways to experience the supernatural or, more explicitly, God. But whether visiting the grave of Rabbi David U-Moshe in Timzerit, Morocco; Rabbi Menachem Mendel Schneerson ("the Rebbe") in Brooklyn, New York City; or Rabbi Nahman of Bratslav in Uman, Ukraine, it is a ritual based in mysticism, an important dimension of the Jewish tradition.

What Is Mysticism?

One way to understand mysticism is as communication with God experientially, rather than only intellectually—a way to directly experience the Divine. According to scholar Lawrence Fine, five characteristics apply to mysticism at large:

1. Mystics aspire to understand God in as deep a way as possible, an endeavor that goes well beyond the confines of rational thought. They want to experience God "in a way that is intuitive, direct, and intense."
2. Mystics believe that God resides in all living and nonliving things. This means that one way to access God is through oneself, internally; through one's own body and mind.
3. Mystics commonly see the world holistically, as a single entity. Anything that might seem to be a distinct component in fact exists only within God's oneness; its separateness is an illusion.

4. Mystical practices are often quite regimented and detailed.
5. Mystical practices include various forms of prayer.

What Is Jewish Mysticism?

Despite the use of the word *God* in this description, not all Jewish mystics believe in a personal, higher power. Rather, many mystics regard such theistic notions of God as *pshat,* the most literal way to understand the Divine, and believe that the deepest layers can only be found through *sōd.* (As explained in chapter 2, *sōd* is the mystical way of approaching Torah, with *pshat, remez,* and *drash* making up three other common paths.)

Some scholars are quick to point out, however, that there is no single thread called Jewish mysticism; there are only Jewish mysticisms. The preeminent twentieth-century scholar of Jewish mysticism, Gershom Scholem, said that there are as many notions of the term *mysticism* "as there are writers on the subject." Scholar Arthur Green explains that Jewish mysticism never developed linearly, and even fundamental mystical texts such as the *Zohar* (discussed below) present multiple understandings of God.

Important distinctions can be made between Jewish mystical thought and mysticisms connected to other religious traditions. Apart from its core texts, Jewish mysticism is different in two particular ways:

- The restraint with which Jewish mystics have portrayed experiencing God, exemplified by the lack of mystical autobiographies or attempts to personalize mystical experiences (aside from the Hasids of the eighteenth and nineteenth centuries);
- The belief that the Hebrew language—and the Torah as the most important Hebrew text—is a mystical medium, one of the primary ways God interacts with humans.

Origins of Jewish Mysticism

The first Jewish mystical text is the Torah. As discussed in chapter 2, the Five Books of Moses form the core of all Jewish thought; everything else is dependent on and built upon this foundation. Jewish mysticism is a way to interpret the Torah, which is understood as the word and message of God. In some sense, all Jewish mystics aim to experience God "face to face," as Jacob and Moses did, or as the Israelites did during the revelation at Mount Sinai, when they "saw the sounds of thunder and lightning."

SPECIAL TOPIC 6.1
EZEKIEL 1:1–26

[1]In the thirtieth year, on the fifth day of the fourth month, when I was in the community of exiles by the Chebar Canal, the heavens opened, and I saw visions of God. [2]On the fifth day of the month—it was the fifth year of the exile of King Jehoiachin—[3]the word of God came to the priest Ezekiel son of Buzi, by the Chebar Canal, in the land of the Chaldeans. And the hand of God came upon him there. [4]I looked, and lo, a stormy wind came sweeping out of the north—a huge cloud and flashing fire, surrounded by a radiance; and in the center of it, in the center of the fire, a gleam as of amber. [5]In the center of it were also the figures of four creatures. And this was their appearance: They had the figures of human beings. [6]However, each had four faces, and each of them had four wings; [7]the legs of each were [fused into] a single rigid leg, and the feet of each were like a single calf's hoof; and the sparkle was like the luster of burnished bronze . . . [15]As I gazed on the creatures, I saw one wheel on the ground next to each of the four-faced creatures. [16]As for the appearance and structure of the wheels . . . [26]Above the expanse over their heads was the semblance of a throne, in appearance like sapphire; and on top, upon the semblance of a throne, there was a semblance of a human form.

Jewish mysticism is built upon the Bible, historically and literarily, as well as upon Mishnah, Talmud, and Midrash. Scholem explains this further: "To the mystic, the original act of Revelation to the community—the, as it were, public revelation of Mount Sinai, to take one instance—appears as something whose true meaning has yet to unfold itself; the secret revelation is to [the mystic] the real and decisive one." This vision of gradual unfolding is especially true for the most important mystical text from the medieval period through today, the *Zohar.* Its study necessitates familiarity with both the Bible and rabbinic writings.

Stairway to Heaven: *Merkavah* Mysticism

One of the earliest genres of Jewish mystical texts is generally called *Merkavah* literature. Described by scholar Moshe Idel as the "mystical visionary experience of the divine realm," this way of experiencing God is traced by some to specific passages in the Bible, such as ones from 2 Samuel or Ezekiel (special topic 6.1). The word *merka-*

ff

Curribus igni-comis ſurſum Thesbita levatur,
Palliolum cujus mox Heliſæus habet.   2 *Regum.*   *Hoc ſiccis pedibus Iordanis flumina tranſit:*
                                    Cap 2. vers 11.   *Vatum et diſcipulis obviat in Iericho.*
                                   Viſscher Excudebat.

FIGURE 6.2. *Elijah Carried to Heaven in a Chariot of Fire.* This seventeenth-century depiction of the biblical Elijah ascending to heaven, by Nicolas Ryckemans, is based on 2 Kings 2:11–12: "And as they went on and talked, a chariot of fire led by horses separated them and Elijah went up to heaven on it surrounded by a whirlwind."

vah translates to "throne" (as in "the throne of God") or "chariot," sometimes understood as a vehicle that can take one to the heavens (as in the chariot that Elijah went up to heaven on; fig. 6.2). Some of these texts also touch on ideas such as the ascendance of souls.

Scholars debate whether the Bible contains the earliest texts of Merkavah literature. Some claim that this genre evolved out of the apocalyptic (foretelling the end of the world) literary tradition that emerged as early as the destruction of the Second Temple (sixth century BCE) or as late as the fall of Jerusalem in the first century CE. Others maintain that those who wrote the Dead Sea Scrolls, dated to the second century BCE through the second century CE, were also engaged in forms of Merkavah mysticism.

According to scholar Rachel Elior, this esoteric genre of mystical ideas was transmitted through a priestly lineage that existed for centuries. Scholar Peter Schäfer, in contrast, maintains that this mystical school did not emerge linearly from any previous tradition. Part of the problem, says Schäfer, lies in the difficulty in categorizing distinct textual genres under the single umbrella of Jewish mysticism (or even the sub-umbrella of Merkavah literature). Scholem argues in a different direction, asserting that much of Merkavah literature appeared during the third and fourth centuries CE, alongside the emergence of the Palestinian Talmud. Ultimately, Scholem says, we have no way of knowing for certain.

Medieval Mysticism

By the tenth century, Jews had dispersed throughout the Mediterranean and Europe. In turn, new centers of Jewish mysticism emerged in the Muslim- and later Chris-

Some scholars contend that ideas emerging out of Zoroastrianism, an ancient Persian-based religion, played a role in the development of Jewish mysticism, such as various approaches to evil. Others have focused more on the influences of medieval ideologies. For example, thirteenth-century Spanish Jews were living under Christian rule. Although tolerant at times, many Christians felt that they needed to show Jews "the light" and bring them into the Christian fold by "saving" them. Some hold that the most important book of medieval Jewish mysticism, the Zohar, should be seen as a "grand defense of Judaism, a poetic demonstration of the truth and superiority of the Jewish faith."

The intolerance of Christians during this time may be one reason that the Zohar is replete with passages reflecting prejudice against non-Jews, especially in the text's treatment of non-Hebrew and non-Israelite characters in the Torah, such as the "mixed multitude" (Exod. 12:38) of Hebrews and non-Hebrews, Israelites and non-Israelites, that hastily left Egypt while being chased by Pharaoh and his soldiers. Much, if not all, of this contempt is implicit, perhaps because the Zohar's author(s) understood that being more forthright could lead to a violent backlash against Jews.

At the same time, some Jewish mystics integrated Christian thought into their mystical ideas. There is also evidence of clear connections with Muslim mystical and philosophical literature. Most passages linking Jewish and Islamic forms of mysticism are implicit, but particular forms of meditation illustrate obvious links with Sufism (Islamic mysticism), such as practices in which a mystic meditates on a particular name of God (e.g., *hazkarah* and *dhikr*). For example, in thirteenth-century Egypt, Maimonides's son, Abraham, and grandson, Ovadiah, openly refer to their reverence for and study of Sufi practices and their unifying of them into their own.

As for Hindus, there is no historical evidence of actual meetings between them and medieval Jews in France and Spain. However, a small yet growing body of scholarship points to ideas in Jewish mystical thought that clearly predate the medieval period and are present in ancient Hindu texts. For example, a number of notions in the Book of Formation or Sefer Yetzirah run parallel structurally to ancient Hindu texts; there are also Hindu equivalents for the sefirot and the Ein Sof (see later in chapter). Two of the most overt links between Hindu and Jewish mysticism are as follows: First, in a book attributed to a renowned twelfth-century halakhic jurist and mystic, Abraham Ibn Ezra, the author unambiguously notes how the astrological system he and his colleagues were using was based on Hindu mathematical systems. Second, in one of Moses De León's texts—he is credited with writing a number of books aside from the Zohar—*Sefer Mishkan ha-Edut,* the author mentions *ḥakhmei hodu ha-kadmonim* (the ancient Indian sages), seeming references to the Hindu doctrine of maya or the illusory dimension of the world. (Chapter 7 briefly looks at further interaction between Indian Jews and Indian Hindus.)

---

tian-ruled Iberian Peninsula (today's Spain and Portugal) as well as Christian-ruled France and Germany. As to the connection between these medieval mystical schools and those preceding them, Scholem originally argued that although certain thematic ideas are present in Jewish mystical writings from both the first few centuries CE and the twelfth and thirteenth centuries, no continuous mystical tradition was passed from the rabbinic period to the medieval period. Later he reversed his position, partially due to the unearthing of Merkavah literature from the seventh through eleventh centuries, particularly in Babylonia. For our purposes, it is most important to note that mystical texts from the medieval period clearly did build upon previous ones.

In twelfth- and thirteenth-century Germany in particular, then home to the emperors of the so-called Holy Roman Empire, many German Jewish mystics, commonly referred to as Hasidim or *Ḥasidei Ashkenaz,* lived in small communities committed to the study of Jewish mysticism accompanied with ascetic practices. (Note that this group is not connected to the Hasidim of eighteenth-century Russia discussed later in the chapter; they only share the same signifier, *Hasid,* which is Hebrew for pious.) Some of their mystical literature clearly echoed content from earlier mystical texts.

These German Jewish mystics also communicated with Spanish Jewish mystics, and each clearly influenced the other's mystical ideas. At the same time, new ideas came about and were included in the growing canon of mystical literature. Both German and Spanish Jewish mystical schools were also influenced by non-Jewish communities. While German mystics, for example, integrated aspects of their experiences living during the Christians' Crusades into their worldview, Spanish mystics were shaped by Muslims and Christians. The later sixteenth-century Safed-based mystics, as well as mystical traditions that emerged among Hasidic Jews in eighteenth- and nineteenth-century Russia and Poland, would similarly be influenced by non-Jewish communities. (See special topic 6.2 for a discussion of some of these influences.)

Kabbalah

Many date the genesis of Kabbalah to medieval France and Spain, when Jewish mystical texts materialized as a new genre of writing, emerging in multiple different forms. Today, Kabbalah is often popularly used to mean Jewish mysticism as a whole. However, the major scholars of Jewish mysticism are virtually unanimous that this is inaccurate. They explain that in rabbinic literature, the term *Kabbalah*—translated as tradition, reception, or acceptance—commonly refers to books in the Bible aside from the Torah, and during the medieval period mystics in Spain and France were using the term in this manner. In this chapter, I too use the term *Kabbalah* narrowly, to refer specifically to Jewish mystical literature that emerged in medieval Spain and France.

The *Book of Illumination (Sefer ha-Bahir)*

One of the earliest and most important books from the era of Kabbalah is called *Sefer ha-Bahir* or the *Book of Illumination* (also translated as the Book of Brilliance or Book of Clarity). During the twelfth century, this book circulated in France (though it probably originated elsewhere). Made up of interpretations of biblical verses as well as agaddic and midrashic passages (see chapter 5), the *Book of Illumination* seems to have been written over a long period of time; notions of Jewish mysticism change throughout its pages. It lays out various manifestations of God and the world through which we experience God, such as the "seven voices" or the "ten spheres *[sefirot]*" (described later in the chapter).

Scholars underscore the linkages between this text and Gnosticism, a religious ideology that originated in the first few centuries CE in Palestine, known for positing, among other things, that there are two forces, or Gods, in the world, one good and one evil. One of these connections is the symbols that appear in both the *Book of Illumination* and Gnostic writings. Although there is no clear evidence of the relationship between Gnostic literature and this book, some of the early Gnostics were undoubtedly Jewish, so it isn't farfetched to make this association.

According to Arthur Green, the mystical writings of the Kabbalists were entirely unique to the Jewish community. It was an innovative, extraordinary, and fresh way to understand God and reality. In Green's words, "The image of God that first appears in *Sefer ha-Bahir*—to be elaborated by several generations of *Kabbalists* until it achieved its highest poetic expression in the *Zohar*—is a God of multiple mythic potencies, obscure entities eluding precise definition but described through a remarkable web of images, parables, and scriptural allusions. . . . The *Bahir* and other early *kabbalistic* writings refer to a secret inner life of God, lifting the veil from the ancient Jewish insistence on monotheism and revealing a complex and multifaceted divine realm."

The *Zohar (Book of Radiance)*

Although the *Book of Illumination* is clearly a foundational medieval Jewish mystical text—as is the *Book of Formation* or *Sefer Yetzirah,* a text that explains, among other things, how God created the universe using only the twenty-two letters of the Hebrew alphabet—the most important mystical text from the medieval period is undoubtedly the *Zohar,* also known as the *Book of Radiance* or *Book of Splendor* (or as *Ha-Zohar ha-Qadosh [The Holy Zohar]* in Hebrew). Over time the *Zohar* has become one of the most important books in the Jewish textual canon, long believed by mystics to be on a par with the Bible and Talmud in terms of importance. Some hold that since its emergence, the *Zohar* has had more commentaries and explanations written about it than any other Jewish text other than the Bible.

Sometimes called a "mystical novel," the *Zohar* presents many of its ideas through the narrative of a Talmudic rabbi with mystical, even magical, powers, in discussion with his disciples. For centuries, many thought that the *Zohar*'s author, as well as the text's main figure, was the second-century Shimon bar Yochai. Many other esoteric texts similarly claim direct connections to earlier figures to enhance their authority.

Aside from marginal naysayers, this story of the *Zohar*'s origins stuck for centuries, until it was shattered in the twentieth century. Based on the text's medieval grammar and its vocabulary composed of a mixture of

Hebrew and a unique form of Aramaic, for a while scholars thought that the *Zohar,* or at least much of it, was written by a single author, posited to be a Spanish Jew named Moses De León. More recently, however, it has been suggested that the *Zohar,* like the *Book of Illumination,* was written over a longer period of time by different authors, as the text has changing notions of Jewish mysticism.

Another reason for dating the *Zohar* to well after the second century and the lifetime of Shimon bar Yochai is that it integrates passages from the Mishnah, Talmud, and Midrash, as well as medieval biblical commentaries such as those produced by Rabbi Shimon ben Yitzchak (Rashi) and Rabbi Moses ben Nahman (Ramban or Nahmonides). Scholars have also noted the influence of various books written by an immediate predecessor of De León's, Maimonides, as well as a clear familiarity with the *Book of Illumination.* Put another way, the *Zohar* integrates all of the major Jewish sacred texts that preceded it.

Further, similar to the organizational system of early midrashim, much of the *Zohar* is a commentary on verses from the Torah (as well as the books of Ezekiel, Ruth, and the Song of Songs), and it follows the division of the Five Books of Moses used in synagogues, sections called *parshiyot,* a system that emerged during the Talmudic era. (See special topic 6.3 for an example of a passage from the *Zohar.*)

Daniel Matt's translation and commentary on the *Zohar* show how it builds upon earlier Jewish texts such as Midrash, the Talmud, the Mishnah, the Writings and Prophets, and, of course, the Torah. For example, in his footnote to the *Zohar*'s passage "Adam cleaved to that impure spirit" (special topic 6.3):

> See *Tanḥuma* (Buber), *Bereshit* 26: "Rabbi Simon said, 'For 130 years Adam separated from his wife Eve, for once Cain was killed, Adam said, "Why should I engender children if they become cursed?" What did he do? . . . Female spirits approached him and heated themselves from him. As the blessed Holy One said to David, ". . . *When he [Solomon] does wrong, I will chastise him with a human rod, with blows of the children of* אדם *(adam)*" (2 Samuel 7:14) . . . , namely the demons'" . . . See BT *Eruvin* 18b: "Rabbi Yirmeyah son of El'azar said, 'During all those [130] years that Adam was under the ban [for having eaten from the Tree of Knowledge], he engendered spirits, demons, and female demons.' Cf. *Zohar* 1:19b, 34b, 55a; 2:231b; 3:76b; Trachtenberg, *Jewish Magic and Superstition,* 51–54."

To clarify, *Tanḥuma* are rabbinic midrashim on the Five Books of Moses; 2 Samuel is a book from the Prophets; BT is the Babylonian Talmud; and *Eruvin* is a Talmudic tractate. But even if little in this footnote makes sense

SPECIAL TOPIC 6.3
CAIN AND ABEL IN THE ZOHAR

The following section of the Zohar explains the narrative of Cain and Abel, in particular the connection between Adam, Eve, the Serpent, and Abel's death:

> Adam cleaved to that impure spirit, while his wife cleaved to it first, receiving, absorbing its slime, from which a son was engendered—son of impure spirit. So there were two sons: one from that impure spirit and one when Adam returned to God; this from the impure side, this from the pure.
>
> Rabbi El'azar said, "When the serpent injected that slime into Eve she absorbed it, so when she copulated with Adam she bore two sons: one from that impure side and one from the side of Adam, Cain resembling both the higher image and the lower. So their paths diverged from one another. Cain was certainly the son of the impure spirit, and deriving from the side of the Angel of Death, he killed his brother. Being from his side, from him emerged all evil haunts, goblins, spirits, and demons . . . Consequently as it is written: *And when they were out in the field* (Gen. 4:8)—this is a woman, as has been said . . . Rabbi Yitzḥak said, 'Come and see: As Cain was killing Abel, he did not know how his soul would expire, as the Companions have established.'"

This passage from the Zohar explains the story of Cain and Abel in terms of the world's mystical layer, sōd. In this telling, the narrative is not so much about two human brothers. Instead, it reflects a much deeper metaphysical struggle, good versus evil. In other words, because God told Adam not to eat from the Tree of Knowledge of Good and Evil, and he nonetheless did so, the world's first humans committed a terrible sin that subsequently passed from Adam and Eve onto their firstborn, Cain. Because Cain was born with the "slime" of the Garden of Eden's serpent, who played a core role in convincing the humans to eat from the Tree, Cain's evil inclination overpowered him. Eventually, he murdered his younger brother, Abel, thereby carrying out a much deeper purpose: of evil challenging good.

to you—indeed, it is a footnote to a passage from one of the more dense and esoteric texts from the medieval period, written some eight hundred years ago!—what should be clear is that the *Zohar* builds upon core sacred texts that preceded it. This is a direct example of the diagram of concentric circles found in figure 2.4.

Clearly, the author(s) of the *Zohar* had a superb fluency

in terms of biblical, Mishnaic, Talmudic, and Midrashic precursors. And when Matt appends a list of related passages from the *Zohar* at the end of this particular footnote, as well as a citation of a contemporary book on magic and superstition published in 1974, he is adding another layer to our image of concentric circles.

Lawrence Fine argues that what distinguishes the *Zohar* from other Kabbalistic texts is the author's extraordinary imagination, which is infused with drama and erudition. Whereas some medieval mystics, such as Abraham Abulafia, wrote texts that explain ways to meditate on God, the *Zohar*'s focus is the object of meditation: God. Green explains that one of the possible reasons the *Zohar* presents such fantastical descriptions of God and the world is that the Torah (in the second of the Ten Commandments) prohibits the use of images, as opposed to words, to depict God. In other words, the *Zohar* approaches the Torah not as a text but rather, says Green, as a "living divine presence, engaged in a mutual relationship with the person who studies" her.

The Ten *Sefirot*

A core idea in both the *Zohar* and other medieval Jewish mystical texts is the doctrine of God's ten *sefirot*—commonly translated as spheres and etymologically linked to the Hebrew word for sapphire, thus alluding to God's brilliance. One way to understand the sefirot is as God's emanations, things that flow from God (fig. 6.3). The sefirot are rooted in something so far beyond human comprehension that it can't be contained. Called the *Ein Sof,* whose literal translation is "without end," this "something" is perhaps best understood as infinity.

These ten spheres are not divisions of God, for God is always one, but they are God's external traits, which, with a great deal of practice, one can even access. All except for the *Ein Sof,* that is, which lies just beyond the highest *sefirah*. Sometimes called *Keter,* or crown, and sometimes called *Ayin* or *Ein,* meaning "the root of all roots," this highest sphere connects with both the *Ein Sof* of God and to the other nine sefirot.

EIN SOF AND NOTHINGNESS

Some mystics use the idea of emptiness or nothingness (as in no thingness) to explain the *Ayin,* akin to an idea found in other religious traditions, such as Buddhism. However, the term *nothingness* does not imply that Kabbalists believed that the world does not inherently exist; rather, God pervades the entire world, and there is noth-

ing in it that is separate from God because God is everything. The fourteenth-century Kabbalist David ben Abraham ha-Lavan, wrote, "Nothingness is more existent than all the being of the world. But since it is simple, and all simple things are complex compared with its simplicity, it is called *Ayin*." In other words, the idea of nothingness does not support the doctrine of nihilism, which holds that not only does God not exist, but there is no meaning to existence (and there are no religious or moral principles).

Attributing nothingness to the world also acknowledges the limits of our intellectual understanding of God and underscores the need for the entire endeavor of mysticism. As Scholem explains, "Essentially, this nothingness is the barrier confronting the human intellectual faculty when it reaches the limits of capacity. In other words, it is a subjective statement affirming that there is a realm which no created being can intellectually comprehend, and which, therefore, can only be defined as 'nothingness.'"

THE OTHER *SEFIROT*

As for the other spheres, each touches on a different attribute of God, such as wisdom, understanding, love or greatness, power or judgment, beauty or compassion, endurance, splendor, and foundation. They also exist in structural pairs, to balance one another out (e.g., judgment and compassion). The lowest sefirah, *Malkhut*—the one closest to a pshat perception of the world—is God's kingdom, often referred to in the *Zohar* as the Congregation of Israel. For nonmystics, Malkhut is the world we see around us, and for mystics, it exists in and through God. It is also sometimes called *Shekhinah,* God's presence. In some descriptions, each of the ten sefirot is linked to a letter in the Torah; in others, to different biblical characters; and in still others, to parts of the body.

Clearly there are paradoxes in the doctrine of the sefirot, such as the fact that while God is beyond human comprehension, humans are able to understand aspects of God; or that even though God is one, there are seemingly separate components to God. But the Kabbalists were unique in attempting to explain God's various energies or forces, the way God ebbs and flows within the world while simultaneously being omnipresent.

Souls and Reincarnation

Perhaps unsurprisingly, the Kabbalists also wrote about the relationship between the human soul and God.

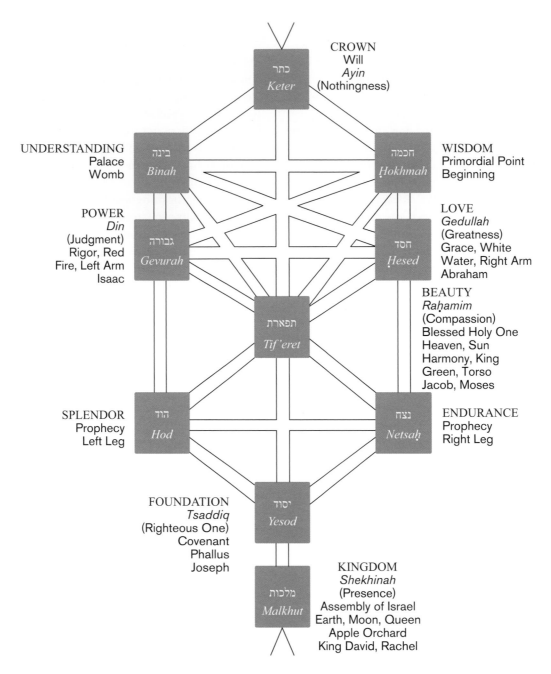

CROWN
Will
Ayin
(Nothingness)

כתר
Keter

UNDERSTANDING
Palace
Womb

בינה
Binah

WISDOM
Primordial Point
Beginning

חכמה
Ḥokhmah

POWER
Din
(Judgment)
Rigor, Red
Fire, Left Arm
Isaac

גבורה
Gevurah

LOVE
Gedullah
(Greatness)
Grace, White
Water, Right Arm
Abraham

חסד
Ḥesed

BEAUTY
Raḥamim
(Compassion)
Blessed Holy One
Heaven, Sun
Harmony, King
Green, Torso
Jacob, Moses

תפארת
Tif'eret

SPLENDOR
Prophecy
Left Leg

הוד
Hod

ENDURANCE
Prophecy
Right Leg

נצח
Netsaḥ

FOUNDATION
Tsaddiq
(Righteous One)
Covenant
Phallus
Joseph

יסוד
Yesod

KINGDOM
Shekhinah
(Presence)
Assembly of Israel
Earth, Moon, Queen
Apple Orchard
King David, Rachel

מלכות
Malkhut

FIGURE 6.3. The ten *sefirot*.

Going back to the Torah, we find three Hebrew words connected to the metaphysical nature of a soul: *nefesh, ruaḥ,* and *neshamah.* The latter two terms are found in Genesis in relation to the creation of humans, whereas the word *nefesh* is used to describe an animal's soul. These three Hebrew terms have been translated in various English versions of the Bible as breath, life, spirit, and rushing-spirit. In the Prophets and Writings, they become relatively interchangeable. In general, however, it seems the Bible's approach to humans is that they

are made up of both a body and a soul. The Talmud and Midrash continue this thread. Rachel Elior contends that Greek notions of the soul's ability to exist irrespective of the body—especially after the body dies—entered Jewish texts during the Talmudic period as well.

During the medieval era, Jewish mystics added new layers to this centuries-old discussion. In one description, the development of a human soul is said to go through three stages: intercourse (when the soul comes into being), pregnancy (when the soul gestates), and birth (when the soul is infused in a body). This explanation, as well as others from this time, is based in the belief that God is the source of all human souls, and human souls reflect the image of God. Some also approached the human soul as a reflection of the ten sefirot. In this account, human attempts to reunite with God are efforts to re-fuse one's soul with the Soul of all Souls, the creator of the universe.

The *Zohar* picks up on the Talmudic tradition that *nefesh, ruaḥ,* and *neshamah* are all words for a human soul, adding that they are different components of the same thing, arranged hierarchically. The *Zohar* continues by explaining the role of transmigration of the soul, today commonly called reincarnation or *gilgul*. According to the *Zohar,* the human soul cannot return to God until it has fully evolved. If one's body dies before reaching this state, one's soul transmigrates into a new body. Such is the process until the soul achieves its ultimate goal.

The Larger Context: Medieval Jewish Philosophers

Historically, Kabbalists have often been described in scholarship as having been generally at odds with other Jews, specifically those we loosely refer to as philosophers (as they were many other things). (The dominant academic perspective is now that these schools were much more integrative than oppositional.) One of the tensions between these two groups seems to have been based on philosophers' misunderstandings of mystical thought. Although the ten sefirot describe aspects of God, the Kabbalists were clear that there was only a single God. Some philosophers from this period, however, wrote that the sefirot implied polytheism, the belief in multiple gods.

Other points of discord, however, were due to a real divergence in perspective. For instance, whereas some Kabbalists believed human beings could affect God, for philosophers such as Maimonides (chapter 5), this was a blasphemous idea. Maimonides said that God did not *care* one way or another whether Jews observed the mitzvot as God does not have human feelings. Orienting toward God in anthropomorphic terms, he argued, was a superficial way to understand the creator of the universe. (What may have been lost on those who critiqued this perspective is that Kabbalists generally agreed with this point of view, commonly writing that because God was well beyond human comprehension God could not accurately be described as having human emotions.)

Yet as we have seen, on certain doctrines they came together in agreement. Some in both camps felt that Jewish philosophy and mysticism were not oppositional

schools of thought but rather complementary. For example, many Kabbalists and philosophers approached God through the lens of monism (chapter 2), maintaining that God exists beyond human comprehension and is completely dissimilar from humans, without a form or body.

Maimonides, for one, believed that the most advanced way to worship God was through rational and logical means, with one's intellect. In his own words: "Know that the description of God . . . by means of negations is the correct description, a description that is not affected by an indulgence in facile language and does not imply any deficiency with respect to God. . . . You come nearer to the apprehension of [God] . . . with every increase in the negations."

Although they didn't feel Maimonides's writings were as important as, for example, the *Zohar,* some mystics felt that Maimonides's most famous text, *The Guide for the Perplexed,* could serve as a doorway into Jewish mysticism, and some even thought of it as a Kabbalistic text.

Some reputable halakhic authorities accepted by masses of Spanish Jews integrated Kabbalistic ideas into their thinking. The foremost example is the Ramban (Moshe ben Nahman or Nahmonides), who worked mystical ideas into his commentary on the Bible. Such individuals helped mystical thought gain a greater acceptance and respect among thirteenth-century Spanish Jews. Similarly, in the sixteenth century, farther east, Joseph Karo, who wrote one of the most important books on halakhah in Jewish history, the *Shulḥan Arukh,* was a mystic who incorporated mystical thought into his writing (see chapter 5).

Sixteenth-Century Safed and Isaac Luria

Following the expulsion of Jews from Spain and Portugal in the fifteenth century (see chapters 1 and 7), some Jews moved east, eventually settling in Ottoman-controlled Palestine. By the sixteenth century, perhaps due to improved treatment Jews received from these Muslim rulers (in contrast to Christian rulers), approximately ten thousand Jews were living in Palestine. One of the cities with the highest populations of Jews was Safed. Located in the Galilean mountains, Safed was much cooler than other places in the Middle East, even during the hot summer months. For this and a number of other possible reasons—including the *Zohar's* claim that the messiah would arrive in this city before any other—Safed became a center of sixteenth-century Jewish mystical learning, attracting thinkers who built upon Kabbalistic texts from centuries prior.

During this era Jewish mysticism was popularized, a process that helped give birth to the Hasidic movement of the eighteenth century and continues to play a significant role today. Although Jewish mystical thought began to reach the masses during the medieval period with, for example, the Ramban's explanation that even ordinary people could attain oneness with God, as described in the *Zohar,* for a number of reasons it did not take hold until the sixteenth century and thereafter.

One popular practice that emerged at this time was the veneration of saints (described in beginning of chapter). According to common legend, a number of Talmudic sages are buried in and around Safed, including on Mount Meron, where the original alleged author of the *Zohar,* Shimon Bar Yochai, may himself be buried. Some sixteenth-century mystics spent time near the graves of such figures, hoping to have metaphysical experiences. Ascetic practices—such as lengthy fasts, self-flagellation, extensive meditation, and wearing sackcloth or rolling naked in the snow—also gained momentum during this period. Some may have engaged in such practices as a self-imposed penance for becoming a Converso, a Jew in Spain or Portugal who pretended to convert to Catholicism while continuing to practice Judaism in secret (see chapters 1 and 7).

But halakhah ensured that mystical ascetics could not become maximally austere. Among other mitzvot are the biblical directives to marry (and procreate) and celebrate Shabbat, the Jewish Sabbath. Many Safed mystics, indeed, focused more on celebrating and enjoying ritual rather than engaging in ascetic actions. Some, of course, embraced both ascetic actions and joyous approaches to halakhic observance, all perceived as ways to properly worship God.

One of the most important figures from this time and place was Isaac Luria, also known as *Ha-Ari,* The Lion, who made his way to Safed from his birthplace, Jerusalem, via Egypt. Before arriving in Safed, Luria had been a rabbi and self-identified mystic, as well as a businessman; like the rabbis of the Talmud, he was not a paid rabbi in the contemporary sense, but had other "day jobs." Shortly after Luria moved to Safed, one of the giants of his day, Moses Cordovero, died; this created a leadership vacuum, which he quickly filled. (There were a number of major mystical teachers during this time aside from Luria, all of whom built their ideas upon texts such as the *Zohar.*)

Although Luria was only in Safed for less than three years before he died (at the age of thirty-eight), he had a number of disciples, ten or so at any given time. In contrast to the Spanish Kabbalists or the eighteenth- and nineteenth-century Hasids, a small number of these students were women, some of whom are said to have had visions of spirits and angels, like their male counterparts. After Luria died, Haim Vital, Luria's most famous student, moved to Damascus, where he continued his teacher's traditions.

For Luria, the most important mystical text was the *Zohar,* which, among other things, teaches that humans play a role in the transformation of the world, helping God to reconnect with Godself. By some accounts, Luria took this idea to a new level. He and his devotees understood themselves to be a microcosm of the universe. As such, they felt an urgent responsibility to help heal the world, including through the observance of mitzvot.

In fact, one of the reasons Lurianic understandings of mysticism spread may have been that he and his devotees were explicitly committed to halakhic observance. Acts of charity and Torah study were among the more important practices of Luria's group, and all of the biblical directives were adhered to strictly, as was the study of halakhah itself. In addition, Luria is credited with creating new rituals, including many linked to Shabbat, and the Lurianic mystics considered all such rituals to have cosmic consequences. They believed that each action they completed—every mitzvah observed—played a role in the world's healing of itself, thereby moving creation toward redemption.

Luria also added a new and influential component to mystical understandings of the creation of the world. Inverting an idea found in the Talmud and early midrashim and building upon the *Zohar*'s discussion of the creation of the world through a divinely sacred spark, Luria proclaimed that God birthed the world through an act called *tzimtzum,* in which God contracted or withdrew into Godself, thereby creating a space for the world to emerge. Once God created this space—created, in other words, this absence of God wherein God could generate a new world—God sent vessels into the space that were supposed to contain God's light.

This leads to a complementary Lurianic idea, the "Breaking of the Vessels." Put simply, God's light was too powerful for the vessels, and they shattered, sending both the broken pieces and the light all over the newly created world. God needs humans' help to release the light now hidden in our world, thereby helping re-form and mend the vessels, a process known as *tikkun olam,* or healing the world. Another way to understand this concept is that even the smallest act of righteousness plays a role in transforming the world toward its potential.

Everything we do is therefore important and has macrocosmic repercussions. This is a radical concept: God needs humans in order to perfect Godself.

Another act of major importance in this process, says Luria, is prayer. Through prayer, humans can ascend into sefirot beyond the Shekhinah. Among the new ritual practices Luria added to the halakhic canon was habitually meditating privately, sometimes while invoking God's various names. Luria also presented a detailed system related to the role one's intention, or *kavannah*, plays in this process.

Luria and his disciples also attempted to commune with the souls of deceased tzadikim at their graves. Not surprisingly, Shimon Bar Yochai's grave outside Safed was one they visited often. Such practices were interwoven with earlier doctrinal beliefs in reincarnation, or *gilgul*. Luria believed that through reincarnation, souls have multiple opportunities to assist in releasing the world's sparks. Only when one fulfills the mitzvot in their entirety is one released from this process. (Or for non-Jews, as they, too, have a role to play in healing the world, when one follows the "Seven Mitzvot of the Sons of Noah," rather than the 613 biblical directives.) If one commits sinful acts, one's soul potentially transmigrates into a lower form of animal, or it might even descend into a realm most easily explained as akin to hell.

In many ways, the Safed mystics paid more attention to the future than their medieval Spanish Kabbalist predecessors. In particular, they focused on the roles humans can play in bringing about the messianic age. This helps explain the resurgence of the messianic belief over the next few centuries (chapter 4). Some of Luria's predecessors, such as Isaac Abarbanel, turned to the future immediately following the mass expulsion of Jews from the Iberian Peninsula, even explaining the expulsions of the 1490s in terms of messianic doctrine. Although belief in a messiah is not explicitly linked to mysticism, it didn't take long before the two schools of thought—messianism and mysticism—became intertwined. Indeed, it was only half a century after the Inquisition that Jewish mysticism took on a new life in Safed.

Jewish mystics in the sixteenth century also had a great deal of interaction with Christian mystics, particularly those living in Italy. Some Christians even composed their texts in Hebrew in an effort to integrate the mystical thought of both traditions. The interaction of these two communities may well explain why this century was one of the most creative in the history of Jewish mysticism. Nevertheless, like the *Zohar* before it, elements of Lurianic mysticism were clearly discriminatory against non-Jews, a thread further developed by an early founder of Hasidism, Shneur Zalman. Whether this can be explained away—apologetically or not—as a form of resistance to Christian proselytizers and persecutors is another topic altogether.

Hasidism

As mentioned in chapter 4, when Hasidism emerged in eighteenth-century Russia, it quickly became an influential new movement within the Jewish collective. Although there are different theories as to the relation of this movement with the messianic failure of Sabbatai Tzvi (insofar as he did not herald in the age of redemption), it is clear that from its inception Hasidism embraced Jewish mysticism, including elements that were anti-Sabbatian in nature.

But Hasidism is renowned for a number of other things, some of which built upon previous Jewish practices and ideologies:

- Saint Veneration. Although the veneration of saints goes back at least to the Talmudic era, and sixteenth-century Safed mystics observed this practice, Hasidic Jews more than any other group rapidly popularized this practice. Most often referred to as tzadikim, the rabbinic leaders of each respective Hasidic dynasty are approached by their devotees as if they are the human embodiment of God (fig. 6.4). The preeminent saint, of course, for all Hasids, is the founder of their movement, the Baal Shem Tov. But within a few short generations after Hasidism's birth, a remarkable number of unique leaders of Hasidism emerged, each with a distinct personality.
- Accessibility. Hasidism made Jewish mysticism much more accessible to the masses. For example, Hasidic leaders have habitually translated mystical ideas using the formulation of parables, stories that sound similar to those from the ancient Greek collection of Aesop's Fables.
- Experiencing God Trumps Textual Learning. The Baal Shem Tov famously taught that experiencing, or communioning with, God is more important than studying Jewish texts. As many of the masses were illiterate, this proclamation invited them into the fold. (Luria maintained a similar idea.)
- Popularizing Movement-based Prayer. Hasidism also popularized forms of ecstatic movement in prayer, making such practices available to the masses.

This said, Scholem writes that aside from what the founder of Chabad, Rabbi Shneur Zalman, who was a dis-

FIGURE 6.4. One of the many Hasidic rituals illustrating a community's veneration of their rebbe, or *tzadik,* is called a *tisch.* Literally meaning table, in this practice a rebbe (here, the leader of the Belzer Hasids, Rabbi Yissachar Dov Rokeach, seated at the head of the table during the holiday Purim) is surrounded by his male devotees, who sing joyous songs in an effort to honor and celebrate him. During a Friday-night *tisch* it is common for the rebbe to eat his dinner during this time; some consider it praiseworthy to eat his crumbs.

ciple of a disciple of the Baal Shem Tov, contributed (special topic 6.4), Hasidism produced very little new mystical thought. Other scholars, such as Moshe Idel, disagree, noting that although Hasidism built many of its mystical notions upon those that preceded it—in particular Lurianic mysticism—it also added new understandings to the larger canon of mystical thought.

The Hasidic movement, of course, had its detractors, both *Mitnagdim* (Opponents), traditionalists whom we might retroactively call non-Hasidic Orthodox Jews, and *Maskilim* (Enlightened ones), Jews who embraced many of the "nonreligious" ideas and texts that had begun to take hold in the larger non-Jewish milieu at this time (see chapter 8). Some of the critiques of Hasidic practices charged them with disobedience with regard to halakhah and the study of Torah, despite evidence to the contrary. Some Mitnagdim, such as the eighteenth-century Rabbi Elijah of Vilna (better known as the Vilna Gaon, or Genius of Vilna), were Jewish mystics who studied the *Zohar.* During the eighteenth and nineteenth centuries, mysticism was not limited to Hasidism whatsoever.

Israel ben Eliezer, also called the Baal Shem Tov [lit., Master of the Good Name], was born at the end of the

seventeenth century in Międzybórz, a small town in what is today called Poland. (This is one reason why the Hasidic movement has almost exclusively shaped Ashkenazi Jews; see special topic 6.5.) Much about the Baal Shem Tov has been shrouded in Hasidic legend, and, according to scholar Louis Jacobs, founder of Masorti Judaism in the United Kingdom (see chapter 8), during his lifetime in Eastern Europe there were a number of charismatic leaders, of whom he was only one. However, says Jacobs, the Baal Shem Tov's "teachings and way of life so influenced like-minded followers that the other groups eventually vanished from the scene."

Aside from the Baal Shem Tov and Shneur Zalman, perhaps the most important Hasidic figure in terms of mysticism was Rabbi Nahman of Bratslav, the Baal Shem Tov's great-grandson. Born and raised in the Ukraine, Nahman was also rare among Hasidic teachers in that some of his greatest teachings resemble what might be called "fairy tales" today; these texts, however, are thought by Bratslav Hasids to be deeply mystical. The Bratslav Hasids are unique among their fellow Hasids in that after Nahman died (in 1810), they did not appoint a successor. Thus, for over two centuries, this community, sometimes referred to as "dead *Hasidim,*" have not had a liv-

Hasidic rabbis have added more layers of understanding of Judaism's sacred texts (i.e., see fig. 2.4), as shown in the following passage about the Cain and Abel narrative. Here, Shneur Zalman, the first rebbe of the Lubavitch sect of Hasidic Jews, builds his understanding of Cain and Abel upon what has been written in other important Jewish texts, including, of course, the Zohar and the Torah:

> The interaction between Moses and his father-in-law, Jethro, begs for explanation. Why does Moses bow to Jethro, the priest of Midian? And why does he show such affection for him, kissing him, etc.? The answer is that Jethro's soul transcends that of Moses. It is written in *Likutei Torah* [written by Isaac Luria] that the soul of Jethro stems from the realm of Cain, while Moses stems from Abel [Zohar 1:28b]. . . .

> The realm of Cain is much loftier than that of Abel. As it is written in *Shaar Hagilgulim* [also written by Luria] . . . all souls of the realm of Cain are extremely lofty souls. Thus Moses, who is of the realm of Abel, bows to Jethro.

Content aside (like the Zohar passage on Cain and Abel in special topic 6.3, this text is not very accessible), not only does this nineteenth-century Hasidic rabbi integrate texts written by the sixteenth-century mystic Isaac Luria, but in the continuation of this passage (see accompanying note, found online) he also integrates mystical understandings of the Cain and Abel narrative from the Zohar, which liken each brother to one of the ten sefirot, and ritual practices performed by the Baal Shem Tov, including how the founder of Hasidism wore his prayer shawl.

Like so many cultural institutions, Hasidism has taken many forms since its birth. One of the more notable permutations has been the emergence of a Hasidic sect (otherwise a through-and-through Ashkenazi phenomenon) among non-Ashkenazi Jews—specifically, a community largely made up of Moroccan Jewish Israelis that practices a form of Hasidism referred to by one scholar, quite logically, as "Moroccan Hasidism."

In short, during the twentieth century a Hasidic rabbi (who was Ashkenazi) named a Moroccan Jew his successor—thus birthing a new, non-Ashkenazi lineage of Hasidism. Though they are few in number (estimates number them at no more than a few hundred devotees), the emergence of this strand of Hasidism is notable, especially in light of tensions between Moroc-can Jews and Ashkenazi Jews in Israel that go back decades (see chapters 1 and 10). That said, not all of this small group's members are of Moroccan descent; some identify straightforwardly as Ashkenazi.

One of the group's most important rituals is an annual pilgrimage to the Israeli grave of the biblical prophet Habakkuk, located in the Galilee, a practice they refer to, like other Moroccan pilgrimages, as a hillula. A number of formalities performed at this hillula are common to Hasidic sects, such as the observance of a tisch (fig. 6.4). The ritual fusion of Ashkenazi and non-Ashkenazi Hasidism is also evident in the biannual pilgrimages made to the grave of Shimon Bar Yochai, on Mount Meron (also in the Galilee), a customary practice of a number of other Jewish communities.

ing leader, but have continued to communicate with him via prayer and meditation. In fact, even though the cemetery he was buried in was destroyed during the twentieth century, his devotees continue to make pilgrimages there today. Nahman's devotees are also known today for their proselytizing activities in Israel, as well as for dancing fervently in public.

Mysticism and Prayer

For many Jews, mystics or otherwise, one of the many ways to reunite with God is through prayer. But what does "prayer" mean exactly? For the medieval Kabbalists and their successors, the primary meaning of prayer was radically different from a dominant norm of the rabbinic period (at least among the Talmudic rabbis), animal sacrifice. For instance, many mystics believed that the observance of mitzvot, including the directive to pray, meant not only that people could ascend to God, but also that they might affect God in turn, an idea most medieval Jewish philosophers considered heretical.

As for the act of prayer itself, if we define prayer (*tefilah* in Hebrew; the reflexive verb form, *lehitpallel*, means to judge oneself) as a devotional act of gratitude toward, praise for, or a request of God, Jewish mystics added (or perhaps enhanced) rituals best described as meditative, ones in which thoughts are focused on the metaphysical aspects of God in a controlled manner. Through meditation, mystics have aimed either to remove thoughts from their mind entirely or to ensure that they are thinking only about God. In this sense, meditative prayer looks to God from within.

For the most part, Jewish mystics remained fully committed to dominant Jewish rituals. This applied to prayers as well as other aspects of halakhah. Although by the tenth century the text of prayer books was somewhat fixed, mystics continued to add new prayers. (Prayer books were not standardized until much later because printing in Hebrew did not become commonplace until, at the earliest, the late fifteenth century.) In addition, sometimes mystics would recite a particular prayer with such devotion and contemplation that what took a few minutes for a nonmystic might take a mystic a few hours to recite, a tradition found as far back as the Talmud. In this sense, although largely unaware, many Jews—even those in the twenty-first century—engage in what we could call Jewish mystical practices when they pray (see "Jewish Mysticism Mainstreamed," below).

Mysticism and Evil

Jewish mysticism focuses on the concepts of good and evil more than other Jewish textual genres. To contextualize mystical approaches to this issue, we can look to the ways good and evil are first introduced in the Torah, in the Garden of Eden, specifically in relation to the Tree of Knowledge of Good and Evil. It is not clear whether evil exists as a part of God's creation at large or within human beings specifically as connected to free will; texts from the rabbinic period present a range of answers to this important question. Later in the Bible, in Isaiah 45:7, well after the narrative of Adam and Eve, we are told that God created evil.

But nowhere is there any discussion affirming that evil is controlled by an equally powerful entity that exists apart from God (such as Satan). In general, the Bible explains evil as a manifestation of particular types of behavior. In other words, if one performs God's biblical directives, the mitzvot, one is doing good; if not, one is doing evil. The pshat of the Bible indicates that one is rewarded for doing good and punished for doing evil. Not only is this stated explicitly a number of times in the Torah, but examples also abound of individuals rewarded for good deeds and punished for evil ones.

During the rabbinic period, the Talmud introduced the term *yetzer hara,* the idea that there exists in all humans an inclination to act in evil ways. But once again, this is not something that exists outside God or even humans. Rather, it lies within each person and can be overcome. Further, it has the potential to play a positive role in people's lives. The rabbis explained that yetzer hara also drives one's passion, creativity, and ambition; without it, we wouldn't be able to engage in business, build homes, marry, or have children. Channeled appropriately, it can help in the performance of certain mitzvot.

Other texts from the rabbinic period further entangle the concept of reward and punishment with good and evil. The rabbis explained that negative events, such as the destruction of the Temple, happened to the Jewish community because Jews were not properly observing God's laws. Unjust punishments, such as a righteous person inflicted with a hideous disease, were commonly understood as something that would be sorted out in the world to come, where such an individual would be rewarded. (Alternatively, unjust punishments might be explained as just treatment for some sort of bad behavior performed in secret or as something beyond human comprehension.)

During the medieval period there were, of course, additional points of view. The philosopher Maimonides, for instance, compared one's good inclination, *yetzer hatov,* with reason and intellect, and yetzer hara with imagination. But medieval mystics commonly focused more of their thought on good and evil than did nonmystics. Not surprisingly, they usually explained these forces in cosmic terms.

For some Kabbalists, what seems to be evil to humans is not so in actuality, a strand of thought that emerged in the rabbinic period. According to Scholem, some Kabbalistic texts maintain that evil exists apart from sinful acts, whereas others clearly say that evil only arises due to sinful acts. For example, both *Sefer ha-Bahir* and texts attributed to Isaac the Blind, a Kabbalist from the medieval era, explain that when the sefirah of understanding was birthed out of judgment, destructive forces also appeared.

The *Zohar* takes a similar approach, insofar as it understands evil to be an existing reality, not merely an illusion. In examining the origins of evil, the text suggests a number of possibilities: evil is akin to the "leftovers" from previous worlds God had already created and destroyed; it came about as a by-product of creation, a metaphysical form of waste; it emerges due to a disequilibrium among the sefirot (e.g., when judgment is not counterbalanced by other sefirot); it was introduced to the world when Adam ate from the Tree of Knowledge of Good and Evil; it is a result of humans focusing too much on themselves, which creates false realities.

As for how to deal with evil, the *Zohar* offers a number of remedies, commonly also clarifying that it is humans' responsibility to separate evil from good. One way to do this is by engaging in moral acts, such as the mitzvot, which have the potential to transform evil into good. Another is to avoid evil, even though it is an element of existence.

Luria took considerations of evil to another level, focusing on the role of human agency in ridding the world of evil altogether. He also explained the connection between evil, creation, and the "Breaking of the Vessels." The idea that humans are born into a world with evil, found in both Kabbalah and later forms of Jewish mystical thought, is largely contrary to the rabbinic period's idea of yetzer hara. Many Hasidic texts continued Lurianic ideas. Luria and earlier Kabbalists also wrote about ideas such as hell, Satan, demons, and angels.

Mysticism, Gender, and Sexuality

Jewish mysticism, according to Scholem, "is a masculine doctrine, made for men by men." In contrast to Islamic mysticism and Christian mysticism, there are almost no documented female Jewish mystics. Aside from some of Luria's and Vital's students, as well as a number of saints in Morocco, women have been excluded from Jewish mystical communities, and there are only a handful of Jewish mystical texts attributed to women.

Among these may be a group of texts from the seventeenth through nineteenth centuries, a time when some Jewish women had learned to read Yiddish and studied Yiddish translations of Lurianic ideas. This opened a short-lived entrance of women into, to use a phrase of scholar Lawrence Kushner's, the Jewish mystical imagination. One prayer in particular, called *Thkine Imrei Shifre,* contains explicit Kabbalistic imagery, language clearly taken from the *Zohar.* Though we don't know the author, the publisher, or when precisely it was written,

scholar Chava Weissler, an expert in this area, argues convincingly that the prayer was written by a woman (or multiple women), even though the text also makes the case that the only way a woman can access Jewish mystical thought in full is by becoming, or pretending to be, male.

As for feminine representations within Jewish mystical thought, it is notable that the ten realms of God in *Sefer ha-Bahir* are gendered, each sefirah being labeled either male or female. In addition to the sexualized element of the sefirot, such as the explicitly phallic nature of *Yisod,* the *Zohar* uses terms such as conception and procreation, bride and bridegroom, king and queen. Only when male and female sefirot come together, through intercourse, are new sefirot able to be born. (When humans have sexual intercourse, thus, they are reflecting the birthing of the cosmos itself.) At one point the *Zohar* even explains that when Moses encountered God, the physical nature of their meeting was a form of sexual intercourse (i.e., with God as the Shekhinah).

Perhaps the most important of the female sefirot is the tenth sefirah, the Shekhinah. She is symbolized by such things as the moon, the sea, the Temple, and the Community of Israel. She is passive, in her capacity as a receptacle, and is the aspect of God to which Kabbalists devote themselves. One possible reason the earthly sefirah of God—the Shekhinah—is female lies in homophobia; i.e., males may have been more comfortable publicly discussing their love for a female God than a male one.

Green suggests that this idea may have been reappropriated from Christianity, in terms of the Virgin Mary. But in contrast to Mary's chastity, the Jewish description of the female aspect of God is quite erotic. Indeed, says Green, the metaphor of the marriage of the Shekhinah and her partner, sometimes described as Israel, was actually a veiled critique of the Christian doctrine of monasticism.

Daniel Matt notes that the transmitters of the Shekhinah were probably not proto-feminists. In fact, he says, some contemporary feminists are suspicious of the feminized elements of God found in Jewish mysticism, whether because the Shekhinah is understood as the passive receptacle of God's masculinity or simply because God exists beyond and above gender. Matt adds, "*Shekhinah* represents a partial, yet significant corrective to patriarchal religion. God's maleness was no Jewish invention. The transition from Goddess to God, from dominant female deities to dominant male deities, occurred long before the composition of the earliest books of the Bible. . . . The Goddess may have been expunged from the official religion of biblical and rabbinic Judaism, but She reemerges as *Shekhinah* in Kabbalah."

Although not claiming that pre-Hebrew and pre-Israelite forms of worship were centered on a female God (i.e., a Goddess), Matt underscores the importance of the *Zohar's* focus on the feminine. "She is a leading character in the masterpiece of Kabbalah, the *Zohar,* which devotes more space to Her than to any other *sefirah.* She fascinated the *Zohar's* male composer, Moses ben Shem Tov de León, who realized something radically obvious: God cannot be adequately described in solely masculine terms. Today, seven hundred years later, de León's theological critique is still widely unheeded."

Jewish Mysticism Mainstreamed

Jewish mystical ideas have entered the non-Jewish mainstream in some startling ways. For instance, in seventeenth-century England, after the massive fire in London, the city was rebuilt based on the schema of the sefirot. In the United States, the Kabbalah Centre, headquartered in Los Angeles, has influenced a number of important cultural icons, including Madonna (see chapter 11). It should come as no surprise then that over time components of Jewish mysticism have become integrated into dominant forms of Judaism as well. Part of what began as an esoteric strain of Judaism, limited to an elite few, worked its way into the practices of Jews worldwide.

This process may have begun in sixteenth-century Safed, when the mystics focused their energy on mainstreaming mystical thought within nonmystical communities. As scholar R.J.Z. Werblowsky notes, "The social habits and values of the Safed *Kabbalists* helped to integrate the individual mystic in an ideal, normative community which gave him spiritual security and support, and which provided him with a fund of energy and discipline on which he could constantly draw." Fine adds: "There is reason to believe that the rules and rites that these groups practiced were intended, at least in part, to encourage members of the wider community in Safed and even beyond to engage in similar pietistic activities."

The mainstream idea of tikkun olam, loosely understood as social justice activism, is directly linked to the Lurianic idea of the "Breaking of the Vessels" and is a defining value of twentieth- and twenty-first-century Judaism. A number of rituals also owe their beginnings to Jewish mystics. For example, in houses of mourning it is common to study a Jewish text, such as a mishnah, in honor of the deceased person; on the holiday Shavuot, many communities have a late-night or even all-night study session; many verbal forms of prayer use an order based on practices first developed in Safed; and countless contemporary graveside rituals and forms of meditation were originated by Jewish mystics.

In addition, many prayers written by Jewish mystics are found in prayer books in Reform, Conservative, and Orthodox communities among other denominations (in particular, a prayer recited regularly on Friday nights to welcome the Sabbath Queen, called *Licha Dodi,* part of a Kabbalistic service referred to as *Kabbalat Shabbat*). One could argue that many prayer rituals—especially those framed as meditative—are mystical in origin and intent, ways everyday Jews attempt to communicate with God in a realm beyond words.

Perhaps the most important addition the Jewish mystics made to the larger Jewish canon lies in rituals connected to Shabbat. The Safed mystics saw Shabbat as a way to pivot from the mundane to the sacred, from exile to the metaphorical Land of Israel. Consequently, on Shabbat one's home is transformed into an otherworldly realm in preparation to receive the Shekhinah. One's body, too, becomes a reflection of cosmic shifts related to Shabbat, with practices related to cutting one's nails, bathing, and putting on special clothing. Even the practice of eating three meals on Shabbat goes back to Safed.

The imprint that Jewish mysticism has left on Judaism is perhaps best explained by scholar Adin Steinsaltz: "The truth is that Kabbala permeates every aspect of Judaism, and the 'esoteric wisdom' has been a basic ingredient of scripture, ritual, and prayer. . . . The mystical contents of Kabbala are not necessarily restricted to *sefirot* and angels and 'other-wordly' forces; they are also in the familiar constituents and motions of the body, they are in the bible and the Talmud, they are in all the many vehicles of the Torah."

Whether Jews are even aware, Jewish mysticisms have played, and will continue to play, a fundamental role in Jewish identities, perhaps for all time.

Cultures

Contents

Key Ideas

• Jews have created and recreated Jewish cultures and subcultures historically, a phenomenon that has, no doubt, played a role in this community's long-standing survival and led to its intensely diverse nature. Though some Jewish subcommunities have attempted to isolate themselves from dominant non-Jewish cultures, and others have chosen to assimilate into said non-Jewish cultures (some to the point of no longer identifying as Jews), substantial numbers of Jews have opted for integrationist practices whereby Jewish and non-Jewish cultures have cross-fertilized.

- Although there are dominant Jewish cultures, especially among the 80 percent of Jews worldwide who live in the United States and the State of Israel, there are multiple Jewish subgroups. For example, whether speaking about Indian Jews, Iraqi Jews, or Yemenite Jews, each one of these Jewish subcommunities has a number of subdivisions, such that every Jewish subgroup is heterogeneous in its own right.
- Jewish subcommunities often have their own dominant narratives that have not extended to the entire Jewish community.

An American Jew Dreaming of a White Christmas

As a little boy growing up in the United States, I loved Christmas. Although we were Jewish, every few years my brother and I traveled to Chapel Hill, North Carolina, with my mother to see my maternal grandparents, where we celebrated Christmas together. Part of my childhood self knew Santa Claus wasn't real. Nonetheless during these times, each Christmas Eve we set out cookies and milk for the white-haired, white-bearded, roly-poly old man in a red suit, and each Christmas morning, as soon as we opened our eyes, we were downstairs in a flash, snatching our red felt stockings down from above the fireplace.

We knew there would be a tangerine or two, as well as peanuts (unshelled, of course) inside; for us, mere stocking stuffers, but actually a historical remnant of times when such goodies were rare and appreciated. There were also small gifts hidden in the oversized sock, such as face paint or, one year, a wooden popgun, à la Peter and the Wolf.

The rule was that we couldn't open any of the wrapped presents, which seductively waited for us underneath the decorated tree, until everyone in the house was awake. Only after the grown-ups had some breakfast were we allowed to commence with the ravaging of paper and cardboard boxes. This way we could all open our gifts together, making it a family ritual with enhanced meaning.

As mentioned in chapter 5, my mother converted to Judaism. So my maternal grandparents were not Jewish. Even though an infinitesimal number of my friends in my East Coast Jewish parochial school and summer overnight camp were raised in similar situations, I didn't think it was strange. Perhaps because no one ever explicitly told me that I wasn't as Jewish as another child based on the fact that not everyone in my family was Jewish, it wasn't until I was older that I gained a deeper appreciation of how this family dynamic both challenged and deepened my social identities.

FIGURE 7.1. First airing in 1965, *A Charlie Brown Christmas* was a standard for many kids—Christian and non-Christian alike—who grew up in the United States from the latter half of the sixties through the turn of the century. One of the most famous scenes is Linus's explanation of the "true meaning of Christmas," in which he quotes a passage from the gospel of Luke.

Growing up, my Jewishness was never in doubt. It defined me internally and it shaped countless aspects of my everyday life. Yet even if my maternal grandparents hadn't been culturally Christian, and even if they hadn't celebrated Christmas, as a child of the seventies and eighties I grew up looking forward to the annual television showings of *Frosty the Snowman; Rudolph, the Red-Nosed Reindeer; A Charlie Brown Christmas* (fig. 7.1); and the like. Like other Americans, I grew up knowing the words to numerous Christmas songs, not because anyone had formally taught them to me, but simply because the United States is so imbued with Christian culture. Come December—or these days, as early as the day after Thanksgiving—one would be hard pressed not to proverbially inhale Christmas when out in public.

Like many other Americans, neither my Grammie nor Grampie was a member of a church, nor did they even distantly espouse devotion to a particular Christian ideology. There were no crosses in their house, or religious symbols of any kind. When we marked Christmas, we weren't performing a belief in Jesus Christ. For that matter, we weren't even focusing on Jesus's birth. Their Christmas decorations consisted of a few green fir wreaths, red stockings above the fireplace, and a small pine tree dressed in multicolored bells and other nonspecific holiday ornaments. They had no nativity scene outside their home displaying a baby Jesus. In fact, I can't remember such religious symbols in their entire neighborhood.

Rather, all of us experienced this ritual as something that was culturally American. Even if my mom had attended Christmas Midnight Mass every year while growing up (which she hadn't), well before she had converted to Judaism, as a child in the American South she considered going to church to be a social act, not a religious one. My brother and I experienced semi-annual childhood Christmas rituals as fun. If anything, we embraced them as Americans. These visits were about family, presents, and Santa, in that order.

From Jewish American Culture to Worldwide Jewish Cultures

Many American Jews today identify as Jews "ethnically" or "culturally" as opposed to "religiously." Consequently, they experience many communal rituals mainly as social, even those framed as religious. This is one explanation for the sizable number of American Jews—those subsets who identify with more than one tradition (Judaism and Christianity) or whose parents identify in this way—who have Christmas trees or "Hanukkah bushes" in their homes (fig. 7.2).

The latter is a ritual blending of two distinct holidays and dates back in the United States to at least the 1870s. But this hybridization has not been unique to America. Though perhaps nominally different in form, a number of prominent European Jews, such as Theodor Herzl (founder of contemporary political Zionism; chapter 10) and Gershom Scholem (a scholar of mysticism cited in chapter 6), grew up in families that had Christmas trees. In Europe, this was a sign of identifying with the larger non-Jewish collective culturally but not necessarily religiously.

Today, many Jews in the United States and Israel, the two countries where 80 percent of the world's Jews live, reject the notion that Judaism is solely their religion. In fact, widely accepted data collected on the Jewish American community of the last two decades, the 2000–2001 NJPS (National Jewish Population Survey), suggest that about 25 percent of U.S. Jews identify more with a Jewish ethnicity than a Jewish religion, a number that is much higher among younger Jews specifically, according to an October 2013 Pew Center study.

This chapter addresses two large questions: What are some of the ways that Jews have created and re-created distinct cultures and subcultures historically? Given this community's great diversity, to what extent—if any—do its members share a common cultural or ethnic bond? To address these issues, this chapter looks at both familiar

FIGURE 7.2. Hanukkah bushes come in many forms. Often they have six-pointed "Jewish stars" embedded in them (see "Complications: Categories and Contexts" later in chapter). Other times they are decorated with *dreidels* (spinning tops used in a game played on Hanukkah) or Hanukkah menorahs (a candelabra with nine candles, also called a *hanukiah*). Some, like the one here, are more "tree" than "bush."

and lesser-known Jewish communities, with an emphasis on the latter.

Within the past two millennia, a dominant way of understanding the diversity of Jews worldwide has been to group them according to whether they lived in Christian-majority or Muslim-majority societies. This may well be more useful for contextualizing twenty-first-century Jews than any other framework, but such a scheme leaves out the experiences of Jews living in communities prior to the birth of Christianity (first century CE) and Islam (seventh century CE), as well as those living in non-Christian-majority and non-Muslim-majority communities.

With this in mind, this chapter begins by examining Jewish cultural identities in Greco-Roman Palestine, Babylonia, and Persia, the regions closest to the geographical birthplace of the Hebrews and Israelites. Both Babylonia and Persia, encompassed by Iraq and Iran today, eventually became Muslim-majority areas. Thus, there are specific elements of overlap between them and other Jewish communities who have lived in areas that became Muslim-majority, such as Yemenites and Egyptians, who are discussed later on. Significantly, between the twelfth and nineteenth centuries estimates are that as many as 85 to 90 percent of Jews lived in Muslim-majority societies, a phenomenon no longer reflective of today's realities.

Afterward, we look at Jews living in Christian-majority regions, beginning with Ethiopian Jews—whose presence in eastern Africa probably predates the rise of Christianity yet who, probably since the fourth century, have lived under Christian rule—and continuing with the birth of the moniker *Sephardi Jew* (which was also discussed in chapter 1). Finally, the chapter ends with a look at two lesser-known, but no less important, Jewish communities, both living in non-Christian- and non-Muslim-majority regions in Asia—specifically, India and China (the two most populated countries in the world).

Please note that the attention to marginalized Jewish subgroups (and sub-subgroups) should in no way be understood as an attempt to exoticize them, a standard response to groups people do not know much about. Rather, the goal of this chapter is to challenge and reevaluate biases regarding the Jewish "norm," and to shed light on how Jewish culture has continuously developed in relationship with larger non-Jewish communities.

Culture: A Working Definition

Before continuing, we need to consider the definition of the amorphous term *culture*. Scholar David Biale, editor of the three-volume *Cultures of the Jews,* offers the following definition:

> Culture is an elastic term that can be stretched in many directions. . . . One way to define culture is as the manifold expressions—written or oral, visual or textual, material or spiritual—with which human beings represent lived experiences in order to give them meaning. But culture is more than just the literary or aesthetic products of a society. As one witty adage goes, "Culture is how we do things around here." From this point of view, culture is the practice of everyday life. It is what people do, what they *say* about what they do, and, finally, how they understand both of these activities.

Culture, like ethnicity, is also one of the ways we attempt to categorize people's identities, both others and our own. The terms *culture* and *ethnicity* bleed into one another. Each reflects how people perform identities in and through behavior, beliefs, customs, emotions, ideas, language, and values. (To complicate matters, once we bring belief, custom, and meaning into a discussion about culture the lines between religion and culture also become blurred.)

Perhaps above all else, one's culture reflects a larger, shared communal narrative with which one identifies. At times, specifically in regard to minority communities (such as Iraqi Jews or Ethiopian Jews), it also expresses the tension between the dominant narratives of a larger collective and that of a subcommunity. Practically speaking, culture plays out in terms of the clothes one wears, the food one eats, the language one speaks. It permeates one's opinions and thoughts, and even can inform one's take on the purpose of life.

For Jews, there is not, nor has there ever been, a single Jewish culture (or ethnicity), only cultures (or ethnicities). The diversity of Jewish culture is due at least in part to Jews having been a minority for virtually all of recorded history (until the establishment of the State of Israel in 1948). Even if a minority group attempts to isolate itself entirely, which Jews have rarely done of their own accord, a majority group's culture still plays a fundamental role in shaping a minority's identities. Jews have always interacted with non-Jews. Sometimes Jews have taken on the identities, and accompanying culture, assigned to them. Other times their identities have developed in reaction to such forced exchanges. Because Jewish identities have never existed in a vacuum, the cultures of Jews have always been "inseparable from [those] of their Canaanite, Persian, Greek, Roman, Christian, and Muslim neighbors." Similarly, dominant Jewish communal narratives have always been changing.

Culture and Religion

Although many Jews call themselves culturally Jewish, others often say that identifying as a Jew cannot be a statement of one's culture but instead reflects only one's religion: a connection to or belief in the tenets of Judaism. This framing is deeply ingrained in dominant American narratives. There are a number of reasons for this trend, two of which are discussed here (others are explored in chapters 8 and 10).

First, as scholar Melanie Kaye/Kantrowitz argues, approaching Jewish identity as one's religion (or "faith") is common among those living in Christian-dominant countries such as the United States, where almost 80 percent of the population identifies as Christian. This has also been the practice in Europe, where for centuries people were categorized as either Christians or heathens—

with Jews, of course, being grouped within the latter. One reason why many Americans, Jews and non-Jews alike, approach Jewish identities in a similar fashion is that dominant groups often shape common discourse. Further, subordinated groups—in this case, Jews—often accept ideas learned from dominants.

Second, because Christianity is the de facto religious identity of America, it has a monumental influence on American culture. In his important collection of essays *Theology of Culture,* Paul Tillich explains how societies' cultures are infused with "religion." Pop culture alone illustrates this point; for example, Easter and Christmas are part of the lives of characters in American television programs and influence what songs are played on the radio. Moreover, there has never been a president of the United States who was not Christian.

It is not simply happenstance that each year there is an Easter egg hunt outside and a Christmas tree inside the White House. Whether expressed in the American English language or through American symbols, says Tillich, "the Church and [American] culture are within, not alongside, each other." One of the reasons Jews and non-Jews categorize Jewish identity within the context of religion is that Jews have had this identity classification system imposed upon them.

A Cross-Cultural Spectrum

For most of their history, Jews (and proto-Jews such as Hebrews, Israelites, and Judeans) have lived as a minority. Through this process, they have interacted with dominant cultures in multiple ways. On one end of the spectrum are those Jewish communities that have isolated themselves; on the other are those that have assimilated, sometimes to the point of abandoning their Jewish identities completely. Most often, however, Jews have fallen somewhere between the two poles, integrating components of non-Jewish cultures into their own and vice versa.

The isolationist approach is epitomized by ultra-Orthodox Jews who attempt to create a bubble around their community, detaching themselves from everyone else, including non-ultra-Orthodox Jews and sometimes even other subgroups of ultra-Orthodox Jews. Today, most of these communities live in the State of Israel and the United States. The primary reason for isolation is the group's fear that without segregating itself from what it perceives to be the moral decadence of the "outside world," their way of life will be lost. But even isolationists interact with outsiders in minor ways. In the twenty-first century, it is quite difficult for a community to cut itself off from the outside world completely, especially if one wants access to basic amenities such as energy, food, and water.

On the other end of the spectrum are assimilationists, those Jews who—for as long as there have been people who have identified as Jews—have adopted and internalized the customs and attitudes of a dominant non-Jewish culture. Some assimilationists end up leaving the Jewish community altogether; others maintain a Jewish identity but don't instill it in their children; still others straddle the line between their Jewish and non-Jewish identities to various degrees. As an individual, it is possible to both assimilate and maintain one's identities. Often, however, this plays out differently in public and in private; for example, one might conduct oneself outwardly according to the dominant norms of the surrounding culture though internally express an emotional connection to a minority identity or perhaps even enact a "hidden" identity.

Between isolation and assimilation lies integration. In this model, community members attempt to maintain their traditional culture while incorporating aspects of a dominant "other." Such individuals commonly identify with the conventional or mainstream culture in which they live but simultaneously work to have the culture they were raised with be recognized as different and unique. Although such people adopt attitudes and behaviors of the larger culture, they do not necessarily do so at the expense of their own heritage. Whether for the purposes of survival or not, integration means that Jews from Azerbaijan to Zambia, Botswana to Yemen, and China to Wales express aspects of identity that distinguish them from other Jews, most often learned from the non-Jews among whom they live.

Of course, particular rituals or communal practices may be more or less assimilationist or isolationist, rather than wholly lying in one of these categories alone. Whether a group of Jews interacts with a dominant non-Jewish community as isolationists, assimilationists, or integrationists, there is always the potential for cultural interchange. In fact, the primary difference between assimilation and integration for Jews seems to lie merely in the degree of cross-fertilization. This holds true for many other minority populations as well.

Complications: Categories and Contexts

Before continuing, we need to consider some qualifications about categories and contexts. First, just like identity itself, the categories of isolationism, assimilationism, and integrationism are *constructs*. As scholar Max Weinreich once observed, "More often than not, it appears, the distance between Jewish and non-Jewish patterns is created not by a difference in the ingredients proper but rather by the way they are interpreted as elements of the given system." In other words, sorting Jews into these three categories is an interpretive act, as, for that matter, is calling something "Jewish" and something else "non-Jewish." Nonetheless, this framework is helpful because it gives us a starting point.

For our purposes, most important—and perhaps most interesting—are integrationist Jewish cultural practices, which is the focus of this chapter. In what follows, rather than sticking to the categories of "Jew" and "non-Jew," I will attempt to show how cross-fertilization has always been a central component of Jewish identities.

Second, framing cultural practices as "Jewish" or "non-Jewish" presupposes that we can identify cultural practices as such; it assumes we can definitively put a ritual in one specific category only. Many things thought to have originated with group X may in fact have been appropriated —and thus actually have emerged from group Y. One example is the so-called Jewish star, or Star of David. This six-pointed shape is a modern symbol for Jews, but, according to Gershom Scholem (chapter 6), it can only be dated back definitively a few centuries, and there is no evidence that it originated in ancient Israel. A second example is the swastika. Although many Europeans and Americans immediately think of Nazis when they see this symbol, it in fact pre-dated twentieth-century Germany by thousands of years. Moreover, in these other contexts, such as in South Asian Buddhist, Hindu, and Jain communities, it had (and continues to have) positive meanings. In short, everything is contextual, and usually—especially when the origins lie in the ancient past—culturally dense, embodied with multiple meanings.

Third, it is important to point out that each Jewish subgroup encompasses multiple subfactions. As an example, consider the following various genres and subgenres of music: e.g., within Jazz one can identify Blues-Jazz vs. Swing-Jazz vs. Bebop-Jazz vs. Soul-Jazz vs. Post-Bebop-Jazz vs. Psychedelic-Jazz vs. Acid-Jazz vs. Jazz-Funk based on noteworthy characteristics. The same is true of humans. Whether talking about Ashkenazi Jews, Babylonian Jews, or Indian Jews, each subgroup has multiple subdivisions within it.

"Like Everyone Else, Only More So"

As the biblical prophets foretold, Jews were scattered from the Land of Israel to the "four corners of the earth."

Jews currently live in 70 percent of the world's almost two hundred countries. Since their community of fifteen million comprises only about 0.2 percent of the earth's population, it is remarkable that they are as dispersed as they are. Consequently, Jewish culture can be said to be as varied as the number of cultures there are in the entire world. This has perhaps led to the adage "Jews are like everyone else, only more so." Although this is a simplification, and might even imply a certain anti-Jewishness by employing the stereotype of Jews' crafty and shape-shifting nature, there is some truth to the comment.

In most twenty-first century societies, Jews do not live separately from non-Jews. In this way, they are indeed "like everyone else." At the same time, paradoxically, many maintain distinct cultural connections, identifying with both Jewish and non-Jewish communities simultaneously. As scholar Shaye Cohen said in regard to ancient Jewish communities—a maxim that still applies—Jews want "to be the same as everyone else while also being different than everyone else." Perhaps the best way to understand this paradox is to look at particular examples of integration and assimilation. It is in these places where I believe some of the most notable, and perhaps most sustainable, aspects of Jewish cultures have developed.

Greco-Roman Jews and Judeans

A new chapter of intercultural integration for Middle Eastern Jews began in the late fourth century BCE with Alexander the Great's defeat of the Persian Empire, followed a couple centuries later by the Greeks' defeat at the hands of the Romans (see fig. 7.3). It is widely held that at this time most Judeans were assimilated into the dominant Greek culture. Some Greek practices had in fact been adopted by Judean society when Jews were still living under the Persians, such as the use of Greek coins, symbols (e.g., the Athenian owl), ceramics, which soon became the regional norm, and the sculpting of Greek figures.

Some Judeans, often referred to as Hellenists (those who identified as Greek culturally but not ethnically or tribally), were, ironically, able to maintain a Judean identity because "Jewish" culture and practice had been translated into Greek, both literally and metaphorically. Scholar Erich Gruen argues that for most Jews living outside the Land of Israel yet still within the Greco-Roman Empire it was not difficult to interweave Greek and Jewish identities together. Philo, a famous Alexandrian Jew from this era (first century BCE to first century CE), wrote

FIGURE 7.3. This mosaic floor, in what may have been a synagogue, in Tiberias, Israel, dates back to the third century CE. Encircled by a number of Zodiac signs, the figure in the center of the floor is Helios, the Greek god of the Sun, who rules over time (days and years) and seasons. Part of his body is damaged (so you only see his upper half). There are at least seven other ancient Judean buildings in the State of Israel with an image of Helios surrounded by Zodiac symbols, all thought to have been synagogues.

that the Jews of his day were both strangers to and no different from non-Jews living in the Greek Empire.

A number of examples reflect such ancient hybrid identities. For instance, because few Jews outside the Land of Israel knew Hebrew, the Torah was translated into Greek in this period (circa third to second centuries BCE). Some ritually observant Jews even recited the Shma (see special topic 5.1), a central Jewish prayer, in Greek, thereby obeying (or perhaps generating) a halakhah outlined in the Mishnah that permitted them to do so. In addition, many Jews studied Greek "wisdom literature" rather than Torah. Perhaps unsurprisingly, even some of the structures of legal reasoning laid out in the Talmud, which have been used to interpret the Torah ever since, have precise parallels in, and are perhaps derived from, Greek logic texts.

Some Judean Hellenists were perceived as heretics by other Judeans such as the Hasmonean leader Mattath-ias. (The Hasmoneans were a semi-autonomous Judean group living in the Land of Israel under Roman control.) At times, this attitude led to instances of what today we might call hate crimes, where Hasmonean Jews murdered Hellenist Jews. And yet many Hasmoneans, like their Judean Hellenist brethren, also took on Greek names and integrated Greek symbols into their daily lives.

Perhaps to the Hasmoneans' chagrin, it is generally assumed that even the Temple's architecture was influenced by Roman designs of the day. Jewish tombs from this era, for those elites who could afford one, also imitated Greek and Roman architectural forms and symbols. Archeologists have unearthed synagogues from this period with Greek pictorial representations, such as a mosaic floor with a Zodiac circle found in a synagogue in the Galilean city of Tiberias (fig. 7.3). According to the Talmud, Palestinian rabbis were well aware of this practice and did not prohibit it. At the same time, non-Jews were adopting Jewish-specific ideas, such as incorporating Yahweh into their pantheon.

Of course, it is difficult to distinguish ideas and rituals from this period by way of the categories "Greek," "Roman," and "Jewish." Some scholars reject the notion that what we now refer to as the Jewish community was anything other than "Judean," a label that had a different meaning in terms of today's understandings of ethnicity and religion. As in twenty-first-century America, in many ways these cultures commingled. Cross-cultural integration may have been encouraged by the fact that Palestinian rabbis, who were leaders in the Judean community, took on many Greek and Roman practices themselves.

Unlike Babylonian- and Persian-based rabbis, Palestinian rabbis interacted with Roman rulers. According to scholar Richard Kalmin, they even accepted idolatrous practices (prohibited in the Ten Commandments). For example, according to a section from the Mishnah, a Roman soldier found Rabban Gamliel, a central member of the rabbinical court, bathing in a pool dedicated to the Greek goddess Aphrodite. When asked how a Jew could support idolatry, Gamliel responded that he didn't think of the site as a sacred space devoted to a Greek deity, but rather as an ordinary bath.

Greek Jews Today

For centuries prior to their decimation during World War II, the majority of Jews in Greece were centralized in two cities, Athens and Salonika. Of those who remain in Greece today, a small group claims a direct lineage back to Jews from the Greco-Roman era and identify as Romaniote Jews. The rest assert being descendants of those who arrived there during the fifteenth and sixteenth centuries or later and identified as Sephardi Jews. (The latter are discussed below in the "Jews among Christians" section.) Because of their deep roots in the region, Romaniote Jews are thought to have embraced more Greek cultural habits than Sephardi Jews. For instance, for many Greek was their primary language. Consequently, a notable percentage of Romaniote Jews who immigrated to the United States in the early part of the twentieth century fought their community's assimilation into the dominant English-speaking Ashkenazi American milieu, maintaining aspects of their "Greek identities." Even today, many of their descendants continue to speak Greek and identify as "Greek Jews," unlike most of their Sephardi Greek brethren.

From at least the sixteenth century through the beginning of World War I, when parts of modern-day Greece were still part of the Ottoman Empire, more Jews lived in Salonika than in any other Greek city. In fact, some contend that Salonika was one of the most important centers of Jewish intellectual life in the world during the sixteenth century. (There were at least thirty synagogues there at the time.) That said, sixteenth-century Salonikan Jews were heterogeneous—there was no single Salonikan Jewry, only Jewries—and could be divided into a number of different subgroups. For example, aside from Romaniote Jews, among Sephardi Salonikans there were Conversos and non-Conversos; those from northern Spain (Catalonia) and those from southern; those who arrived in the 1490s and those who came during the sixteenth century; those more lenient with halakhah and those more stringent. Within a few centuries there were also Jewish immigrants from such places as Livorno, Italy, who made their way to Salonika through commerce and trade, only some of whom identified as Sephardi.

As for Jews in Salonika today? Most estimates are that a larger percentage of Jews were wiped out at the hands of the Nazis in Salonika than in any other European city: 96 percent of them perished in the Shoah. (Sephardi and Romaniote Greek Jews were two of a small number of non-Ashkenazi Jewish subgroups in Nazi death camps.) Before World War II, there were 70,000 Jews living in Salonika and Athens, 50,000 of them of Sephardi descent. After the war, most survivors emigrated to the State of Israel. Today, Jews account for less than 1 percent of the total population of Salonika. Most of the cultural evidence of Salonikan Jewish culture was destroyed during the Shoah.

Babylonian Jews

Even before the Land of Israel came under Greek influence, there were Jews (or proto-Jews) in Babylonia, an area that today includes parts of Iraq, Syria, and other regions, such as Kurdistan. Many maintain that this community embodies the longest unbroken Jewish communal presence in history, dating back to the sixth century BCE and the destruction of the First Temple. (Some put Ethiopian, Indian, Jerusalem, and Syrian Jews in this category as well.) Lest we forget, the biblical character Abraham, perhaps the first recorded Hebrew, is from the city of Ur in ancient Mesopotamia, an area that includes modern-day Iraq.

The primary contemporary group identifying as

FIGURES 7.4A–C. Syrian Jewry in Damascus. Middle Eastern Jews commonly integrate Islamic and nationalistic icons into their cultural practices. I took these photos in January 2002. *Left:* Entrance to a Jewish family's home in Damascus, Syria, painted in the same style as other homes in this largely Muslim neighborhood. Above the door is the Arabic phrase "Masha'allah" (Praised be God). *Center:* An inside wall of the same home, with a framed image of a Hebrew name for God, YHWH or Yahweh; to the right of God's Hebrew name is a metal plate with an image of former Syrian president Hafez al-Assad. To the left of God's name was a photo (not seen herein) of the home's patriarch with the president of Syria, Bashar al-Assad; I was not permitted to take a picture of this framed photo (or of the man whose home it was). *Right:* Entrance hall to a Jewish school, Madrasa Ibn Maimon (Moses Son of Maimon or Maimonides School), where, alongside scores of Syrian flags, hang photos of Hafez al-Assad. The school was open as recently as 1999, and in 1992, before the last large group of Damascus Jews immigrated to New York City, it had close to 1,000 students. In January 2002, there were fifty or so Jews still living in Damascus.

descendants of Babylonian Jews are Iraqi Jews. However, a number of other communities are thought to have had origins in ancient Babylonia, including Syrian Jews (figs. 7.4) and Kurdish Jews. Although these other two communities do not generally identify as Babylonian Jews, many trace their lineage back to ancient Babylonia; indeed, their ancestors may have even arrived there prior to the destruction of the First Temple, circa 586 BCE, perhaps as early as the eighth century BCE.

Despite this variety, when people speak of Babylonian Jews today, they largely focus exclusively on Iraqi Jews. Culturally speaking, Iraqi Jews were part of the Arab milieu, a term now virtually invisible in discussions of Jewish immigrants to Israel from Middle Eastern lands in the 1950s (on this exodus, see below). Whether members of this community identified then or identify now as Arabs is a politicized question, which is explored more in chapter 10.

One member of the larger Arab Jewish community, Albert Memmi, a well-known Tunisian Jew, explains,

"Because we were born in these so-called Arab countries and had been living in those regions long before the arrival of the Arabs, we share their languages, their customs, and their cultures to an extent that is not negligible." Similarly, Jewish Israeli author Sami Michael, who was born in Baghdad, Iraq, says, "We perceived ourselves as Arabs of a Jewish descent. Just as there are Christian Arabs [or Muslim Arabs], we were Jewish Arabs."

Prior to immigrating to Israel, Iraqi Jews' first language was Arabic and they often had Arabic names, such as Abdallah or Abdul (servant of God). One of the most renowned Iraqi chief rabbis of all time was Abdallah Somekh, who lived during the nineteenth century. Their greatest poets, journalists, and other writers wrote in Arabic. Two musician brothers who gained popularity in the 1930s, Salah and Daud Al-Kweiti—described as the "creators of modern Iraqi music"—were firmly ensconced in the non-Jewish milieu in Iraq.

The food of Iraqi Jews reflected, and today continues to reflect, Iraqi cuisine, integrating the herbs and spices of

FIGURES 7.5A–B. Iraqi Jews. *Left:* Two Jewish men in Mosul, Iraq (c. 1870–1963). *Right:* Family of Iraqi Chief Rabbi Hakham Ezra Dangoor, Baghdad (c. 1910); from left to right, Muzli (granddaughter), Saleh Basri (grandson), Farha Shaoul Basri (daughter), Hakham Dangoor, and Habiba, the rabbi's wife.

the region, such as cardamom, cinnamon, ginger, basil, mint, dill, and lemon. Staple victuals such as *kemar* (a thick cream spread on bread and topped with sugar, possibly originating in Mongolia) and *ambah* (a spicy sauce made with pickled mango, perhaps a fusion of Indian and European dishes) were (and are) often central to their meals.

In Iraq, they also adopted non-Jewish norms with respect to the social roles of women. For instance, outside the home most female Iraqi Jews covered their head and face (with a veil) and body (with a cloak). Until the end of the nineteenth century, Iraqi Jewish girls were commonly married by age twelve or thirteen; by the early twentieth century fifteen was a more common marriage age. The size of one's dowry played a major role in this endeavor. As for divorce, it was quite rare. Finally, polygyny was permitted. For example, if a married man died childless, his widow was obligated to marry his brother (her brother-in-law), even if he was already married, an ancient law described in the Torah and Talmud called Levirate marriage. Once practiced in Ashkenazi communities as well, this tradition continued in Iraqi Jewish communities for a long time. By the beginning of the twentieth century, however, this Iraqi Jewish custom had virtually vanished.

Of course, there were nuanced cultural differences within the Iraqi Jewish world based on whether one lived in Baghdad, Basra, or Mosul. For most of history, these distinctions were quite important to Iraqi Jews, though less so today.

Iraqi Jews Today

During the 1940s virtually all of the world's 140,000 or so Iraqi Jews lived in Iraq. Between 1948 and 1951, roughly 123,000 of them immigrated to the State of Israel, most airlifted from Baghdad to Tel Aviv via Operation Ezra and Nehemiah (also called Operation Ali Baba), owing to a rare agreement between the governments of Iraq and Israel permitting Iraqi Jews to leave. Another 6,500 arrived over the following two years. Today's estimates put the number of Jews in Iraq at fewer than 10, whereas in Israel the number hovers around 250,000, some 175,000 of whom were born in the Jewish State (figs. 7.5).

After immigration to Israel, regional differences among Iraqi Jews have become less significant. Most Iraqi Jewish Israelis, especially those under the age of forty, identify as Iraqi much more than as Baghdadi or Mosuli. This has everything to do with the phenomenon of identity formation in Israel, where Jewish families largely trace themselves back to Middle Eastern countries rather than specific cities. (This is common among immigrant groups in general, such as Mexican Americans in the United States.)

Ironically, the process of assimilating into Israel's dominant *Jewish* culture—where they are legally free to practice Jewish rituals—has caused much of the Arab culture of Iraqi Jews to be lost. A similar phenomenon of acculturation and marginalization occurred among Jews arriving in Israel from Algeria, Egypt, Iran, Kurdistan, Lebanon, Libya, Morocco, Syria, Tunisia, and Yemen. Whereas there were some 800,000 Jews living in Middle Eastern countries in the 1940s, prior to the establishment of Israel (1948), by the 1950s this number had dropped to less than 50,000, as most communities relocated to the State of Israel and, to a much lesser extent, the United States. Much smaller populations of Jews from these various countries also exist in the United States, Canada, and England.

Iraqi Jewish Culture in Israel

Once in Israel, Iraqi Jews changed many cultural customs, both voluntarily and involuntarily. The most obvious example was language: many parents and grandparents did not want their children to speak Arabic, which in Israel was too often conflated with Palestinian and not Jewish identities, but instead focused on their learning Hebrew. Members of the first immigrant generations often changed their names as well. For example, many who were named Abdallah now went by a Hebrew equivalent, Ovadiah. (See further in chapter 10.)

The roles of women also changed. Whereas in Iraq, Jewish girls' families commonly prohibited them from attending school, in Israel there was compulsory education for all. This led to rapid increases in women's employment, decreases in birth rates, and a rise in the age when Iraqi women married. The cumulative effect was more independence for these women, as well as a greater potential for upward social mobility.

Another difference is that the cultural influence Iraqi Jews had enjoyed before immigrating to Israel did not transfer. As one Iraqi Jewish Israeli author, Samir Naqqash, harshly noted, "I don't exist in this country, not as a writer, neither as a citizen nor human being. I don't feel that I belong anywhere, not since my roots were torn from the ground [in Baghdad]." Although this feeling is not universal, many Iraqi Jews living in Israel share a similar sense of alienation, particularly those who were not born in the Jewish State.

Another reason for negative feelings is the allegation, factual or not (and likewise not held by all Iraqi Jewish Israelis), that they were deceived into leaving their Muslim-Arab-majority homeland by the Mossad (the Israeli covert intelligence agency, akin to the American CIA). According to a number of scholars, the Mossad planted bombs at important Baghdadi Jewish sites around the same time as the mass immigration (1950s) to demonstrate that the alternative to moving to Israel was death.

Even today, some Iraqi Jewish Israelis consider this allegation to be true. Whatever the case, during the 1948–1949 war in Israel and Palestine (see chapter 10), when a small military brigade from Iraq challenging the nascent Jewish State was defeated, Jews' status in Iraq worsened, all but forcing many Iraqi Jews to leave.

Jewish Culture in Kurdistan

Kurdistan today encompasses parts of five modern nation-states: Armenia, Iran, Iraq, Syria, and Turkey. Prior to emigration (see below), many of their customs, such as their dances, reflected influences of the larger non-Jewish Kurdish milieus in which they lived. Men wore turbans with colorful scarves, and women wore striped gowns and decorated their arms, hands, and legs with gold and silver jewelry. It was not uncommon for women to have tattoos and nose rings. This community was also renowned for storytelling, especially of generations-old folk tales. In contrast to most other Jewish groups, Kurdish Jews, men and women alike, were commonly farmers and shepherds who worked from sunrise to nightfall. Many lived in abject poverty. As recently as the twentieth century, some Kurdish Jews spoke a neo-Aramaic dialect, in addition to speaking Arabic, Hebrew, and Kurdish. They also celebrated a distinct holiday called Seharane, which some link to the Persian holiday Nowruz (see "Persian Jews" below).

Kurdish Jewish Culture in Israel

Although there have been Kurdish Jews in the Land of Israel since at least the seventeenth century, most immigrated to the Jewish State in the 1950s, in two separate waves, alongside Iraqi and Iranian Jews. It is estimated that before the mid–twentieth century there were 50,000 Kurdish Jews in Kurdistan, most of whom have since left the region. Because the Israeli government only categorized immigrants in terms of their country of origin (Iran, Iraq, Syria, and Turkey), a practice that continues today, the actual number of Kurdish Jews in Israel is unknown. Unofficially, some estimate that there are between 100,000 and 200,000 Kurdish Jews in Israel today.

In general, Kurdish Jews have assimilated into the dominant Jewish Israeli culture. One of the few national holidays Kurdish Jewish Israelis still observe is Seharane—a celebratory holiday originally marking the end of winter and beginning of spring—which had fallen into neglect but was revived in the 1970s. At that time, because it landed on the same day as another post-Passover holiday, Mimouna, widely observed by Moroccan Jews, Kurdish Israelis began celebrating Seharane in the fall, which gave it new life, and to some degree a new incarnation (no longer used to celebrate the beginning of spring). Over the past few years, a small handful of Kurdish Jews have returned to Kurdistan after decades in Israel.

Persian Jews

During the sixth century BCE, the Persian Empire defeated the Babylonians. At first, this was a case of Jews living under Persian rule. Over time, however, these two signifiers—Persian and Jew—morphed into the Persian Jew, who still exist in sizable numbers today.

Instances of this cultural synthesis are found in what is perhaps the most famous of all Persian Jewish stories, found in the Scroll of Esther, a biblical tale of assimilation, among other things. The names of the two main Jewish characters in this book, Mordechai and Esther, derive from the names of two Babylonian gods, Marduk and Ishtar. Likewise, the name of the main villain of the story, Haman, also has a Persian source.

The tomb of Esther and Mordechai continues to be an important pilgrimage site for Persian Jews, as do the resting places of the prophets Daniel and Habakkuk, two other biblical figures believed to have been buried in what today we know as Iran. (Habakkuk is thought to be buried in the State of Israel as well; see special topic 6.5.) These sites are also sacred for many Muslims.

While it is difficult to pinpoint exactly when Persian Jews began integrating non-Jewish rituals into their observances, we do know that for centuries, if not millennia, Persian Jews have practiced two customs rooted in Zoroastrianism, the dominant Persian religion prior to the spread of Islam in the seventh century CE: the celebration of Nowruz and the burning of *esphand,* an herbal seed, to ward off the "evil eye."

An annual holiday that often overlaps with Pesaḥ (see chapter 1), Nowruz is sometimes called the Iranian New Year. Traditions include the preparation and eating of "the seven dishes" (each one beginning with the Persian letter *sinn,* e.g. *sabze,* sprouts; *samanu,* creamy pudding; *sib,* apple) and the placement on a ceremonial Nowruz table of a number of objects linked to rebirth and renewal, including coins, a basket of painted eggs, an orange in a bowl of water, and a flask of rose water. In addition, depending on how one identifies within the Iranian collective, one places important books on this table, such as the Hebrew Bible (Jews), the Qur'an (Mus-lims), or a book of poetry by a Persian non-Jew, such as Hafez or Rumi.

According to scholar Saba Soomekh, one of the intentions behind the Jewish celebration of Nowruz is to honor the sixth-century BCE King Cyrus, under whose rule the ancestors of Persian Jews were alleged to have been treated well. This holiday is even mentioned in the Jerusalem Talmud. (For more on whether King Cyrus treated Jews under his rule with dignity and respect, as many Persian Jews today maintain, see chapter 3).

As for esphand, although a minority of Persian Jews make a point of not observing Nowruz because of its non-Jewish roots, even the most orthodox and "non-superstitious" Persian Jews continue to follow this protection-seeking tradition today.

Persian Jews Today

Contemporary Persian Jews, especially those still living in Iran, are similar to their non-Jewish neighbors, in appearance, in culture, and in language. For instance, Jews in Iran, as well as most first-generation Persian Jews in Israel and the United States, speak Farsi.

The largest waves of Persian Jews left Iran and immigrated to America in the years following the 1979 Iranian revolution; most settled in the greater Los Angeles area (what some call Tehrangeles as a result). There are about 80,000 Persian Jews in the United States today, a fraction of whom refer to themselves as Iranian Jews rather than Persian Jews. As for those remaining in Iran, some estimates are as high as 30,000, though the 2011 Iranian government census listed them at slightly fewer than 9,000. As of 2011, estimates of the Persian Jewish population in Israel ranged from 137,000 to 250,000; any figure within this range makes this the largest community of Persian Jews in the world.

As with all communities, there continue to be nuanced differences within the Persian Jewish community. First, as with Iraqi and Moroccan Jews, there are distinctions based on what city one's family emigrated from, whether Tehran, Hamadan, Esfahan, or another place in Iran, particularities much more important to older generations than younger ones. Each of these communities had its own dialect, among other differences. Second, there were also Iraqi Jews and Kurdish Jews living among Persian Jews in Iran as recently as the late twentieth century, thus further complicating what it means to be a Persian Jew. Third, while there is a dominant narrative among Persian Jews, there are a multitude of subnarratives as well. For example, many Persian Jews in Los Angeles fear for the lives of those Jews still living in Tehran, although Jews in

FIGURE 7.6. Uzbek Jews. A Jewish teacher with his students in Samarkand, Uzbekistan (c. 1905–1915).

Tehran do not necessarily have such fears. Of course, there are also socioeconomic and other types of differences.

A number of today's Jewish communities are thought to be descendants of Persian Jews, such as Afghani Jews; the "Mountain Jews" of Azerbaijan; Bukharan Jews, who commonly trace themselves back to the location of the modern nation-states of Uzbekistan (fig. 7.6) and Tajikistan; Kazakhstani Jews; and Pakistani Jews (see below). However, some of these communities claim a direct lineage to Israelites or Judeans, whether exiled in the eighth, seventh, or sixth century BCE, rather than a familial connection to Persians per se. All of these subgroups have cultural characteristics both unique in the Jewish world and similar to their local, non-Jewish neighbors.

Jews among Muslims: Yemenites and Egyptians

Islam first emerged during the seventh century CE in today's Saudi Arabia. By the time a forty-year-old man named Muhammad proclaimed that God was commu-nicating to him through the angel Gabriel, Jews were already firmly ensconced in Arabian society. They spoke Arabic and are thought to have been physically indistinguishable from their non-Jewish neighbors. In other words, they were Arab through and through.

Within a few generations, Islam spread from the small city of Mecca to Medina and then onto the entire Arabian Peninsula. Though many Jews maintained their Jewish identities, others—by some accounts, most Jews living among Muslims—eventually joined the new dominant identity and converted to Islam. (Conversion is not always about faith alone; it is also linked to economic and political access.) Scholarly opinions are mixed as to whether the Muslim Arab Empire—which, over the next century, spread to regions as far west as Spain and Morocco and as far east as Afghanistan—forced conquered populations to convert. Whatever the case, we know that Jews were affected by the new hegemonic power, though it is likely that the process of cultural Islamization and Arabization took not decades but centuries. Some estimate that by the twelfth century CE as many as 85 to 90 percent of all Jews worldwide lived in Muslim-majority countries, a trend that lasted until the nineteenth century. Such a statistic underscores how these Jews shaped the Jewish discourse in countries around the world.

Although Jews were treated differently across Muslim-controlled regions, their de jure status was similar. Along with Christians and other minorities, Jews were understood to be *Ahl al-Kitāb,* People of the Book, which gave them a status above those communities that did not pledge allegiance to a single God, who were considered heretics and sometimes killed (or forced to convert). At the same time, they were categorized as *dhimmi,* or non-Muslim citizens of an Islamic state, and treated according to specific rules, essentially "second-class citizens."

For example, they had to pay various taxes to their Muslim rulers that Muslims were not obligated to pay. Other consequences of their dhimmi status included prohibitions against building synagogues, working in particular professions, and bringing evidence against a Muslim in an Islamic religious court. Some of these restrictions are rooted in the so-called Pact of Omar, probably concretized as early as the seventh century.

But as with most generalizations, there were exceptions across place and time. There are examples of Jews having permission to do all of these things, even hold political office. Some scholars point to how dhimmi were protected, whereas others focus on ways in which they were persecuted. Today, those who reduce centuries of Jews living among Muslims to one or the other end of the spectrum often have an underlying agenda based in polemics or apologetics. (It is also not uncommon today for scholars to make sweeping generalizations that compare how Jews were treated under Muslims to how they were treated under Christians.)

Jewish Culture in Yemen

Some Yemenite Jews trace their presence in the Arabian Peninsula (where Yemen is located) to the sixth century BCE, when they arrived there from the Land of Israel after the Babylonian Exile. One of the more unique attributes of Yemenite Jews is related to food. They are one of the only known Jewish communities to have regularly embraced the halakhically sanctioned precept to eat locusts; without this practice, many Yemenite Jewish subcommunities would have starved to death. Although Yemen is the most fertile land of the Arabian Peninsula, because of its intense dependence on rainfall Yemenites,

Jews and non-Jews alike, have suffered from severe food shortages for centuries. This affected Yemenite Jews differently depending on their socioeconomic status. If they were poor, locusts were the main component of their diet; if they were wealthy, locusts were occasionally served as part of dessert.

Aside from access to food, other factors played important roles in the shaping of Yemenite Jewish identities. First, because no Christians lived in the Arabian Peninsula, these Jews were the only non-Muslim group in the region, a fact that set them apart from other Jewish communities living as dhimmi. Although theoretically this might have meant better treatment, for most of their history this status did not turn out well for them.

One of the worst periods in Yemenite Jewish history occurred in the late seventeenth century. In an act often described as fanatical, Imam Ahmad al-Mahdi exiled all of the members of the Yemenite Jewish community to a remote coastal region in western Arabia called Mauza, known for its extreme heat. Many non-Jewish tribes opposed the decree, and some chose to protect those Jews living among them. After one year, the law was annulled, but by that time, three-quarters of Yemenite Jews had died as a result of the exile. In the interim, most of their synagogues and other Jewish-owned buildings had been destroyed.

Second, prior to the mid–twentieth century, Yemenite Jews—though few in number (some 60,000 in all)—were dispersed throughout Yemen. Roughly 80 percent lived in small villages, sometimes made up of a few isolated families. (The two largest communities were based in Aden and Sana'a.) Because many Jewish customs necessitate living in a community with others (for example, certain prayers can only be said if there is a quorum of, typically, ten men; see chapter 8), this sometimes limited the rituals that Yemenite Jews could observe. This dispersal also accounts for their heterogeneity in terms of "customs, physiognomy, vernaculars, socio-economic structure, and living style."

Though geographically far from Babylonian Jews, these Yemenite subcommunities held a deep admiration and respect for Babylonian rabbis, illustrated in the safekeeping of what are the oldest existent copies of the Babylonian Talmud in the world and the acceptance of halakhot codified by the ninth- and tenth-century Babylonian rabbi Saadia Gaon. Another similarity was the custom for males to wear *pe'ot,* sidelocks, in a unique fashion (fig. 7.7a). Today, they are arguably the only Jewish group to continue this custom in this precise way.

FIGURES 7.7A–B. Yemenite Jews. *Top:* Jews outside a synagogue in the capital of Yemen, Sana'a, c. 1911. *Bottom:* A Jewish Yemenite bride in Israel wearing traditional wedding garb, c. 1958.

Yemenite Jewish Culture in Israel

As for their lives outside of Yemen, from as early as the first decade of the twentieth century, Ashkenazi Jews and Yemenite Jews living alongside one another in Ottoman-controlled Palestine sometimes did not get along. According to scholar Yoav Peled, between 1904 and 1914 Ashkenazi Jews brought a relatively small number of Yemenite Jews to Palestine in order to replace the non-Jewish Palestinian "Arab labor" and serve as a substitute working class; they considered Yemenite Jews "natural" workers. Needless to say, these Yemenite immigrants were treated as inferiors, arguably from that point through today. (See below and chapter 10 for more recent examples of intra-Jewish oppression in Israel.)

During the 1950s, almost all of the 60,000 Jews in Yemen immigrated to Israel. Prior to this time, their largest relocation to the Land of Israel took place in 1882, when approximately 200 Yemenite Jews moved to Ottoman-controlled Palestine. (According to some, after the Ottoman Empire conquered Yemen, the Jews living there were given new freedoms in regard to legal migration. Along with the opening of the Suez Canal for Jews in Egypt, this created an opportunity for Yemenite Jews to travel to the Land of Israel much quicker than previously. Some Yemenite Jews saw this as an unfolding of the messianic age and thus wanted to hasten it.)

By 1940 the community living in the Land of Israel (then British-occupied Palestine) had grown to 15,000, largely due to other waves of immigration. A 2011 estimate of the Yemenite Jewish Israeli community put their population at 150,000. With the secret immigration of another 151 Jews from Yemen between 2009 and 2013, estimates are that fewer than 90 Yemenite Jews remain in Yemen, half of them living in the capital, Sana'a.

Firmly ensconced in the Yemenite Jewish Israeli narrative is an event commonly referred to as the "Yemenite Babies Affair." Just as many Iraqi Jews in Israel continue to maintain that the Mossad played a nefarious role in encouraging them to leave Iraq in the 1950s, Yemenite Jews today continue to allege mistreatment in the 1950s. This episode, however, is arguably much more heinous.

According to this claim, upon their arrival in the Jewish State, even though they were one of the poorest communities of Jewish immigrants, many of their possessions were taken away from them and given to non-Yemenite Jewish Israelis. Some were also put in "secular reeducation" transit camps, aimed at stripping them of their "primitive" religious beliefs; physical violence was employed. But much more shocking—and something that many Jewish Israelis, both Yemenites and non-Yemenites alike, believe to be true—is the allegation that hundreds, if not thousands, of babies were taken from the newly arrived immigrants.

Since that time, a vocal group of Yemenites have claimed that when they reached Israel they were told that their babies needed to be taken to the hospital for health reasons. Shortly thereafter, they were told that their children had died. These people say that in many cases not only were their babies still alive, but they were actually handed over to Ashkenazi Jewish families. Some go so far as to assert that experiments were conducted on these babies. Three different Israeli government administrative commissions, the last of which concluded in 2001, deny these allegations. Nonetheless, to this day, some Jews of Middle Eastern descent, especially Yemenites, consider the kidnapping of Yemenite babies to be true (as do many outside these communities). To not include these events in the teaching of Jewish history, they believe, is a form of double oppression.

Egyptian Jews

Although some date this community back to the biblical Hebrews, most date it to the sixth century BCE and the Babylonian Exile. One of their subcommunities, Karaite Jews, has been in Egypt since at least the tenth century CE (see chapter 11). More recently, during the nineteenth century CE, Jews immigrated to Egypt from North Africa and Europe. All of this means that aside from the geographical diversity of Egyptian Jewry—whether they lived in Cairo or Alexandria, the Nile Delta or Upper Egypt—prior to the 1950s there had been distinct groups, such as Romaniotes (who spoke Judeo-Greek), Corfiotes (who spoke a Venetian Judeo-Italian dialect), Francophones (who spoke French), and "Arab Jews" (who spoke Arabic), in Egypt for some time.

Within these groups, some identified as Ashkenazi, some as Sephardi, and some as neither. Occasionally, Jews from the same subcommunity identified as either Ashkenazi or Sephardi, such as those arriving from France or Morocco. There was such intra-Jewish diversity that between 1877 and 1948 more than seventy Jewish newspapers and periodicals were published in Egypt, including at least twenty-two in Arabic, twenty-six in French, six in Hebrew, six in Ladino, and four in English.

As in Iraq, during the nineteenth and twentieth centuries Jews played key roles in the development of Egyptian culture, such as the journalist and dramatist Yaqub Sanu, who has been called "the father of Egyptian theater and one of the founders of satirical Arabic journalism." In contrast to other Jewish communities, Jewish women figured prominently in Egypt, primarily from the end of the nineteenth through the mid–twentieth century, such as Esther Lazari-Moyal, the first feminist activist in Arab journalism. One reason for this was Egyptian females' access to higher education.

All of these differences led to more intra-Jewish cultural stratification than probably existed in other pre-1948 Middle Eastern Jewish communities. For instance, various subgroups of Egyptian Jews, especially ones from higher socioeconomic classes, often looked down upon those Jews who spoke Arabic, instead embracing the French and English languages and cultures, which they deemed to be more "civilized."

There were two major migration waves of Egyptian Jews in the twentieth century: in the 1950s, after Egyptian president Gamal Abd Al-Nasser "nationalized" all private property (i.e., seized it on behalf of the government), and in the late 1960s, immediately after the 1967 War with Israel. Prior to the 1950s there were about 80,000 Jews in Egypt, about 10,000 of whom were Egyptian citizens. Of the rest, some 30,000 were foreign nationals, and the remaining 40,000 were stateless, most of them poor, Arabic-speaking Cairines and Alexandrians. By 1961, all but 10,000 Egyptian Jews had left, most for Israel and others for Europe, North America, and South America, numbers that dwindled to less than 1,000 post-1967 War. Today's best estimates put the number of Jews left in Egypt at fewer than fifty.

Jews among Christians

The Roman Empire began the process of Christianization in the fourth century CE, when Emperor Constantine converted. Prior to that point, Christian Jews were persecuted alongside non-Christian Jews. As Christianity spread, however, and Christian Jews became a distinct non-Jewish community (see chapter 4), Jews living in places where the regional authority identified as Christian were singled out. Eventually the Roman Empire declared it illegal to practice certain aspects of Jewish life, such as studying Mishnah. From that time into the medieval period and through the twentieth century, Jews generally experienced oppression in Christian-majority societies, especially in Europe (see chapter 9).

Two important Jewish communities living under Christian rule were Ethiopian Jews and Sephardi Jews, the latter a key Jewish identity today, with roots in the Christian-ruled medieval Iberian Peninsula (see chapter 1).

Ethiopian Jews

Contemporary Jews and non-Jews alike are intrigued by the notion of the "Lost Tribes of Israel," that is, contemporary Jewish communities that claim to descend from one or more of the ancient Israelite tribes that became separated from the group that eventually became the Jewish mainstream (see chapter 3). One of the oldest groups in this category—as well as one of the oldest Jewish populations in general—is Ethiopian Jewry.

Most maintain that Ethiopian Jews are the descendants of the Israelite tribe of Dan, a position accepted in 1973 by the chief Sephardi rabbi—but denied by the chief Ashkenazi rabbi—of the State of Israel. According to this tradition, during the eighth century BCE the Assyrians sent this group south from the Land of Israel into exile; they ended up in the land of Cush, thought to coincide with today's nation-state of Ethiopia. Others date Ethiopian Jews back to the biblical reign of King Solomon (c. 1000–950 BCE), arguing that this proto-Jewish subgroup was birthed through the union of Solomon and the Queen of Sheba. There is no proof for either of these theories.

For most of history, non-Jewish groups have attempted to assimilate Ethiopian Jews, as in the fourth and fifth centuries CE, when a large number of Ethiopian Jews, along with most Ethiopian non-Jews, converted to Christianity. Since that time in Ethiopia, rather than be called *Beta* (House of) Christian, as were the early Christian Ethiopians, Ethiopian Jews have been called Beta Israel. (Feres Mura, a subcommunity of Ethiopian Jews, are of Beta Israel descent yet are most commonly not referred to by this broader term because they also often have an externalized Christian identity; see below.)

In 1984, following reports that Ethiopian Jews were being persecuted because of their Jewish identity, the State of Israel began airlifting them to the Jewish State. More than 4,000 Ethiopian Jews died en route from Ethiopia to the Sudan, where they were met by Israeli government officials. During this time there were two major airlifts, one in 1984–1985 and a second in 1991, the latter organized due to concerns that the country's political destabilization would lead to a life-threatening situation for Ethiopian Jews. The total number of Ethiopian Jews in Israel today is estimated at more than 125,000, about two-thirds of whom were born in Ethiopia and have since received Israeli citizenship.

Jewish Culture in Ethiopia

Most research attempting to uncover the meaning of Ethiopian Jewish culture prior to their mass immigration to Israel focuses on the lives of Ethiopian Jews only over the last two centuries. Largely based in northwest Ethiopia, according to scholar Hagar Salamon, Ethiopian Jews regularly interacted with Ethiopian Christians for centuries. Yet demarcation lines existed (and continue to exist) between the two groups, most notably in Ethiopian Jewish prohibitions against physical contact and the sharing of food with non-Jews, practices based on their particular understanding of biblical (not Talmudic) notions of purity and kashrut. (It is generally maintained that because these Jews immigrated to Cush prior to the Talmudic era, where they lived largely in isolation from other Jews, it wasn't until the twentieth century that Ethiopian Jews even learned of the existence of the Talmud.) In turn, the Christian majority also established boundaries, such as the prohibition against Jews owning land, which continues to ensure the relegation of Jews to a lower social status. There were also a number of proscriptions regarding proper ways to celebrate events with non-Jews, whether holidays or weddings. According to Salamon, such practices were becoming less strict in the years leading up to the mass migration of Ethiopian Jews to Israel between 1984 and 1991.

Although Ethiopian Jews had other laws separating them from their Christian neighbors—such as confining menstruating women in designated "blood huts," areas cordoned off by stone walls—a non-Ethiopian outsider would have seen them as simply Ethiopian. Indeed, evidence suggests that they did not look different from their non-Jewish neighbors. As for their diet, like most Ethiopians, a core part of their meal has been *injera,* a type of spongy bread that is distinctly Ethiopian (and Eritrean). The style of their homes and clothes has also been typically Ethiopian. In sum, although they have been a minority in Ethiopia, they have been Ethiopian nonetheless.

Ethiopian Jewish Culture in Israel

In Ethiopia, these people were accepted as Jews. However, even though the Israeli government went to great lengths to "return" these "lost Jews" to their ancient homeland, upon arrival in Israel they were forced to go through a ritual conversion; without it, they could not gain citizenship. In other words, their Jewishness—the very thing that allowed them to move to Israel in the first

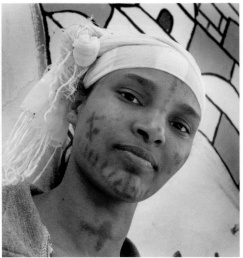

FIGURES 7.8A–B. Ethiopian Jews. *Left:* A 2012 protest by Ethiopian Jewish Israelis over being repeatedly denied housing by the Israeli government, one of the institutional forms of discrimination they continue to experience. *Right:* In Ethiopia, it used to be a custom of Feres Mura Jews to have Christian symbols engraved on their bodies, especially on their faces and necks, in an effort to show their allegiance to the country's Christian majority, despite privately maintaining a Jewish identity.

place—was challenged by other Jews. According to the rabbinic authority of the Jewish State, conversion was necessary because Ethiopian Jewish ritual practices, from the slaughter of animals to the "blood hut," had been devoid of rabbinic interpretations—that is, their understanding of Jewish law was not based in the Talmud.

Some Ethiopian Jews immigrating to Israel had been owned by other Ethiopian Jews and treated as slaves. Part of the practice of Ethiopian Jews owning slaves in Ethiopia (non-Jewish Ethiopians also owned slaves) included converting the slaves to Judaism. According to Salamon, as of the mid-1990s these former slaves continued to maintain a clear subcommunal status among Ethiopian Jews living in Israel.

In Israel, Ethiopian Jews of all stripes are often seen not simply as Jews but as "Black Jews." Most Ethiopian Israelis maintain that the biggest challenge of living in Israel is the prejudice they have experienced because of their blackness, a pattern which, for them, began with their required conversion to an identity they had maintained for centuries. (Prior to arriving in Israel, Ethiopian Jews understood their skin color to be "reddish-brown," not black.)

Conversion aside, two infamous examples of structural discrimination at the hands of the Israeli government have been the systematic disposal of Ethiopian blood donations by the Israeli Ministry of Health, due to the groundless fear that they were contaminated with the HIV virus, first reported in 1996, and the same ministry's failure to inform Ethiopian women that the mandatory injections they received in transit to Israel were long-term forms of birth control, first reported in 2008. Whether or not these events were explicitly linked to prejudice, Ethiopian Jews also experience higher levels of poverty, lower levels of unemployment, and higher incarceration rates than other Jewish Israeli subcommunities. (Fig. 7.8a depicts a 2012 protest by Ethiopian Israelis.)

A subset of Ethiopian Jews continues to be embroiled in controversy with the Israeli government. Called the Feres Mura or Falasha, these people are descendants of a small number of Ethiopian Jews who converted to Christianity in the nineteenth and twentieth centuries (fig. 7.8b). According to the Israeli government, most Feres Mura are not Jewish as they are deemed to be far too estranged from their Jewish roots; thus, until 2010 their citizenship was denied officially. Many in this group claim that their ancestors' conversion to Christianity had been a ruse without which they would have been killed, as with the Conversos in fifteenth- and sixteenth-century Spain and Portugal. Other Feres Mura admit that their ancestors converted to Christianity in an effort to assimilate, but maintain that they themselves are committed to Judaism. Between 2010 and 2013, the Israeli government brought what was thought at the time to be a final group of 8,000 Feres Mura to Israel. As of mid-2015, approximately 12,000 Feres Mura remained in Ethiopia, almost all of whom claim to be Jews and have applied for and been denied Israeli citizenship. In November 2015, the interior minister of the State of Israel, Silvan Shalom, submitted a draft proposal for an additional 9,146 Ethiopians in Ethiopia to be granted legal permission to become Israeli citizens.

Ethiopian Jewish Israeli culture is shaped not only by such instances of prejudice but also by unique ritual practices that pre-date their immigration to Israel. Perhaps the most notable are connected to their prayer services (although these have started to change, especially during services in synagogues frequented by non-Ethiopian Jews as well) and to a one-of-a-kind Jewish holiday called Sigd. Regarding the former, most of their prayers are said in Ge'ez (and/or Amharic, a dialect thereof), an ancient language that few Ethiopian Jews today still understand. Music is also core to their prayer services, to the extent that most prayers are sung rather than spoken. They also integrate musical instruments into their prayer services in unique ways.

As for Sigd, this is an annual Ethiopian holiday observed in the fall, fifty days after Yom Kippur (the Day of Atonement), that this community maintains dates back to the time of the prophets Ezra and Nehemiah. Pre-immigration, Sigd observance necessitated the ascent of one of the highest mountaintops in northwest Ethiopia, where people would pray, read passages from the Hebrew Bible, and proclaim their desire to return to Zion. Post-immigration, Sigd is much more of a celebration, during which Ethiopian religious leaders—called *Kessim* (sing. *Kes*)—declare gratitude to God for bringing their community to Israel and beg forgiveness for both their community's wrongdoings as well as those of all Jews. In 2008, Sigd became an official Israeli state holiday.

A final point worth mentioning—applicable to almost all Jewish Israeli minorities—is that for Ethiopian Jewish Israelis, marrying a Jew from outside their subcommunity is often seen as a form of intermarriage, almost as if one is marrying a non-Jew. A 2009 survey by the Israeli government found that 93 percent of male Ethiopians and 85 percent of female Ethiopians marry other Ethiopians. Of course, this pattern also reflects the attitudes of non-Ethiopian Jewish Israelis, almost 60 percent of whom said it would be unacceptable for their daughters to marry an Ethiopian (a statistic that dropped to 40 percent when it came to their sons).

The Birth of "Sephardi" Jews

Perhaps the most significant premodern example of Christian mistreatment of Jews took place in the fifteenth century: what came to be called the Spanish and Portuguese Inquisitions, an era that gave birth to the Sephardi Jew. (*Sepharad* is the modern Hebrew word for Spain.) At the time, Jews were given three choices: convert to Christianity, leave the Iberian Peninsula, or die. (At times, too, Jews were murdered outright without being given any choice whatsoever.)

Many date the Spanish Inquisition to 1492 and the Portuguese Inquisition to 1495. But the Catholic Church had been conducting inquisitions against a variety of alleged Jewish heretics since at least the twelfth century. Further, quite a few scholars contend that as far back as the beginning of the fourteenth century, Jews in the northern parts of what are today Spain and Portugal were already facing the three narrow options of convert, leave, or die.

As mentioned in chapter 1, among those who chose conversion were the Conversos, a small number of families who identified as Catholic publicly but Jewish privately. (A small number of Catholic converts returned to Judaism a few decades later.) As for those who were expelled, most ended up in Christian-majority countries to the north, Muslim-majority countries to the south, and a handful of countries to the east—both Christian- and Muslim-majority—that border the Mediterranean Sea.

Most of their descendants have identified as Sephardi ever since. But because of the diversity within communities self-described as Sephardi, when twenty-first-century Jews in Israel or America claim this identity, it actually tells us less about their Jewish background than does claiming to be Ashkenazi. Further, evidence suggests that fifteenth-century Iberian Jewish identities—pre-Inquisitions—were much more complex than the single signifier "Sephardi" can cover. As scholar Jonathan Ray notes, "At no point did a Sephardi community exist that operated in a politically cohesive manner, nor was there anything that might be described as a Sephardi consciousness."

Ray argues that the label Sephardi was retroactively inserted into discussions about previous generations of Jews who traced themselves back to the Iberian Peninsula. This means that the ancestors of many of today's Sephardi Jews, the so-called original Sephardi Jews, would not have labeled themselves as such. Initially, this moniker was utilized to point to a geographical designation, not a particular subculture.

The Inquisitions led to yet another dispersal of Jews to countries around the globe, from the Middle East and North Africa (Morocco, Tunisia, Algeria, Libya, Egypt, Palestine or the Land of Israel, Syria, Lebanon, Turkey, Iraq, Iran) to South Asia (India) to the Americas (Argentina, Peru, Cuba, Jamaica). Some of these groups spoke Ladino, a dialect mixing medieval Castilian Spanish and Hebrew (also called Judeo-Spanish). It is widely taught that aside from Conversos, no Jews lived in Portugal or Spain for centuries thereafter.

Everywhere, these Jews had to reestablish their identities, whether as Jews or, for those no longer identifying as such, as non-Jews. Centuries later, when Jews from all over immigrated to Israel and the United States, vestiges from the medieval period played a role in these distinct communities being grouped together as Sephardi, despite their vast differences. In fact, some who are called Sephardi Jews—especially by non-Sephardi Jews—never identified as Sephardi, such as Syrian Jews, many of whose families had lived in Syria for centuries prior to the fifteenth and sixteenth centuries. (See chapter 10.)

Scholar Ben Zion Netanyahu muddles up the reformulation of Jewish identities in this particular time and place. He argues that at the time of the Spanish and Portuguese Inquisitions most Jews who were expelled were already Christian. He is one of a few scholars who assert that the Inquisitions were aimed specifically at Conversos, those Jews "hiding in plain sight." Ironically, he argues, these new laws had a perhaps unintended consequence: if not for said policies, the Conversos most likely would have assimilated into the dominant Christian milieu within a short period of time. Some, however, returned to their previous public Jewish identities as a result of their having been singled out.

Netanyahu also suggests that Jews had been immigrating away from Spain and Portugal for a few centuries prior to the Inquisitions, and continued to do so for a few centuries thereafter. There is also evidence that during the sixteenth and seventeenth centuries Jews were able to return to the Iberian Peninsula. These notions all challenge the simplistic yet widely held contention that at the end of the fifteenth century Sephardi Jews were summarily exiled from Spain and Portugal, never setting foot there again. Whatever the particulars, the truth inevitably lies in the complication of Jewish identities rather than the simplification.

Jews in Asia: India and China

The history of Jews in Asia—specifically in India and China—though unique, is at the same time comparable to the history of other Jewish communities. Most scholars contend that Jews living in India and China, unlike their associates living in Muslim- and Christian-majority areas, generally lived lives free of persecution and

oppression. Nevertheless, the process by which these Jews cross-fertilized culturally with non-Jews has been somewhat formulaic.

Indian Jews

Another lesser-known group of Jews is Indian, among whom, as with Ethiopians, there is a tradition that one of their subgroups is a "Lost Tribe." Just as other Jewish subcommunities can be additionally subdivided, three basic subcommunities of Indian Jews are recognized, each of which can be subdivided even further (figs. 7.9):

- "Cochinis," from the southwestern Indian state of Kerala;
- "Bnai Israel," whom some consider a "Lost tribe" and who have lived as recently as the last century in Karachi, Pakistan; the Indian cities of Ahmedabad, Mumbai (Bombay), and New Delhi; and an area encompassing a section of northeastern India, Bangladesh, and Myanmar (Burma); they are the largest Jewish subcommunity in India;
- "Baghdadis," the most recent of the three subgroups to arrive on the Indian subcontinent, who have lived in the vicinity of the Indian cities of Mumbai, Pune, and Kolkata (Calcutta), as well as southern Myanmar.

As an indicator of Indian Jewish diversity, scholars need to be versed in Arabic, Hebrew, Hindustani, Judeo-Arabic, Malayalam, and Marathi, among other languages, to be able to study these communities.

"Cochini" Indian Jews

Over time, Cochini Jews have lived in a range of port cities in the area now encompassed by the Indian state of Kerala. Yet for the last few centuries, most have lived in one city, Cochin, hence their name. (At points, Cochin was formally the name for a larger region in southeast India as well, another possibility for their name.) According to their traditions, the community dates back to biblical times, though precisely when is not clear: accepted versions point to a time when King Solomon conducted trade with India, which led to the founding of a new Jewish community there, or to the era following the destruction of either the First Temple, in the sixth century BCE, or the Second Temple, in the first-century CE, when Middle Eastern Jews fled to India and resettled. The primary evidence for any of these possibilities is extensive travel and trade between ancient Israel, ancient Greece, ancient Rome, and

FIGURES 7.9A–B. Indian Jews. *Top:* Bnai Menashe Indian Jews in an Israeli absorption center in December 2012. *Bottom:* A traditional Bnai Israel pre-wedding Mehndi (henna) ceremony at Shaar *Hashamayim* Synagogue in Thane, India, in 2012.

southwestern India. (For example, there are at least forty-five references to Indian spices, such as pepper, in the Talmud, some of which were used in temple rituals.) Medieval Egypt and Persia have also been posited as possible origins for this population.

Whenever and wherever they came from, scholars agree that there have been Jews in Kerala since at least the eleventh century. In the fifteenth century, they were given a plot of land in the city of Cochin, eventually dubbed Jew Town, a name that carries through to today, even though few Jews live there now. From that time onward, they were also involved in the Dutch East India Company.

As far back as at least the sixteenth century, "white" and "black" Jews living in Cochin have often had bitter relations. The white Jewish subgroup, largely of Sephardi descent, was much smaller in number and higher up the socioeconomic ladder than the black subgroup, also called "Malabar" Jews (named after another region in southern India). Scholar Nathan Katz attributes this social stratification to the Indian caste system as well as to racist influences that made their way to Cochin from Europe. Whatever the reasons, Jews who arrived after these tensions began—such as Converso Spanish and Portuguese Jews who came during the seventeenth century—identified as white or black after making Cochin their home.

Regarding particular Cochini rituals, many of their songs and prayers are in Malayalam, a local language of Kerala, and their synagogues have resembled Hindu temples. They share the custom of removing their shoes before entering a synagogue, similar to their Muslim and Hindu neighbors' practice of removing footwear before entering their houses of worship. In the Paradesi Synagogue, the only remaining synagogue in Cochin—built in the sixteenth century by a subgroup of white Jews also called "Paradesis," hence the building's name—there was also a second *bimah* (prayer stage), specifically designed for those in the separate "women's section," one of only two remaining synagogues in the world constructed in this way. (The other is in Anatolia, Turkey.) There are also life-cycle rituals for women, such as wearing a ceremonial sarong for her wedding, and eventually again for her funeral. (Post-funeral and pre-burial, the sarong is taken to the woman's synagogue and hung up and placed on display.)

Cochini Jews are also known for being quite strict in their observance of Passover. They begin to clean for Passover immediately after the end of Hanukkah, some one hundred days before Passover begins—the only Jewish group known to start this process so early. They also set aside a separate room in their homes to store Passover dishes, to ensure that no *ḥametz*—foods prohibited on Pesaḥ—touches these special plates, utensils, etc. So careful are they with their food that they examine each grain of rice individually to ensure there is no accompanying ḥametz. Each year, too, they repaint their houses (safeguarding themselves from potential ḥametz on their walls), purchase new household items (such as cushion covers), purify their water, and isolate themselves completely from their non-Jewish neighbors, to make sure ḥametz doesn't transfer into their food during Pesaḥ.

Bnai Israel Indian Jews

According to one tradition, the founders of the Bnai Israel Jewish community were survivors of a ship that originated in the Land of Israel and sank off the western coast of India (near today's Mumbai) in the second century BCE. Another narrative, sometimes linked to the shipwreck tradition and sometimes not, is that they are the descendants of the ancient Israelite tribe of Menashe (or Ephraim). A third tradition traces the lineage of Bnai Israel Jews back to China, Afghanistan, and Persia. Whatever the case, as of the early twentieth century Bnai Israel Jews were spread out across the places we now call Pakistan, northern India, and northeast India/Bangladesh/Myanmar.

Some scholars note important distinctions among these three geographically differentiated subcommunities of Bnai Israel Jews. For example, there are those who say that the subgroup based in northeast India/Bangladesh/Myanmar (commonly called Shinlug, Zu, or Chin-Kuki-Mizo) is ethnically part of a larger non-Jewish group, known by non-Jews as *Shanwar Telis,* loosely translated as Saturday Oilmen, reflecting the fact that they abstained from pressing oil on Shabbat.

One of the largest communities of Bnai Israel Jews before 1948, when many immigrated to the State of Israel, was in Bombay (Mumbai), where their first synagogue was built in 1796. Those who lived in this area, as well as in the Indian state of Goa to the south, identified as white Bnai Israel Jews, while those in the area now encompassed by Pakistan considered themselves black Jews. During the eighteenth and nineteenth centuries those living in Bombay began to become more conventional in their Jewish practices, integrating dominant forms of Judaism, largely those practiced by Cochini and British Jews, into their own.

At the beginning of the twentieth century, when the territory was still called India, there were roughly 2,500 Bnai Israel Jews living in Karachi; by 1968 there were still 250 Jews in Pakistan, most identifying as Bnai Israel and living in Karachi. As of 2001, only a handful of Jews remained in Pakistan. Aside from the Bnai Israel subcommunity, even in 1953 there were other Jewish subgroups living in Pakistan, such as Persian merchants and European World War II refugees.

Perhaps most noteworthy in terms of ritual is the great importance the Bnai Israel Jews place on the biblical prophet Elijah, more than any other Jewish group. This aside, a number of Bnai Israel rituals resemble those of their non-Jewish neighbors in India. For example, many Bnai Israel songs are chanted in the style of the Indian *kirtan* (a call-and-response form of recitation), with both songs and prayers performed in Marathi, a local language. One ritual, called the *Malida,* is practiced on special occasions—Jewish holidays such as Tu B'Shvat (today akin to a Jewish Earth Day; traditionally, the Jewish new year for trees, celebrated on the fifteenth of the Hebrew month *Shvat,* hence the holiday's name), life-cycle events, the end of Shabbat—by making a dish called *malida* (a sweet dough mixed with ghee, milk, and nuts), topping it with fruit, and after making an "offering" to God, eating it. This practice is similar to Hindu and Muslim Indian rituals. Other rituals the Bnai Israel share with their fellow non-Jewish Indians include painting a bride with henna prior to her wedding ceremony (fig. 7.9b) and doting on pregnant women by bringing them sweets, beautiful clothes, and brushing their hair.

"Baghdadi" Indian Jews

The Jew who started what became known as the "Baghdadi" Jewish Indian community was not from Baghdad, but from Aleppo, Syria. Ironically, aside from Iraq, members of this group came from Afghanistan, Bukhara (in today's Uzbekistan), Kurdistan, Persia, Syria, Tunisia, Yemen, and even Cochin, most arriving during the mid–eighteenth century. Although they first put down roots in Surat, 150 miles north of Bombay, they later moved to Bombay and Calcutta (Kolkata), in eastern India, as well as Myanmar and Bangladesh.

The Baghdadi Jews were unusual in their identification with British colonialists in India. Eventually they asked the British to legally categorize them as European and/or Sephardi, rather than Indian or Middle Eastern. Wealthier Baghdadi Jews dressed "Western" and started speaking English instead of Arabic and Hindustani, while those from lower socioeconomic classes maintained their native languages. (Estimates place the number of Baghdadi Jews who lived in poverty as high as 50 percent.) This assimilation no doubt played a role in the harsh ways they treated Indian Jews that did not take on such dominant non-Jewish behaviors, such as Bnai Israel Jews, particularly those living alongside them in Bombay and Rangoon, Burma, whom they distanced themselves from as much as possible. Regarding particular rituals, most Baghdadi Indian Jews did not identify with the larger Indian or smaller Indian Jewish communities but maintained customs that reflected trends among Sephardi and Mizraḥi Jews (see chapter 1).

Many scholars agree that Baghdadi and Cochini Indian Jews never experienced anti-Jewish sentiment, no small thing considering both the treatment of Jews in other places (see chapter 9) and the way other minorities, such as Muslims, were treated under Hindu rule (and have been treated by Hindu-majority governments since independence). Whether factual or not, most attribute this tolerance to the general ethos of Hinduism.

Indian Jews Today

Most Cochini and Bnai Israel Indian Jews moved to Israel after 1947–1948, following Indian independence and the founding of the Jewish State, while Baghdadi Indian Jews mostly immigrated to England, with a small subgroup choosing Israel instead. Population figures for these groups vary widely, but best estimates are that there are currently 70,000 Indian Jews in Israel, and less than 5,000 still in India (neither figure is differentiated by subgroup). In England, ironically, Baghdadi Indian Jews were perceived as "too Indian," something they had said about Bnai Israel Jews only a few years before. For the most part, none of these Indian Jewish groups had to undergo a ritual conversion prior to becoming citizens of Israel. At the same time, Bnai Israel Jews (but not the other two groups) have been told that if they marry a Jewish Israeli outside their community, the Israeli government would treat such a marriage as if the Bnai Israel Jew was a non-Jew (thus they have had to convert beforehand in order for the wedding to be accepted by the state as halakhically valid).

Chinese Jews

As is the case with other small, isolated Jewish communities such as the Ethiopian and Indian groups, the beginnings of the Chinese Jewish community are shrouded in mystery. Its origins have been dated to anywhere from the third century BCE to the tenth century CE. What is clear is that by the sixth century CE, the city of Kaifeng,

the home of China's oldest known community of Jews, had become an important city on the famed Silk Road (fig. 7.10). According to the Babylonian Talmud, Jews settled along the Silk Road as early as the fourth century CE, if not earlier. Other sources confirm this Jewish presence, such as one noting Persian Jews who lived along the Silk Road in China as of the ninth century.

Approximately 325 miles west of the East China Sea and 400 miles south of Beijing, Kaifeng lies on the Yellow River, China's second-largest river, in a flat, non-mountainous region, close to three other rivers. This confluence of geographical advantages led to Kaifeng's becoming a stopover on the ancient Silk Road "highway" and, from the tenth through twelfth centuries, the capital of China as well. It is likely that Kaifeng became important to Jews because of their involvement in trade and commerce.

Many contend that the founders of Kaifeng's Jewish community were of Babylonian or Persian descent. The few surviving material objects from the community point to this lineage, such as Judeo-Persian words found in prayer books and in an old Haggadah (Passover prayer book). Another theory is that Kaifeng's Jews are descendants of Bukharans (an area located in today's Uzbekistan), who may themselves have descended from Persians. Most agree that Kaifeng's Jewish community was established during the tenth through twelfth centuries, when Kaifeng was China's capital. There is also general agreement that in 1163 CE they built their first, and perhaps only, synagogue.

Whether living under the Tartars or Mongols, or during the Yuan, Song, Han, or Ming Chinese dynasties, Chinese Jews fared the same as other non-Jewish locals. By the fifteenth century, for example, they were using names that were typical for their country, similar to adaptive practices of Jewish subgroups worldwide. The Kaifeng Jewish community's lingua franca was a local dialect of Mandarin, though they also used Hebrew, as is evident from artifacts engraved with Chinese expressions using Hebrew characters.

With the abandonment of the Silk Road, Kaifeng gradually became isolated and less important. When the Yellow River flooded in 1642, the third time in as many centuries, almost the entire city was wiped out, leaving, at best, about two hundred Jews, all of whom had one of seven surnames, a lineage that continues to this day. By the nineteenth century, only eight Jewish families remained, most of them living in poverty. At their height there were probably—at best—no more than 4,000 Jews in Kaifeng, approximately 500 extended families.

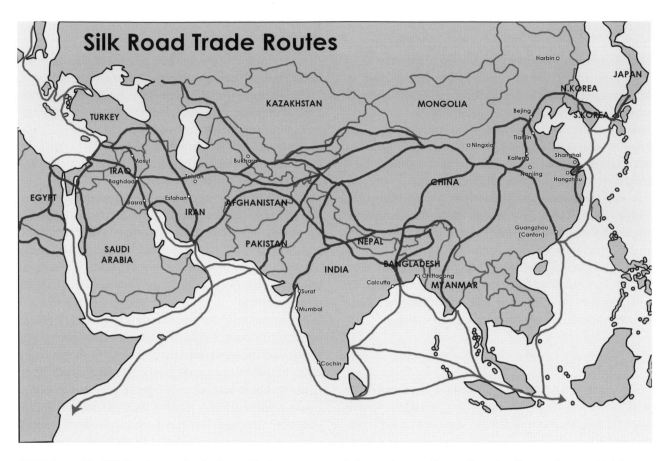

Silk Road Trade Routes

FIGURE 7.10. The Silk Road was not a single road but was composed of countless smaller roads and pathways. Some maintain that China's first Jews arrived there while conducting business along the Silk Road.

According to scholar Xu Xin, as of 1980 only sixty-five Jews remained.

Chinese Jewish Culture in Kaifeng

Like other groups of Jews living as a minority, the Kaifeng community developed in relation to the culture at large. A number of elements of Jewish cultural life point to an integration of halakhah within the larger non-Jewish Chinese milieu. The Jews of Kaifeng integrated Chinese architectural designs into their synagogue (fig. 7.11a), Chinese foods into their diet, Chinese clothing into their attire (although at certain points in history they were required to wear different clothes than non-Jews), and so on. There is also evidence that they integrated Chinese philosophies into their Jewish belief system. In one fifteenth-century text written by a Kaifeng Jew, for example, an inscription on a stone tablet that stood in the courtyard of the city's main synagogue and explained the origins of the community, the author relies more on books central to Confucian thought, such as the *Book of Changes* and the *Analects of Confucius,* than on the Talmud or Torah. According to scholar Irene Eber, by the eighteenth and nineteenth centuries Kaifeng Jews were indistinguishable from non-Jews (figs. 7.11).

These Chinese Jews had other distinctive practices that reflected their immersion in Chinese culture. For example, on Passover they used to eat an actual "paschal lamb" (a directive found in the Torah that has not been practiced with any frequency by Jews for quite some time), in addition to serving a bitter-tasting soup as a substitute for *maror* (bitter herbs). For burial, they followed a local Chinese custom of only marking graves for nonlocals (i.e., if a nonlocal Jew needed to be buried in Kaifeng, the individual's grave would be marked). A Scroll of Esther depicting the characters of the biblical narrative as indigenous Chinese remains one of the most interesting Jewish sacred texts in existence. Unfortunately, most other Kaifeng customs and artifacts have been lost to history.

FIGURES 7.11A–C. Chinese Jews. *Top:* A model of the Kaifeng synagogue from the Beit Hatfutsot museum (see chapter 3) in Tel Aviv, based on an eighteenth-century sketch of the original. *Bottom left:* Chao Tzu-fang and family, Kaifeng, China (c. 1910). *Bottom right:* Jin Guangzhong and his family celebrating Shabbat in 2012. They are among the few remaining members of the Jewish community in Kaifeng.

Jews Living in Other Cities in China (and Hong Kong)

Jews also lived in other Chinese cities beside Kaifeng. In addition to Ningbo and Yangzhou, southeast of Kaifeng, there were Jews in Hangzhou during the twelfth century and in Nanjing and Quangzhou in the fourteenth century (southeast China), as well as in Ningxia in the fifteenth century (northern China, west of Beijing). It is also likely that some Jews traced themselves back to ninth-century Canton, a province in southern China. Further, we know that Jews were present in nineteenth-century Tianjin, a port city eighty miles southeast of Beijing (we also know they built a synagogue there in 1939); and in Harbin, in the far northeastern corner of China, most of whom arrived from Russia. By the mid–nineteenth century there was also a group of Jews living in Shanghai, most of whom were of Iraqi and Egyptian descent. (Fig. 7.10 includes the locations of these cities.)

Finally, Jews have lived in Hong Kong dating back to the nineteenth century, some of them relocating there from nearby Canton after it was conquered by the British. (There were also Jews in Nagasaki, Japan, at this time.) During the 1930s, many Jews fled to Hong Kong from Japanese-occupied areas such as Shanghai. The Jewish population of twenty-first-century Hong Kong is estimated at 6,000.

The Many Other Jewish Communities

Whether going back millennia or mere centuries, there have of course been many other Jewish communities. Whether we're talking about Jews who lived in Muslim-majority areas, such as in Algeria, Lebanon, Libya, and Tunisia, or those who, with the spread of European (Christian) colonialism or because of the Shoah, ended up in places such as Australia, Mexico, the Philippines, South Africa, and South Korea, Jews have dispersed around the globe. Each community has a unique history, usually including the absorption of "new" Jews over time, who have added new layers to the earlier community's culture. Until the twentieth and twenty-first centuries, this geographical diversity was the rule rather than the exception.

A Common Jewish Culture?

As of today, however, 80 percent of the world's Jews live in two countries—the United States and Israel—a historically unprecedented phenomenon that has not only cre-

ated new Jewish cultures and subcultures, but also led to the dominance of specific Jewish narratives. Jews in these countries have reinvented themselves in new ways, a process that is discussed further in chapters 10 and 12. But this situation has also led to the marginalization, and even disappearance, of some unique Jewish subcommunities that existed for much of recorded history.

From the vantage point of the twenty-first century, given the sheer breadth, depth, and length of Jewish history, it would be erroneous to say that there is such a thing as a single Jewish culture. At given times and places, to be sure, there have been dominant trends within particular Jewish communities. But that is all. The descriptions of select Jewish subgroups in this chapter, which merely scratches the surface regarding the myriad types of Jewish cultural practices throughout history, don't even begin to address the twentieth- and twenty-first-centuries phenomenon of intra-Jewish partnering.

Because of the major shift in Jewish geography that has put most of the world's Jews in just two nation-states, an Iraqi Jewish Israeli whose parents were born in Baghdad can pair off with an Ashkenazi Jewish American whose parents are from Poland; a Chinese Jew of Persian descent from Shanghai can pair off with an Egyptian Jew of Sephardi descent whose family was living in Cairo just a generation ago; an Argentinian Jewish American of Syrian descent with ties to Aleppo can pair off with an Ethiopian Jewish Israeli born in Gondar. Though these examples are not the norm, the fact that they are happening at all is extraordinary.

All of this diverts attention away from one of the most common ways Jews pair off today, which is with non-Jews. Whether or not children produced from such partnerships will have Jewish identities—to say nothing of "strong" or "weak" ones—is explored more in chapters 10 and 12. But whether a commitment is made between two Jews from different Jewish backgrounds or between a Jew and a non-Jew, new hybrid identities continue to be added to the vast canon of Jewish cultural expressions as we speak.

Does this mean that there is no "culturally Jewish" common denominator to connect a single, lower-class, Jewish Moroccan man of Sephardi descent living in Casablanca to a married, middle-class, Jewish African American woman living in New York City? As Biale notes, "Culture would appear to be the domain of the plural: we might speak of Jewish *cultures* instead of culture in the singular. And, yet, such a definition would be missing a crucial aspect of Jewish culture: the continuity of both textual and folk traditions throughout Jewish history and throughout the many lands inhabited by the Jews. The multiplicity of Jewish cultures always rested on the Bible and—with the exception of the Karaites and the Ethiopian Jews—on the Talmud and other rabbinic literature." In other words, one premise is that a core set of common texts links Jews worldwide. At the same time, however, Biale goes on to challenge his own assertion, quickly adding that "the Jewish library cannot be reduced to a single 'essence.' . . . Myth and magic occupy as much room on its shelves as law and philosophy." So where does this leave us?

We can certainly say that one of the most important pillars of Jewish culture (as opposed to *cultures*) is the characteristic of adaptability. Whether identifying as isolationist or integrationist, all living Jewish groups adapt. For instance, the Satmar sect of ultra-orthodox Jews, isolationist by any account, played an important role in the 2013 race for New York City mayor. Adaptability also accounts for the diversity of synagogues throughout the world, most mirroring the architectural structure of their surroundings, and for the number of Jewish-specific dialects, including Judeo-Arabic, Ladino, and Yiddish. Another similarity, perhaps, between Jews of different subcultures is that many feel as if they live in exile, whether living inside or outside the Land of Israel (see chapter 3).

To take this conversation in a theoretical direction, another reason there is a Jewish culture is because Jews identify with one another. Despite incredibly different subcultures, Jews identify with other people who claim the same signifier. In other words, something that connects all Jews is that they call themselves Jews. Similarly, as photographer Frédéric Brenner once noted, the thing that links all Jews is their differences. Along the same lines, to quote Jean-Paul Sartre on Jews and Jewish identities: "If they have a common bond, if all of them deserve the name of Jew, it is because they have in common the situation of a Jew, that is, they live in a community which takes them for Jews."

Of course, all group identities can be understood as such. It is profoundly postmodern to say that anyone who calls herself X is part of community X. All collectives are made up of disparate individuals who are connected by virtue of their desire to connect with a common group. If people believe themselves to be part of a community—if this is how they identify—then they are, to some degree or another.

Such a postmodern approach, however, has its limits. One is that identities are shaped by others—those outside a group—as much as they are by those within a group. As an example, if group X is murdering members of group Y, no matter what an individual from group Y might say in her own defense, when group X labels her a member of group Y, she surely will be killed. The role of the other in shaping identities is explored more in chapters 9 and 11.

The second limit is that there *are* borders to the Jewish collective. Not everyone who identifies as a Jew is accepted as a Jew by other Jews. Consider the example at the beginning of chapter 5, where an individual raised as a Jew from birth, who attended thirteen years of Jewish parochial school, spent ten summers at a religiously affiliated Jewish overnight camp, and studied in a number of Orthodox seminaries, was told that due to a technicality in his mother's conversion his Jewish identity was potentially suspect. This idea is explored further in chapter 11.

Movements

Contents

Key Ideas

• Many members of the Jewish community identify as Jews in terms of their religion; many do not, instead identifying as Jewish ethnically, culturally, etc. Similarly, categorizing someone as a religious Jew or a secular Jew does not necessarily tell us anything about the person as it is overly simplistic.

- Although current Jewish denominations only began taking shape in the nineteenth century, the notion of Jewish (or proto-Jewish) sectarianism is ancient.
- The development of Jewish movements has largely been shaped by non-Jewish communities' ideas and influence.
- The so-called founders of Reform, Orthodox, Conservative, and Reconstructionist Judaism did not necessarily intend to start new denominations. Further, the growth of modern Jewish denominationalism has been slow and gradual.

From Movement to Nonmovement

I grew up in the Conservative movement: I went to a Conservative-affiliated synagogue, summer overnight camp, and parochial primary school. Yet by the time I graduated from a nondenominational Jewish high school, I could only give a simplistic (and no doubt inaccurate) explanation of the differences between the three largest Jewish denominations of the last century: Conservative, Reform, and Orthodox.

In college, I spent much more time in Orthodox environments, while simultaneously maintaining an allegiance to the liberal streams of my youth. For a Jewish American in the 1980s and 1990s, identifying as a liberal Jew—that is, as Reform, Conservative, or even Reconstructionist—was the norm. (The fact that I went to a Jewish parochial school and religious summer camp made me somewhat unusual statistically, however.) Then for most of my twenties, I did not associate with a particular synagogue. If I wanted to participate in Jewish communal prayer, which I did on occasion, I was most comfortable in a setting similar to those of my youth. In my thirties, I remained unaffiliated; only right before my partner and I had our first child did we formally join a synagogue.

I share all of this not because these parts of my Jewish life are particularly interesting. (They're not.) Rather, in terms of affiliation, my experience falls within the Jewish American statistical norm for the period since the 1970s. Most Jews under the age of forty, in both the United States and Israel, do not affiliate with a particular movement. My personal choices regarding marriage and having children also fall within socially accepted standards.

Today, heteronormative American Jews, like non-Jews, most commonly get married and have children in their thirties, and at around the same time most decide to join a synagogue, most of which are affiliated with a denomination. People often feel a greater responsibility to engage with their Jewishness once they have children. As scholars Steven Cohen and Ari Kelman put it, "The organized Jewish community, like other religious communities in America, is heavily structured around and built for (and by) married couples with children." If one is single, it is more difficult to fit in (except, perhaps, with other singles).

Yet even though my experiences reflect recent Jewish American norms, they are different from the dominant Jewish communal trends of the last two centuries. For Jews over forty today, and for virtually all Jews of the last two hundred–plus years, a primary way to define Jewishness, at a minimum in relation to other Jews, has been via denominational attachment. Although twenty-first-century Jews are rapidly moving away from such affiliations, it would be impossible to unpack the current state of Jewish identities if we didn't look at some of the overriding trends that got us here.

Meanings of "Religious Identity"

In October 2013, the Pew Research Center published a study about twenty-first-century American Jewish identities. When asked whether they identified with a particular religion, 22 percent said no. In addition, sixty-two percent said they would frame Jewish identity in terms of "ancestry/culture," 15 percent in terms of "religion," and 23 percent as both. While fascinating data, one basic flaw in this study—and most studies that poll "religious identity"—is that the terms *religion* and *religious* have many meanings.

Most definitions of "religion" are God-centric, focusing on an organized system of beliefs, rituals, and rules related to the worship of a God or group of Gods. However, not only are there different ideas about the divine (chapter 2 touches on differences between theism and monism, for example), but God-centric definitions exclude nontheistic religions such as Buddhism, Jainism, and Confucianism. (At a large meeting at the University of California, Santa Barbara, in 1991, the Dalai Lama publicly proclaimed, "We Buddhists are atheists.")

If we take God out of the equation, per se, we're left with religion as an organized system of beliefs, rituals, and rules. This resembles the definition of renowned cultural anthropologist Clifford Geertz: religion is a structure whereby humans organize the world into a meaningful worldview. He also distinguishes between a "religious belief in the midst of ritual, where it engulfs the total person, transporting him, so far as he is connected, into another mode of existence, and religious belief as the pale, remembered reflection of that experience in the midst of everyday life." In other words, even when we

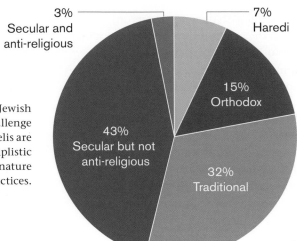

FIGURE 8.1. Self-defined religiosity of Jewish Israelis (2009). Data such as these challenge the oft-cited notion that Jewish Israelis are either secular or religious, an overly simplistic binary that fails to reflect the fluid nature of identity in terms of ritual practices.

enact a ritual without being aware of doing so—such as, for instance, not eating a certain food based on what we were taught about it as children—it is still a ritual.

Scholar Ninian Smart observes that religion is a human phenomenon with multiple dimensions, each of which can be isolated and examined. Likewise, when talking about Jews as a religious community or a religious identity—whether faith-based, cultural, or ethnic—being Jewish is one of many aspects of one's social identity. Moreover, when someone says that Judaism is their religion, as many did in the Pew Center study, this really only tells us how they identify and not what they believe.

"Secular" and "Religious" Jews in Israel and the United States

Jewish identities also have different meanings in different countries. For example, Jewish Israelis are often described as either *dati* (religious) or *ḥiluni* (secular), with the former usually equated only with Orthodoxy or ultra-Orthodoxy. A 2009 poll asking Jewish Israelis how they defined themselves "religiously" found that 43 percent identified as "secular, but not anti-religious" (fig. 8.1). Those who so identified commonly keep kosher dietary laws, observe Shabbat, regularly study Jewish texts (i.e., Torah, Talmud), and "feel religious." Even 25 percent of Jewish Israelis who identified as "secular and anti-religious" observe Jewish rituals "to some extent." In contrast, Jewish Americans who observe kashrut and Shabbat in a "traditional manner" are often regarded as "religious."

Although nearly half of Jewish Israelis identify as secular, more than 80 percent "always" or "frequently" make an effort to be with their family on Shabbat, 85 percent

say it is "important" or "very important" to observe Jewish holidays according to tradition, 70 percent keep kosher, 94 percent deem it "important" or "very important" to perform a *brit milah* (ritual circumcision) for newborn males, and 91 percent think having a Bar Mitzvah is "important" or "very important."

The same poll found that 67 percent believe that Jews are the "chosen people" and 65 percent believe that the Torah and the mitzvot were "God-given." This means that a number of "secular" Jews in Israel believe things that might be considered foundationally "religious." In contrast, although 62 percent of Jewish Americans explain Jewish identity as based in ancestry or culture, and not religion, 40 percent believe that the Land of Israel was "given by God to the Jewish people."

In other words, in Israel and the United States—as in countless other places—although many Jews do not identify as religious, they share beliefs with those who do and perform countless "religious" observances. To understand the "religious" dimensions of Jewish identities, it may be best to approach beliefs and ritual observances as marks on a spectrum rather than as an all or nothing proposition, noting further that over the course of a year, or a lifetime, people can go through many phases in regard to their personal beliefs and practices. This perspective characterizes this chapter's survey of the movements within Judaism.

"Movements" or "Denominations"?

Scholars of modern Jewish groups often make a distinction between the terms *denomination* and *movement*. The former, they say, is a word appropriated from the

Protestants, used to describe differences among Christians. Partly for this reason, when speaking about Jewish groups there has been a shift over the last few decades toward the term *movement* instead. Similar debates echo scholars' discussions about first-century CE Palestine-based Jewish groups, and whether it is more accurate to call them sects, movements, or something else altogether.

For our purposes, what is most important is that, whether in the first or twenty-first century CE, the factions that Jews have affiliated with only differentiate them from, and are most important for, other Jews. All subgroups are social collections of people with dominant narratives and general agreements; each one reflects aspects of the larger collective narratives of the entire Jewish community, though each one also has attributes that differentiate it from other Jewish subgroups. At the same time, further gradations exist within subgroups themselves. This chapter begins with a glance at some Jewish groups in ancient Palestine before moving to the development of the Reform, Orthodox, and Conservative movements; it concludes with three smaller twentieth-century Jewish movements, all of which were first established in the United States.

Ancient Movements

From as far back as the Hebrews, Israelites, and Judeans, the Jewish community has never been homogeneous. Although most of this chapter focuses on Jewish movements of the last few centuries, let us start by touching on two brief periods in the ancient Land of Israel to illustrate how heterogeneity has always been the norm, not the exception, among Jews (and proto-Jews). First is second-century BCE Palestine, where a group of Judeans called the Hasmoneans lived semiautonomously under Greek and Roman control. As mentioned in chapters 3 and 7, although often described as a passionate group of proto-Jews who fought together against the ruling power for independence, this subcommunity was in fact composed of distinct Jewish subgroups, including, for example, Zealots and non-Zealots, Maccabees and non-Maccabees, Hellenists and non-Hellenists. Then, in first-century CE Palestine, less than two hundred years later, rather than a number of subgroups under the larger umbrella of Hasmoneans, there were a handful of Jewish groups with different names, such as Christians, Essenes, Pharisees, Sadducees, and Zealots.

Jewish identities in the ancient Middle East, clearly, were different from those of today. But if we approach movement affiliation as a conventional pattern of being a member of a particular Jewish subgroup, no matter the era, heterogeneity becomes the focus. Whether called a denomination, movement, or sect, these ancient subgroups—as well as, perhaps, today's—are trees in the forest of Jewish history and identities.

Hasmonean Heterogeneity

According to dominant Jewish narratives today, when Jews were living under the Greeks in the second-century BCE Land of Israel, during what some historians refer to as the Hasmonean period of Jewish history, a Judean family called the Maccabees emerged that decided to cast off Greek hegemony. Over time, a story about this family morphed into an entirely new Jewish holiday, what many consider the first nonbiblical one: Hanukkah. During the annual contemporary celebration of this holiday, Jews often tell one another the story of how a small family challenged the mighty Greek army in an against-all-odds David-and-Goliath-type battle. When this family recaptured the Temple, which had been desecrated by the Greeks with idols and pigs' blood, they noticed that the Temple candelabra, which did not have enough oil for more than a day, had miraculously remained burning for eight consecutive nights.

Not only is there reason to doubt many parts of this narrative, but we do not even know just when Hanukkah became popularized among Judeans. Like all Jewish holidays, this ritual, and its accompanying story, developed and changed over time. To be sure, the earliest celebrants of the holiday were not eating *latkes* (potato pancakes) and *sufganiyot* (jelly-filled donuts) nor showering their children with chocolate coins and presents, all customs connected to Hanukkah today. In fact, virtually everything from this ancient period is up for debate. For example, some contend that one of the Greek rulers, Antiochus IV, declared harsh edicts against the Judeans in reaction to their rebelliousness; the Judeans, in other words, were the instigators, not the other way around.

Most relevant for us, the core of this ancient story dramatizes the internal schisms within the Israelite and Judean-Israelite communities—i.e., there were Judeans who took up arms against the Greeks and those who did not, not to mention Samaritan-Israelites (as opposed to Judean-Israelites)—which eventually spilled out into the larger non-Judean milieu. (For instance, some contend that during the second century BCE tensions between the Samaritan-Israelites and Judean-Israelites came to a head when a Judean Maccabean king named John Hyrcanus destroyed the Samaritan temple on Mount Gerizim; see chapter 11.) The Books of Maccabees dispute such assertions, maintaining that "it was the Greeks vs. Maccabees, not the Maccabees against other Jews!," justifying, and even glorifying, the Maccabees as heroes who fought against the evil Greek empire. (Somewhat ironically, it is the Greek translation of these books that survived to the modern era.)

But lest we think that clear lines separated these proto-Jews from people outside their community, after a Judean region was reestablished during the Hasmonean period (part of the larger region formerly called Judea) and a group of non-Judeans called the Idumeans were captured, many of them became part of the Judean community. According to scholar Shaye Cohen, they were brought into the Judean milieu not as members of a new ethnicity, but as citizens of an area newly under Judean control. (One ancient text, the book of Judith, however fictional, says that even the Greek ruler Antiochus chose to become a Judean.) What is perhaps most probable is that some Idumeans opposed Judeans, while some Judeans were pro-Greek. In any event, the lines were much more nebulous than the standard Hanukkah narrative suggests.

Pharisees, Sadducees, Essenes, Zealots

A few centuries later, during the first century CE, the Jewish community continued to be made up of a number of subgroups. Estimates of the population of Jews in Palestine at this time range from hundreds of thousands to 2,500,000. Many who teach about this era in Jewish history list the following distinct Jewish groups (or sects) as the most important: Christians, Essenes, Pharisees, Sadducees, and Zealots. They are usually described in the following manner:

- Christian Jews believed Jesus was the messiah (though they weren't known by this moniker at the time).
- The Essenes lived in Qumran, an area adjacent to the Dead Sea; they are usually credited with having written the Dead Sea Scrolls.
- The Pharisees are commonly considered the rabbis referred to in the Mishnah and Talmud.
- The Sadducees were the Temple priests, a position that gave them a much higher socioeconomic status than other Jews.
- The Zealots (sometimes called the Sicarii, from the Latin word for dagger) may have been descendants of the Hasmoneans and/or Maccabees. They were

extremist Jews who targeted both Romans and those Jews they considered to have assimilated too far into the larger non-Jewish milieu. They became perhaps most well known for taking over a fortress on a Dead Sea mountain top called Masada, where they fought off the Romans for a number of years (see chapter 10).

These communities have been the subject of a great deal of scholarly debate. One reason for the lack of certainty is the dearth of sources from this time. Aside from texts discussed in chapters 2 and 5, such as the Mishnah, Talmud, Apocrypha, Pseudepigrapha, Josephus's writings, Dead Sea Scrolls, and other Jewish texts commonly referred to as rabbinic, most sources describing the first century CE are actually from the second and third centuries CE, such as the Synoptic Gospels (Matthew, Mark, Luke, and John). Hence, a number of scholarly giants maintain that the boundaries between Hellenistic Jews (those who identified as Greek culturally but not ethnically or tribally; see chapter 7) and rabbinic Jews—schisms that began prior to the Hasmonean period and continued well beyond this era—were not clear or uniform.

The facts about any of these groups may never be known. For example, many contend there is a basic lack of evidence for today's common claim that the Pharisees were either the proto-rabbis or the rabbis of the Mishnah and Talmud. Although after 70 CE (following the destruction of the Second Temple; see chapter 3) the rabbis may have felt the need to link themselves to Moses in an unbroken chain of authority, they themselves never explicitly say that their predecessors were the Pharisees.

Shaye Cohen argues that the Pharisees were most likely heterogeneous and had subcommunities, such as those deemed "anti-Roman" (e.g., devotees of Judas the Galilean, who demanded autonomy from proxy-Roman rulers such as Herod) and "pro-Roman" (who subjugated themselves to the Romans, sporadically offering minimal resistance). Other scholars have described seven different subdivisions among the Pharisees, not just two. Some point to evidence of a Pharisaic subgroup intentionally killing non-Pharisaic Jews with whom they disagreed. Still others contend that they were "revolutionaries" or, quite the opposite, that they kept their heads down and did their best not to stir the pot.

We aren't even positive about the origins of the name Pharisee, which is rooted in the Aramaic for "set apart." One theory is that the name was given retroactively to the group of Jews who opposed the Sadducees, but it was not a name they used themselves—just as eighteenth-century CE opponents of the Hasidic movement never actually called themselves Mitnagdim (lit. Opponents; see later in this chapter). This idea is supported by the fact that usually when the Pharisees are mentioned in the Talmud they appear in tandem with the Sadducees, espousing different opinions regarding a halakhic issue. Another theory is that their name distinguished them not from the Sadducees but from the masses, referred to as *am ha-aretz* (lit. people of the land, in the Talmud referring to uneducated Jews), particularly in regard to ritual observances related to purity.

Then there are the Zealots, or as some call them the Sicarii or the Fourth Philosophy (though these may have been either two or three separate groups). Some say that the boundaries between the Zealots and the Pharisees were shaded in gray and that they agreed on issues related to Jewish law. Our main, and perhaps only, source for the Zealots' existence is Josephus, and at times his descriptions are contradictory. Some historians maintain that members of this group not only carried out regular attacks on Romans, but also attacked fellow Jews they considered to be overly assimilationist or traitorous.

Trying to piece together events from two thousand years ago is difficult. The bottom line regarding these ancient Jewish subgroups is that we don't know anything for sure. But regardless of the varied interpretations of the historical records, what is clear is that heterogeneity is an ancient characteristic of the Jewish community.

The (Jewish) Enlightenment

To continue this history of intra-Jewish diversity, let's fast-forward to eighteenth-century Western Europe and the Age of Enlightenment. Intellectual trends such as the Scientific Revolution (e.g., Charles Darwin's *Origin of Species*) were in full swing, as were political developments like the rise of the nation-state, which was accompanied by notions of citizenship and equal rights. European Jews were among the minorities granted legal equality in country after country during this period, which in Jewish history is commonly called the Emancipation.

Two centuries after Martin Luther had sparked the Protestant Reformation, European Catholics—now symbolizing all that was wrong with religion—had become a minority, while religious ritual and practice had been made more accessible to the masses (via Luther's concept of the priesthood of all believers). Although biblical criticism—whether understood as the idea that humans wrote the Bible or that despite the Bible's divine origin its transmission had been corrupted (see chapter 2)— had not yet been mainstreamed, "reason" had become

central to everyday conversations, especially those on religion.

All of these changes in European society, which took shape from the sixteenth through eighteenth centuries, also influenced the Jews living there. The literal and metaphorical walls of the ghetto—isolated areas in urban centers that Jews had been required to live in for centuries, sometimes while wearing yellow stars—had begun to crumble. For some Jews, this meant choosing to no longer follow ritual halakhic observances. (Special topic 8.1 includes a description of some of the many Jewish ritual practices of eighteenth-century Europe.)

France, the Netherlands, Belgium, and Greece began considering making Jews citizens, which included giving them legal rights, such as owning private property, that they had been denied for centuries. In 1791, the second year of the French Revolution, Jews in France indeed received full civil rights as citizens of the state. "France is our Palestine," one French Jew wrote, "her mountains our Zion, her rivers our Jordan." However, to exercise their new rights, Jews had to publicly declare that they were French first and Jews second.

Jews began to proudly profess "Enlightenment" ideas that only decades earlier they had considered sacrilegious. For example, in 1670 the Dutch Jew Baruch Spinoza had published his controversial *Politico-Theological Treatise,* a book that not only rejected the divine election of any people, Jews included, but went so far as to claim that the Torah was not authored by God. Within a century, arguably, many of these ideas had become normative. The eighteenth century is also when the so-called scientific study of Judaism—*Wissenschaft des Judenthums*—emerged as a reputable field of scholarship. Building on Spinoza's work, which previously many thought was heretical, textual criticism began to be applied to sources as sacred as the Hebrew Bible. According to scholar Jacob Neusner, *Wissenschaft des Judenthums* was not yet a "university discipline, though it aspired to academic status," an eventual precursor to today's academic area called "Jewish Studies." (In Jewish circles, the Enlightenment commonly went by its Hebrew name, the *Haskalah,* and its adherents were called *maskilim.*)

In the German Jewish community, a man named Moses Mendelssohn, a ritually observant Jew who was also a philosopher and art critic, came to embody the ethos of integration (fig. 8.2). Fluent in both German and Hebrew, credited with translating the Torah into German, on a first-name basis with giants of the age such as Immanuel Kant, he both pushed European Jews to embrace their respective nation-states and encouraged non-Jews to give Jews political equality.

As scholar Todd Endelman explains in *Broadening Jewish History,* though there were major transformations in European Jewish life during this era, such changes did not keep pace with those experienced by their Christian neighbors:

> At first glance, middle-class Jews in Berlin, Paris, London, Amsterdam, Vienna, and Budapest were indistinguishable from their non-Jewish counterparts. They wore the same clothes, spoke the same language, visited the same cafes, museums and concert halls, educated their children at the same schools, and enjoyed the same leisure-time activities. . . . Yet despite these advances in institutional integration and social mixing in public forums, Jews remained a people apart in terms of their most fundamental social ties. . . . The situation was not radically different among the wealthiest Jewish families. . . . Judaism, even after emancipation, was not a religion in the same way that Christianity was. It retained a collective social dimension and encompassed customs and laws. . . . It regulated behavior in which Christianity took little interest, for example, in matters of diet and Sabbath and festival rest.

Of course, as with all times and places, there is no one-size-fits-all. Generally, for example, French Jews were less ritually observant than English Jews. And among the latter, wealthy Ashkenazi Jewish men were more likely than their middle- and lower-class counterparts to shave off their beards, dress like non-Jews, engage in non-Jewish social customs (e.g., attending the opera and theater), and ignore somewhat or altogether kashrut and Sabbath laws. Similarly, English Sephardi Jews, many of whom had been "immersed in the social and cultural life of the non-Jewish world prior to their settlement in England," were more negligent in observing these Jewish ritual laws than their Ashkenazi countrymen and countrywomen. At the same time, in some places, such as Warsaw, Poland, in Eastern Europe, lack of ritual observances among middle- and lower-class Ashkenazi Jews led to conversions to Christianity.

Laxity among British Ashkenazi Jews at large didn't manifest until the mid–eighteenth century, however. Prior to that time, it was German Jews who had gone farther than most in terms of changing, or even disregarding, many ritual practices (see "Reform Judaism" later in the chapter). Yet through the end of the nineteenth century, although most British Jews were practicing what could then be described as Reform understandings of halakhah rather than Orthodox, they refused to identity as Reform. Indeed, no more than 10 percent of England's Jews identified as Reform through the mid–twentieth century, until after World War II.

In the mid–nineteenth century, a Russian Jewish *maskil* named Judah Leib Gordon proclaimed, "Be a Jew in your home and a man outside it," an idea that Mendelssohn would have supported. But not all Jews in eighteenth-century Europe agreed. Some tried to isolate themselves from all non-Jewish ideas, and others renounced their Jewish identities altogether. The famous German poet Heinrich Heine, a contemporary of Mendelssohn's, for example, shed his Jewish "skin" and had a Christian baptism. (Presciently, Heine famously said, "Where books are burned, in the end people will be burned.") Even four of Mendelssohn's six children married non-Jews and/or converted to Christianity. Of course, the broad strokes painted here are simplifications. Although Mendelssohn was surely one of the most important German Jewish voices of his era, he was also an exception, especially in terms of how he was accepted by the non-Jewish intellectual elite. In fact, German Jews didn't achieve full legal equality until 1871.

It is within this context that Reform Judaism was born.

Reform Judaism

Like the founders of other new movements, it does not seem that the founders of Reform Judaism intended to start a new denomination. All the reformers were committed Jews, and all were concerned about the manner in which European Jews were integrating Haskalah ideas into their lives, with some choosing to leave Judaism altogether. They realized that the Jewish community was changing and that if they, too, didn't change and make ritual practices more relevant, Jews might assimilate into oblivion.

FIGURE 8.2. This painting by Moritz Daniel Oppenheim (c. 1856) portrays a 1763 imagined meeting of three scholars in the library of Moses Mendelssohn in Berlin—Mendelsohn *(left)*, Gotthold Ephraim Lessing *(center, standing)*, and theologian Johann Kaspar Lavater *(right)*. Over the doorway, where the domestic attendant is holding a tray, there is a Hebrew blessing from the Torah (Deut. 28:6), one of many images in the painting that reflect the presence of religious belief in a "modern" European setting.

Western Europe

The early reformers were laypeople, not rabbis, who began making changes in their own Jewish communal practices by shortening prayer services, integrating choruses with organs, and ensuring sermons and prayers were delivered in the local language. One of the most important of these reformers was Israel Jacobson, who founded a school in Seesen, in central Germany, to educate both Jewish and Christian children. From 1810, the services conducted in the school chapel included these innovations, and after 1815 he continued such services in his home in Berlin, 180 miles to the east. In 1818, the Hamburg Temple adopted them as well, becoming the first Reform synagogue.

Although the reformers' innovations were controversial, most were not actually new ideas. Translating Hebrew prayers into the dominant, non-Hebrew language of a community is laid out in the Mishnah. Nor was the practice of abbreviating prayers original. For most of Jewish history, there wasn't just one Jewish prayer book, there were many, and prayers came in various versions and lengths. Even integrating a choir into prayer services was not anathema to *halakhah* (Jewish law; chapter 5). Still, many communities resisted change. For some, the most challenging new practice was having a musical instrument—in this case, an organ—as part of a Shabbat service.

To explain why these challenges were halakhically permitted, a rabbi in Dessau, Germany, Eliezer Lieberman, published halakhic *teshuvot* (responses)—legal questions followed by answers from one or more rabbis. In one of these teshuvot, an Italian rabbi said that the recent practice of using an organ was appropriated from Christians but then added that Christians had first learned the ritual of playing music during prayer from first-century Jews worshiping in the Temple in Palestine, so it was actually, in its original form, a Jewish custom.

These early "reformers" were trying to make Jewish ritual more relevant to the Jews of their time. Moreover, they were working from the assumption that halakhah was obligatory. From their perspective, all of their innovations were permissible, justified according to the rules and logic of the halakhic system. None of them would have called themselves "Reform Jews," just Jews. In fact, if we used contemporary terms to retroactively categorize these Jews, we would say that they were Orthodox. (Remember, there were no Reform Jews or Orthodox Jews yet; these labels were not yet used.)

There was a range of opinions within this German-based proto-Reform movement, and over the first half of the nineteenth century the movement's perspectives broadened further still. On one end of the spectrum were those such as Eliezer Lieberman who were committed to working within the halakhic framework, making changes only if they could justify them halakhically. On the other end were those more comfortable adapting ideas from the larger non-Jewish milieu without necessarily substantiating them with halakhic arguments. This group was eventually in favor of more dramatic changes, such as removing notions of messianic redemption from prayers; swapping the name *synagogue* with *temple* to reflect the fact that they did not want to rebuild the Temple in Jerusalem; and substituting the observance of the Jewish Sabbath from Friday/Saturday with Saturday/Sunday, to be more in line with Christian communities' *day of rest*.

In 1844, the Reform movement became official when the reformers held their first rabbinical conference in Breslau, Germany, which was followed by annual conferences in 1845 and 1846. Thus the century's most radical European Jewish ideologues began to lay the groundwork for an organizational infrastructure.

Meanwhile, new camps within the movement emerged. One was represented by such people as Rabbi Abraham Geiger, who argued that the Jewish community was always changing because ideological development was an organic process of evolution; change in small steps, he said, was not only best but was historically normal. On the other side of the debate, Rabbi Samuel Holdheim of the Berlin synagogue *Reformgemeinde* (lit. Reform Congregation) asserted that what was happening was not evolution but revolution. Although there were "eternally valid religious elements" in the Torah, Holdheim said, there were also anachronistic laws, rituals practiced by the biblical Hebrew community some three millennia prior that were no longer relevant. At the 1846 conference, Holdheim led the charge in suggesting that the entire movement embrace the Saturday/Sunday observance of Shabbat, a practice his synagogue had adopted the previous year.

United States

Jews began coming to America during the early colonial period, establishing their first congregation—which predated modern denominations and was thus not affiliated with a particular movement—in New York City in 1654 (Congregation Shearith Israel). These Jews, largely of Dutch, Portuguese, and Spanish Sephardic descent, also set up *mikva'ot* (ritual baths; sing. *mikveh*), kosher slaughtering facilities, Jewish burial societies, and more. But theirs was a relatively small community.

Estimates of the Jewish population in the United States' first three-quarters century are as follows: 1790—1,200 (.03% of the total population); 1818—3,000; 1840—15,000; 1848—50,000 (.2% of the total population). Then, between 1880 and 1910, one million–plus Ashkenazi European Jews arrived in the United States from Russia and Eastern Europe: 1880—230,000 (.5%); 1888—400,000 (.6%); 1900—1,058,000 (1.3%).

While it is unclear to what extent early-nineteenth-century Jewish Americans were influenced by German Jewish reformers, the proto-Reform movement in the United States was starting to take off at the same time. The same perspectives were being voiced, but the landscapes for change were starkly different. In Germany, aside from two synagogues that started up as new institutions (in Hamburg and Berlin), the reformers were working exclusively within established Orthodox communities, trying to make change from within. In contrast, in the United States entirely new communities could be (and were being) created.

In 1824, a few members of a synagogue in Charleston, South Carolina, founded the Society of Reformed Israelites after the synagogue's board of trustees rejected their request for changes to their prayer services. As in Germany, this group was led not by a rabbi but by a layperson, Isaac Harby. However, possibly the most important person to lay the groundwork for today's American Reform movement was another man, Rabbi Isaac Mayer Wise, who immigrated to the United States in 1846.

Wise did not initially intend to start a new movement; for example, he did not call himself or his ideas "Reform" or even "Liberal." Initially, he wanted simply to create a new, unified Jewish American community, not launch intra-Jewish denominational opposition. One of his first efforts, in 1857, was to publish a new prayer book, *Minhag America* (*minhag* meaning custom), which offered one way American Jews could literally get on the same page. To be more in line with American society and its six-day workweek, in 1869 he pushed to change the core community weekly prayer service from Saturday morning to Friday evening, thinking that more Jews would be willing to go to synagogue if it didn't conflict with their work schedule.

By 1873, Wise had founded the first national organization of Reform synagogues, the Union of American Hebrew Congregations (UAHC; now known as the Union for Reform Judaism, or URJ). He started the Reform movement's first rabbinical school, Hebrew Union College (HUC), in Cincinnati in 1875, and the first national organization of Reform rabbis, the Central Conference of American Rabbis (CCAR), in 1889.

While Wise was successfully driving the establishment of American Reform institutions, ideologically the movement was moving more in a direction laid out by another figure, Rabbi David Einhorn, the American ideological equivalent of Germany's Samuel Holdheim. For example, in 1892, when deciding on its official prayer book, the CCAR chose not *Minhag America* but one proposed by Einhorn, now called the *Union Prayer Book*.

Even more important, although Einhorn died in 1869, his ideas are credited as a foundational influence on the 1885 "Pittsburgh Platform," which became the unofficial organizational platform for the Reform movement for decades thereafter. One of the most notable ideas articulated in the Pittsburgh Platform is the commitment to the Torah's "moral laws," regulations based in justice and righteousness (and also, by and large, dictated by American civil law). In contrast, laws dealing with diet, dress, priestly behavior, and animal sacrifices were no longer obligatory for Jews, being "primitive," "foreign," and not based on reason or science. In addition, the Pittsburgh Platform did not support a "return to Palestine" or a restoration of a Jewish state of any kind. Many scholars contend that this new set of ideological statements reflected those espoused by countless American Protestant churches of the time. Scholar Lance Sussman describes it as "clearly a Judaic parallel to the New Theology of the Protestant modernists."

Since 1885, the Reform movement in the United States has become the epicenter for Reform Judaism worldwide. It has gone through a number of official and unofficial ideological changes, some of which are outlined in the Columbus Platform of 1937 and the New Pittsburgh Platform of 1999. Several of these adjustments have to do with

gender equality, both de jure and de facto. The German Reform movement was the first to ordain a female rabbi, Regina Jonas, in 1935; in 1972, Sally J. Priesand became the first American female rabbi (fig. 8.5). Although there has never been a female president of the URJ or HUC, in 2003 Rabbi Janet Marder was elected president of the CCAR, the highest position a woman held in any major Jewish movement, Reform or otherwise, until January 2014, when Rabbi Deborah Waxman began serving as president of the Reconstructionist Rabbinical College, the Reconstructionist movement's seminary and congregational institution (see below).

As for how the Reform movement has approached queer issues—those related to sexual, sexed, and gendered variances (see special topic 0.2)—the same year as Priesand's ordination, 1972, the world's first gay and lesbian synagogue, Beit Chayim Chadashim, was founded in Los Angeles. The Reform movement accepted it as a member congregation, while simultaneously proclaiming that the movement did not need gay- and lesbian-specific synagogues, that such individuals were welcome in any Reform community. The following year New York City's Congregation Beth Simchat Torah was established.

In 1977, the movement called for an end to discrimination against gays and lesbians in terms of civil law; in 1982, it approved gay and lesbian converts; and although in 1985 it declared opposition to gay and lesbian Jewish marriages, that position was formally reversed in 1993. In 1989, the Union for Reform Judaism declared that the "union of [Reform] congregations must be a place where loneliness and suffering and exile end," and the following year openly gay and lesbian rabbinical students were accepted into Reform seminaries, followed in 2003 by the acceptance of bisexual and transgender rabbinical students. (In 2000, Reform rabbis were granted permission to marry gay or lesbian couples.) In March 2015, Rabbi Denise Eger became the CCAR's first openly gay president.

Arguably, however, this movement's most controversial decision came in October 1983, when the CCAR passed a resolution that redefined the centuries-old parameters of who is a Jew. In a detailed responsum, the CCAR explained that

- During biblical and postbiblical eras, patrilineal descent was the primary way of determining a Jew's identity.
- It is unclear when the shift was made from patrilineal to matrilineal descent;
- nor do we know the historical reasons for this change.

- During the nineteenth and twentieth centuries, Jews confronted situations entirely different from the past, and unions between Jews and non-Jews became not only not rare but common.
- Jews have always reshaped communal laws based on changing realities.

With this justification, the CCAR decided that an individual needs to have only one Jewish parent—either mother or father—in order to be accepted as a Jew. This decision meant that the Reform movement and the other two major American movements, Orthodoxy and Conservatism, no longer had a common answer to the basic question of who is a Jew.

Orthodox (as in Not Reform) Judaism

While the reformers in nineteenth-century Germany were starting to voice their ideas, some nonreformers were digging in their heels, vociferously maintaining their opposition to what they perceived were radical modifications. But just as the initial reformers are framed as founders of the Reform movement only in retrospect, we can't accurately call the nonreformers "Orthodox" either. They, too, were simply Jews, some of whom believed in traditional doctrines, some of whom didn't, but all of whom felt Reform Jews were going too far with their changes to conventional Jewish practices, and were moving closer and closer to Christianity. Only over time, once the reformers began to label themselves Reform (and/or Liberal), did this other subgroup go by the name Orthodox. (Some in this subgroup eventually founded Conservative Judaism, as we see in the next section.)

Western Europe

Opponents of the reformers in Germany often understood that the reformers were sincere in believing that by making changes to Jewish practices they would preserve Judaism. But the opponents disagreed with the reformers' methods, arguing that these changes—most of which they thought were extreme—would instead destroy Judaism.

In 1851, Rabbi Samson Raphael Hirsch, who later became known as a founder of Modern Orthodoxy (or Neo-Orthodoxy), moved to Frankfurt to head a synagogue that soon became one of the most prestigious in all of Europe. Born during the Haskalah, Hirsch was familiar with its ideas, but he didn't agree with all of them. He

even said that because the Emancipation had led many Jews to assimilate into the larger non-Jewish community, and sometimes leave the Jewish fold altogether, it would have been better if Jews had never been "emancipated" in the first place.

Hirsch and his ideological colleagues differed from what would later be called ultra-Orthodoxy (see chapter 7)—those isolationists who created, and continue to create, a bubble around their community, detaching themselves from everyone else, including sometimes other subgroups of ultra-Orthodox Jews—in that they were not telling Jews to remove themselves from non-Jews entirely and remain in a literal ghetto. Rather, like Moses Mendelssohn, he felt it was possible to observe halakhah while also participating in the modern world. Unlike Mendelssohn, however, Hirsch cautioned that one's Jewish identity—as well as the building blocks that help shape it, such as the Torah and Talmud—were ultimately more important than Enlightenment-era literary works emerging from the non-Jewish world. Mendelssohn, in contrast, seems to have been pushing for a true synthesis of the two.

United States

The American Jewish Orthodox community was going through some of the same challenges in the nineteenth century as were Jews in Western Europe. Yet just as there was a greater range of thought among American Reform Jews than among European Reform Jews, so too was American Orthodoxy more varied. For instance, a group of East Coast Jewish leaders who met in 1886 in New York City to discuss what they should do to counter the growth of the Reform movement had little in common with one another besides calling themselves rabbis who were not Reform. Some had received Reform training; others had not. Some interacted with both non–ritually observant Jews and non-Jews; others did not. Some were flexible regarding the less observant halakhic practices of many American Jews; others were not.

With the growth of Reform Judaism, these non-Reform Jews knew that in order to build Orthodoxy into the fabric of American Jewish life they needed to take a page out of the Reform movement's handbook and establish their own seminaries and rabbinical councils. A few months after the meeting in New York City, also in 1886, a collective of Orthodox rabbis founded the Jewish Theological Seminary (JTS), modeled on the Jewish Theological Seminary of Breslau, Germany, founded in 1854.

The Union of Orthodox Jewish Congregations of America (now known by the abbreviation OU) was launched in 1898, akin to the Reform movement's UAHC, started twenty-five years earlier. OU had a number of organizational principles that directly refuted those laid out in the Reform movement's Pittsburgh Platform of 1885. These clearly stated that halakhah is binding, the Torah is a divine document from God, Judaism is a religion and collective national body, the messiah will be a personal individual, and a return to Zion is an obligation.

By the turn of the twentieth century, three streams of Jewish thought and practice had emerged within Orthodoxy: (1) the group that eventually became the founders of the Conservative movement (see below); (2) those we can loosely call an Americanized Orthodox rabbinate; and (3) the "Old World" Orthodox rabbinate. Whereas most of those in the first two camps originated in Western Europe, most in the latter were from Russia and Eastern Europe. Many in the first two camps identified with the Union of Orthodox Jewish Congregations of America, whereas most in the third joined another group, *Agudat ha-Rabbanim,* or Union of Orthodox Rabbis of the United States and Canada, which was founded in 1902 and excluded English-speaking, Western-educated rabbis. All three groups largely lived side by side in the Lower East Side of New York City.

Other important Orthodox institutions were founded during the first half of the twentieth century, such as Yeshiva College in 1928 (a males-only undergraduate institution combining a liberal arts education with the study of traditional Jewish texts, such as Talmud and Torah, that now resides within Yeshiva University); the Rabbinical Council of America in 1935 (the product of a merger between two Orthodox rabbinical organizations that eventually became one of the most important Orthodox institutions in the United States); and the Ramaz School in 1937 (a coeducational, dual-curriculum K–12, parochial school that became a model for Jewish schools around the country, both Orthodox and non-Orthodox).

Orthodox Submovements

In looking at Orthodoxy from the 1800s through today, it needs to be underscored that this community is made up of multiple subgroups, including those we might call Hasidic, non-Hasidic, ultra-Orthodox, Modern Orthodox, and Maskilim. Each one of these subgroups can be further divided. In fact, today there is perhaps more sectarian diversity within the Orthodox community than in any other Jewish movement. All of these groups began coming to the United States and Canada as early as the beginning of the nineteenth century, some even prior.

One thing that continues to distinguish Orthodox subgroups from one another is their varied approaches to modernity. For instance, although Hasidic Jews in Eastern Europe were under assault by their critics, the Mitnagdim, as early as the late 1700s, by 1810 these schisms had become less hard and fast, especially in the United States. The Haskalah affected Hasidic and Mitnaged Jews alike. Whether in the old country or the new, both groups believed their common enemy was modernity. In contrast, Modern Orthodox Jews (as one might intuit from the name) embraced many more aspects of modernity, much as Mendelssohn and Hirsch proposed. And as we know from chapter 6, there were mystics and mystical ideas within each of these subgroups; Hasidic Judaism did not corner the market on Jewish mystical thought.

Some argue that today's Hasidic Jews—those twenty-first-century Jews who descend from the Hasidic dynasties of the eighteenth and nineteenth centuries—should only be called ultra-Orthodox or *Haredi* (those who fear God) and not Hasidic owing to their many differences from their predecessors. More specifically, the reasoning is that their ancestors embraced the Baal Shem Tov's pluralistic, open-minded, compassionate approach to Judaism, but today's Hasids are much more narrow and judgmental in their halakhic methodology. This shift in the dominant Hasidic discourse seems to have been the result of their struggle with modernity. As Enlightenment ideas began to exert an influence in their communities Hasidic and Mitnaged Jews, in an attempt to protect their communities' ways of life, isolated and insulated themselves from others, becoming more strict and rigid in the process.

Conservative Judaism

From the 1840s onward, within the group we retroactively call "Modern Orthodox," there were a number of rabbis who supported the "positive-historical method" of Torah study, explicitly recognizing God's positive role in helping humans shape halakhah over the course of history. Decades later, this group became the founders of Conservative Judaism—though, as with other Jewish movements of the time, they undoubtedly were not looking to start a new denomination.

Western Europe

Some cite a mid-nineteenth-century rabbi named Zechariah Frankel as the initial leader of the positive-historical approach. Like Samson Raphael Hirsch, the founder of Modern Orthodoxy, Frankel was a rabbi in Germany at the time of the Reform rabbinic conferences of the mid-1840s. Although he skipped the first conference in 1844, he attended the second, held the following year, in an effort to influence the group's decisions. After disagreeing with an important resolution that the attendees proceeded to pass, he left the conference in an act of protest.

Less than ten years later, in 1854, Frankel helped establish the Jewish Theological Seminary of Breslau, which was not affiliated with the reformers. In fact, not only did Reform leaders criticize Frankel for being too conservative, but Hirsch also criticized him for being too liberal. (Some say this critique has been the Conservative movement's Achilles' heel ever since.) Frankel, of course, was equally critical of these other approaches. In 1859, he published what some consider his magnum opus, *Darkhei HaMishnah* (Ways of the Mishnah), in which he outlined how (a) halakhah was a living body of law that changed continuously in response to new historical conditions and (b) the authority to make halakhic changes was in the hands of human communities. For Hirsch, this work made it abundantly clear that Frankel was moving toward Reform Judaism, despite Frankel's vociferous objections to the contrary.

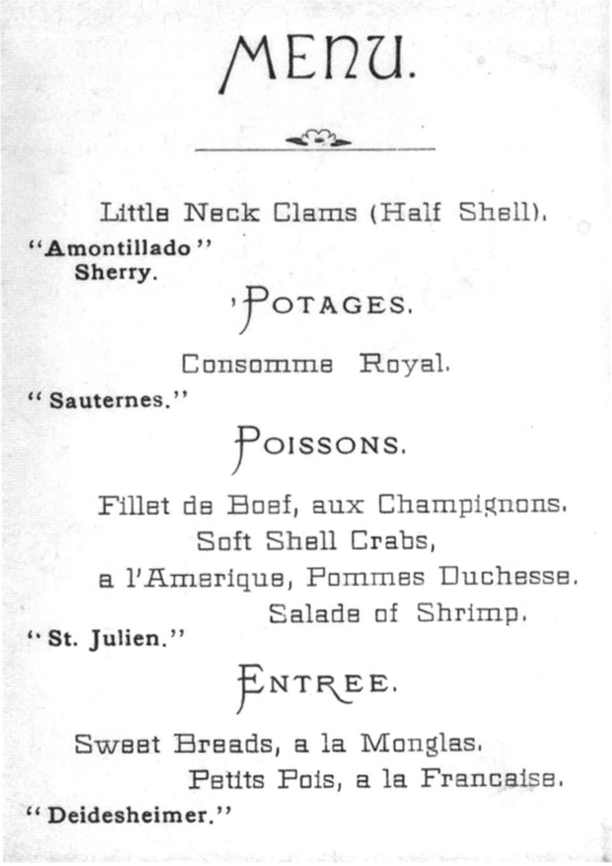

United States

Like Reform Judaism, Conservative Judaism took off in the United States rather than in Europe. One historical event in particular is generally credited with setting the new movement on its course away from Reform Judaism. In 1883, the Reform movement held a gala in Cincinnati to honor the first rabbinical school graduates from Hebrew Union College and to celebrate the tenth anniversary of the founding of Union of American Hebrew Congregations. According to lore, a group of rabbis attending the banquet dramatically stormed out of the building upon realizing that the caterers were serving nonkosher food, known in Yiddish as *treif* (lit. torn). For them, the food wasn't just unkosher but was *really* unkosher: clams, crab, shrimp, and frog's legs, as well as nonkosher beef served with dairy (fig. 8.3). Scholars continue to debate what role the so-called *Treifa* Banquet played in the founding three years later in New York City of the Jewish Theological Seminary (JTS) and the further rad-

icalizing of Reform Jewish practices thereafter (special topic 8.2).

Although JTS (est. 1886) would go on to become the central institution of Conservative Judaism, it was founded by Orthodox Jews (though they may not have self-identified as such just yet). Its first president, Rabbi Sabato Morias, and faculty were thoroughly Orthodox in intent and practice, and Reform founder Isaac Mayer Wise referred to the new seminary as an "orthodox Rabbinical School." Only one of JTS's initial faculty members, Rabbi Alexander Kohut, had received rabbinic ordination in Germany from Rabbi Zechariah Frankel, the pioneer of the positive-historical approach. According to scholar Neil Gillman, whereas Morias was the proto-Conservative movement's institutional founder, Kohut was its ideological one. Like Frankel, both Morias and Kohut publicly censured Reform ideologies. At the same time, they were also attacked for being too liberal.

MENU.

Little Neck Clams (Half Shell).
"Amontillado" Sherry.

POTAGES.

Consomme Royal.
"Sauternes."

POISSONS.

Fillet de Boef, aux Champignons.
Soft Shell Crabs,
a l'Amerique, Pommes Duchesse.
Salade of Shrimp.
"St. Julien."

ENTREE.

Sweet Breads, a la Monglas.
Petits Pois, a la Francaise.
"Deidesheimer."

FIGURE 8.3. The *Treifa* Banquet menu. Held on July 11, 1883 in Cincinnati, this gala honored the first ordination class of the Reform rabbinical school, Hebrew Union College. This is the first page of that evening's menu, which includes many nonkosher food items. See special topic 8.2.

As of 1900, there were still only two denominations
in the American Jewish community: Reform and not-
Reform—though both encompassed a range of perspectives. The not-Reform group started to self-identify as
Orthodox only in reaction to the reformers. Although
they began naming their American-based national institutions, such as OU, using the word *Orthodox* as early
as 1898, they still chiefly understood themselves as
Jews rather than Orthodox Jews or Conservative Jews.
Indeed, the establishment of OU was announced in 1898
at the first of a series of conferences held in partnership
with New York's Jewish Theological Seminary, an orga-

nization all the attendees then supported (i.e., JTS was
Orthodox).

By 1900, out of the eleven synagogues that supported
JTS at its founding, six had officially become Reform.
By JTS's third conference, in 1902, differences regarding various issues—such as whether to hold the conference in English or Yiddish and whether to officially com-
mit the institution to "positive-historical Judaism"—had
led to a mass schism. Those who preferred Yiddish and
opposed the "positive-historical" approach left the JTS
fold, including OU.

That same year, one of the most respected scholars
of Judaism, Solomon Schechter, moved to New York
City to become JTS's president, a position he held until
1915, when he died. Scholar Michael Cohen argues that
the Conservative movement only came about after this
schism took place and Schechter took over; thus, he
should justly be thought of as the new denomination's
founder, more so than any of his predecessors. Supporting this argument is the fact that it wasn't until 1913 that
JTS established an institution to represent its synagogues,
equivalent to the UAHC and OU, called the United Synagogue of America (now called the United Synagogue of
Conservative Judaism).

Others say that the line separating Conservative Judaism from Modern Orthodoxy didn't start to materialize
until the late 1940s; indeed, JTS was still regularly placing its rabbinical school graduates in Orthodox synagogues into the 1950s, and the seminary didn't even
require a course on Conservative Judaism until 1975.
Perhaps the most cogent argument against JTS having
started a new denomination in the early twentieth century is the fact that it had not yet said what its movement officially stood for, or how it differed from both
Reform and Orthodox Jewry. Although Reform Jews had
laid out a platform in 1885, and a subgroup of Orthodox Jews did the same in 1898 with the establishment
of OU, it wasn't until 1988 that the Conservative movement published its first official platform, *Emet ve-Emu-
nah* (Truth and Faith).

In 1900, the JTS community was clearer about what
it didn't believe than what it did. Representing the center, it comprised a wide range of perspectives. Schechter's first public address at the seminary, delivered in
1902, might even lead us to frame JTS's ideology at the
time as "Modern Orthodox." The community was clear
about its separation from Reform but not from Orthodoxy. Scholar Jeffrey Gurock adds, "Orthodox rabbis, in
[JTS's] view, did not truly understand the demands of the
acculturated, and Reform rabbis had yet to be sensitized

FIGURES 8.4A–B. Synagogues today feature a range of *meḥitzah* designs, all intended to separate males from females during prayer services. *Left:* The women's-only balcony section in the B'nai Jacob Synagogue, Ottumwa, Iowa. Only males are permitted to sit down below. *Right:* The women's section of the Western Wall in Jerusalem is on the right; males and females are separated by a metal *meḥitzah*. As of 2014, women were arrested by the Israeli police if they prayed with a Torah, even on their own side, as this is contrary to ultra-Orthodox custom (an ultra-Orthodox man is the Chief Rabbi of the site). In early 2016, the Israeli government decided to create a new mixed seating area at the southern expanse of the Western Wall. See special topic 8.3.

to their fears of assimilation and of intermarriage [Jews marrying non-Jews]."

Explaining why people were drawn to the proto-Conservative movement, addressing such issues as "mixed seating" (figs. 8.4, special topic 8.3), Gurock continues:

> [By] offering its communicants a sociologically sophisticated mixture of liturgical traditionalism and ideological liberalism, [JTS] attracted vast numbers of second-generation Jews uncomfortable with their parents' European-looking Orthodoxy and put off by the "church-like" religious radicalism of Reform. American Jews were good family men who wanted to pray seated next to their wives and family. And they found in Conservatism a theology and practice attuned to the slowly developing suburban life-style, prepared to make religious accommodations to America's work clock and transportation revolution and yet still remain philosophically and practically within older Jewish traditions. Masses of Jews saw in the Conservative rabbi an adroit mediator between the ancestral faith of the past and the exigencies of the American future. These leaders could communicate their approach in impeccable English understandable to Jews and Gentiles alike.

Scholar Jack Wertheimer offers a sociological analysis of the development of Conservative Judaism, arguing that the movement originated less from a "religious impulse" than a "broadly social one": ". . . namely, the upwardly mobile aspirations of the second generation of East European Jews whose families had arrived during the great mass migration that lasted from the 1870's to America's imposition of entry quotas in the 1920's. As the children of these immigrants climbed the socioeconomic ladder, they grew disenchanted not with Reform but, on the contrary, with East European–style Orthodoxy and its Yiddish-speaking rabbis."

Since its inception, the Conservative movement has been criticized by Reform Jews for being too conservative and by Orthodox Jews for being too liberal, thereby embodying the adage that one who performs more mitzvot than another is a fanatic, whereas one who performs fewer is a heretic. Nonetheless, from the early 1900s onward the Conservative movement grew by leaps and bounds. Between 1915 (when Schechter died), and 1972, when JTS's fourth president and later chancellor, Louis Finkelstein, passed away, the school increased from twenty students to five hundred; their congregations in the United Synagogue grew from twenty-two to eight hundred; and the Rabbinical Assembly (akin to the Reform movement's CCAR), founded in 1901 as JTS's alumni association, grew into an international body of more than 1,300 rabbis.

Largely in response to the changing social norms among Americans generally and Jewish Americans specifically, in 1984 JTS began admitting women; one year later, Amy Eilberg graduated as the Conservative movement's first ordained female rabbi (fig. 8.5). A group of JTS faculty opposed to admitting women founded what eventually became, though was not necessarily intended to be, a new Jewish organization called the Union for Traditional Conservative Judaism (now called the Union for Traditional Judaism). In 1990 they established their own rabbinical school, the Institute for Traditional Judaism.

In 2007, JTS began accepting openly gay and lesbian rabbinical students. Conservative-affiliated schools, including ones in Buenos Aires (Argentina), Jerusalem, and Los Angeles, have historically had their own institutional standards regarding applicants, slightly different from those of JTS. Five years later, the halakhic authority of the Rabbinical Assembly (the Conservative movement's rabbis) officially sanctioned same-sex unions.

SPECIAL TOPIC 8.3
MIXED SEATING IN THE MOVEMENTS

One of the practices upon which the Reform, Orthodox, and Conservative movements have differed concerns the seating of men and women in ritual settings
(primarily for prayer services). It is widely thought
that, for centuries prior to the modern period, men
and women sat in separate areas of a synagogue or on
opposite sides of a partition called a meḥitzah (figs.
8.4), which is still present in almost all Orthodox synagogues. Today, the overall trend, Orthodoxy aside,
is toward mixed seating, even though the pace and
manner of making this change has differed among the
movements.

Some say a synagogue in Charleston, South Carolina, in 1784 was the first in the United States to per-
mit mixed seating. Others credit the Reform Congregation of Berlin with being the first in modernity, in
1845, to do away with both a separate women's balcony
section in a synagogue and a physical meḥitzah. But
many synagogues, Reform among them, maintained
a virtual meḥitzah—with men sitting on one side and
women on the other—for decades thereafter. For example, in 1900 one of the most important synagogues
in the European Reform movement, the Hamburg
Temple, "refused a donation of one million marks
from the American banker Henry Budge . . . because
the sum was conditional on 'men and women sitting
together' in the new edifice." Thus, the evolution in
Reform settings went from meḥitzah to no meḥitzah
but still separate seating to mixed seating (also called
"family seating").

In the United States, the practice of mixed seating in Reform synagogues came more quickly than
in Germany, even though some Reform synagogues
initially disagreed on the issue (and one community
was even taken to court over the matter). When New
York City's Reform synagogue Emanu-El was established in 1845, it did not include a women's balcony,
but men and women still sat separately. Less than ten
years later, in their new building, Emanu-El instituted
mixed seating. Similar changes taking place in Protestant churches seem to have influenced Reform's practices. (Notably, Emanu-El's new building was a former
church, so when the congregation moved in, pews

where Christians had worshiped in mixed seating
were already present.)

Historian Jonathan Sarna argues that although the
Reform movement probably instituted mixed seating
because they wanted to be more like Christian Americans, Reform leaders at the time denied such assertions, arguing that the new practice was a logical reflection of the move toward full equality between men
and women. Whatever the case, by 1890 all American
Reform synagogues had mixed seating.

In the Conservative movement, soon after Solomon
Schechter took over at the Jewish Theological Seminary, he publicly declared that the use of a meḥitzah
was outdated and would be replaced by "separate seating." He did not go so far as to allow mixed seating,
however. It wasn't until 1921 that the Conservative
movement's Rabbinical Assembly officially adjudi-
cated the matter, saying that Conservative synagogues
were allowed to introduce mixed seating. By 1955,
mixed seating had become the norm in Conservative
environments across the United States.

Yet even then, in the mid–twentieth century, the
issue of mixed seating alone did not help distinguish
clear lines between Conservative Judaism and Modern Orthodoxy. During this time, JTS was placing its
rabbinical school graduates in Orthodox synagogues.
Further, there were scores of Orthodox-identifying
synagogues with rabbis ordained by Orthodox rabbinical schools, and many of these, too, permitted mixed
seating. For some, it was an intentional decision made
to attract younger, "modern" Jews to their prayer services. According to one source, as of 1954, 90 percent
of the rabbinical school graduates of the Orthodox-
affiliated Chicago Hebrew Theological Institution and
50 percent of those from Yeshiva University had positions in synagogues that allowed mixed seating. According to another, in 1961, 250 Orthodox synagogues
had mixed seating.

Despite all this, twenty-first-century narratives surrounding the history of mixed seating in the United
States remain unnuanced. Many in Conservative and
Orthodox settings are unaware of the movements'
overlap through the 1950s and beyond.

Smaller Twentieth-Century Movements

During the twentieth century a number of smaller, yet
arguably no less important, Jewish movements emerged,
three of which are described here. Given that Reform,
Orthodox, and Conservative Judaism all developed in

the United States, perhaps it is unsurprising that all three
of these smaller movements also emerged in the same
country. But what may be surprising to many is that ideas
from these three movements have played a role in shaping Reform, Orthodox, and Conservative Judaism.

FIGURE 8.5. Breaking the rabbinic glass ceiling. Seated left to right are Rabbi Sally Priesand, Rabbi Sandy Eisenberg Sasso, Rabbi Amy Eilberg, and Maharat Sara Hurwitz. The first three are the first women to be ordained as rabbis by American rabbinical schools affiliated with the Reform, Reconstructionist, and Conservative movements, respectively. The fourth is the first woman to be ordained as a religious leader in an American Modern Orthodox community.

Reconstructionist Judaism

Rabbi Mordecai Kaplan is often regarded as the founder of Reconstructionist Judaism. Much of his life, however, was based in Orthodoxy. Like many of his early-twentieth-century American colleagues, Kaplan, who was born in Lithuania, was raised an Orthodox Jew and received rabbinic ordination from New York City's Jewish Theological Seminary in 1902 (he also received a second rabbinic ordination from Rabbi Isaac Jacob Reines of Lida, Russia, in 1908). After serving for a number of years as a rabbi at a Modern Orthodox synagogue in Manhattan, he began teaching at JTS in 1909, where he remained through 1963, training Jewish educators and rabbinical students. Aside from co-founding "Young Israel," a submovement within Modern Orthodoxy, with Israel Friedlander in 1912, he also served as a congregational rabbi at an Orthodox synagogue until 1921. The next year, he founded the Society for the Advancement of Judaism, with the intention to "reconcile traditional Judaism and modern life," a need that he no longer felt Modern Orthodoxy was necessarily meeting.

In 1934 he published *Judaism as a Civilization,* thought by many to be his most important work and, in some sense, the ideological manifesto of the future Reconstructionist movement. He praised the Reform and Modern Orthodox movements for their willingness to evolve, but criticized the former for shedding too many layers of Jewish identity and the latter for embracing the religious aspect of Jewish identity at the expense of all others. He

agreed with many core components of JTS's orientation, such as the positive-historical method of studying Torah. Eventually, however, he broke from JTS over the issue of halakhah, having come to the conclusion that Jewish law should have a "vote, not a veto." In other words, halakhah should serve as a guide for Jewish practice, but it shouldn't be the central authority a Jew turns to—an idea that was contrary to both Conservative and Orthodox principles.

Perhaps most challenging to traditional beliefs, though, were his understandings of God and Judaism (more broadly). Kaplan challenged theistic, supernatural notions of God, maintaining instead that God is the "worthwhileness of life," which does not transcend nature but is nature itself. "God," Kaplan writes, "is the sum of all the animating organizing forces and relationships which are forever making a cosmos out of chaos." God is not some anthropomorphic entity pulling the strings of all creatures in the universe. Rather, God *is* the universe. There is no separation between our world and God's; they are one and the same. "God is the life of the universe, immanent insofar as each part acts upon every other, and transcendent insofar as the whole acts upon each part."

As for Judaism in broad strokes, Kaplan posited that orienting toward Judaism as if it is only a religion—only a set of obligatory beliefs and rituals—is reductionist. Creeds and practices are but two spokes on the wheel of Judaism, alongside art, culture, customs, ethics, ethnicity, history, language, literature, social institutions, and symbols. Judaism is the totality of Jewish identities and cannot be limited only to whether one believes in God and Torah, and observes halakhah. Because of this complexity, Kaplan argued that each micro-community of Jews needs to build for itself—or reconstruct—a form of Jewish identity and expression that works for it, thereby allowing Jews worldwide to tap into the depths of the Jewish civilization as it suits them and their specific needs and wants.

For some in the JTS establishment, and many within Orthodox circles, Kaplan's ideas were far too radical. An example is the Bat Mitzvah. By the 1940s, approximately one-third of all Conservative synagogues had implemented a Bat Mitzvah ritual ceremony, and by the 1960s it was the norm. But in 1922, when Kaplan's daughter, Judith, celebrated her Bat Mitzvah, at the Society for the Advancement of Judaism, it was widely hailed as the first Bat Mitzvah in Jewish history, and many traditional Jews felt that this was going too far. (It wasn't the first, in fact. According to scholar Francesco Spagnolo, Jewish communities in Italy held Bat Mitzvah ceremonies in Modena in 1844 and Verona in 1846, a practice soon followed by virtually all other major Italian synagogues.)

It wasn't this particular act that led to his public shunning, however. In 1941, after he published *The New Haggadah,* which was his first effort at changing traditional liturgy, his colleagues at JTS wrote a public letter condemning the book's heretical passages. Four years later, a group of Orthodox rabbis affiliated with *Agudat ha-Rabbanim* publicly burned his *Sabbath Prayer Book,* condemning him and the Conservative movement of which he was a part and halakhically excommunicating him. In his prayer book, Kaplan had eliminated traditional passages referring to "Jews as the chosen people, the personal Messiah, a supernatural God who has a role in daily life, divine retribution, and the restoration of the Temple sacrificial cult." Kaplan left JTS in 1963.

The Reconstructionist Rabbinical College (RRC) was founded in 1968, with Kaplan's son-in-law, Rabbi Ira Eisenstein, serving as the first president. (Eisenstein was ordained by JTS.) Many say that Kaplan was initially opposed to a new Jewish denomination, adamantly so. According to scholar David Ellenson, Kaplan "preferred that his Reconstructionist thought permeate and inform all sectors of the American Jewish landscape."

From the outset, RRC accepted women into their rabbinical program, enrolling their first female students in 1969 and graduating their first female rabbi in 1974, Sandy Eisenberg Sasso (fig. 8.5). Starting in 1984 openly gay and lesbian applicants were accepted into the rabbinical program. On January 1, 2014, Rabbi Deborah Waxman, Ph.D., became the new president of the Reconstructionist Rabbinical College, the first woman to serve as president of an institution representing an entire Jewish denomination.

Humanistic Judaism

Many frame Jewish identities in terms of a religion, as for example whether one believes in God or attends synagogue. But what about people who enjoy going to synagogue and find meaning in Jewish rituals but don't believe in God? Since 1963, when Rabbi Sherwin Wine established the first Humanistic synagogue in the United States, there has been a place for Jews who identify as atheist (or agnostic).

Ordained at Hebrew Union College (Reform), Wine started the Birmingham Temple in suburban Detroit to serve those who, to use this own community's language, identify as "cultural but not religious Jews." A few years later, in 1967, Wine founded the Association of Humanistic Rabbis (akin to the Reform's CCAR and Conservative's Rabbinical Assembly), and in 1969 he established the Society for Humanistic Judaism (akin to the Reform URJ and the United Synagogue of Conservative Judaism). In 1985, Wine co-founded the International Institute for Secular Humanistic Judaism (IISHJ), and in 1992 the movement's first rabbinical school was established (akin to Reform's HUC and Conservative's JTS).

Like other branches of the larger Humanist movement, of which Humanisitic Judaism is a part, this movement posits that the "foundation of ethics is human dignity, human survival, and human happiness . . . not God. Ethical behavior consists of relationships between people," regardless of belief in God. What makes this Jewish movement distinct from other Jewish denominations is that its members explicitly identify as Jews only historically and culturally (i.e., ethically, literarily, philosophically, etc.). Although they practice rituals connected to Jewish holidays and life-cycle events, they ensure that any accompanying liturgy is human-centered, naturalistic, and nontheistic. They are committed to universalism (i.e., all humans) and particularism (i.e., Jewish identities specifically), but believe that the former always trumps the latter. They call their core leaders rabbis and gathering places synagogues.

Their understanding of Judaism and what it means to be Jewish echoes ideas found in Kaplan's *Judaism as a Civilization*—that is, Judaism cannot be limited to belief in God and Torah alone but must include art, culture, customs, and more. According to the Society for Humanistic Judaism,

FIGURES 8.6A–B. Renewal Judaism. *Left:* Congregants at Romemu in New York City, "a progressive, egalitarian Jewish community committed to *tikkun olam* and to service that flows from an identification with the sacredness of all life." In this image they have ritually unscrolled a Torah as part of their celebration during the holiday Simḥat Torah. Many Renewal congregations, Romemu among them, subscribe to the notion that although they are affiliated with Renewal Judaism, "Jewish Renewal is a phenomenon not a denomination." *Right:* Members of Romemu in prayer with Rabbi Andrew Hahn, "the kirtan rabbi," who utilizes a unique instrument, called a harmonium, in many of his "Hebrew mystical chants." Both Rabbi David Ingber, the spiritual leader of Romemu, and Rabbi Hahn eschew labels such as "Reform," "Renewal," and the like. (Technically, Ingber was ordained by Zalman Schachter-Shalomi and Hahn by the Reform movement.) Nonetheless, both are deeply connected to, and have been strongly embraced by, Renewal Judaism.

Being Jewish is a consequence of ancestry or choice. Membership in the Jewish people is not a function of belief; it is a function of identification, connection, and loyalty. . . . Judaism is the evolving culture of the Jewish people. There is no single way to be Jewish. What Jews do is called Judaism. What Humanistic Jews do as Jews is Judaism. Pluralism in Jewish life enriches Judaism and enables a more inclusive and enriched Jewish community. . . . The survival of the Jewish people is a consequence of the adaptability of the Jewish people. What has kept us alive is the willingness of the Jewish people to adapt to the dominant culture, while still adhering to the ever changing, yet enduring customs and ceremonies of the Jews. The common history, literature, and fate are all responsible for Jewish continuity.

To distinguish humanitarianism from humanism, Humanistic Jews also note that the latter "is the reliance on people to solve human problems . . . [which] includes [the former,] the act of promoting human welfare and social reform."

As for whether they consider their form of Jewish identity a form of religion, they do. As they put it, "According to the dictionary a religion is a set of beliefs to which people hold fast. Humanistic Judaism is a religion using that definition. In Rabbi Wine's description of religion, Humanistic Judaism falls into the category of an ancestral religion, rather than a salvation religion. Humanistic Judaism is also a religion in its structure, its congregational model, school for children, adult education, and provider of life cycle ceremonies all follow the religious model."

Since 2000, this denomination has been gaining

acceptance in mainstream Jewish institutional circles. Humanistic Jewish leaders have been invited to participate in the United Jewish Communities' annual convention, commonly said to be the largest formal gathering of Jewish American institutions. Further, one of the IISHJ's graduates, Rabbi Greg Epstein, serving as the Humanist Chaplain at Harvard University, gained national attention for his 2009 New York Times bestselling book, *Good without God: What a Billion Nonreligious People Do Believe*. As of 2007, the Society for Humanistic Judaism claimed 40,000 members in more than ten countries worldwide.

Jewish Renewal

Of all American Jewish movements, Jewish Renewal is perhaps the most difficult to describe or categorize (fig. 8.6). Rabbi Marcia Prager, dean of the Renewal movement's rabbinical program, which is run through their umbrella organization, ALEPH: Alliance for Jewish Renewal, explains:

Jewish Renewal is a phenomenon, not a denomination. It resembles Reform Judaism in some ways, Reconstructionism in other ways, and even Orthodoxy—especially Hassidism—in some important ways. But it is not a formal denomination with a formal hierarchy or structure. It is the ongoing creative project of a generation of Jews who are seeking to renew Judaism and bring its spiritual and ethical vitality into our lives and communities, and at the same time embrace a global vision of the role of all human beings and spiritual paths in the transformation of life on this precious planet.

Drawing substantially on the ideas of the biblical Prophets, Jewish mysticism, and contemporary teachers such as Rabbi Zalman Schachter-Shalomi (or Reb Zalman, as he is commonly called, credited as the movement's founder), Jewish Renewal doesn't claim to be halakhic or anti-halakhic, but rather neo-halakhic. It identifies with trans-denominationalism; some of its members belong to denominations while others are nondenominational. Shachter-Shalomi left the cocoon of the Lubavich sect of ultra-Orthodoxy in 1948, at the instruction of the community's religious leader. Along with Rabbi Shlomo Carlebach, he was sent out to connect with Jewish Americans on college campuses—perhaps the first Jewish missionaries in the United States (to exclusively reach out to other Jews). They had no idea that they would help drive the creation of new forms of Jewish identities and play a fundamental role in starting yet another Jewish movement.

Jewish Renewal's proper beginning could be said to be Reb Zalman's founding of the B'nai Or (Sons or Children of Light) Religious Fellowship in 1962. In 1993, two formalized organizations affiliated with Renewal Judaism merged to become ALEPH: Alliance for Jewish Renewal, at the time the core umbrella institution of the movement. ALEPH's rabbinic program was founded a few years later, in 1997. But as with other movements, the precise moment this new denomination began is not clear. Nor did the founders necessarily see themselves as founders until after the fact.

From the outset, Renewal has self-identified as radically egalitarian in terms of gender and sexuality. Former ALEPH president Rabbi Daniel Siegel says that such positions, and others such as liturgical inventiveness, have penetrated into the Jewish American mainstream, though their influence remains unacknowledged. Whether reflected in adaptations of ritual techniques first introduced into Jewish communities by Reb Zalman, such as wearing colored *tallitot* (prayer shawls; sing. *tallit*), integrating meditation into prayer services, or utilizing innovative forms of God-language, Renewal innovations have begun to leave a mark on Reform, Conservative, and even some Modern Orthodox practices.

Jewish Affiliation in the United States: Ebbs and Flows

The denominational descriptions in this chapter, summarized in special topic 8.4 (see also figure 8.7), largely focus on how Ashkenazi Jews identify, not only because many of the initiators of Reform, Conservative, Reconstructionist, Humanistic, and Renewal Judaism are of Ashkenazi descent, but also because most American Jews identify as Ashkenazi (see chapter 1). Most non-Ashkenazi Jews who have immigrated to the United States since the 1950s have either established Orthodox synagogues reflecting their particular subgroup's customs and practices or joined Ashkenazi-dominant Conservative or Orthodox synagogues.

One example is the Persian Jewish community in the greater Los Angeles area. Many of those who immigrated to Southern California in 1979–1980 helped found Beverly Hills's Nessah Synagogue, the largest Persian synagogue in the United States, which describes itself as abiding by "Orthodox, Sephardic Halacha." Many others joined Westwood's Sinai Temple, which until that point had been almost exclusively Ashkenazi but now is made up of approximately half Ashkenazi Jews and half Persian Jews.

Nevertheless, synagogue affiliation is not the best litmus test for understanding American Jewish identities in the twenty-first century, and what a Jewish denomination officially believes and practices does not necessarily reflect the beliefs and practices of its members. In fact, statistics regarding synagogue affiliation have fluctuated quite a bit during the twentieth and twenty-first-centuries. In 1919, fewer than 25 percent of American Jews belonged to a synagogue. From that time through the 1950s, many synagogues even struggled to keep their doors open, largely due to a lack of members.

By the late 1950s, approximately 60 percent of American Jews belonged to a synagogue. But what did this synagogue affiliation even mean? According to one mid-twentieth-century analyst, "The [synagogue] model for the 1950s was nonreligious religion." In other words, synagogue affiliation was not necessarily a good indicator of one's religiosity. As of 2000, adult membership in synagogues had decreased once again, to 46 percent, and as of 2013 membership stands at 31 percent, much closer to the numbers from 1919.

Some attribute changes in Jewish American synagogue affiliation to similar trends taking place in the larger non-Jewish American world, where church attendance has waxed and waned as well. Others, such as scholars Steven Cohen and Arnold Eisen, posit that part of this trend among Jews is a reflection of the American ethos of individuality, which American Jews have embraced. They refer to this phenomenon as the "Sovereign Self," the highly individualistic search for meaning and community practiced by many North American Jews, which concurrently led to less synagogue affiliation.

(Continued on page 166)

SPECIAL TOPIC 8.4

JEWISH MOVEMENTS IN THE UNITED STATES: INSTITUTIONS, SIZE, AND KEY BELIEFS

Movements	Orthodox	Reform	Conservative
Institutions	**1886:** Jewish Theological Seminary (JTS) **1898:** Union of Orthodox Jewish Congregations of America (OU) **1902:** *Agudat ha-Rabbanim* (Union of Orthodox Rabbis of the United States and Canada) **1928:** Yeshiva College **1935:** Rabbinical Council of America **1937:** Ramaz School	**1873**: Union of American Hebrew Congregations (UAHC); now called Union for Reform Judaism (URJ) **1875**: Hebrew Union College (HUC) **1889**: Central Conference of American Rabbis (CCAR)	**1901**: Rabbinical Assembly (RA) **1902**: Founded in 1886, only at this time did the Jewish Theological Seminary (JTS) begin an explicit transformation from Orthodoxy to what eventually became called Conservative Judaism **1913**: United Synagogue of America; now called United Synagogue of Conservative Judaism
What percentage of American Jews affiliate with you?	**1800:** 100%* **1880:** 6% of all U.S. synagogues‡ **1950:** 10% **1971:** 11% **1990:** 6% **2000:** 10% **2013:** 10%	**1800**: 0%* **1880**: 94% of U.S. synagogues‡ **1950**: 25% **1971**: 33% **1990**: 38% **2000**: 35% **2013**: 35%	**1880**: 0%† **1950**: 60% **1971**: 42% **1990**: 35% **2000**: 27% **2013**: 18%
What is your definition of a Jew? (And can one convert to Judaism?)	Someone born to a *halakhically* Jewish woman or who converts to Judaism according to an Orthodox (or perhaps Conservative) understanding of *halakhah*.	Someone who has at least one parent who is Jewish (i.e., both patrilineal and matrilineal descent are recognized) or converts to Judaism according to Reform standards.	Someone born to a *halakhically* Jewish woman or who converts to Judaism according to a Conservative (or Orthodox) understanding of *halakhah*.
What is the Torah's authority?	The Written Torah is the word of God, letter for letter. The Oral Torah is also the word of God, though some believe it is the rabbinic interpretation of the Written Torah, which the Talmudic rabbis had the authority to dictate and which continues to have a divine status.	The Written Torah embodies the relationship between the Jewish people and God. There is a range of official beliefs regarding whether the Written Torah was given by God to humans or was written by humans. Unofficially, most in this movement believe the latter. As for the Oral Torah, it was not divinely given by God but is the rabbinic interpretation of the Written Torah through the ages.	Some believe the Written Torah comes directly from God; others believe it was written by humans. Most contend that the Oral Torah is a manifestation of human interpretation.

* Not all Jews at this time identified as "Orthodox" or attended synagogue. But for those who did, Orthodoxy was the only denomination around, even though it was not yet called Orthodoxy nor did any American synagogue identify as such.

† Did not yet exist as a formalized movement.

‡ Not all Jews at this time identified as "Reform" or attended synagogue. But for those who did, Orthodoxy did not yet have a significant synagogue presence. Immediately thereafter, between 1880 and 1910, one million–plus Ashkenazi European Jews arrived in the United States from Russia and Eastern Europe, most of whom would have identified as Orthodox in terms of today's denominational terms.

Reconstructionist	Humanistic	Renewal
1922: Society for the Advancement of Judaism **1955**: Jewish Reconstructionist Federation (synagogue arm of movement); now part of RRC **1968**: Reconstructionist Rabbinical College (RRC)	**1967**: Association of Humanistic Rabbis **1969**: Society for Humanistic Judaism **1985**: International Institute for Secular Humanistic Judaism (IISHJ) **1992**: IISHJ rabbinical school	**1962**: B'nai Or Religious Fellowship **1993**: Alliance for Jewish Renewal (ALEPH) **1997**: ALEPH rabbinical program § **1998**: Ohalah (Association of Rabbis for Jewish Renewal)
1950: 0%† **1971**: <1% **1990**: 1.3% **2000**: 2% **2013**: 2–3%	**1950**: 0%† **1971**: <1% **1990**: <1% **2000**: <1% **2013**: <1%	**1950**: 0%† **1971**: <1%† **1990**: <1%† **2000**: <1% **2013**: 2–3%
No official position. Since 1968, this movement has accepted both patrilineal and matrilineal descent. As for those choosing to become Jewish, unofficially a ritual conversion is encouraged but not required.	"A Jew is a person of Jewish descent or any person who declares himself or herself to be a Jew and who identifies with the history, ethical values, culture, civilization, community, and fate of the Jewish people. . . . [As for becoming part of the Jewish community,] Humanistic Jews use the term 'adopted' rather than 'converted' because we believe that the person wishing to be Jewish is adopting both Judaism and our community and that the community adopts those desiring to be part of the Jewish people." Further, "we welcome into the Jewish people all men and women who sincerely desire to share the Jewish experience regardless of their ancestry. We challenge the assumption that the Jews are primarily or exclusively a religious community and that religious convictions or behavior are essential to full membership in the Jewish people."	No official position.
"We consider our sacred texts to be the product of inspired experience in the human search for God and holiness in our world. To us, they are neither literal transcriptions from a supernatural being nor anachronisms that are mere constructs and fictions."	"Each Jew has the right to create a meaningful Jewish lifestyle free from supernatural authority and imposed tradition. Humanistic philosophy affirms that knowledge and power come from people and from the natural world in which they live. Jewish continuity needs reconciliation between science, personal autonomy, and Jewish loyalty.... Judaism is an ethnic culture. It did not fall from heaven. It was not invented by a divine spokesperson. It was created by the Jewish people. It was molded by Jewish experience."	No official position. Considers the Torah to be the Jewish community's core sacred text.

(continued)

§ Although the Renewal movement did not have a formalized rabbinical school until 1997, between 1974 and 2007, "112 Renewal spiritual leaders [were] ordained—98 rabbis, three cantors and 11 rabbinic pastors," 60 of whom graduated from the ALEPH rabbinical program.

Movements	Orthodox	Reform	Conservative
What should a Jew's relationship to *halakhah* be?	Jews are obligated to observe *halakhah*.	Jews should make decisions that take *halakhah* into account, but ultimately each Jew has autonomy regarding whether or not to follow *halakhah*. In other words, it is not an obligation. The Union for Reform Judaism states that a common thread between Reform Jews is that they all "share the assertion of the legitimacy of change in Judaism and the denial of eternal validity to any given formulation of Jewish belief or codification of Jewish law. Apart from that, there is little unanimity among Reform Jews either in matters of belief or in practical observance. Conservative and radical positions coexist and enjoy mutual respect."	Reflected in the Conservative motto— "Tradition and Change"— Jews are obligated to observe *halakhah*, though from an Orthodox perspective Conservative Judaism is much more liberal in its interpretation of *halakhah* than is Orthodox Judaism. Another perspective is that Conservative *halakhic* authorities look directly to biblical and Talmudic passages to interpret *halakhah*, whereas Orthodox authorities look to more recent responsa from other Orthodox rabbis.
What is your position on women becoming rabbis?	Prohibited. This said, Yeshivat Maharat, established in New York City in 2009, is the first Modern Orthodox institution in the contemporary world to formally ordain women to be "spiritual leaders and halakhic authorities," who are sometimes referred to as "rabbinic leaders." One's official ordination title is "Maharat," not "Rabbi." (Female graduates of this ordination program have also been called "Rabba.") A handful of other Orthodox seminaries have created similar programs since that time, but none, as of yet, are using the titled "Rabbi." Note: In January 2016, Lila Kagedan became the first ordained graduate of Yeshivat Maharat to use the title "rabbi" in a professional setting. As of 2013, if not earlier, some in the Orthodox American community, in particular those who are socially accepting of women as halakhic authorities, began referring to themselves as part of "Open Orthodoxy."	Permitted. The German Reform movement ordained its first female rabbi, Regina Jonas, in 1935. The American Reform movement ordained its first female rabbi, Sally Priesand, in 1972.	Permitted. JTS began admitting women to its rabbinical school in 1984; one year later, Amy Eilberg graduated as its first ordained rabbi.

Reconstructionist	Humanistic	Renewal
Halakhah has a "vote not veto," and is to be relied upon as a "guide" regarding religious practice. It is not obligatory. Each community and individual decides what the norms are, using *halakhah* as a guide.	*Halakhah* is not obligatory; this movement believes in personal autonomy. They also formally maintain that many Jewish rituals, especially related to Jewish holidays and life cycle events, have great meaning. This movement "create[s] and use[s] non-theistic Jewish rituals, services, and celebrations that invoke the ethical core of Jewish history, literature, and culture. [Its] aim is to foster a positive Jewish identity, intellectual integrity, and ethical behavior among celebrants."	"Jewish Renewal is a transdenominational approach to revitalizing Judaism. . . . We shape *halacha* (Jewish law) into a living way of walking in the world. . . . Renewal is an attitude, not a denomination, and offers tools to all branches of Judaism." "Jewish Renewal is neither 'halakhic' nor 'anti-*halakhic*' but 'neo-*halakhic*.' Just as Rabbinic Judaism involved transcending the *halakhah* of Temple sacrifice, so Jewish Renewal seeks to go beyond the limitations of traditional Rabbinic Judaism to forge a new *halakhah* in which Judaism is conscious of its place in an interconnected world. This new *halakhah*, for instance, includes expansion of the practice of kashrut to include ecological and ethical criteria, a new exploration of the concept of work as it applies to both the personal and societal Shabbat, and reexamination of intimacy and intimate relationships."
Permitted. RRC has always accepted women, ordaining its first female rabbi, Sandy Eisenberg Sasso, in 1974. On January 1, 2014, Rabbi Deborah Waxman, Ph.D., became the new president of this movement (i.e., of their seminary and congregational affiliate institution), the first woman to serve as president of any Jewish denomination.	Permitted. The IISHJ has always accepted women into their rabbinical school.	Permitted. ALEPH has always accepted women into its rabbinical program. "Jewish Renewal has long been committed to a fully egalitarian approach to Jewish life and welcomes the public and creative input of those who were traditionally excluded from the process of forming the Jewish tradition."

Movements	Orthodox	Reform	Conservative
What is your position on queer-identified Jews becoming rabbis?	Prohibited. Openly queer (see special topic 0.2) Jews *may* be accepted as members in some liberal Modern Orthodox communities. However, aside from exceptions such as Rabbi Steven Greenberg, an openly gay man ordained through an Orthodox rabbinical school (he came out many years after receiving rabbinic ordination), the normative Orthodox interpretation of *halakhah* does not permit same-sex sexual relations and thus does not permit openly queer students to study to become rabbis. Similar to positions regarding female rabbis, in 2013, if not earlier, some in the Orthodox community who are socially accepting of queer Jews, though not in terms of halakhically sanctioning same-sex relations, began referring to themselves as part of "Open Orthodoxy."	Permitted. The American Reform movement began accepting openly gay and lesbian rabbinical students to its seminaries in 1990, and openly bisexual and transgender students in 2003. In 2000, rabbis were permitted to officiate in the weddings of gays and lesbians.	Permitted. JTS began accepting openly gay and lesbian rabbinical students in 2007. In 2012, it sanctioned same-sex marriage.
What is your position on Jews marrying non-Jews?	Prohibited. Non-Jews interested in converting to Judaism may be welcomed by Orthodox communities. However, couples made up of one Jew and one non-Jew are often shunned altogether.	Permitted. Historically, in 1909, the CCAR passed a resolution rejecting intermarriage, later changing its official position to embrace families with one Jewish parent and one non-Jewish parent. Today, Reform rabbis are allowed to decide individually whether to perform intermarriages, even though the movement has not passed a resolution formally permitting this practice. As for welcoming non-Jews into the community, as this movement approves patrilineal and matrilineal descent, it is not uncommon for Jewish congregants to have non-Jews in their families.	Prohibited. If rabbis ordained by JTS perform an intermarriage, their rabbinical ordination may be revoked (though no institution in this movement has ever officially taken this action). Halakhic considerations aside, generally it has been assumed that children born to intermarried couples will not be raised as Jews. In 2010, JTS began having public workshops on intermarriage, leading some to speculate that their official position on welcoming intermarried couples into Conservative synagogues may change.

Reconstructionist	Humanistic	Renewal
Permitted. RRC began accepting openly gay and lesbian applicants in 1984. "The Reconstructionist Rabbinical College was the first Jewish seminary to accept openly gay and lesbian students. We retain an unwavering commitment to forming inclusive communities, welcoming to gay, lesbian, bisexual and transgendered Jews as well as multicultural families, Jews of color, and other groups traditionally excluded from full participation in Jewish communal life. Material about gay and lesbian families is included in religious school curricula. Our rabbis are free to perform same-sex commitment or marriage ceremonies if it is their practice to do so."	Permitted. The IISHJ has always accepted queer Jews into their rabbinical school. Likewise, they formally accept queer Jews into all Humanistic Jewish communities. In October 2004, the movement officially resolved: "We support the legal recognition of marriage and divorce between adults of the same sex [and] we affirm the value of marriage between any two committed adults with the sense of obligations, responsibilities, and consequences thereof."	Permitted. Queer Jews have always been accepted into ALEPH and into Jewish Renewal communities.
Permitted. Since 1968 this movement has accepted intermarried couples into their communities. Although they don't encourage intermarriage, each rabbi decides individually whether or not to perform an intermarriage ceremony. It is unclear whether this movement officially allows rabbis to perform an intermarriage with non-Jewish clergy (i.e., it is not uncommon for clergy from different religions to be co-officiating at an intermarriage ceremony). Note: In September 2015, RRC officially changed its policy to accept rabbinical school applicants who have a non-Jewish partner. This decision will no doubt shape other movement policies.	Permitted. "Intermarriage is the positive consequence of a free and open society. If the Jewish community is open, welcoming, embracing, and pluralistic, we will encourage more people to identify with the Jewish people rather than fewer. Intermarriage could contribute to the continuity of the Jewish people." (See also the movement's statement, found above under "What is your definition of a Jew?")	No official position.

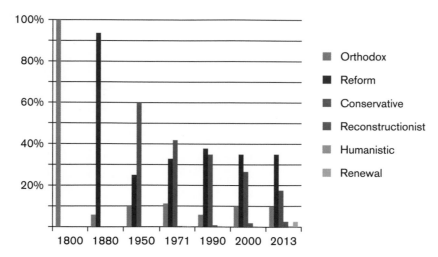

FIGURE 8.7. Percentage of American Jews who affiliate with each movement as listed in special topic 8.4.

In addition to those Jewish Americans under forty who, according to the Pew Research Center's 2013 study, describe themselves as unaffiliated, a small percentage identify as nondenominational or trans-denominational, which sometimes reflects a commitment to attending synagogue but not one of a specific movement. This study also notes that roughly one in three Jewish Americans doesn't identify with a denomination, and the same number consider their Jewish identity not a statement of their "religion" but rather of their culture or ethnicity. (Anecdotally, a number of rabbis ordained via the Conservative and Reconstructionist movements don't identify with a denomination either.)

The 2013 Pew study also raises the issue of generational shifts. Jews between the ages of twenty and forty have different dominant narratives than Jews over forty, a consequence of overall American generational patterns, among other factors. Indeed, to understand how all of the denominations discussed here developed, one must also look to patterns of thought and behavior in the larger non-Jewish communities in which Jews find themselves (but that is beyond the scope of this book).

Problems with Categorization vis-à-vis Movements

Clearly, categorizing twenty-first-century Jews in terms of denominational affiliation (special topic 8.4) is inherently problematic. As this chapter has shown, none of the founders of the major Jewish movements of the last few centuries began with the intention of creating a new movement, nor have the lines separating one denomination from the next always been clear. In terms of using

today's denominational categories, the early founders of Reform and Conservative Judaism were all Orthodox. For much of the twentieth century, faculty at JTS would not have necessarily even identified as Conservative, which has led some to quip that JTS is best described as a school where Orthodox faculty train Conservative rabbis to work with Reform Jews. At the same time, those early founders affiliated with the more liberal wing of American Reform Judaism knew what ritual practices they were choosing to no longer observe. This is quite different from today, when most Reform and Conservative Jews, for instance, would be unable to tell you what ritual laws they are ignoring.

For Orthodox Jews immigrating to the United States between 1880 and 1910, as scholar Hasia Diner explains, "Labels did not mean much. Members of Orthodox congregations violated the Sabbath and consumed unkosher food outside their kosher homes." This was mainly because immigrants needed to earn wages in order to support themselves and their families. According to a 1913 study of New York City Jewish businesses on the Lower East Side, approximately 60 percent were open on Shabbat. This did not mean that such individuals identified as anything other than Orthodox. Rather, it serves as a vivid example of the difference between denominational doctrine and practice for Jews of all stripes.

Most of this chapter has focused on the role movements play in shaping American Jewish identities. Jews in other countries don't have as many denominational options as do Jews in the United States. Israel is the only country that comes close in this way, and even there, aside from in a few major cities, more than 90 percent of all synagogues are Orthodox.

In other places around the world, denominational labels may be different or represent different practices. For example, in Australia, Reform synagogues are called Progressive. Yet if an American Jew visited a Progressive synagogue in Australia, she would probably think of the synagogue not as Reform but Conservative, in terms of the practices followed.

In short, although this chapter explores the shades of gray between Jewish movements as they exist in the United States, each community outside the United States has its own nuances.

Chapter 12 will touch on whether nondenominationalism and transdenominationalism will become a norm for Jews and whether identifying with a specific denomination will perhaps lose meaning entirely.

NINE

Genocides

Contents

Key Ideas

- The genocide of six million Jews in the Shoah (Holocaust)—two out of every three Jews in Europe and one out of every three Jews in the world—continues to play a profound role in shaping twenty-first-century Jewish narratives, whether one is connected to the Shoah through one's family, one's Ashkenazi subidentity, or even one's non-Ashkenazi subidentity. One of the deepest roles it has played is in connection to the establishment of the State of Israel.

- Antisemitism has reared its head multiple times in Jewish history. (Some consider the Shoah to be the culmination of centuries of antisemitism.) Perhaps the three most infamous antisemitic stereotypes about Jews are that they are responsible for "killing Jesus," they are "greedy," and they "control the world." Jews have commonly approached antisemitism through the lens of being either a victim ("it is happening to us again") or a survivor ("we are going to point it out and fight against it"), as well as thinking either that it is something that happens to Jews only (particularism) or it is part of a much larger problem in human societies where specific groups are targeted (universalism).
- Defining something as antisemitic—or as an act of prejudice, for that matter—can be complicated. Negative words lobbed at Jews can sometimes be disregarded and sometimes not, depending on who says them (such as Jewish comedians and so-called "self-hating Jews"). In addition, acts of discrimination can become so commonplace that people don't see them as such (e.g., the Washington Redskins professional football team's name and logo).

Five-Year-Old Fear

One day when I was five years old, I was peering out the second-floor window of my house in Center City, Philadelphia, when an unexpected thought entered my mind. I turned to my dad and asked him when the Nazis were going to come for us. Although my dad does not take the Holocaust lightly, this question surprised him. He responded with a gentle smile. Getting down on one knee, he looked into my eyes and told me that I would never have to worry about such a thing happening to us.

At the time, I was in kindergarten at a Jewish parochial school. I had spent my short life on the East Coast of the United States, largely in the City of Brotherly Love. This was my first year in an all-Jewish school; previously I attended an unaffiliated preschool, where I had both Jewish and non-Jewish friends from a variety of backgrounds.

The Jewish side of my family had immigrated to the United States around 1900 from what are now Belarus, Latvia, Lithuania, and Poland. All four of my dad's grandparents came at this time; his parents were born in Chicago in the early twentieth century, a few years after their families had resettled. Although distant relatives of ours died in the Holocaust, or Shoah, no one from my dad's parents forward knew any of them. In fact, it was not until the late 1980s that we even learned the names of those

family members who had died in Nazi death camps. No one in my family had taught me about World War II or about the members of the Tapper and Scher families who had stayed behind and never made it through the war. I only learned about the Shoah at school, not at home.

What my five-year-old self learned was that the Nazis killed people for being Jewish, and I was Jewish. But what led me to the idea that they might come for me and my family wasn't my family's personal background, but my macro-communal history. As a Jew, I had already started to learn about dominant Jewish narratives, of which the Shoah was—and continues to be—a central component. As a member of the Jewish community, certain events were part of my life, even if neither I nor anyone in my immediate family had experienced them.

This chapter has two focuses: the Jewish genocide, primarily as understood within the Jewish community; and antisemitism, the phenomenon of anti-Jewish hatred that, many Jews believe, culminated in the Shoah. Because more has been written about the Shoah and antisemitism than could be read in a lifetime, this chapter only deals with the history of the Holocaust and antisemitism briefly.

That said, I cannot overstate how important the Shoah and the historical acts of antisemitism that preceded it have been in developing Jewish communities' narratives in the twentieth and even twenty-first century. However, my aim in this chapter is to raise issues related to the Holocaust and antisemitism that are most relevant to the core topic of this book, Jewish identity construction.

What Is Genocide?

The term *genocide* literally means "the killing of a race, tribe, or group." It was coined during the 1940s by the lawyer and law professor Raphael Lemkin, a Polish Jew who had barely escaped World War II; his entire family, aside from his brother, was eventually murdered by the Nazis. Lemkin spent years working to popularize the term on an international scale. For him, it was critical not only to stop the genocide against Jews but to erase the phenomenon of genocide altogether. The idea that this word represents was not a twentieth-century innovation, of course; earlier terms, such as the eighteenth-century *populicide,* meant the same thing. Trained to use a comparative framework in his academic work, Lemkin explicitly grouped the genocide taking place in Europe with the Armenian genocide of World War I. He argued that what was taking place under Hitler's regime was not an isolated occurrence. Although he personally experienced extreme loss—forty-nine members of his family were exterminated—Lemkin considered this phenomenon universal, something that could afflict any group.

Largely thanks to Lemkin's tireless efforts, on December 9, 1948, the General Assembly of the newly established United Nations met in Paris and passed the Convention on the Prevention and Punishment of the Crime of Genocide. Defining the term *genocide* for the first time for an international community, Article II of this resolution states that genocide is "any of the following acts committed with intent to destroy, in whole or in part, a national, ethnical, racial or religious group, as such: (a) Killing members of the group; (b) Causing serious bodily or mental harm to members of the group; (c) Deliberately inflicting on the group conditions of life calculated to bring about its physical destruction in whole or in part; (d) Imposing measures intended to prevent births within the group; (e) Forcibly transferring children of the group to another group."

The Jewish Genocide

The genocide of Jews during World War II is commonly referred to as the Holocaust or the Shoah. The latter term is a transliterated Hebrew word that means catastrophe and usually refers specifically to the Jews who were murdered by the Nazis, not their other victims. (For example, Roma and Sinti, two related groups commonly called Gypsies, prefer the term *Porrjamos* to *Shoah,* the former word meaning "devouring" in some Roma dialects.) As for *Holocaust* (from the Greek *holokauston: holos* 'whole' + *kaustos* 'burned'), it originally meant a sacrifice or burnt offering made to God; by the fifteenth century, it was also being used to refer to a massacre of a group of people. During the 1950s, the term came to denote the large-scale massacre of World War II—no longer *a* holocaust but becoming *the* Holocaust. By the 1960s, the word was mainstreamed.

Under the leadership of Adolf Hitler, the Nazis systematically murdered people labeled as part of "racially inferior" social groups, including Jews, Roma and Sinti, the disabled or non–able bodied (the mentally ill; people with diminished intellectual or physical abilities, including epileptics; the deaf or blind; alcoholics), and Slavs (e.g., Poles and Russians). Other targets were Communists, Socialists, Jehovah's Witnesses, and homosexuals. All in all, between 1939 and 1945 the Nazis exterminated eleven million humans, six million of whom were Jews. (Roughly fifty million people died during World War II more broadly.) Most relevant for our purposes, the genocide of approximately six million European Jews

was equivalent to two of every three Jews in Europe and one of every three Jews in the world.

The Nazis' Definition of a "Jew"

Adolf Hitler and the Nazi party didn't emerge in a vacuum. Nor did their death camps spring up overnight. Rather, the process, on both counts, was gradual. Appointed chancellor of Germany in January 1933, Hitler began laying the groundwork for his racist ideology immediately. One month after he took office, Germany became a police state; civil rights were suspended. By July, the Nazi party was the only political party left in the country. The following year, after the death of president Paul von Hindenburg, Hitler assumed the presidency, while also holding onto the chancellorship. He was now Germany's sovereign, bar none.

Within a few years, Germany's legal definitions of "Jew" would determine whose private property could be seized by the state, and eventually who would be exterminated. As in the United States for most of its history, the Nazis classified people into strict racial categories; some were superior, such as "Aryans" and "Germans," and others were inferior. In 1933, laws regarding the category of "Jew," a group that was "unworthy of life," were established. By the end of 1935, the Nazis' definition had become quite elaborate (fig. 9.1). As historian Richard Miller notes, "Precise legal definition of a targeted group is crucial to the destruction process."

Initially, the Nazis defined two types of Jews: the "Jewish crossbreed" and the "Jew." A crossbreed was one who "descended from one or two grandparents who were racially full Jews" and participated in Jewish communal activities. A Jew was one who "descended from at least three grandparents who were racially full Jews." Those married to a Jew or born to a Jew, even through an extramarital relationship, were almost always considered Jews. In 1935, crossbreeds were still considered German citizens, though with far fewer rights, but Jews were not. Eventually, the Nazis expanded their definition of a Jew to be anyone with at least one Jewish grandparent.

Jews were gradually prohibited from using public transportation and were permitted to shop for food only during specific hours. They could sit only on Jewish-designated benches in public parks. They were prohibited from marrying or even having sexual intercourse with "pure" Germans (i.e., non-Jews). In order to legally prove one's "race," one needed to acquire an official "certificate of racial composition" from the state. (Germany's discriminatory laws in c. 1935 echoed those in the United

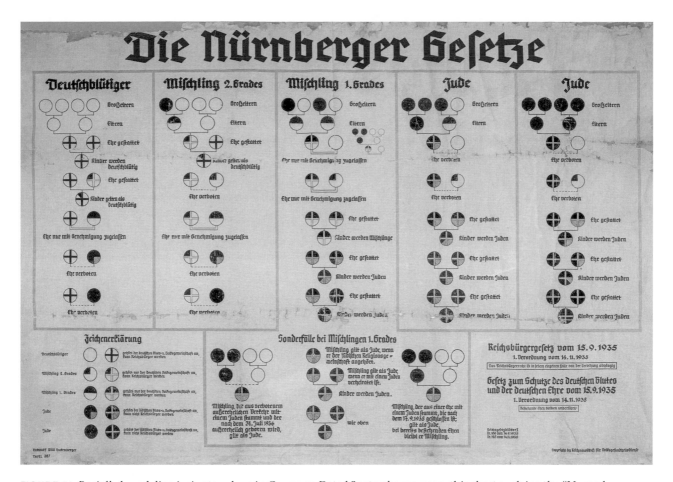

FIGURE 9.1. Racially based discriminatory laws in Germany. Dated September 15, 1935, this chart explains the "Nuremberg Laws," which defined the legal parameters for "Jews," "Jewish crossbreeds," and "pure" Germans.

States regarding who counted as a "Negro," an "Indian," or a "Chinese" person, designations that determined who could be married, own private property, and exercise countless other rights).

Laws against sexual relations between people of "different races"—in both the United States and Germany—were based, at least partly, on the nineteenth-century theory of eugenics, the idea that the best way to "purify" a superior race was to isolate it from inferior ones. According to Nazi ideology, inferior groups, such as Jews, were inherently flawed and needed to be wiped out altogether. By killing all "inferior" people, Germany would be able to ensure genetic superiority, thereby creating a "master race." Some nineteenth-century "scientific" theories, such as phrenology, claimed that a person's intelligence and personality traits, like honesty and greediness, could be deduced from an individual's physical characteristics, such as skull size. The Nazis asserted that Jews could be easily identified by other traits as well: they had big noses and flat feet, and males had circumcised penises.

However, as scholar George Mosse points out, research in 1870s Germany showed that the distinct "races" weren't so distinct: "An estimated 11 percent of German Jews were 'pure blonds' and 42 percent black-haired, while (Christian) Germans divided into 31.8 percent blonds and 14.05 percent black-haired. Most striking, however, was the finding that the largest number of both Christians and Jews fit into a 'mixed type' category, neither pure blond nor pure black-haired—47 percent of Jews and 54.1 percent of Christians." In other words, decades before the Nazis took power, most Germans could not be classified into strict categories based on such physical characteristics as hair color. According to Mosse, "The *German Anthropological Review* found [the similarity between Jewish Germans and non-Jewish Germans] so disturbing that they suppressed the data and fudged, simply reporting that the Jewish population had fewer blonds than the German population."

Germans who fit the legal category of Jew, even if they did not define themselves as such, were de jure Jews. This

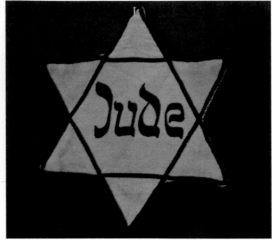

FIGURES 9.2A–B. Prisoners in Nazi death camps often had to wear badges that delineated specific social identities. For example, Jehovah's Witnesses wore purple triangles and homosexuals pink triangles *(left)*. In certain areas of Europe, Jews were required to wear yellow badges with the word *Jew* (here in German) written on it *(right)*.

included people whose grandparents had been born into Jewish families but had converted to Christianity and identified only as Christian. All designated Jews were required to carry identity cards, and some were given new middle names if their first name was not "recognizably Jewish" (Israel for males and Sara for females). Eventually, Jews in many Nazi-controlled areas were required to wear yellow stars with the word *Jew* written on them (fig. 9.2b), and in death camps most had numbers tattooed onto their arms. Meanwhile, the Nazis were promoting an understanding of German nationalism that did not include Jews or other "inferior" groups, ensuring that "real" Germans understood that the "lesser" people in their midst were the enemy.

Is the Shoah a One-of-a-Kind Genocide?

It is not uncommon for some to argue that the Shoah is unlike any other genocide in terms of the proportion of the target population killed, the amount of suffering inflicted, and the goal of wiping out a single target population worldwide (as opposed to all of community X in one country only). For example, consider the story a colleague in the field of Jewish Studies (who teaches at a university in one of the most populated cities in the United States) recently shared with me. A few years ago, two people representing a Holocaust education resource center requested a meeting with him. Because this is a reputable not-for-profit organization that collects Holocaust artifacts and paraphernalia, documents testimonials from Holocaust survivors, and coordinates a Holocaust speaker bureau, he set aside time for them.

As expected, two people came to his office, the president and the chair of the board of directors of the organization. They wanted to relocate their center to the university where he taught. Knowing how big a task this would be, he asked a number of questions. One was whether the Holocaust center's resources could potentially lay the foundation for a larger genocide studies center, something he felt the university would be more inclined to accept than a focus only on the Shoah. He asked them if they felt the Holocaust was sui generis, an event that could not be compared with any other. Without missing a beat, both individuals firmly said that nothing in the history of humankind can be compared to what happened to the Jews in the Holocaust.

Another example involves a national controversy around a Shoah commemoration at a high school in Tel Aviv, Israel. It was Yom Hashoah (Holocaust Memorial Day), May 1995. For the first time, this school decided to incorporate acknowledgment of other genocides into their Shoah ceremony—such as those that decimated Native Americans, black American slaves, Roma, and Armenians. Each of these genocides was mentioned alongside the Jewish genocide, and seven candles were lit: six for the six million Jewish victims of the Shoah, and one for all other genocides. The event incited a national uproar. (One of the criticisms in the convoluted controversy was that only Ashkenazi Jews had the authority to approach the Shoah in this manner, and not non-Ashkenazi Jews such as the predominantly Sephardi and Mizraḥi students, or the principal, a Jewish Israeli of Moroccan descent, of the school in question.)

This incident raised, for the first time in Israeli public discourse, the question of whether the Jewish genocide is exceptional. Some argued that just as every human being is unique, so too is every historical event, genocide or otherwise. This response isn't particularly helpful in terms of analysis, however, as it quashes attempts to compare any two things, which are always, by definition, different.

As for those who argued that the Shoah is unique, for starters, even scholar Steven Katz—who asserts that the Shoah is the only intentional genocide in history—notes that proportionally, Native Americans were massacred in equal, if not greater, numbers. The same is true, he says, of the African slave trade. Even if one argued that in decimating two-thirds of all European Jewry, a greater proportion of Jews died in the Shoah than in any other genocide, this, too, would be inaccurate. The killing that took place during the 1994 genocide in Rwanda was much faster than the slaughter of Jews in the Shoah, and some 80 percent of Rwandan Tutsis were murdered, as opposed to 66 percent of European Jews.

Such lines of reasoning can lead to problems beyond mere inaccuracies. Comparing atrocities, whether in terms of human suffering or numbers of victims, challenges moral sensibilities. Scholar Yehuda Bauer explains that "the suffering of victims of all genocidal massacres or mass murders is always the same. There is no gradation of suffering. No genocide is better, or worse, than another genocide. No murder is worse than another. No torture is better than another torture. The Jews did not suffer less, or more, than Tutsis in Rwanda, or Armenians in the Ottoman Empire. To argue otherwise is not only morally unacceptable, but in actual fact provides a platform for an essential distortion of the Holocaust by setting it apart, outside of history."

A few years ago, Bauer, renowned in the field of Holocaust Studies, publicly announced that he would no longer use the term *unique* when referring to the Shoah because it implies something that "happened just once in history, and will not be repeated in the future. But the Holocaust . . . was caused by humans for human reasons, and it can therefore be explained by other humans." He suggested another word, *unprecedented,* because it points not to the one-of-a-kind nature of the Shoah but to the characteristics that make it replicable. He acknowledged that there were exceptional details about the Shoah, such as the Nazi use of poisonous gas. But, he went on to explain, perpetrators always use the best weapons available to them. In this respect, he says, the Germans were no different. What was unprecedented was the Nazi Germans' intention to carry out the genocide of Jews worldwide.

The United States Holocaust Memorial Museum (USHMM)—one of the most important organizations documenting and educating the public about the Jewish genocide and genocide more broadly—addresses the question of the Shoah's uniqueness this way: "A study of the Holocaust should always highlight the different policies carried out by the Nazi regime toward various groups of people; however, these distinctions should not be presented as a basis for comparison of the level of suffering between those groups during the Holocaust. One cannot presume that the horror of an individual, family, or community destroyed by the Nazis was any greater than that experienced by victims of other genocides. Avoid generalizations that suggest exclusivity such as 'The victims of the Holocaust suffered the most cruelty ever faced by a people in the history of humanity.'" The USHMM has held a number of events focusing on genocides of the last thirty years, such as that taking place in the Sudan's Darfur region.

If the Shoah is considered historically "unique," how does this help the study of genocide? How does it help to end ongoing genocides? Does this mean that the Jews are hated more than other groups? Or does it mean that Jews have been oppressed more than other groups? And what are the theological implications of such a proposition? Does making this claim mean that the Jews deserved it? Was God punishing them?

Yet comparing genocides can have other negative implications. As scholar David Biale argues, pointing to similarities between the Shoah and other genocides may "dilute Germany's special moral burden after the Holocaust by arguing that others perpetrated similar atrocities: If the Holocaust is not unique, then Germans are not more culpable than others."

Is the Shoah Relevant for All Jews?

The Shoah and Israel's "Declaration of Independence"

The issue of the uniqueness of the Shoah leads to another fundamental question: Is the Shoah relevant for all Jews? May 14, 1948, was the official end of Great Britain's occupation of Palestine (also known as the British Mandate). The same day, a group of Jews gathered in Tel Aviv to proclaim the establishment of a new nation-state, the State of Israel (see chapter 10). Through the Declaration of the Establishment of the State of Israel this collective offered an explanation of the need for a Jewish-identified country, including this passage: "The catastrophe

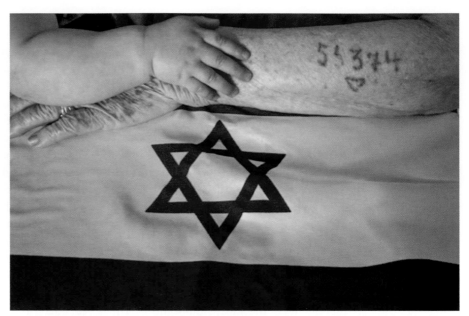

FIGURES 9.3A–B. *Top:* This image, of Daniela Har-Zvi's tiny hand resting on the arm of her great-grandmother, Dora Dreiblatt, atop an Israeli flag, is often used to promote community events related to the Shoah or Israel. Born in Poland in 1922, Dreiblatt is a survivor of the Nazi death camp Auschwitz; Har-Zvi was born in Israel in 2007. *Bottom:* This image, used by Stand with Us, an American "pro-Israel education and advocacy organization," explicitly links Shoah prisoners and members of the Israeli military. For many Jews, these two images embody the direct connection between the Shoah, the State of Israel, and the future of the Jewish people.

that recently befell the Jewish people—the massacre of millions of Jews in Europe—was another clear demonstration of the urgency of solving the problem of its homelessness to re-establishing in *Eretz Yisrael* [the Land of Israel] the Jewish State. . . . Survivors of the Nazi holocaust in Europe . . . never ceased to assert their right to a life of dignity, freedom, and honest toil in their national homeland." This foundational document concretized the explicit connection between the Shoah and the creation of Israel (see figure 9.3); for many twenty-first-century Jews, the narratives of the Shoah continue to be inseparable from the narratives of the State of Israel.

The Shoah and Non-Ashkenazi Jews

Since roughly half of Israeli Jews, and twenty percent of American Jews, are not Ashkenazi, and because the Jewish genocide primarily affected Ashkenazi Jews, it is important to ask whether the Shoah is relevant to non-Ashkenazi Jews. Over the last few decades a number of self-identified Mizraḥi novelists and scholars have begun to raise this very question. According to scholar Yochai Oppenheimer, the second generation of Mizraḥi Jewish Israelis, in contrast to the first, has rejected the Shoah as an Israeli narrative both because it did not happen to them and because it overshadows their own Jewish-specific narratives.

Other non-Ashkenazi Jewish Israelis have gone in a different direction. In 2001, the leaders of Israel's largest Sephardi political party, Shas, proposed a bill in the Knesset (Israeli Parliament) to build a memorial in Israel for Jews who were abused or murdered as a direct result of actions taken by Muslim Arab-majority governments in the 1940s and 1950s. Their aim was not only to spotlight the group traumas experienced by Sephardi and other non-Ashkenazi Jews but also to offer another justification for the existence of the State of Israel: the need for a safe haven not just for Shoah survivors but for Israel's "other" survivors as well. The bill did not pass. By many accounts, one factor at play was the bill's challenge to the exceptionalism of the Shoah.

Government-Sanctioned Shoah Education

For decades, Holocaust education (discussed below) has been required in both Israeli schools and the Israeli military. In other words, Jewish Israelis—and even Palestinian Arab citizens of Israel, commonly called Israeli Arabs (see chapter 10)—are taught to incorporate the Shoah into their identities. (Mandatory military service includes educational seminars at Yad Vashem—the country's Holocaust memorial museum—which is run through the museum's Office of Holocaust Education for Israel's Defense Forces.)

This was not always the case. In the years immediately following the establishment of Israel, not only were many Shoah survivors silent about their traumatic experiences, but other Jews often looked down on them for having been part of a Jewish generation perceived to go passively like "lambs to the slaughter." Following the trial of former Nazi officer Adolf Eichmann in 1961—which captivated Israelis and non-Israelis alike due to the symbolism of putting Nazi atrocities on trial—and the rise to power of a new political party, Likkud, in 1977, the Jewish genocide began to make its way into state-sanctioned curricula. In 1985, it became a mandatory subject in Israeli high schools. As of 2014, it is a requirement for children in grades kindergarten through twelfth grade.

Arguments for Why the Shoah Is a Jewish, and Not Ashkenazi-Exclusive, Experience

Like all countries, Israel has crafted a master narrative for its citizens. (Because it is the Jewish State, many con-

tend it has also done so for Jews worldwide; see chapter 10.) For some, however, the question remains: why is the Shoah understood not as an Ashkenazi tragedy but as a Jewish one? There are several arguments, the most obvious being that it was one of the worst calamities ever to befall the Jewish community. In terms of the history of humanity, likewise, the systematic extermination of millions in the Shoah is shocking.

A second argument is that Hitler's ultimate goal was not to exterminate only all European Jews, but all Jews everywhere. (Historians generally agree that by 1941 this idea, the so-called Final Solution, was an explicit Nazi goal.) Hitler thought that all Jews—no matter whether Ashkenazi, Sephardi, Mizraḥi, or something else—were subhuman. Although he and his army didn't succeed, this doesn't make his goal any less horrific. Even when defeat was imminent, the Nazis continued to murder Jews.

In a related argument, a third reason why the Shoah has become a core component of Jewish narratives is that following World War II, some Israeli Jews worried that Jews living in Muslim-majority countries would suffer a "second Holocaust." Israel's second president, Itzhak Ben-Zvi, pointed to how Armenians and Assyrians were treated under the Ottoman Empire, saying that Jews living in North Africa and the Middle East were also susceptible to genocide. (Some Jews continue to maintain this fear, whether in terms of Jews being murdered in Muslim-majority or Christian-majority countries.)

A fourth argument is connected to the dominant Zionist doctrine of death and rebirth, dispersion and return, exile and redemption. The idea of Jews not only surviving the Shoah but in many cases literally emerging from the ashes, complements (or embodies, depending on one's perspective) this storyline. But this only works if it is the Jewish story and not just the Ashkenazi Jewish story.

A fifth explanation is that the master Zionist narrative was largely shaped by Ashkenazi Jews. Dominant subgroups commonly imprint their particular narrative onto the larger group's narratives, presenting subcommunal experiences as national ones. Further, the more that subordinated groups assimilate into the larger one, the greater the cultural hegemony.

Holocaust Denial

"Holocaust denial" is a faux-historical field that tries to prove the Shoah never happened. Those who espouse this idea say that it was a worldwide hoax orchestrated by Jews. Even though the Shoah is one of the best-documented genocides in history, deniers assert that the number six million is massively exaggerated and artifacts such as the diary of Anne Frank are forgeries.

The denial of the Jewish genocide is not unique. A number of other genocides have been repudiated. For instance, the early-twentieth-century Armenian and Assyrian genocides, carried out under the Ottoman Empire, continue to be denied by the Turkish and Iraqi governments, respectively. In 2007, the International Association of Genocide Scholars declared that "the denial of genocide is widely recognized as the final stage of genocide, enshrining impunity for the perpetrators of genocide, and demonstrably paving the way for future genocides."

Cultural and Spiritual Genocide

Raphael Lemkin also raised the notion of cultural genocide, which he defined as the systematic attempt to destroy the cultural heritage of a group, embodied in "language, the traditions, the monuments, archives, libraries, churches . . . the shrines of the soul of a nation." Although some say that the Nazis were primarily interested in the physical extermination of Jews, it is certain that they also wanted to ensure that European Jews could no longer perform their Jewish identities (except as dehumanized prisoners in death camps).

The term *cultural genocide* has also been used outside a Jewish context. For example, a 2013 opinion column in the *New York Times* notes that in 1972 the National Association of Black Social Workers declared that transracial adoption was the embodiment of cultural genocide. In context, the assumption is that when white Americans raise black children in a white cultural context, they help erase black culture.

Jews such as those affiliated with the Jewish missionary organization Aish Hatorah (who proselytize exclusively to other Jews) say Jewish cultural genocide—and even spiritual genocide—is rapidly occurring through assimilation and intermarriage (see chapter 12). Although some abhor comparisons between the genocide of World War II and intermarriage, many rabbis from this community consider this equivalency to be apt. Take, for example, this statement, made by one of their outreach educators: "There is a spiritual Holocaust facing the Jewish people today no less devastating in its implications for the *Am Hashem* [nation of God] than the physical extermination of six million Jews in the Holocaust. Those six million constituted approximately one-third of the Jew-

ish nation. At least two-thirds of Jews today have little connection to the Jewish people, certainly not enough to prevent them from intermarrying. . . . The 'spiritual Holocaust' is no metaphor."

Similarly, some in the ultra-Orthodox community referred to one of the most famous Jewish American intermarriages of the early twenty-first century, that of Marc Mezvinsky and Chelsea Clinton (daughter of former President Bill Clinton and former Secretary of State Hillary Rodham Clinton), in terms of a "spiritual Holocaust." Even those identifying as Modern Orthodox, such as the former president of Yeshiva University, Norman Lamm, warn of spiritual genocide: "With a diminishing birth rate, an intermarriage rate exceeding 40%, Jewish illiteracy gaining ascendance daily—who says the Holocaust is over? . . . The monster has assumed a different and more benign form . . . but its evil goal remains unchanged: a *Judenrein* [free or clean of Jews] world."

A second type of cultural genocide taking place among Jews, argue scholars such as Sami Shalom Chetrit, Ella Shohat, and Sammy Smooha, has been taking place on an intracommunal, rather than intercommunal, level. In the United States and Israel, they say, "Ashkenazi dominance and cultural hegemony" is wiping out non-Ashkenazi Jewish cultures. Chetrit notes that since Israel's founding, Ashkenazi Jews have dominated not only Israeli cultural institutions, but also Israeli social, economic, and political structures. For decades, non-Ashkenazi Jews have had parts of their Jewish identities marginalized and even erased.

Shohat calls this trend a "cultural massacre." She adds that some scholars have attempted to justify this "'desocialization' (or erasure of [non-Ashkenazi] cultural heritage) and 'resocialization'—that is, the assimilation to the Ashkenazi way of life" by explaining that this is a normal outcome of relationships between dominants and subordinates. Like Chetrit and Shohat, Smooha notes that by the 1970s non-Ashkenazi Jews in Israel started to have a greater ability to perform their pre-Israel cultural identities. One example is the partial inclusion of "Mizraḥi heritage" in Israeli government-sanctioned school curricula. These scholars argue, however, that such additions, though a form of progress, are far from equitable.

While Chetrit, Shohat, and Smooha, perhaps because of the gravity of physical genocide, do not use the words *Holocaust* or *genocide* when discussing the marginalization of non-Ashkenazi Jewish identities, other Mizraḥi Israelis are not as cautious. A number of novelists identifying with this community have explicitly used the term *Holocaust* to refer to the way their community has been treated by Ashkenazi Jews. Whatever the case, the intention here is not to argue whether these expressions are accurate; rather, it is simply to raise these issues, which lie at the core of the larger question of what it means to identify as a Jew.

What Is Antisemitism?

The Shoah is an ultimate act of antisemitism, the worst-case scenario of anti-Jewish violence. But most all Jewish communities—whether Ashkenazi, Ethiopian, Mizraḥi, Persian, Sephardi, etc.—have experienced antisemitism to one degree or another. Some Jews quip that Jewish holidays can be summed up thus: "First they tried to kill us, but we survived. Let's eat." There is an element of "truth" to this not-so-funny joke.

Examples of Antisemitic Acts

Jews, like most minorities and all subordinated groups, have been persecuted historically in a variety of ways:

- confiscation of property
- destruction of property (books, homes, synagogues)
- prohibitions against owning property
- prohibitions against employment
- prohibitions against acceptance to educational institutions
- arrest
- expulsion
- death (lynchings, riots)
- and genocide.

Although the term *antisemitism* wasn't coined until the mid–nineteenth century, anti-Jewish discrimination dates back to at least the third century BCE, when Greeks persecuted Jews and outlawed many Jewish ritual practices (chapter 7). From the vantage point of the twenty-first century, all of the acts in the above list are understood as antisemitic. An antisemitic crime is a hate crime that targets Jews for being Jewish.

The antisemitic events most often mentioned by Jews today are the maltreatment received when living in Christian-majority European countries and Muslim-majority Middle Eastern countries; the mass murder of Jews during the medieval Crusades; the pogroms (organized mob attacks commonly sanctioned by the local authorities) of nineteenth- and twentieth-century Russia and Eastern Europe; the Shoah; and contemporary "anti-Israelism."

Anti-Israelism

Many antisemitism watchdog groups, such as the Anti-Defamation League (ADL), label anti-Israelism (also referred to as anti-Zionism), or criticism of Israeli governmental policies, as "the new antisemitism." Even though some people who are critical of the State of Israel and its policies are motivated by antisemitism, certainly not all are. However, these watchdog groups tend to assume that all criticism of Israeli governmental policies is equivalent to antisemitism; many also call Jews who engage in such criticism "self-hating Jews," an effort that sometimes marginalizes Israel's critics.

Such strategies for combating antisemitism are not necessarily constructive. Indeed, some argue that they are counterproductive. In the words of reporter Ami Eden:

> Jewish organizations and advocates of Israel fail to grasp that they are no longer viewed as the voice of the disenfranchised. Rather, they are seen as a global Goliath, close to the seats of power and capable of influencing policies and damaging reputations. As such, their efforts to raise the alarm increasingly appear as bullying. . . . For more than half a century, Auschwitz has rightly stood at the heart of virtually every moral argument put forth by spokesmen for the Jewish community, a powerful testament to the consequences of otherwise decent people remaining silent in the face of evil. Yet this legacy is in peril, threatened by an increasing reliance on raw political muscle over appeals to conscience.

Antisemitic Stereotypes

Prejudice against a group cannot be justified—contextualized, perhaps, but not justified. That said, three of the best-known charges used to justify antisemitism are that

- "Jews killed Jesus Christ."
- "Jews are greedy and obsessed with money."
- "Jews control the world."

"Jews Killed Jesus Christ": The Christian Bible

The first of these claims has been core to Christian doctrine—both Catholicism and Protestantism—for centuries. With one-third of all people worldwide currently identifying as Christians, this has on occasion had catastrophic consequences. Christianity became the dominant religion of the Roman Empire in the fourth century, after Emperor Constantine's conversion. Previously, the Christian Bible—the Synoptic Gospels (Matthew, Mark,

FIGURE 9.4. Jews and the Blood Libel. This fifteenth-century image depicts a group of Jews draining the blood from a helpless non-Jewish child, ostensibly in order to make *matzah* for the holiday Passover.

Luke, and John) and the other books canonized soon thereafter—contained a number of passages that condemned Jews for the death of Jesus, an idea millions have historically accepted as literal and true. In other words, prior to the spread of Christianity by the Roman Empire, there was already fuel for the antisemitic fire because the Christian Bible charged Jews with killing Christ. How could Christians respond to Jews except by punishing them? (See online Notes regarding the Catholic Church's 1965 proclamation that Jews were/are not responsible for the death of Jesus.)

"Jews Killed Jesus Christ": The Blood Libel

Some link the so-called Blood Libel to this same hatred. According to this myth, which first emerged in twelfth-century Europe and has subsequently been revived numerous times, each Passover Jews round up non-Jewish children, murder them, and use their blood to make *matzot,* the unleavened bread central to the holiday (fig. 9.4). If a child went missing in an area where Jews lived among Christians, this accusation was likely to surface. Perhaps this libelous refrain is linked to the calendrical proximity between Passover and Easter. Historians note

such episodes throughout medieval Europe—in places such as England, France, Germany, Spain, and Poland—each time ending with a mob attacking Jews. During the nineteenth century, the Blood Libel emerged in the Middle East (Damascus, Syria), where, in certain circles, it is still propagated today.

"Jews Are Greedy and Obsessed with Money"

A second common antisemitic stereotype, that Jews are greedy and obsessed with money, is also centuries old. Some say it is connected to the Christian Bible's description of Judas betraying Jesus for thirty pieces of silver. Others point to the fact that a disproportionate number of moneylenders in medieval Europe were Jews. The prohibition against Jews owning property may be behind this phenomenon: locked out of other professional opportunities, lending money was one of the few ways Jews could generate capital. In many places, they were also not allowed to become citizens. Because of these legal restrictions, the nobility generally believed that Jews could never garner enough financial power, even as moneylenders, to be a threat; thus they didn't need to worry about Jews using this profession to gain societal influence. Further, this also set up Jews to receive any ill will projected onto moneylenders, something nobles were only too happy to displace onto somebody else.

But Jews were not the only moneylenders in Christian Europe. According to scholar Norman Roth, despite a number of twelfth-century laws that imposed harsh penalties for Christians charging interest on monetary loans, a practice known as usury, even "churches, monasteries, bishops and the popes themselves" engaged in such practices. In fact, not only did Christian moneylenders outnumber Jewish ones, but the former group often charged much higher interest. While it is true that some Jews charged excessive rates, says Roth, they were the exception.

The stereotype of greedy Jews has been reincarnated in a number of popular literary works over the centuries, including the characters Shylock in William Shakespeare's *The Merchant of Venice* and Fagin in Charles Dickens's *Oliver Twist.* But perhaps what has kept this myth alive is the fact that, because of their role in moneylending, Jews were particularly well situated for the modern economic shift, in Europe and the United States, toward a capitalist market. Partly because of this historical anomaly, Jews in the United States have been disproportionately represented in spheres of economic power, a trend that persists to this day (see further chapter 10).

"Jews Control the World"

A third common antisemitic stereotype, that Jews control the world, is more historically recent than the other two. It is usually attributed to a book called *Protocols of the Elders of Zion,* published in Russia in 1905 (a truncated version appeared in 1903). *Protocols* presents itself as the "minutes" of an annual meeting of a group of powerful Jews who come together to decide the fate of the world in the upcoming year. Planning economic schemes, international conflicts, and political successes and failures, this fictitious cabal manipulates the world based on its own interests and those of the Jewish community at large.

The book appeared in Europe and the United States following World War I. In the United States, automotive pioneer Henry Ford based portions of his notoriously antisemitic book *The International Jew* on the *Protocols.* Decades later, Hitler turned to both the *Protocols* and Ford's text in developing his own racist ideology. Despite conclusive evidence provided by the *Times of London* in 1921, a Swiss court in 1935, and the United States Senate in 1965 that this supposed Jewish conspiracy is sheer fabrication,

the book continues to circulate around the globe today, the most pervasive antisemitic text of the twentieth and twenty-first centuries. In Cairo and other major cities in the Middle East, one can still purchase it from street bookstores (booksellers whose wares are laid out on the ground rather than in a store in a building).

Parsing Antisemitism

Native Americans and Discrimination

Whether an act is considered antisemitic or not is part of the much larger question of defining acts of discrimination. Consider, for example, the Washington, DC, professional football team, the Redskins, which first encountered national controversy in 1992, when the team made it to the NFL Super Bowl. At issue was the team name and the team symbol, the head of a Native American. Since then, including as recently as 2013, a number of lawsuits have been brought against the team's various owners, each one claiming that both the name and mascot are racist, that they disparage Native Americans, whether intentionally or not. Every owner has denied the charges, always alleging that the team's identifiers are a "shout out" to Native Americans and reflect respect for their courage and strength. Statisticians have conducted polls on whether fans and Native Americans agree with the team's various owners. As of 2014, virtually every study has confirmed that a majority of non–Native Americans think the team's name and mascot are not racist. (As to what Native Americans think, the findings are mixed.)

During a recent round of the controversy, the National Congress of American Indians (NCAI) generated the graphic reproduced in figure 9.5. Clearly intended to compare different types of discrimination, the campaign implied that all stereotypical characterizations of groups—such as Native Americans, Jews, or Chinese—are equally offensive. This leads to an important question: Can there be objectivity in determining whether something is racist (or antisemitic)?

Antisemitism and Jewish Comedians

A related question arises as well: Is it acceptable for people from group X to belittle others from that same group? Does it matter if people from group Y are in the audience? For example, is it okay for Sacha Baron Cohen, Sarah Silverman, or Jerry Seinfeld—to name only three of countless Jewish comedians—to make jokes that take aim at other Jews?

FIGURE 9.5. Baseball caps used as part of an advertising campaign by the National Congress of American Indians (NCAI) to draw attention to "derogatory and harmful stereotypes of Native people—including sports mascots—in media and popular culture." The caption reads: "No race, creed or religion should endure the ridicule faced by the Native Americans today. Please help us put an end to this mockery and racism by visiting www. ncai.org."

In the 2006 film written and produced by and starring Baron Cohen, *Borat: Cultural Learnings of America for Make Believe Glorious Nation of Kazakhstan,* quite a few scenes make fun of Jews (as well as Kazakhstanis, Americans, and other groups). In one, the film's main character, Borat (fig. 9.6), decides to stay at a bed-and-breakfast owned by a Jewish couple. In the middle of the night, he flees out of fear of what they might do to him. Before climbing out the window, we see Borat throw money at two cockroaches (ostensibly the Jewish couple transformed) while commenting that the Jews' horns must be hidden.

Perhaps Baron Cohen's most famous scene featuring derogatory language aimed at Jews is from his British television program *Da Ali G Show,* where, as Borat, he sings a song at the Country West Dancing & Lounge, in Tucson, Arizona, called "In My Country There Is Problem," better known by the song's refrain, "Throw the Jew Down the Well." The lounge patrons respond not with disgust but with cheers and applause. (According to verifiable sources, many of those at the bar were in on the joke.)

Are these scenes antisemitic? In an interview with *Rolling Stone* magazine, Baron Cohen said: "I think part of the movie [*Borat*] shows the absurdity of holding any form of racial prejudice, whether it's hatred of African-Americans or of Jews. . . . By being anti-Semitic, [*Borat*]

lets people lower their guard and expose their own prejudice, whether it's anti-Semitism or an acceptance of anti-Semitism." Is that a sufficient justification?

Deborah Lipstadt and other scholars of antisemitism and the Shoah weighed in at the time, echoing Baron Cohen's interpretation. The ADL, in contrast, issued a statement declaring that such content could incite people to be violent toward Jews. According to their logic, some viewers might not be able to tell whether Baron Cohen was condoning antisemitism or spotlighting how absurd such discrimination is.

"Self-Hating Jews"

Some call figures such as Baron Cohen "self-hating Jews"—Jews who are allegedly so uncomfortable with being Jewish that, in some sort of Freudian sublimation, they express that angst by mocking the community to which they belong. As we saw above, Jews sometimes call other Jews "self-hating" in relation to Israel. More than a century ago, Theodor Herzl, widely hailed by Jews as having lit the modern Zionist match that eventually led to the establishment of the Jewish State, accused some of his fellow Jews of being antisemites, in particular those who opposed the ideas presented in his 1896 book *The Jewish*

„Was kann mer doch alles machen mit die Gojim! Ihren Christus haben unsre Lait gehenkt am Kreuz und aus seinem Geburtstag machen wir ä Riesen-Geschäft . . . .”

FIGURES 9.6A–B. Is this antisemitism? *Left:* Sasha Baron Cohen playing Borat, a character known, among other things, for habitually making flippantly antisemitic remarks. *Right:* A 1929 German cartoon encouraging people not to purchase goods from Jewish-owned businesses. The caption reads: "One can do anything to those *goyim* (non-Jews). Our people crucified their Christ on the cross, and we do a great business on his birthday . . . "

State. A few years later, the same accusation was leveled at Herzl himself, first for allegedly focusing too much on Jews' differences from non-Jews, and later for suggesting that the Zionist movement should first found a country in a non–Middle Eastern location, such as Uganda, before claiming the Land of Israel as its final home (see chapter 10). Perhaps British writer Howard Jacobson put it best: "No one hates a Jew or a Jewish organization like another Jew or another Jewish organization."

Scholar Sander Gilman explains that the phenomenon of the self-hating Jew is a result of internalized oppression, something members of subordinated communities often experience. According to this argument, groups persecuted by others eventually come to see such prejudice as the "truth"; that is, they begin to view themselves through the eyes of their oppressors. In Gilman's words, Jewish self-hatred emerged because "Jews see the dominant society seeing them and . . . they project their anxiety about this manner of being seen onto other Jews as a means of externalizing their own status anxiety."

Two Ways that Jews Deal with Antisemitism

Victims and Survivors

In dealing with antisemitism—including what many Jews perceive as the culmination of centuries of such persecution, the Shoah—people tend to respond in one of two general ways (aside from humor, described previously): as victims or as survivors. Compare the definitions of these terms, offered by the *Oxford English Dictionary* (special topic 9.1). While *victim* connotes weakness, rigidity, transience, and surrender, *survivor* is characterized by strength, adaptability, permanence, and a will to live. Victims are prey; survivors are not to be messed with.

Collectively, Jews today oscillate between these two poles when it comes to the Shoah. In general, those who perished in the Shoah are called victims, and those that made it through, survivors. And yet at times, Shoah survivors have also been regarded as victims. In the United States and Israel, especially in the years immediately after World War II, those who made it through the Shoah alive were sometimes treated as weak, as having given themselves up to the Nazis. Other times, they were considered strong and indomitable.

Until a few years ago, it was commonly believed that in the first few decades after World War II Shoah survivors in the U.S. didn't even speak about the atrocities they had experienced. Perhaps due to "survivor's guilt"—feeling responsible for not having saved others or for having lived while others died—the trauma of having lost countless loved ones in a genocide and experiencing some of the worst evils humans are capable of inflicting on one victim \ˈvik-təm\

  a person harmed, injured, or killed as a result of a crime, accident, or other event or action: *victims of domestic violence* | *earthquake victims.*

  a person who is tricked or duped: *the victim of a hoax.*

  a person who has come to feel helpless and passive in the face of misfortune or ill-treatment: *I saw myself as a victim* | [as *modifier*]: *a victim mentality.*

  a living creature killed as a religious sacrifice: *sacrificial victims for the ritual festivals.*

survivor \sər-ˈvī-vər\

  a person who survives, especially a person remaining alive after an event in which others have died: *the sole survivor of the massacre.*

  the remainder of a group of people or things: *a survivor from last year's team.*

  a person who copes well with difficulties in life: *a born survivor.*

  Law: a joint tenant who has the right to the entire estate on the other's death.

another, those who made it through could not bear to offer testimonies of the evil they had lived. (According to scholar Hasia Diner, however, survivors started talking about their experiences immediately.)

In Israel, survivors had a different experience. There, educational curricula focused on examples from World War II in which Jews fought back against the Nazis. Those developing lesson plans for students wished to highlight the strength and courage that Jews showed during the Shoah. Israeli Jewish youth, so went this approach, could not be taught that the new Jewish immigrants had gone like "lambs to slaughter." And yet, contrary to these efforts—at the same time—survivors were often treated precisely as those lambs, in the sense of blaming the victim. This mixed view of survivors continues in Israel today.

Israeli psychiatrist Hillel Klein, a survivor who treated other survivors as his patients, also found negative stereotypes: "In many circles," he wrote, "the survivors were seen as 'bad, guilt-ridden, envious, jealous, greedy for compensation, imposters, overbearing,' etc. As individuals, they aroused in non-survivors a diversity of feelings from shame, pity, and guilt to anger and irritation, very much as non-Jews saw Jews."

Many of these negative feelings came from Zionist Jewish Israelis who had left their families behind in Europe, before the outbreak of World War II, to help establish the Jewish State; for those whose families had perished in the Shoah, some felt it was somehow their fault. Klein is one of many who documented the myriad ways in which survivors were culturally silenced by their fellow Jews in Israel. Most add that attitudes started to change after the Israeli government's trial of former Nazi Adolf Eichmann in 1961, though even then not particularly quickly. Over time, the Shoah became more central to Jewish narratives in Israel than in the United States, partly because the survivors moving to Israel embodied the Zionist plotline of the rebirth of the Jewish nation in the Land of Israel.

Holocaust Education

In Israel, the primary method of transmitting the historical and societal importance of the Holocaust has been through the Israeli state educational system. One way the Israeli Ministry of Education has kept the Shoah relevant to younger Jewish Israelis has been through government-sponsored trips to death camps in Poland, such as Auschwitz. Such programs began in the 1960s, stopped after the 1967 war (when Poland began denying travel visas to Israeli citizens), and started again in 1987 in an expanded form, involving many more students. In one of the annual trips, called "March of the Living," Israeli and non-Israeli (i.e., "Diaspora," see chapter 3) Jews make a three-kilometer walk between two Nazi death camps, Birkenau and Auschwitz, on Israel's Holocaust Remembrance Day (fig. 9.7).

These trips have been criticized for supporting the commercialization of these death camps (the Polish government has renovated some of the sites' buildings for the explicit purpose of tourism). Others object that financially supporting Poles is equivalent to putting money in the pockets of former "murderers." In a different type of critique, some say that these programs are forms of "political manipulation." Some even argue that the Holocaust has become a centerpoint, or even a Godhead, of Israel's civil religion; Holocaust education broadly, and taking a trip—or making a pilgrimage—to a former death camp specifically, are enacted rituals that affirm the sacredness of places such as Auschwitz. Whatever one's stand, these educational voyages have played a profound role in shaping Jewish Israelis' self-identities and collective identities. A 2009 study found that 77 percent of students and 96 percent of teachers in Israeli high schools consider the Shoah to be central to their worldview.

Trauma, Memory, and the Future

"Never Again"

Jews (and non-Jews) often say, "Never again," when speaking about the Shoah. But the phrase, generally, has two meanings. For some it means, "Never again should something like the Shoah happen to us Jews." For others, "Never again should genocide happen." The first is a particularist perspective; the second, universalist (fig. 9.8).

Those who gravitate toward a universalist orientation see what happened to Jews as something that can happen to any group. The poem attributed to German pastor Martin Niemöller, popularized since World War II, is an example of this perspective:

> First they came for the socialists, and I did not speak out—
> because I was not a socialist.
> Then they came for the trade unionists, and I did not
> speak out—
> because I was not a trade unionist.
> Then they came for the Jews, and I did not speak out—
> because I was not a Jew.
> Then they came for me—and there was no one left to speak
> for me.

Collective Memory

What individual Jews mean by "Never again" reflects their orientation toward the collective Jewish memory. As Hannah Arendt explains in *Between Past and Present,* the act of memory is the nexus between the "truth" of the past and the potential for the future. The past is the accumulation of everything that has happened, such as the persecution of Jews for centuries, and the murder of one out of every three Jews in the world in the Shoah.

The question, however, is to what extent should the Jewish community allow its collective memories of persecution to define its present and future? Perhaps the answer lies in the space between the following two sentiments. The first is expressed in the 2009 film *Defamation:*

FIGURE 9.7. A "March of the Living" group walking underneath the infamous sign found at the entrance to a number of Nazi death camps, including Auschwitz, that reads colloquially: "Work Will Set You Free."

FIGURE 9.8. As illustrated in this image, multiple genocides have occurred since World War II, challenging the sincerity of repeating the phrase "Never again."

Anti-Semitism, the Movie by an unnamed Jewish Israeli guard accompanying a group of students on a trip from Israel to World War II death camps in Poland. He says:

> We [Jews] live with the feeling that death is always with us. . . . It is always hanging over us, and here in Auschwitz you see how it became an industry, an industry of death. The Germans started it all, and we are perpetuating it. I thought a lot about this yesterday, whether this "March of the Living" is good or bad, this death industry, and I said something about this yesterday evening [to the students]. . . . We perpetuate death, and that's why we will never become a normal people: because we emphasize death and what happened. We have to remember, no doubt, but we live too much in it, and it's preventing us from being a normal people.

The second sentiment was made by Pope John Paul II: "May it enable memory to play its necessary part in which the unspeakable iniquity of the Shoah will never again be possible."

Whereas the guard's statement addresses what it means to perpetrate the "death industry," Pope John Paul II focuses on the adage that those who don't remember history are destined to repeat it. Holding on to the memory of the Jewish genocide has both constructive and destructive ramifications. The tension between remembering genocide in order to protect one's community from such a trauma, on the one hand, and remembering it in order to safeguard all communities from such horror, on the other, continues to be central to Jewish narratives in the twenty-first century.

Powers

Contents

Key Ideas

- Jews can have simultaneous self-perceptions of themselves as weak/powerless and strong/powerful, embodied in the biblical characters David and Goliath, respectively. The Shoah, for example, reflects both victimhood and survival. Similarly, Jews commonly think of the State of Israel as at once a source of strength and a country that could be destroyed at any minute.
- Historically, Jews have never had more power than they do today, in both the United States and the State of Israel. In the United States, Jews are disproportionately represented in the spheres of academia, government, media, and pop culture. In Israel, Jews have established a new Jewish-majority country, an event that many Jews consider the greatest miracle in Jewish history.
- Although Zionism is no doubt a dominant creed in Jewish communities today, during the nineteenth century and first half of the twentieth century Zionism was often unpopular among Jews; at times, it was a marginal ideology altogether.
- With the establishment of a new Jewish-majority country came shifts in Jewish identities—such as the creation of a new identity, the Israeli Jew (both a cultural and legal signifier), and major decline of the "Arab Jew"—and the emergence of new non-Jewish identities, such as the "Israeli Arab."

David or Goliath?

A few years ago, I participated in a conference call with a group of Muslim Americans and Jewish Americans. Our goal was to finalize details regarding an educational project for Muslim and Jewish high school students. The two dominant voices in the conversation were a Jewish man, Sam, and a Muslim man, Adam, both in their fifties. At one point Sam said something that, though tangential to the topic at hand, caught Adam's attention. He abruptly interrupted the discussion and said, "Hold on, Sam. You think that Jews are a minority?"

Sam did not hesitate. "Are you kidding? Of course we are. There're barely any Jews in the world. Muslims and Christians make up more than half the people on the planet. Jews are no more than one-fifth of one percent of humanity."

Adam, sounding surprised, replied: "But here, in the United States, do you think of yourself, as a Jew, part of a minority? Do you think of Jews as a small and powerless group?"

Sam said, "Well, we are certainly a minority. That's indisputable. We're only two percent of the American population" (fig. 10.1). He continued. "As for being powerless, I wouldn't say that. But we certainly aren't as powerful as Muslims."

"Muslims?" Adam said incredulously. "You don't actually think that Muslims have power in the United States, do you? I can tell you, at least from my experience as an Arab Muslim American, that ever since 9/11 it has not been easy to live as an Arab or as a Muslim in this country. Only really in the past decade did I begin to understand what it must be like to be black in the U.S."

Sam said, "I can't speak for you, of course. But how can you see Arabs and Muslims as powerless when there are literally billions of you throughout the world?"

As our time together was short, and we had clearly gotten sidetracked from the task at hand, someone else on the call acknowledged the importance of the discussion that Sam and Adam were having, suggested they continue it at another time, and asked us all to refocus.

For me, a proverbial fly on the wall, the two men's exchange was both unanticipated and fascinating. I had known both Sam and Adam for a few years, and although I had never spoken about concepts of power with either of them, their opinions were telling. Whereas Sam had spent almost his entire life in the United States, mostly in New York City, Adam was born in the Middle East, moved to the United States as a boy, and grew up in Washington, DC. Both men were sharp, successful, and well spoken, and both were sound critical thinkers.

I wouldn't have thought to call either one culturally sheltered; if anything, each was exposed to many points of view and open-minded about them. Yet the two narratives they expressed were mirror opposites. It seemed that until this moment neither had ever given serious thought to the possibility that other people saw their respective communities as powerful and dominant. Rather, each thought it obvious that their particular collective was small, relatively powerless, and oppressed. Both thought of their own group as the embodiment of the biblical David, not Goliath—the small, overmatched boy as opposed to the strong, overpowering giant.

Neither Sam nor Adam said anything that others hadn't said before. Their perspectives reflected their American groups' dominant narratives. Many Jews, in Israel and the United States, fail to think of the Jewish community as a powerful collective, but instead focus on how few Jews there are in the world, basing their understanding of power on population size. Further, many have been so traumatized by the Shoah that they forever see non-Jews

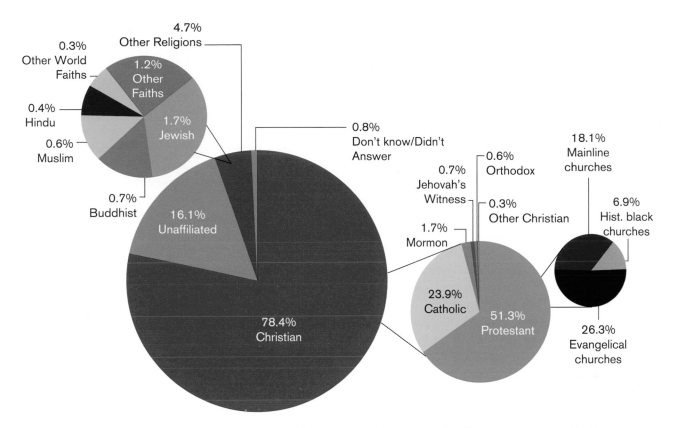

FIGURE 10.1. Sizes of major religious groups in the United States. Jews make up somewhere between 1.7 percent (the figure shown here) and 2.2 percent of the U.S. population.

as potential oppressors. It certainly doesn't quell those fears when anti-Jewish acts are carried out in places such as Copenhagen and Paris, to mention but two that took place in early 2015.

No doubt, Sam was also channeling aspects of the era into which he was born, when the Shoah's effects were still felt by Jews worldwide and the State of Israel had only just been established. In the United States, Jews were really struggling; they were still being locked out of colleges and universities, as well as important professions, such as medicine and law. Sam was looking at the present largely through the lens of the past.

Twenty-First-Century Jews and Power

Twenty-first-century Jews are not powerless. On the contrary, for the first time in history there is a modern Jewish-majority country, and in many ways Jews' status in perhaps the only remaining superpower, the United States, is quite strong, especially relative to their population size. (Some would even say that the Jewish subnarrative within America is a metaphor for the American

experience itself. As literary critic Leslie Fielder notes, "The Jew has become on all levels [in American literature] the symbol in which the American projects his own fate.") Israel and the United States contain approximately 80 percent of Jews worldwide. Israel is one of the most important players in the Middle East, an essential region of the world geopolitically speaking. And the United States is currently one of the most powerful and influential nation-states in existence.

Yet many American and Israeli Jews of Sam's generation habitually express feelings of disempowerment and alienation, perhaps partly because of continuing instances of antisemitism and the fears that these engender. This paradox raises a number of questions, which lie at the core of dominant Jewish narratives: Will the State of Israel survive the twenty-first century, or will it be destroyed? Will there be another Shoah? Or will something else altogether, such as intermarriage and assimilation, lead Jews to eventually disappear?

These questions are rooted in the trauma of the mass genocide of Jews during World War II as well as in the community's centuries-old experiences as a minority that has been discriminated against time and time again. This historical maltreatment cannot be discounted. Yet it is anyone's guess whether the Jewish community's empowerment since the mid–twentieth century will reorient their relationship to the 97.8 percent of the United States and 99.8 percent of the world as a whole that is not Jewish.

The paradox that lies at the heart of this chapter is the tension in dominant Jewish narratives between power and powerlessness, survival and victimhood, fact and "truth." Although the narrative of victimhood has been enabled in part by current events, this chapter is not focused on the oppression of Jews; rather, it aims to explain how a group that has experienced remarkable progress in social mobility, both in the United States and internationally, can continue to feel powerless and vulnerable. (This is not to ignore historical oppression, but that subject was addressed in chapter 9.)

This chapter, therefore, explores the anomaly of Jewish power in the twentieth and twenty-first centuries, a period when Jews have achieved unprecedented success, not only compared to other minorities but also when viewed against the rest of Jewish history. We will explore the emergence of the modern movement of Jewish nationalism (Zionism), the establishment of the State of Israel, the emergence of new Jewish identities (i.e., the "Jewish Israeli"), the decline in historical Jewish identities (i.e., "Arab Jews"), and ways that particular ideas (e.g., specific forms of Zionism) have become dominant.

This chapter will focus more on the State of Israel than the United States, for two basic reasons. First, several chapters have already addressed important aspects of the Jewish experience in the United States, which cannot be said for the Jewish State. Second, the relationship between Jews and power in Israel is much more fraught with challenges than in the United States, since it is a state that, de jure and de facto, was established for Jews. As with chapter 9—which focused not on the dates, facts, and figures of the Shoah, but rather on how the Jewish genocide is understood within the Jewish community— the goal of this chapter is not to cover the history of the State of Israel or the Israeli-Palestinian conflict (and related wars with Egypt, Jordan, etc.). Instead, most of the issues raised in this chapter are presented within the context of this book's core topic: the ongoing construction of Jewish identities.

What Is Power?

Many see power as existing at the core of all human relationships, such as in the dynamic between dominant groups and subordinated ones. Yet it is difficult to measure power, or even to qualify it. In and of itself, power is neither positive nor negative; rather, it can be used both constructively and destructively. It is an ethereal resource that can be possessed, shared, and hoarded. Power differences may be visible, emerging from particular decisions (e.g., taking a toy away from a child), or invisible, rooted in an ideology (e.g., teaching a child to believe that one country is more important than another).

One scholar who has explored the omnipresence and complicated nature of power in depth is the French philosopher Michel Foucault. He contends that power goes hand in hand with knowledge—or in the framework of this book, "truth." Just as there have been shifts in the scientific understandings of things—from believing that the earth is flat to maintaining that it is round, for example—"truth" is always changing, not of its own accord, but in relation to power.

Generated within the domains of academia, government, the media, the military, and elsewhere, "truth" does not exist in isolation. Rather, it is shaped by dominant narratives, reinforced by the repetition of scripts used to organize the world and our place within it. Power is so ensconced in social structures that it is often taken for granted; we often accept a given authority as unchallenged fact. For Foucault, power exists everywhere. Or as one scholar puts it, "Foucault believes that there is no outside to power."

When we say that during the twentieth and twenty-first centuries Jews have gained a great deal of power, this does not mean merely that some Jews have gained the ability to control or influence things. Not only does such a thesis reinforce the falsehoods propagated in books like the *Protocols of the Elders of Zion* (see chapter 9), but reducing the idea of power to control alone is simplistic. Certainly, power can exist in the control of one thing over another, such as through military might. But there is also cultural or ideological power, which is linked to certain ideas taking precedence over others. Most news headlines focus on the abuse of power, but often power is given, not taken.

From Powerlessness to Power

Power's Forms—Jews in the United States

Since World War II, Jews have steadily achieved more societal power than ever before in terms of both self-determination and cultural capital. In the United States, Jews' upward social mobility over the last half century has gradually led them to become disproportionately represented in some of the most important spheres of American social influence, including academia, government, the media, and pop culture (specifically, movies, music, and television). In American higher education, some estimate the proportion of Jewish students at the most elite colleges and universities, such as Harvard, Princeton, and Yale, to be as high as 25 percent. (This is especially notable given that these same schools once had harsh quotas to guarantee that that those with "Jewish-sounding names" would account for no more than 5–10 percent of the student body.) Similarly, the proportion of Jewish faculty at American colleges and universities, elite or otherwise, has been estimated at anywhere from 10–17 percent in 1969 to 5–13 percent in 2006.

In terms of government representation in the United States, whether as mayors of major cities (as of 2013, Chicago's Rahm Emanuel, Los Angeles's Eric Garcetti, and New York City's Michael Bloomberg), congressional representatives (during the 112th Congress, 2011–2013, Jews accounted for 6 percent of the House of Representatives and 13 percent of the Senate), or Supreme Court justices (as of 2013, three of the nine justices are Jews), Jews appear in far greater proportion than in the overall population. Scholar David Luchins notes, "Part of the new mythos of American Jews is that we're not a minority anymore. . . . We have access. The president of the United States meets regularly with the Jewish leadership. That's an incredible thing." Even President Obama's first chief of staff, Rahm Emanuel, and senior advisor, David Axelrod, both explicitly self-identify as Jews.

In Hollywood, Jews not only founded major studios, but they continue to run many of them today. Some commentators claim that this form of influence, which spills also into television, plays a greater role in shaping American culture than any other. Writer J.J. Goldberg puts it this way: "If anybody can genuinely be said to control Tinseltown, it's probably the 25 people who run the 12 main film studios—that is, the chairman (in one case, two co-chairmen) and president of each. Of those 25, 21 are Jewish, or 84%." Outside Hollywood, Jews are also disproportionately represented on the governing boards of directors of Fortune-1000 corporations, and some 11 or 12 percent of the richest individuals in the world are Jews.

Yet contrary to the claims of the *Protocols of the Elders of Zion,* there is a major difference between disproportionate representation and a "secret strategy" that Jews have to manipulate worldwide events for their own purposes. Many negative stereotypes regarding Jews are interconnected and, thus, self-perpetuating. Alongside the notion that Jews "control" things is the fiction that Jews exist in large numbers. According to a poll conducted in the 1990s, 40 percent of Americans thought that Jews make up not 2 percent but 20 percent of the U.S. population. Another poll, published by the Anti-Defamation League in 2014, found that 18 percent of people surveyed in more than one hundred countries think that Jews make up more than 10 percent of the world's population; an additional 30 percent put the number at between 1 and 10 percent. (As said previously, Jews make up 0.2% of the world.)

Although many Americans are aware of American Jews' power in terms of wealth, few, including Jews themselves, are aware of the numbers of Jews in the United States who are poor. New York City, home to more Jews than any other city in the United States (and second in terms of cities worldwide, behind only Tel Aviv, Israel), has the largest number of socioeconomically disadvantaged Jewish Americans. In the early 1990s, for example, out of New York City's 1.1 million Jews, roughly 145,000 (13 percent) were living with "serious economic deprivation." That percentage had changed very little as of 2011. Nationwide, moreover, in 2007 approximately 15 percent of Jewish Americans were living at or near the federal poverty line, on par with the U.S. population as a whole.

Power, Recognition, and Responsibility

In a 1995 essay, "The Ethics of Power," scholar Irving Greenberg asks what Jews have done with their newfound power: "We are at the beginning of a fundamental change in the Jewish condition: the assumption of power." He continues: "After almost two millennia, Jews are again exercising sovereignty in their own land. In the Diaspora and Israel, the Jewish people is taking responsibility for its fate in the realm of politics and history."

Greenberg begins by acknowledging this monumental change, but the rest of the piece ignores the unprecedented challenges that Jews face as a consequence of their newfound power. For instance, he justifies the abuse of power, which he describes as Jewish soldiers "deliberately beat[ing] Arabs on the hands" and "smash[ing] the arms and legs of some [Palestinian] civilians," saying that it is "inescapable," the only "alternative to death." He refrains from offering a self-critical analysis of power's potential to corrupt, instead saying that such situations are "morally tolerable." He ignores the effect this has had on Palestinians or Israeli Jews, disregarding an exploration of the responsibility that comes with power. He also repeatedly refers to the Shoah, as if surviving this genocide should be the driving force behind Jewish responses to their new situation.

In contrast, scholar Carl Sheingold acknowledges this new power and at the same time addresses its ability to corrupt. He notes a "Jewish loss of innocence" in the twentieth century, which arrived in tandem with power, adding that Jews should be cautious about assuming that this new era in Jewish history is anything other than a mere moment; it can just as quickly disappear. He then goes further, addressing the need for accountability, specifically in terms of the Israeli government's treatment of Palestinians living in Israel and the occupied West Bank and Gaza (the latter regions commonly called Palestine). Scholars who write about power generally echo Sheingold's argument that the "denial of one's power is only a small step away from the abuse of it." When power differentials become overly asymmetrical, these inequities occasion the abuse of power. Over time, they become destructive.

Both these viewpoints recognize the current status of Jews in the United States and Israel, but only one raises the issue of responsibility. Commentators like Greenberg explain away misuses or abuses of power as acceptable and understandable, while those like Sheingold recognize that with this new status comes a requisite conscientiousness.

Of course, some Jews are not on this spectrum at all, denying or unaware of any significant rise in social mobility and power. As Goldberg explains in *Jewish Power* (1996), "To this day, American Jews remain largely oblivious to the sea change in the status of the Jewish community in the last half-century. Much of the world views American Jewry as a focused bloc of influential, determined believers, firmly entrenched in the American power structure. The average American Jew views his or her community as a scattered congregation of six million-odd individuals of similar origins and diverse beliefs, fortunate children and grandchildren of immigrant tailors and peddlers." Still others admit Jews' lopsided presence in positions of power but, in a sign of seeming cognitive dissonance, simultaneously point to Jews' vulnerabilities.

Israeli Jews: Zionisms from Theodor Herzl to the Jewish State

The modern nation-state of Israel (special topic 10.1) is central to Jewish identities today. Along with the status of Jews in the United States, it is core to any discussion about Jewish power. It is not uncommon in twenty-first-century

America for a Jew's position relative to Israel and Jewish nationalism (i.e., Zionism) to be the primary means of acceptance into dominant forms of Jewish communal life (see, e.g., "From Zionisms to Zionism" below). Growing from a marginal European social movement into a Jewish-majority country, the rapid erection of the State of Israel is a noteworthy part of twentieth-century history.

A great deal has been written about the various conflicts linked to the State of Israel. (In terms of American media coverage, some contend that this strife gets more attention than any other.) But in looking at Jews and their relationship with the State of Israel, including how it impacts their identities, we need to backtrack. Where did the State of Israel come from? How did a relatively unimportant Jewish reporter convince his community, along with imperial powers such as the United Kingdom, to support a new settlement project in the Middle East? Is this even what happened? And once the new country was founded, how did Jews design this society to ensure not only their physical survival but also their demographic staying power? What new Jewish identities did they create in the process? What older ones did they marginalize? And what political alliances did they form in order to become militarily and economically strong well beyond their wildest imaginings?

Herzl and the Rise of Jewish Nationalism

Theodor Herzl is commonly credited with turning the modern idea of political Zionism into an international movement that eventually led to the establishment of the State of Israel in 1948. The following represents a common narrative told about Herzl and how he blazed the path that led to the Jewish State:

> In 1894, Herzl, then a young Jewish reporter in Vienna, was sent to Paris to cover the infamous Dreyfus trial, in which a Jewish officer in the French army, Alfred Dreyfus, was falsely accused of espionage. Herzl was shocked at the overt displays of antisemitism by the French masses toward Dreyfus and Jews in general.
>
> In a self-described moment of clarity, he concluded that the only place European Jews would ever be safe was in their own Jewish-majority country. Believing in the supreme value of the nation-state, Herzl felt that Zionism, a national movement for Jews based on the framework of European national movements, was the best way to achieve this goal. Shortly thereafter, in 1896, he published and disseminated his now famous pamphlet *Der Judenstaat* (The Jewish State). The following year, he gathered more than two hundred Zionists from around the world for the first conference of the World Zionist Organization.

SPECIAL TOPIC 10.1
NAMING ISRAEL AND PALESTINE

A number of different terms are used to refer to the land between the Jordan River and the Mediterranean Sea. For centuries, Jews have referred to this general geographical region as the "Land of Israel," a territory that some believe was promised by God to Abraham and his descendants, as laid out in the Torah. Aside from the problematics of considering an ancient sacred text to be historical evidence, one difficulty with this position is that, as mentioned in chapter 3, the Torah and the Prophets identify different borders for the Land of Israel (e.g., Gen. 15:18–21, Num. 34:1–15, Deut. 11:24, as well as Josh. 1:4 and Ezek. 47:13–20). A second difficulty is that these biblical descriptions cannot be reconciled with contemporary topography.

In contrast to the "Land of Israel," the "State of Israel" (also called the Jewish State) is a nation-state founded in 1948, an internationally recognized country with distinct borders. (The United Nations voted to accept this country as a member state in May 1949. Although the State of Israel isn't legally recognized by a number of other member states—as of 2008, 34 countries—Israel has diplomatic relations with 159 countries and a few other countries recognize it but lack diplomatic relations.)

Between the ceasefire in 1949 and 1967, the West Bank, also called by the biblical names Judea and Samaria, was controlled by Jordan, and Gaza, sometimes called the Gaza Strip, was controlled by Egypt. Since the end of the June 1967 war, the State of Israel has occupied (special topic 10.2) the West Bank and Gaza, leading some to call these two noncontiguous areas the Occupied Territories or the Occupied Palestinian Territories. In 2005, the State of Israel withdrew all of its Jewish Israeli citizens from Gaza—a group commonly referred to as "settlers" (also the term most often used to refer to Jewish Israelis living east of the "Green Line," the armistice line agreed to by Israel and Jordan during the 1949 ceasefire, in the West Bank)—

and relocated them inside Israel. Since then the Israeli government has played a central role in controlling access into and out of Gaza by way of land, air, and sea. (Since 1967, Israel has also controlled access into and out of the West Bank.)

As for "Palestine," some use this signifier to refer to the West Bank and Gaza, a practice that points to a future Palestinian state in those areas. Former U.S. president George W. Bush was the first American president to use the term Palestine in this manner. Others use the term to refer to the entire area between the Jordan River and the Mediterranean Sea. Jews (and others) commonly understand this second usage to mean nonrecognition of the State of Israel, which indeed is sometimes the case.

During the time this area was controlled by Great Britain, between the end of World War I and 1948, it was formally referred to by the ruling authority as British Mandate Palestine (called British-occupied Palestine in this book). Prior to this era, it was ruled by the Ottoman Empire and often called Ottoman Palestine (referred to as Ottoman-controlled Palestine in this book). Some also use the term "historic Palestine" when referring to Ottoman-controlled or British-occupied Palestine.

Throughout *Judaisms* I have chosen to distinguish between the State of Israel and the Occupied Palestinian Territories (i.e., the West Bank and Gaza). One reason behind this decision is to point out that although the West Bank and Gaza are still controlled by Israel, and although there are now approximately 500,000 Jewish Israeli "settlers" living in the West Bank (and none living in Gaza), these pieces of land are not part of the State of Israel from the de jure perspective of the Jewish State. (East Jerusalem was part of the pre-1967 West Bank and has been partially annexed by Israel, but the Jewish State has not formally annexed the West Bank or Gaza.)

But facts on the ground show that Herzl's path toward Zionism was a bit more indirect than this popular narrative suggests. Although Herzl himself claimed in 1899 that the Dreyfus affair led him to write *The Jewish State,* his personal diaries, among other evidence, indicate that this account was a case of revisionism. A variety of factors beyond his experience in Paris led him to the conclusion that Jews needed their own country, including European nationalisms of the time, which he felt did not include Jews, and his own experiences with antisemitism

growing up in the Austro-Hungarian empire. Some argue that in the context of these other nationalisms, modern Zionism was quite unexceptional, an ideology rooted in "colonialist settler" discourse like any other.

Nonetheless, curricula sanctioned by the Israeli government, in particular in the first few decades after the Holocaust ended and Israel was born, not only embellished Herzl's narrative of Jewish exceptionalism, underscoring the idea that the new country was created to protect Jews from antisemitism, but went so far as to portray

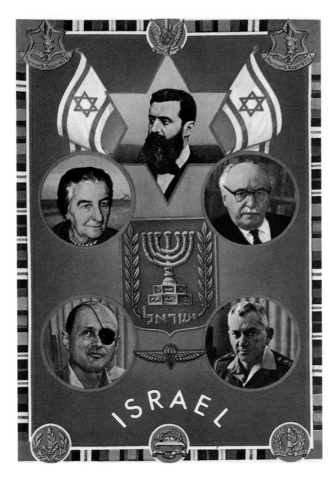

FIGURE 10.2. Israeli notables, headed by Theodor Herzl. *From bottom left, clockwise:* Moshe Dayan, Israeli military chief of general staff, defense minister, and foreign minister; Golda Meir, Israel's fourth prime minister; Theodor Herzl; Zalman Shazar, Israel's third president; and Haim Bar-Lev, Israeli military chief of general staff. This image reflects the foundational symbolism that Theodor Herzl continues to have today as a progenitor of the State of Israel.

him as the most important figure in modern Jewish history, both before and after the state was founded (fig. 10.2). As is true of many "national biographies" (see chapter 1), the first curricula even fabricated parts of his life, claiming that as a young boy he had prophetic visions of the creation of a Jewish State. Most biographical narratives of Herzl also leave out the fact that in the 1890s, before he declared allegiance to Zionism, one of his solutions to Jewish survival was the mass conversion of Jews to Christianity.

Herzl didn't even hold that the only place the Jewish State could be established was in the Land of Israel. (Special topic 10.1 discusses the term *Land of Israel* further.) He gave serious consideration to a number of alternative

locations, such as Argentina, which he first suggested in *The Jewish State.* Over the first few decades of the twentieth century, other Zionist leaders proposed various sites for the new country as well, including Angola, China, Cyprus, Egypt's Sinai Peninsula (the El-Arish Project, which Herzl sometimes called "Egyptian Palestine"), Morocco, Mozambique, Peru, South Africa, the former Soviet Union (including an area established for Jews by Joseph Stalin called Birobidzhan), and Uganda.

At the 1903 World Zionist Congress, when Uganda was first given serious consideration, several Eastern European Zionists not open to any location for the new Jewish-majority country other than the Land of Israel called Herzl a traitor for offering this proposal. Disagreements over this issue played a pivotal role in the Zionist movement's early intracommunal factionalism, reflected in the emergence of new organizations, such as the Jewish Territorial Organization (ITO), the Jewish Colonization Association, and the Jewish National Fund (JNF). (Of the three, the JNF, established in 1901, continues to this day.)

The fact that Israel might have been established in a place different from its current site is significant, not only because the Jewish State might then have avoided problems with Palestinians, but also because such discussions reveal the access Herzl and his colleagues had to imperial powers. (Of course, such a new country would likely have confronted challenges no matter the location.) Even if these European governments agreed to Herzl's requests for meetings mainly for the possibility that the Jewish community could be used to their political advantage, the fact that they considered proposals made by such a marginal group reflects Herzl's social capital.

As for why the Zionist movement was open to establishing a new country outside the Land of Israel, there are two basic reasons. First, acts of antisemitism in Europe and pogroms (organized massacres commonly sanctioned by local authorities) in Russia and Eastern Europe meant that many Jews had an immediate need for a safe haven. Second, despite the Zionist slogan "a land without people for a people without a land," early-twentieth-century Zionists in Ottoman-controlled and/or British-occupied Palestine were well aware that there was a large non-Jewish population living there and that that group was not willing to leave. Efforts made abroad to convince Jews to relocate to the Land of Israel rarely included information about the local non-Jewish inhabitants (fig. 10.3).

Thus, Israel's pre-state history is much more complicated than dominant Zionist and Jewish narratives let on. The intention here is not to dissect this past, but sim-

FIGURES 10.3A–B. Two of hundreds of posters from the early twentieth century that encouraged Jewish Zionists to travel to British-occupied Palestine and settle the land. The one on the left is from 1936; the one on the right, c. 1935, written in Romanian and Hungarian, reads: "Toward a New Life / The Promised Land / The first movie ever filmed in Palestine."

ply to point to the circuitous historical path that was followed from Herzl's *The Jewish State* to 1948. As in most of history—especially with regard to a country's founding—the road was anything but clear, clean, and simple.

Anti-Zionisms

When Herzl first began his campaign for the establishment of a new Jewish country, many European and Russian Jews were not only skeptical but vehemently opposed. From the 1890s through the 1930s (and some would say the 1940s), the Jewish collective worldwide seemed anti-Zionist. Even those Jews who had moved to Ottoman-controlled Palestine pre-1890s weren't Zionists in terms of wanting to establish a new nation-state. For them, the Land of Israel was a sacred space that Jews had had a connection to going back centuries (fig. 10.4).

Reform Jews in Europe opposed Zionism mostly because they were trying to become more integrated into

FIGURE 10.4. Three Jewish men in Jerusalem, Ottoman-controlled Palestine, c. 1914.

their particular nation-state. They favored other forms of nationalism and maintained that the creation of a new country based exclusively on Jewish identities ran counter to such ideologies. In the United States, Reform Jews starting new lives in a new place wanted to become American. This view is reflected in their 1885 "Pittsburgh Platform" (see chapter 8), which became the unofficial organizational platform for the Reform movement for decades thereafter: "We recognize, in the modern era of universal culture of heart and intellect, the approaching of the realization of Israel's great Messianic hope for the establishment of the kingdom of truth, justice, and peace among all men. We consider ourselves no longer a nation, but a religious community, and therefore expect neither a return to Palestine, nor a sacrificial worship under the sons of Aaron, nor the restoration of any of the laws concerning the Jewish state."

In 1889, a professor at Hebrew Union College (HUC), the Reform movement's rabbinical school in the United States, remarked: "A sober student of Jewish history and a genuine lover of his co-religionists sees that the Zionist agitation contradicts everything that is typical of Jews and Judaism." Similarly, in 1916 HUC's president said: "Ignorance and irreligion are at the bottom of the whole movement of political Zionism." From these perspectives, Zionism's contention that Jews should have their own Jewish State contradicted the idea that Jews in the United States should be seen as Americans. In other words, such Jews didn't orient toward the Jewish community as a nation nor were they interested in starting a Jewish nation-state. (Some say Modern Orthodox Jews such as Samson Raphael Hirsch had similar reasons for opposing Zionism.) The Reform movement's Central Conference of American Rabbis (CCAR) did not lift the ban on public support for Zionism until 1935. Even then, this was a far cry from official endorsement. (By 1937, however, the Reform movement declared it an "obligation of all Jewry to aid" in the "upbuilding" of a "Jewish homeland.")

For very different reasons, Modern Orthodox and ultra-Orthodox Jews in Europe, Russia, and the United States in the late nineteenth and early twentieth centuries were also opposed to the idea of a Jewish State. Believing that only the (Jewish) messiah could initiate the biblical prophecy to "ingather the exiles" and thereby redeem the Land of Israel, many Orthodox Jews resisted any movement that favored a "return" to Zion without an accompanying messianic figure. A Jewish State based in civil, rather than halakhic, law was contrary to their messianic doctrine. Such an occurrence was thought to be heretical, and such subcommunities compared Zionist leaders to false messiahs.

In 1889, for example, a famous Ashkenazi rabbi, Dov Baer Soloveitchik, said that the Zionist movement was "a new sect like that of Sabbatai Tzvi" (see chapter 4). Perhaps partly because of this position, only 1 percent of the Jews leaving Russia at the end of the nineteenth century and beginning of the twentieth century immigrated to Ottoman-controlled Palestine; the majority went to the United States instead. Even after the 1917 Balfour Declaration, which declared British support for a "Jewish homeland" (a critical event in terms of the eventual establishment of a Jewish State), most anti-Zionists remained unswayed. This rejection of Zionism continued for decades. Indeed, during the Shoah, a number of ultra-Orthodox rabbis asserted that the mass murder of Jews was a direct result of misdeeds carried out by Zionists.

Anti-Zionists were so opposed to Zionist thought that some accused Zionists of allying themselves with the Nazis. This harsh claim turned out to be accurate in one notable way. In the 1930s, a small number of Zionists did collaborate with Nazis to assist German Jews in immigrating to British-occupied Palestine, weighing the value of saving Jews from death and settling the Land of Israel over partnering with the Nazi regime.

After 1948, when the State of Israel was officially established, and to a larger extent following the war of June 1967, many ultra-Orthodox anti-Zionists became non-Zionists instead. Rather than actively fighting against Zionist ideologies, they simply removed themselves from the debate. As of the twenty-first century, very few ultra-Orthodox groups continue to publicly decry Zionism. For the most part, with the establishment of the State of Israel the Zionist question of "should there be a Jewish State?" was replaced with more practical concerns, such as "now that there is a Jewish State, how can it be sustained and thrive?" or "how can it become halakhic?"

Meanwhile, the majority of Orthodox, Conservative, and Reform Jews—in the United States and Israel—have been self-identified Zionists for decades (see chapter 12 for more on shifts in this phenomenon).

Zionisms

After Israel was founded in 1948, Zionism developed a dominant definition, more or less based on Herzl's idea of Jews needing a Jewish-majority and Jewish-controlled nation-state. Yet from the 1890s through the 1940s, the Zionist community was deeply divided over which of the many understandings of Zionism would become dominant—including whether a nation-state should be created at all. In other words, until Israel's establishment, Zionism had multiple meanings. Early in the twentieth century it was implicit that whichever subgroup's Zionist ideology "won" this battle would dominate what would happen in the Land of Israel.

Zionists such as Herzl, who were pushing for a new Jewish-majority country, are often called "political Zionists." Mainstream "political" Zionism, he said, was focused on creating a country like other countries—similar to Germany, a state for Germans, or France, a state for French people—rather than one rooted in the ethics of Jewish culture. Others, like Asher Ginsberg, better known by the pen name Ahad Ha-am (One of the People), are described as "cultural Zionists"; they called for the Land of Israel to become a Jewish cultural epicenter, but not necessarily a nation-state, for Jews around the world. Ahad Ha-am supported the Jewish "religion" in a cultural sense. He believed in a spiritual humanism based in biblical and modern literature, as well as in science, agriculture, and other components of the "civilization" of Jews. Whether Jews established an actual country was beside the point; such efforts, he argued, should be at best secondary.

Building upon Ahad Ha-am's ideas were other nonpolitical Zionists such as Martin Buber, individuals who were quite sensitive to the issue of Palestinian Arabs. After defecting from Herzl's Zionism, Buber spoke openly about not a literal Zion, embodied in land, but a "Zion of the soul." Scholar Maurice Friedman explains Buber's Zionist position in this way: "[Buber held that the] Zionist movement must be broadened to include all the factors and movements of spiritual rebirth, and at the same time deepened by leading it from the rigid and empty formalities of superficial activism to an inward, living comprehension of the people's being and the people's work. Zion must be reborn in the soul before it [could] be created as a tangible reality. . . . The Jewish Renaissance [was] the goal and meaning of the Jewish movement; the Zionist movement [was] the consciousness and will that lead to Renaissance." Like Ahad Ha-am, Buber challenged Zionists who wanted the Jewish nation to be similar to other nations. Such a political ideology, he said, was focused entirely on "preserving and asserting itself"; it was a form of "national egoism" rather than "national humanism."

Along with other important intellectuals in Ottoman-controlled and British-occupied Palestine—including Chaim Kalvarisky, director of the Palestine Jewish Colonization Association; Judah Magnes, chancellor of the Hebrew University of Jerusalem; Gershom Scholem, one of the most important Jewish Studies scholars of the twentieth century (see chapter 6); Henrietta Szold, founder of Hadassah, the women's Zionist Organization of America; Jacob Thon of the settlement department of the Jewish Agency; and Robert Weltsch, editor of the most important journal of the German Zionist movement—Buber was a member of Brit Shalom, a Palestine-based organization calling for a "binational state," a single state from the Mediterranean Sea to the Jordan River, which would contain both Palestinian Arabs and Jews as equal citizens. Even Israel's first president, Chaim Weizmann, publicly pledged his support for this idea prior to the founding of Israel. Although Brit Shalom eventually disbanded, and some of these individuals changed their positions over time, the notion of binationalism was core to the platform of the pre-state political party Ihud (Unity), and continues as a potential "solution" to the Israeli-Palestinian conflict today.

Similar to the cultural and spiritual Zionism of Ahad Ha-am and Buber, respectively, was that espoused by Mordecai Kaplan (chapter 8), who advocated for a "stateless"—or non-nation-state—form of Zionism. Writing prior to the establishment of the State of Israel, Kaplan noted: "Current concepts of nationalism are deeply problematic because they are based upon the misleading assumption that nationhood is synonymous with statehood, which makes it impossible to be considered a nation unless it is represented by a state." Whereas some Zionists pointed to Nazi Germany as evidence for why Jews needed their own country, Kaplan used Nazi Germany as an example of the corrupt nature of nation-states: "With the organization of modern nations there has been a return to the sub-human principle of the herd." Germany's actions during World War II were an argument against the formation of a new nation-state, said Kaplan, rather than the reason a Jewish State based on this same structural model was necessary.

On the other end of the Zionist spectrum from Buber were individuals such as Ze'ev Vladimir Jabotinsky. Commonly described as more "hawkish" than David Ben-Gurion, Israel's first prime minister and the primary figure responsible for integrating Herzlian notions of Zionism into the newly established Jewish State, Jabotinsky broke from the mainstream Zionist Executive Council in the 1930s and founded the New Zionist Organization (NZO). Shortly thereafter, the NZO launched the Irgun, which is commonly depicted as a paramilitary group (or, by some scholars, as "terrorists") that fought for the establishment of the Jewish State and is credited with multiple antagonistic operations carried out against "Zionist enemies," such as the British occupying forces.

Israeli Jews: Independence and Shaping the Jewish State

Pre-Independence and the Palestinian Arab "Other"

The core Jewish narrative promoted by political Zionists, whose vision of Zionism ultimately won out, has been that those Jews who between 1880 and the 1930s immigrated to their ancestral land were returning "home." Yet as a future prime minister of Israel, Moshe Sharett, crudely admitted as early as 1914, a major problem was on the horizon: "We have forgotten that we have not come to an empty land to inherit it, but we have come to conquer a country from people inhabiting it, that governs it by the virtue of its language and savage culture."

Indeed, a monumental obstacle was the existence of another sizable population living in the area known to Jews as the Land of Israel (at the time, a population much larger than Jews; see below). Sharett was far from alone in testifying to this fact (or in describing the local population using derogatory language). During this era many notables, including David Ben-Gurion, Martin Buber, Ahad Ha-am, Theodor Herzl, and Ze'ev Jabotinsky, also said that the relationship between Jews and Palestinian Arabs was the most important issue to solve in terms of establishing a new country.

This observation was also quite obvious. In 1880, the proportion of Jews to Palestinian Arabs in Palestine (i.e., the area between the Jordan River and the Mediterranean Sea) was roughly 25,000 to 300,000 (1:12); in 1922, it was 84,000 to 666,000 (1:8); and by 1947 it was 640,000 to 1,300,000 (1:2). (The Jewish population grew quickly because of pre- and post-WWII immigration of Jews coming from Europe and the Russian Empire. Increasing population rates among Palestinians have been attributed to a number of other factors, such as improvements in health care and, as a result, increases in longevity.)

This meant that the Zionist Jews coming to Palestine confronted not just the presence of a significant non-Jewish group, but also the fact that they were outnumbered anywhere from twelve to one (1880) to two to one (1947). Partly because of these demographics, the Jewish-Palestinian (or Zionist-Palestinian) conflict has defined both of these Middle Eastern communities since well before 1948. Some historians argue that it is only possible to explore early modern Zionist history in Palestine, or Palestinian Arab history during the same period, in terms of "relational history," a process whereby one group can be accurately understood only in relation to another.

With regard to dominant Jewish narratives, especially in light of "relational history" and their connection to Palestinians, throughout the first half of the twentieth century there were periods when Jews and Palestinians lived together peacefully and others when there was violence. Many Jews today point to events that took place in August 1929 in Hebron as an early example of conflict between these two groups. Called the "Hebron massacre" by Jews, this three-day spate of violence ended with Palestinian Arab mobs having murdered sixty-seven Jews. The impetus for the attacks, according to scholar Benny Morris, lay in orchestrated rumors that Jews were attacking Palestinian Arabs—in Jerusalem, among other places—or that they were storming the Noble Sanctuary, al-Haram al-Sharif, the area immediately above the Western Wall, the third holiest site in Islam (called the Temple Mount by Jews). Dominant Jewish narratives focus exclusively on those killed, though many Palestinians helped save their Jewish neighbors during the violence (an estimated 450 survived).

Within dominant Palestinian narratives, in contrast, the phrase "Hebron massacre" points not to August 1929 but to February 1994, when Israeli Jew Baruch Goldstein murdered twenty-nine Palestinians, and injured more than one hundred more, in the Ibrahimi mosque at the Cave of the Patriarchs in the Old City of Hebron.

A Challenge to Independence

The State of Israel was established in 1948. By the following year, when a ceasefire was agreed upon, the Jewish demographic within the borders of the new Jewish State (an area smaller than the region between the Jordan River and the Mediterranean Sea; fig. 10.5) had changed drastically. Jews now outnumbered Palestinians roughly four to one within the State of Israel. Of the total population of 800,000 citizens of the new Jewish State, almost 20 percent, 154,000 of them, were Palestinian (renamed by the Israeli government "Israeli Arabs"; see below).

This demographic shift is primarily attributed to the dispossession of approximately 800,000 Palestinian Arabs from their homes. Jewish military forces physically removed many of them and threatened others, which caused them to leave (arguably the current dominant academic historical position, a shift that began in the 1980s, when Israeli government archives were first made

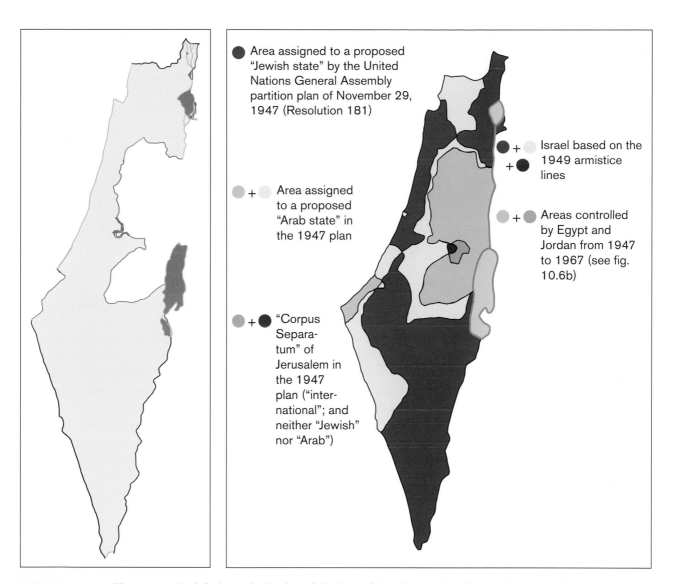

FIGURES 10.5A–B. The map on the left shows the borders of the State of Israel in 1949, based on various armistice agreements made by the Israeli government and the governments of Egypt, Jordan, Lebanon, and Syria. These "Armistice Demarcation Lines" are different from the international borders in existence prior to the 1947–1949 violence and, according to the armistice agreements, were to have been "provisional" rather than "permanent." Partially because agreements as to permanent borders between Israel and Egypt and Jordan did not take place for decades thereafter (and due to the fact that agreements with Lebanon and Syria have never taken place), from the perspective of the Israeli government these lines have been the de facto, and to some degree de jure, borders ever since. Sometimes these borders, in particular the one separating Israel from the West Bank, are referred to as the Green Line, a name based on the original color used on one of the main maps during negotiations. *Right:* This map shows the borders of British-occupied Palestine in 1947 (the entire territory shown here), at the time the British left the region, juxtaposed to the proposed United Nations borders for a Jewish state alongside a Palestinian Arab state (which never came to fruition) and the 1949 borders of the armistice agreements.

available officially). Some fled owing to the general dangers linked to war. Invading Arab armies are also considered responsible for ordering some Palestinians to leave. Many now identified as refugees, having relocated from the new Jewish State to the West Bank, Gaza, or other surrounding countries, such as Lebanon, Syria, and beyond. Much of this history continues to be debated today. For some, the question of whether Palestinians chose to leave or were forced to do so defines their position regarding the Israeli-Palestinian conflict.

The "Miracle" of Independence

By some accounts, during the years immediately after Israel's founding the American Jewish community supported the new Jewish State only nominally; over time, however, the establishment of Israel has become core to dominant Jewish narratives, with many Jews considering it one of the greatest events in Jewish history. Indeed, many twenty-first-century Jews regard the establishment of Israel as a "miracle," even those who do not identify as religious (see below and chapter 8). In this collective's story, Israel's founding is the culmination of a long journey that began with the biblical Israelites, an embodiment of prayers to "return to Zion" made for close to two millennia (chapter 3).

In accord with this particular narrative, Jews commonly refer to the fighting that went on between 1947 and 1949—whether against local Palestinian Arabs or armies from nearby countries, such as Egypt, Iraq, Jordan, Lebanon, and Syria—as the War of Independence. In contrast, Palestinian and non-Palestinian Arabs generally call it Al-Nakba (the Catastrophe). Whether dated to May 14, 1948 (the day Israel was officially declared an independent country, coinciding with the end of the British occupation of Palestine), or July 20, 1949 (when the fourth and final armistice was agreed to by the new Israeli government and the bordering countries that had invaded only fourteen months before; see fig. 10.5), for many Jews around the world the establishment of the Jewish State embodied—and continues to embody—the community's wildest hopes and dreams.

From Independence to Stability

Despite what many Jews see as the extraordinary "miracle" of Israel's establishment, not until after the 1967 war, almost twenty years later, did Jewish Israelis begin to truly see themselves—collectively—as a strong people, an empowered nation in charge of its own future. As reflected in countless documents from the time, in the years after independence Jewish Israelis often felt that Israel's existence was precarious.

For example, consider the following description by Ariel Sharon, a former Israeli prime minister and venerated military officer, speaking of the period before the 1967 war: "In those days [Jewish] Israelis shared a nearly universal belief that the only possible way to survive in the midst of our hostile neighbors was to stand firmly on our rights." Regarding the time following the 1967 war, though, Sharon said:

Neither the uncertainty about the future of Samaria and Judea [the West Bank] nor anything else could dampen the euphoria of those days. It was as if the country was collectively celebrating the most joyful period of its existence. Certainly it was the happiest time I had known. There was a feeling that we had finally broken free from the noose that had been around our necks. Up until then everyone had always felt the fragility of this narrow, vulnerable place we lived in. . . . For me personally the feelings of those days were far more intense than those that had accompanied the end of the War of Independence. Then I had felt that our victory was incomplete . . . [that] we had eked out for ourselves a tenuous existence. Now—nineteen years later—the world seemed to have opened up before us.

Sharon is one of the more important symbols of the State of Israel, perhaps the archetype of a Jewish Israeli hard-liner. Born in 1928 in British-occupied Palestine, Sharon fought in every Israeli war from 1947 through 2005, eventually rising to the most powerful position in the Israeli government, prime minister. (In January 2006, he had a stroke while serving as prime minister. Between then and January 2014, when he died, he was in a state of "minimal consciousness.")

Yet Sharon is far from the only Jewish Israeli who experienced elation following the 1967, rather than 1948, war. By claiming the Sinai Peninsula and Gaza from Egypt, the Golan Heights from Syria, and the West Bank from Jordan as a result of the 1967 war (which Jews refer to as the Six-Day War and Palestinians as Al-Naksa, the Setback), Jews achieved power over land they had not controlled for millennia. According to dominant Jewish narratives, from the era when the Land of Israel was ruled by the biblical proto-Jewish kings David and Solomon through to 1967, Jews lacked power over, and nontransient access to, the Old City of Jerusalem and the West Bank, the most important parts of the Land of Israel according to the Bible, containing such cities as Bethlehem, Hebron, and Jericho, to name a few. As a result of a war that lasted less than one week, the Israeli government more than doubled its geographical size.

One cannot overstate the impact that the 1967 war had not just on Jewish Israelis but also on Jewish Americans and the United States government. As Benny Morris writes, "The war did wonders for the [Israeli] state's international standing, almost overnight converting it from a miniscule backwater into a focus of the world's attention. Israel was now seen by the West, and primarily Washington, as a regional superpower and a desirable ally among a bevy of fickle, weak Arab states. . . . The war also generated a surge of unity and self-confi-

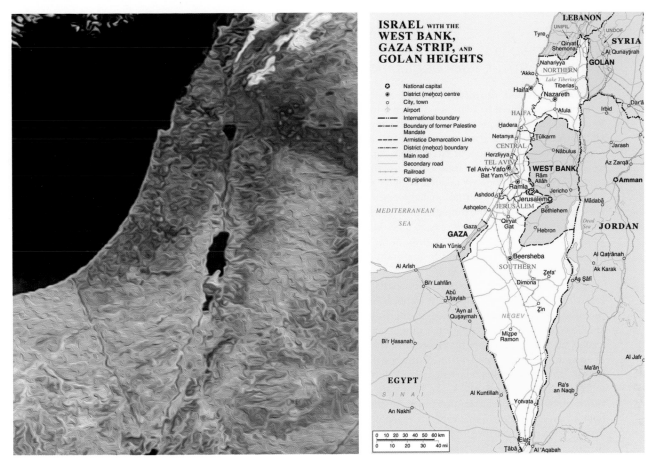

FIGURES 10.6A–B. Israel and the occupied West Bank and Gaza (the latter two regions also commonly called Palestine; see special topic 10.1). *Left:* A satellite image of Israel, Palestine, and surrounding areas. *Right:* The same area of land but with the State of Israel distinguished from three of the four areas conquered by the Israel military during the June 1967 war: Gaza, the West Bank, and the Golan Heights, taken respectively from Egypt, Jordan, and Syria. (The fourth area, the Sinai Desert, which is partially shown in the map and which the Israeli military also conquered in 1967, was ceded to Egypt in the 1979 Camp David Accords.) When people today speak about the Occupied Palestinian Territories, they are commonly referring to the West Bank and Gaza, the same areas most often considered to be the land encompassed by a future state of Palestine, perhaps with a corridor connecting them (the so-called "two-state solution").

dence among the world's Jews; it even gave rise to a modest wave of immigration to Israel from western Jewish communities."

Jewish Israelis felt as if they had finally reestablished Jewish sovereignty, not just temporarily but for the long term. An editorial in the Israeli newspaper *Haaretz* dated June 8, 1967, expressed this feeling: "The glory of past ages is no longer to be seen at a distance but is, from now on, part of the new state, and its illumination will irradiate the constructive enterprise of a Jewish society that is a link in the long chain of the history of the people in its country. . . . Jerusalem is all ours. Rejoice and celebrate, O' dweller in Zion." Today, many scholars continue to refer to this war as a "tremendous victory" for Israel.

Stability to Instability and Military Occupation

Conquered land aside, arguably the most significant consequence of the Jewish State's newfound power following June 1967 was its control of one million Palestinians—360,000 in Gaza and 670,000 in the West Bank—who had been under the authority of Egypt and Jordan, respectively, since 1948 (fig. 10.6). The narrative of Israel as the underdog began to shift, and questions began to emerge: Given its new status in terms of military dominance, in the David/Goliath construct how could Israel truly still be David? Who but Goliath would have been able to conquer land held by three different countries, and in only six days? Who but Goliath would be able

SPECIAL TOPIC 10.2
A NOTE ABOUT THE TERM *OCCUPATION*

The term *occupation*, broadly speaking, is a technical military term applied to a situation when a military force conquers an area previously not under its control and, rather than grant the resident population independence, semi-autonomy, or citizenship, continues to control the area and the rights of its inhabitants, commonly through a newly created military administrative body. Various international agreements deal with this situation (e.g., the Hague Convention of 1907 and the Geneva Convention of 1949, to name but two). Special topic 10.4 is a brief explanation of the Israeli government's ongoing decision to maintain such a state of military control since 1967.

Use of the term occupation in relation to the Israeli-Palestinian conflict has important implications. Although some claim that Palestine (i.e., the West Bank and Gaza) is not under occupation, a number of Israeli leaders have used precisely that word over the years. In 2003, for example, then–Prime Minister Ariel Sharon said the following in referring to the Palestinians living in the West Bank and Gaza: "You cannot like the word, but what is happening is an occupation—to hold 3.5 million Palestinians under occupation. I believe that is a terrible thing for Israel and for the Palestinians. . . . It can't continue endlessly. Do you [Jewish Israelis] want to stay forever in Jenin, in Nablus, in Ramallah, in Bethlehem? I don't think that's right."

In fact, ever since the end of the 1967 war, various Israeli politicians have argued that the Israeli military should return to the pre-1967 borders and end the occupation. For instance, in 1971, former prime minister Ben-Gurion said: "If I were still prime minister, I would announce that we are prepared to give back all the territory occupied in the Six-Day War except East Jerusalem and the Golan Heights."

In January 2008, former president George W. Bush declared: "There should be an end to the occupation that began in 1967. The agreement must establish Palestine as a homeland for the Palestinian people, just as Israel is a homeland for the Jewish people. These negotiations must ensure that Israel has secure, recognized, and defensible borders. And they must ensure that the state of Palestine is viable, contiguous, sovereign, and independent." President Barack Obama uses the term occupation regularly in reference to the West Bank and Gaza, as do former U.S. government Middle East foreign policy experts (e.g., Dennis Ross) who work at think tanks such as the Washington Institute for Near East Policy.

Interestingly, many scholars refrain from referring to Egyptian rule over Palestinians in Gaza and Jordanian rule over Palestinians in the West Bank between 1940 and 1967 as "occupation," though an argument could be made to this effect.

---

to occupy one million people and maintain power over them?

Whether one argues for or against Israel's policies in the West Bank and Gaza—calling its actions self-defense or violations of human rights—since 1967 the occupation of these territories has been central to the Israeli-Palestinian conflict (special topic 10.2). For starters, it has further empowered Jewish Israelis and disempowered Palestinians—both those in Israel ("Israeli Arabs") and those in the West Bank and Gaza.

Meanwhile, the Palestinian population has quadrupled since 1967, with approximately 4.4 million Palestinians in Gaza and the West Bank as of 2013. As for the population of Israel, the 2013 census counted 8 million citizens, 6.04 million (75 percent) of whom were Jewish, and 1.66 million (20 percent) Palestinian. (The remaining 5 percent are non-Palestinian Christians and members of other groups, such as Druze, Circassians, Samaritans, etc.) This means that between the Jordan River and the Mediterranean Sea—in Israel and the occupied West Bank and Gaza—there are more Palestinians than Jews, albeit barely. (Even if one argues that there are slightly more Jews than Palestinians in this area, by all accounts the Palestinian birthrate is higher than that of Jewish Israelis; thus, these same issues remain.)

The same issue of demographics that confronted pre-state Zionists continues to haunt many Jewish Israelis today. In terms of electoral politics, if the Jewish State were to incorporate Palestinians living in the West Bank and Gaza—i.e., if it gave these 4.4 million individuals Israeli citizenship—Palestinians would have more votes than Jews. If, in contrast, Israel allowed the Palestinians to establish their own independent state in the West Bank and Gaza, a basic Jewish Israeli (and Jewish American) fear is that Palestine, whether with or without the support of the so-called "fifth column"—the 20 percent of Israel's population who are Palestinians with Israeli citizenship—could potentially attack and defeat Israel. Some venture that even if a future Palestinian country were officially demilitarized, it is always possible to smuggle in weapons. In the long run, there is a lack of trust among Jewish Israelis that Palestinians would keep up their end of a political agreement, as they would always aim to destroy Israel. Such perceptions, rooted in anxiety and even panic, are true for many Jews.

Put another way, from the dominant Jewish Israeli perspective, the question of the status of Palestinians in the occupied West Bank and Gaza is existential. If these 4.4 million Palestinians are integrated into Israel, the Jewish identity of the Jewish State will be in danger, whereas if Palestinians establish an independent Palestinian country, they will destroy Israel. Thus, many Jews believe that the status quo—with Palestinians living under continued occupation in the West Bank and Gaza—is preferable to any other potential reality.

In the current realpolitik, the 4.4 million Palestinians in the occupied West Bank and Gaza do not have Israeli citizenship. Though controlled by the State of Israel, most of them are "citizens of Palestine" (many in the West Bank are also citizens of Jordan), also known as the Palestinian Authority (PA), which means that, theoretically, they are citizens of their own country. But the PA is not fully autonomous, and the Israeli government controls many aspects of Palestinian life in the West Bank and Gaza. (Palestine has declared independence on a number of occasions, but Israel does not recognize its legitimacy, nor does the United States.)

For example, between 2005 and 2014, the Palestinian Authority had virtually no control over deciding what goods could go into or out of the occupied West Bank and Gaza. In addition, the Israeli government controlled the Palestinians' water supply and, when it so chose, their electrical grid. When the Israeli military arrested Palestinians in the occupied territories, they were tried in Israeli military courts. There are also 500,000 Jewish Israeli "settlers," citizens of the Jewish State, living alongside the 3 million or so West Bank Palestinians. As these realities suggest, Jewish Israelis are de jure and de facto more powerful than Palestinians.

For these reasons and more, many Jews believe that the military occupation of the West Bank and Gaza continues to put Israel's political existence in danger. For this reason, according to multiple surveys most Jews in the United States and Israel favor the establishment of an independent Palestinian state in the West Bank and Gaza. Ultimately, in their view, solidifying a political agreement that permits Israel to live alongside Palestine—the so-called two-state solution—will allow Israel greater security.

Based on a number of polls conducted over the decades—where there might be 75 percent of Jewish Israelis in favor of a so-called two-state solution and 75 percent in favor of the continued occupation of the West Bank and Gaza—it is clear that there is a small group of Jews who answer in the affirmative to contradictory scenarios regarding a political end to this conflict. Some might understandably question how someone can maintain two such opposing viewpoints. A simple response to this phenomenon is that many Jews are conflicted about the creation of an independent Palestinian state. Although many are opposed to Israel's occupation, those falling into this subgroup are also fearful that an independent Palestinian state will lead to Israel's destruction. A second reason is that because violence is common in Israel and Palestine, it is not uncommon for someone to answer differently to a pollster when asked the same question over the course of one month's time.

Israeli Jews: The Creation of New Jewish Identities

A New National Jewish Identity: The Israeli Jew

With the establishment of Israel, a new Jewish identity was birthed: the Israeli Jew. There had been ancient Israelites, but that was a much different identity. The Israeli Jew was rooted in a new national narrative, a script that connected ancient Jewish history with the twentieth-century ideology of establishing a Jewish-majority country. (Not all countries are able to assert an ancient connection to the land upon which they are founded.)

The Declaration of the Establishment of the State of Israel laid the foundation for this narrative. Delivered by David Ben-Gurion on May 14, 1948, the declaration connects multiple exiles from the Land of Israel with the twentieth-century Shoah (chapter 9), thereby justifying Jewish autonomy. As scholar Baruch Kimmerling notes, "In Israel, even more than in any other society, the past, present, and future are intermingled; collective memory is considered objective history." This new Jewish Israeli narrative helped to homogenize an incredibly heterogeneous collective of Jews, who had come, quite literally, from all over the world.

In Ben-Gurion's own words:

The diasporas which are being liquidated and are gathering in Israel do not yet constitute a people, but a motley crew and the dust of man, without language, without education, without roots, and without links to the tradition and vision of the nation. It is not a simple task to transform this human dust into a cultured independent nation possessed of vision, and the difficulties are no less than those involved in economic absorption. A prodigious ethical and educational effort is required—an effort that must be accompanied by a deep and pure love to unite these outcasts and inculcate them with the values and principles of the nation.

Ben-Gurion's perception of his fellow Jews is telling. He says that the new Jewish immigrants—those arriving thirty to forty years after himself—were powerless; they were uneducated nomads, akin to "dust," individuals who lacked a common language (or perhaps were deficient in terms of what he considered to be a sophisticated language) and even a rudimentary understanding of the notion of a modern nation-state.

Ben-Gurion imagined empowering this "motley crew" of "outcasts" and shaping them into the foundation for a new country. Such a project meant that there needed to be a "prodigious ethical and educational effort," including the creation of such symbols as a new flag (whose origins actually go back to the 1890s) and a new national anthem (whose origins go back to the 1880s). New genres of music, dance, and literature were likewise needed, and subsequently emerged. Perhaps the most noteworthy innovation was a new dialect, "modern Hebrew" (which is similar to yet distinct from biblical Hebrew). From the first waves of Jewish immigration to Palestine, to those occurring after the state was founded, Jews coming to the Land of Israel spoke scores of different languages. But with a common language, this diverse group had a shared way to communicate.

According to the dominant Israeli national narrative, the individual most committed to a unifying language, even before he immigrated to Palestine, was Eliezer Ben-Yehuda, a scholar who wrote in the introduction to his dictionary of modern Hebrew, "If a language which has stopped being spoken . . . can return and be the spoken tongue of an individual for all necessities of his life, there is no room for doubt that it can become the spoken language of a community." Along with many other new keystones, Hebrew became Israel's new national language.

A New Legal Jewish Identity: The Law of Return

Even before Israel was officially established, Jewish Zionist leaders aimed to ensure that the country's primary identity would be Jewish, especially given that Jews were outnumbered by Palestinian Arabs. Indeed, for many Zionists, creating a country exclusively for Jews was the very purpose of the new state. As the Declaration of the Establishment of the State of Israel puts it, "The State of Israel will be open for Jewish immigration and for the Ingathering of the Exiles." But any legal body—whether a modern government or a religious court—must define its terms. The declaration does not say what Jews are or how they are defined, only that the new country had to embrace them.

A little more than two years after the country's founding, in July 1950, the Knesset (Israeli Parliament) passed the Law of Return, legally permitting any Jew in the world to become a new citizen of the Jewish State. Embedded in the law's name is the dominant Jewish idea that the ancestors of this modern community were exiled and only in their contemporary efforts to relocate to the Land of Israel were they able to return to their land. However, the new bill fell short in terms of defining what a Jew was. Instead, it simply reiterated statements from the founding declaration, adding that if Jews were "engaged in an activity directed against the Jewish people" or were "likely to endanger public health or the security of the State," their application for citizenship would be rejected.

Not until March 1970, twenty-two years after its establishment, did the Jewish State offer a detailed definition of the term *Jew*. This amendment to the Law of Return states: "'Jew' means a person who was born of a Jewish mother or has become converted to Judaism and who is not a member of another religion." The 1970 change also says that relatives of a Jewish person—such as "a child and a grandchild of a Jew, the spouse of a Jew, the spouse of a child of a Jew and the spouse of a grandchild of a Jew"—would also be granted Israeli citizenship, with the exception of those who identify with another religion. Yet the 1970 amendment still left a number of questions unanswered, such as what types of conversions are valid (only those performed by a rabbi? a rabbi of what denomination?) and, of course, the necessary legal parameters for proving that one's mother or grandmother is Jewish.

Since 1950, among the Israeli Supreme Court's most famous cases regarding citizenship have been ones concerning a man born to Jewish parents who converted to Catholicism (Brother Daniel), an American mobster (Meir Lansky), and a family self-identified as "Messianic Jews." The 1970 amendment caused some to note the similarity between the definition of a Jew based on having a single Jewish grandparent and the parameters set by the Nazi regime during World War II. As Haim Cohen, a former Israeli Supreme Court judge, once quipped: "The bitter irony of fate has decreed that the same biological and racist arguments extended by the Nazis, and which

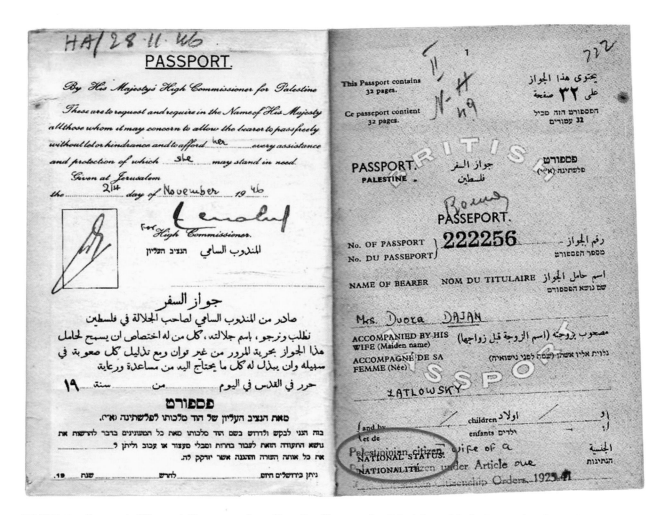

FIGURE 10.7. Passport of Devorah Dayan, mother of Israeli military and political figure Moshe Dayan (see fig. 10.2). On the bottom, circled in red, is her legal status when living in British-occupied Palestine: "Palestinian citizen."

inspired the inflammatory laws of Nuremberg, serve as the basis for the official definition of Jewishness in the bosom of the state of Israel."

Another way some Jews see it, of course, is that this law makes it possible for anyone who would have been murdered by the Nazis to become an Israeli citizen, an opportunity that, had it been in place only a few years prior to 1948, might have saved countless Jews from Nazi death camps. This idea of Herzl's, that Jews needed their own country to serve as a "safe haven," continues to be a core component of Zionist thought today (see special topics 10.3 and 10.4).

(Interestingly, in 2013, Portugal became the second country in the world to pass a "Law of Return," this one permitting the descendants of Jews who were expelled from Portugal in the fifteenth and sixteenth centuries to be repatriated. In 2015 the Spanish Parliament passed a similar law.)

A New National Distinction: Israeli Jew ≠ Israeli (Palestinian) Arab

The process of identity formation includes not only developing the characteristics of Group X, but also distinguishing it from Group Y. Indeed, a major aspect of the politics of identity is a group's defining itself in terms of what it is not (see chapter 11). In the State of Israel— from the start—"Jews" and "Arabs" were sharply differentiated, both de jure and de facto. This process was initiated in the late nineteenth century, when thousands of Ashkenazi Jews began immigrating to Ottoman-controlled Palestine, and it continued in British-occupied Palestine, when Jews were often called "Palestinians" legally (fig. 10.7). A distinction between "Jew" and "Arab" made sense given that most of these Jews weren't of Arab descent and the local population already identified as Palestinian Arabs.

After 1948, the Jewish State became much more methodical than the British in legally separating Jews from Palestinian Arabs. Starting in 1949, all citizens of the new country were given national identity cards. According to scholar Helga Tawil-Souri, "In the aftermath of the 1948 Arab-Israeli war, Palestinians inside the new Israeli state were issued ID cards, while those in the West Bank and the Gaza Strip were usually given temporary documents from Jordanian and Egyptian authorities, respectively. After Israel's occupation in 1967, Palestinians in East Jerusalem, the West Bank, and the Gaza Strip were issued different cards by Israel. . . . All adults in Palestine/Israel [were] issued ID cards [that were] required to be carried at all times."

Each card designated a single "nationality" for the cardholder, a category distinct from citizenship (which is another category on the card)—a practice that was unique to Israel until it changed in 2005. The two most common "nationalities" were "Jew" and "Arab" (though there were/are more than a hundred others). These cards also listed each individual's religious identity—usually Jew, Muslim, or Christian—one of only six countries worldwide to do so. That said, even if Israeli national identification cards didn't distinguish between "Jews" and "Arabs," it was relatively easy to determine this distinction based on other information provided on the card, such as religion, name, and address.

There were a number of reasons for this policy. For starters, it was one way to distinguish those Palestinian Arabs who were citizens of Israel ("Israeli Arabs") from those who were not (i.e., those who lived in the West Bank and Gaza). Second, the Ashkenazi Jews establishing these new laws had been heavily influenced by European worldviews; many had spent their youth in Europe, where Jews and Arabs were often thought of as different ethnicities. Third, it helped distinguish between Palestinian Arab Israelis and Jews arriving from Arab-majority countries. Fourth, Israel was explicitly founded as a country for Jews; as such, it instituted laws that would ensure it remained a state composed of and controlled by Jews.

Reasons for this policy aside, one's national identification card was more than a mere legal document; one's designation had many practical consequences. Between 1948 and 1966, Palestinian Arab citizens of Israel officially lived under "military rule," which meant that they did not have the same de jure rights as Israeli Jews, such as freedom of movement and freedom of the press. In addition, since 1948 "Israeli Arabs" have been excluded from a number of basic legal entitlements, such as social

security. (The government links this legal right to service in the Israeli military, something most "Israeli Arabs" have never had the option of participating in, though it's widely accepted that most would decline if given the choice.) Similarly, since the state's founding, de facto and de jure laws have prevented the sale of government lands—which constitute 93 percent of all the land west of the 1949 armistice border—from being sold to non-Jewish Israeli citizens. According to a number of Israeli human rights organizations, such as Adalah and Sikkuy, these laws are but two of countless examples of government discrimination based on whether one is Jewish.

A New Jewish Distinction: "Arab Jewish Israeli" − Arab = Jewish Israeli

In the twenty-first century, the term *Arab Jew* is incredibly politicized. But until 1948, Jews from Arab-majority countries often identified as both Arabs and Jews without problem. Not only was the primary language of these Jewish communities Arabic (speaking, writing), but historical evidence indicates that they did not perceive Jewish identities to be in opposition to Arab identities (see chapters 1 and 7).

Before 1948, there were about 800,000 Jews living in Arab-majority Middle Eastern and North African (MENA) countries. After the implementation of the Law of Return in 1950, this number dropped to fewer than 50,000, with most of these Jews relocating to the State of Israel (special topic 10.3). Upon arrival in the Jewish State, the Arab component of their identities immediately began to transform.

MENA Jews had immigrated to a country that granted them citizenship precisely because they were Jewish; their Jewish identity was privileged over all other social identities. Intent on generating a new national identity, the Israeli government had no use for the concept of an "Arab Jew," only a "Jew." Thus, these immigrants now became "Israeli Jews." In terms of intra-Jewish interaction, most were now referred to as Mizraḥi (see chapter 1). The same was true for those "Arab Jews" who were present in the Land of Israel before 1948, whether under British occupation or Ottoman control.

About this process, scholar Amnon Raz-Krakotzkin writes: "In Israel, Mizrahim became the new Marranos; in this case, however, it was not their religion that had to be concealed, but their culture. People had to hide their Arabic culture, afraid to listen to the music that preserved their contact to a cultural framework considered hostile and primitive. In other words, they had to aban-

SPECIAL TOPIC 10.3
THE FORGOTTEN REFUGEES?

A core thread within dominant Jewish narratives today is that Jews immigrating to Israel from countries in the Middle East and North Africa (MENA) should be referred to as "refugees." Many of the 800,000 or so Jews who arrived in Israel from these regions (post-1948) were dispossessed of their homes. Some were physically forced to leave, others were threatened, and still others were forced to choose between fleeing or being imprisoned. (Not all left; some 50,000 stayed put.)

Some of these Jews were living in countries at war with Israel (or with the proto-Israeli state) between 1947 and 1949, such as Egypt, Iraq, Jordan, Lebanon, and Syria, and were treated in their home countries as enemies of the state. (This situation is loosely comparable to the American government's treatment of Japanese living in the United States during the 1940s, when the U.S. was at war with Japan.)

Following the establishment of the State of Israel, during the 1950s riots were carried out against Jews in a number of these countries. (The same happened dur-ing the 1940s, prior to Israel's establishment.) Sometimes Jewish-specific buildings were bombed (see chapter 7, "Iraqi Jewish Culture in Israel").

Many Jews arriving in Israel from MENA countries felt that the Jewish State was their "safe haven," their refuge. Yet some Jews resented their new life in the Jewish State, not only because they were mistreated in Israel, but also because some had good relations with their non-Jewish neighbors prior to relocating. In short, there is no one size fits all narrative regarding the lives Jews had in MENA countries prior to the mass migration to Israel.

Since the 1990s and increasingly into the twenty-first century, various Jewish organizations have reintroduced this part of Jewish history into general Jewish discourses. Often these historical experiences are used to buttress the argument that Palestinians who became refugees as a result of the 1947–1949 wars (or even the June 1967 war) have no more right to return to their previously owned homes than do those Jews who lived in MENA countries prior to 1948.

don the culture in whose terms they defined their Jewish identity."

Pressure to assimilate into the new Ashkenazi-dominant society was reinforced by a number of statements made by influential Jewish Israeli leaders, assertions that reflect overt prejudice toward these non-Ashkenazi Jews. Zionist leaders as renowned as Ben-Gurion were outspoken in their desire to de-Arabize these newest Jewish Israelis; in a 1967 interview, for example, Ben-Gurion said, "We do not want the [MENA Jewish] Israelis to become Arabs. We are in duty bound to fight against the spirit of the Levant [i.e., Israel, Jordan, Lebanon, and Palestine], which corrupts individuals and societies, and preserve the authentic Jewish values as they crystallized in the Diaspora."

In a 1965 interview, Ben-Gurion explained further: "Those from Morocco had no education. Their customs are those of Arabs. They love their wives, but beat them. . . . Maybe in the third generation something will appear from the Oriental Jew that is a little different. But I don't see it yet. The Moroccan Jew took a lot from the Moroccan Arabs. The culture of Morocco I would not like to have here. And I don't see what contribution present Persians have to make."

Ben-Gurion was not the only figure to voice this perspective. In an address to leaders of the Zionist Federation of Great Britain in 1964, Golda Meir, Israel's only female prime minister, said:

We in Israel need immigrants from countries with a high standard, because the question of our future social structure is worrying us. We have immigrants from Morocco, Libya, Iran, Egypt and other countries with a 16th century level. Shall we be able to elevate these immigrants to a suitable level of civilization? If the present state of affairs continues, there will be a dangerous clash between the Ashkenazim who will constitute an elite, and the Oriental communities of Israel. This is the most tragic thing that can befall us. We need greater equilibrium and immigrants from countries with a high level.

In countless instances, Ashkenazi Jews called for the sounding of alarms regarding the tainting of the new Jewish Israeli identity by "Oriental" Jews. (Evidence suggests that some Ashkenazi Jews continue to make claims of superiority today.) Some scholars go further, claiming that Jews of MENA descent were brought to Israel to serve as a new working class, thus giving Ashkenazi Jews the opportunity to move up the socioeconomic ladder at their expense.

One way scholars frame Ashkenazi hegemony is through the term *intra-Jewish Orientalism,* resulting in a classification system that has structurally marginalized new Jewish Israeli immigrants from the MENA region (chapter 1). A basic consequence of this bias, scholars point out, was the deliberate segregation and subsequent placement of Jewish immigrants arriving from MENA countries in remote Israeli development towns. It was even official policy in 1950s absorption centers to place immigrant Ashkenazi families of four in the same size apartments as "Oriental" families of eight.

The Otherization—the labeling of a group as different and then treating it in distinct, often unequal, ways—of non-Ashkenazi Jews in Israel's early years has had deep sociological effects. It has led to internalized oppression, manifested in such trends as a lack of progress in education and professional advancement among MENA Jews. (Scholars note that Mizraḥi history is included in Israeli textbooks in only trivial ways.) Similar patterns of discrimination are seen among other groups of non-Ashkenazi Jews who have immigrated to Israel, such as Ethiopian Jews who arrived in the 1980s (chapter 7). One way to begin improving this situation, say some, is to acknowledge that this domination and subordination even exists.

According to two Israeli nongovernmental organizations, the Adva Center and the Association for Civil Rights in Israel, statistical evidence shows that some long-term progress has been made in terms of the treatment of non-Ashkenazi Jews in Israel, at least when compared with the maltreatment of "Israeli Arabs," who fare far worse. But both institutions also note that the Israeli government has a great deal of progress still to make in treating these distinct Israeli subgroups equitably.

Israeli Jews: Secular/Religious and Nationalist/Religious

In exploring Jewish Israeli identities, it is critical to look at the perceived oppositional pairings of secular/religious and nationalist/religious. Scholars commonly categorize nationalist movements such as Zionism, for example, as either secular or religious: thus, the Zionism of Herzl and Ben-Gurion is described as secular, while that of Buber is considered religious. As mentioned in chapter 8, however, this dichotomy is imprecise, especially when applied to Zionism.

Scholar Anthony Smith has explored the convergence of religion and nationalism. He begins by offering a sociological perspective on religion, quoting sociologist Emile Durkheim: "A religion is a unified system of beliefs and practices relative to sacred things, that is to say, things set apart and forbidden—beliefs and practices which unite into one single moral community called a Church, all those who adhere to them." Smith then outlines four "sacred" characteristics that are common to both religious communities and nations:

- Ethnic election—The idea that a given community has been chosen, divinely or otherwise, to carry out a particular task. An example is the nationalistic movement of the French Revolution, a prototype for "secular nationalisms" that see the "nation as the embodiment and beacon of liberty, reason and progress, with a mission to liberate and civilize less fortunate people."
- Sacred territory—The notion that a nation needs to protect its own land because it has more value than other territories. This trait includes the "territorialization of memory," where a "community's past is turned into an integral part of its natural landscape. . . . [Its] natural setting . . . becomes historicized and 'nature' comes to be seen as intrinsic to the community's peculiar history."
- Ethno-history—The fact that nations' narratives are constructed in a sanitized fashion, justifying their existence, and presented alongside a fictionalized "golden age," a time when everything in the community was virtuous, an era that can be achieved again.
- National sacrifice—Those who die for the sake of the nation, the "glorious dead," are memorialized; their deaths give sacredness to their lives, and they become posthumous heroes.

In this sense, all Zionists, whether self-identified as secular or not, can be framed as religious. Further, because figures such as Herzl and Ben-Gurion generally oriented toward the Hebrew Bible as a factual account of history, they were devoted to the Land of Israel as if it were literally the birthright of all Jews—that is, as if it were empirical and established fact and not a theological belief (i.e., fact rather than "truth") that God promised this land to Abraham, Isaac, Jacob, and their descendants, and thus they were legitimate heirs to the land. As scholar Yakov Rabkin notes, most Zionists—secular and religious alike—"used the Torah to justify [their] claims to the Land of Israel."

More to the point, for many Jews, Zionism and Judaism are inseparable. And for others, Zionism, not Judaism, is their "religion" (i.e., their belief system). One paradox is that it is difficult to explain Zionism, especially in terms of establishing a Jewish State in the Land of Israel, without connecting it to Judaism. Zionism doesn't exist apart from dominant Jewish narratives: the Hebrews fled from Egypt to the Land of Israel; they actualized independence from slavery in the Promised Land. The Zionist creed is based on the belief that Jews today are returning to the same land that their ancestors escaped to in search of freedom.

Israeli Jews: From David to Goliath and Back Again

For much of medieval and modern European history, Jews have been portrayed negatively—as diabolic, sneaky, and violent. But another popular antisemitic representation has rendered them as feminized and queer, passive and pathetic. European Christians have consistently disparaged Jews for lacking strength, for being weak. For some Zionists, establishing a country for Jews—putting them on a par with other nations—was the best way to transform these centuries-old negative stereotypes and show the world that Jews are a strong, mighty, and powerful people.

Max Nordau, for example, who co-led the World Zionist Congress in its early years alongside Theodor Herzl, was, according to scholar Michael Stanislawski, interested in "transforming both the 'ghetto' and the bourgeois Jew—both alleged to be effeminate, weak, cut off from nature, cowardly, sickly desexualized—into a physically robust, healthy, and sexually potent man, in the process rebuilding himself, his land and his people." In multiple speeches, Nordau told his fellow Jews that it was time to re-create themselves as *Muskeljudentum* (Jews of muscle).

No doubt, a community needs a great deal of strength (and organizational skills) in order to create the physical infrastructure for a new country. Yet pre-state Zionists also crafted a metaphorical infrastructure, one in which Jews in Ottoman-controlled and British-occupied Palestine became the embodiment of masculine might. Today, the Israeli military is the symbol of Jewish strength: the Jewish man unafraid of anyone, the bold David to the world's many Goliaths. At the beginning of the twentieth century, well before Israel was established, one of the earliest narratives of strength to emerge was rooted in a specific ancient historical event: the siege of Masada.

Masada, Strength, and Masculinity

The story of Masada can be summarized as follows: in 66 CE, a few years before the Romans destroyed the Second

Temple (70 CE), a Jewish group of extremists, the Zealots (or Sicarii; see chapter 8), fled to Masada. Located sixty-two miles southeast of Jerusalem, Masada was a fortified palace that had been built decades earlier into the flat top of a mountain overlooking the Dead Sea as an additional home for King Herod. For several years, some 960 Jewish Zealots living on the palace grounds staved off a Roman army of hundreds, if not thousands. Then in 73 CE, the Roman legions finished building a dirt ramp that connected those on the ground with the mountain top, giving them direct access to the gates of the fortress (fig. 10.8). Once the Romans breached the stronghold's outer wall, they reached the Jews, whom they found dead.

The Zealots, despite having eluded the Romans for so long, had chosen to take their own lives rather than be killed by the Romans, become Roman slaves, or fight an unwinnable battle. According to the only account of this episode we have today, relayed by the first-century CE historian Josephus, the day before the Romans finished their ramp, the Zealots selected ten men to kill everyone in the community. When only these ten remained, the community's leader, Eleazar Ben Yair, killed the other nine, then himself.

Some of Josephus's description of the event is supported by archeological evidence; most is not. Although dominant Jewish narratives commonly reiterate that the Romans didn't find one Jew alive, in Josephus's rendering the Romans found a handful of survivors, including two women and five children. One of these women relayed to the Romans (and Josephus) everything that had happened prior to the breaching of the fortress's outer wall, including a dramatic speech given by Ben Yair before the mass killings began, which Josephus included in his account.

For decades, guides taking Jewish tour groups to Masada, specifically those organized for Americans, have often kept to Josephus's script, which both simplifies and embellishes the story. Details left out of such guided tours are that some in the Masada community hid so as not to be killed (clearly not everyone agreed with the "decision" to carry out mass "suicide"); that shortly before going up against the Romans, the Zealots ransacked the goods of the seven hundred or so Jews who lived in the nearby valley of Ein Gedi and killed them; and that the Talmudic rabbis, who are revered by many today, actually loathed the Zealots.

Perhaps more important, in dominant Jewish narratives this story is often conveyed in a style that praises the Zealots. This approach inverts the horror of mass suicide (or homicide), reframing it as something that reflects

FIGURE 10.8. Masada. On the right is the ramp built by the Romans to reach the top of the mountain during the first century CE.

not weakness but strength. Instead of portraying this group as one that murdered its own members (including those the Zealots considered most helpless—the sick, children, women, elderly), this narrative explains that they took their lives out of bravery. The Zealots are represented as the archetypes of courage and determination, the embodiment of a people ready to fight to the end. It hasn't necessarily mattered that, in fact, they didn't fight until the end. Nor has it been important that before the twentieth century most Jews knew nothing about Masada.

As scholars Jonathan Boyarin and Daniel Boyarin explain,

> The events at Masada, or better the Masada myth, have become, (in)famously, paradigmatic for a certain modern Jewish consciousness. But it was not always so. Indeed, when the Jewish settlement of Palestine was founded in modern times, no one knew how to spell the name Masada in Hebrew, so an early kibbutz (founded 1937)

that took the name used the Greek version. A recent critic notes that the Josephus text was preserved only by Christians and adds: "The story of the fall of Masada thus did not vanish from the records of Jewish history, but it disappeared from the Jews' collective memory."

Today, the Boyarins continue, "the Masada myth has everything to do . . . with manliness." It is held up as a historical example of Jewish strength, a link between modern Jews and Jews from two millennia ago. It represents Jewish power in general and in the Land of Israel in particular; Jews who fought to retain the land at all costs, who fought to control their own destinies. Posters of Masada can be found in synagogues and Jewish schools across the United States. And if one visits Israel as a tourist, a sunrise hike up Masada is likely on the itinerary, followed by the "true"-but-not-factual account of what happened there delivered by a tour guide.

For many Jews, the Zealots have come to symbolize the

classic soldiers, those who go to any lengths to protect their own. They are David to the Roman Goliath. Some of the more militant Zionists fighting the British in the 1930s and 1940s looked to the Zealots for courage. Avraham Stern (of the Stern Gang, an offshoot of the Irgun)—perhaps best known as an anti-British militant—even used the alias Yair in homage to the Masada community leader, Ben Yair. Other Zionists contrasted the Zealots with Shoah survivors who immigrated to the Land of Israel in the 1940s, a group that some criticized for having gone like "lambs to the slaughter" (see chapter 9). To this day, "Masada shall not fall again" is a central mantra of the Zionist enterprise.

The Israeli Military, Strength, and Masculinity

Tourism aside, Masada is also used as a venue for conducting Israeli military ceremonies, which links this ancient site with contemporary Israeli soldiers, the preeminent national symbol of Jewish strength. Most Jewish Israelis perform mandatory military service upon graduating from high school, three years for men and two years for women. Whereas some Jews revel in how quickly the country's military has become one of the strongest forces in the world, others take pride in the fact that Israel is the only country in the world to conscript females. This unique societal decision, and the embedded militarization of Israeli society in day-to-day lives, makes it worthwhile to briefly explore Israel's military in terms of masculinity and femininity.

Not only are women conscripted into the armed forces, but since 1985 they have been permitted to serve in combat positions, and since 2009 have served in Israeli artillery units, rescue forces, and anti-aircraft forces. Almost 50 percent of lieutenants and captains are women. In comparison to other countries' militaries, these policies are extremely rare. Indeed, de jure the Israeli military is one of the most progressive in the world in terms of its treatment of women.

At the same time, the upper strata of the military continue to be male-dominated. The highest-ranking female officer, Major General Orna Barbivay, is head of the military's Personnel Directorate. Says Miri Eisen, a retired Israeli colonel: "The military is a boys club. I think every military is a boys club. It's still a majority of men who are going to choose that way of life." This statement is supported by a study on female combatants' integration into the Israeli military, which found that women commonly "exhibit 'superior skills' in discipline, motivation, and shooting abilities, yet still face prejudicial treatment

stemming from a 'perceived threat to the historical male combat identity.'"

Some point to early policies of the Israeli military to emphasize the undercurrent of gender-related discrimination today. For example, from as early as 1947, tasks that had been open to women in the British army, such as driving heavy vehicles, were forbidden to women in the Israeli military. At the same time, in the wars of 1947-1949, women served alongside men in combat. Things changed by 1951, when the Minister of Defense introduced new regulations prohibiting women from serving in combat, a rule that lasted through 1985. As scholar Dafna Izraeli observes, "The gender regime of the military, which is based on a gendered division of labor and a gendered structure of power, both formal and informal, constitutes and sustains the taken-for-granted role of women in society as help meet [sic] to men." Scholar Orlee Hauser adds that if this male-dominant structure were challenged—for example, by putting women in major military roles—the ties between the military and masculinity would be weakened. As things stand, says Hauser, the current differentiation "between masculine and feminine army roles serves to reinforce the perception of the female as the weaker sex and the male as the soldier protector."

Women are also marginalized in terms of military narratives. For example, one of the most famous pre-state female soldiers was Sarah Aaronsohn, whose mark on history has been largely overlooked in Israeli society. A leader in the pro-British Zionist network working against the Ottomans from 1915 to 1917, she is described in Hebrew sources from the time in relation to her brother, Aaron. In contrast, British and Ottoman intelligence depict her as a core member of the era's largest pro-British espionage association in the Middle East. After decades of obscurity, her story has eventually made its way into the Israeli "national pantheon." That said, the archetype for military power continues to be "'the brave soldier,' tall, sturdy, and handsome"—and male—fighting for the survival of his country.

American Jews: From the Margins to the Center

Aside from the twentieth-century emergence of the State of Israel—a self-identified Jewish country shaped primarily by and for Jews that radically altered the balance of Middle Eastern, and world, power in relation to Jews—the largest indicator of the rise in power of the Jewish community is seen in Jews' changing status in the United States.

Toward Acceptance

As mentioned in chapter 8, between 1880 and 1910 more than one million Jews immigrated to the United States. Yet it wasn't until almost half a century later, between 1944 and 1950, that a dramatic shift took place in how non-Jewish Americans perceived Jews. Through that time, it was not uncommon for Jewish Americans to experience both implicit and explicit antisemitism.

For instance, according to a 1944 poll, 24 percent of Americans considered Jews a "menace to America," and a 1945 poll found that 65 percent of Americans believed that Jews in the United States had "too much power." By 1950, however, those believing Jews were a "menace" had dropped to 5 percent, and by 1962 to just 1 percent. Similarly, when Americans were asked in 1945 if they felt that "anti-Jewish" feelings in the United States were increasing or decreasing, 58 percent said that such prejudice was on the rise, whereas by 1950 this figure was down to 16 percent.

Some have speculated that sharp drops in prejudice against Jews immediately following World War II were a result of what Americans had learned about the heinous crimes committed against Jews by the Nazis. According to this argument, a certain post-Shoah "philo-Semitic" (interest in or appreciation, defense, or love of Jews and things Jewish) cultural trend spread across the United States at this time, which may well have been connected to collective American feelings of guilt (for not doing more to prevent genocide) and sorrow (for the genocide that had just taken place). Another theory attributes this phenomenon to the increased involvement of Jewish organizations in campaigns to quell discrimination of all kinds during this era, something non-Jewish groups, especially ones under attack, appreciated. To this day, all that is clear is that these shifts took place.

Becoming White

Of course, Jewish assimilation during the first half of the twentieth century also played a role in Jews becoming more accepted, as even many of those who had come from provincial Russian *shtetls* (small villages largely composed of Jews) began to dress and act like non-Jewish Americans. In this sense, a third possible reason for the rising acceptance of American Jews after midcentury is the perception that Jews were "becoming white," joining the most powerful social identity group in the United States.

As explored in chapter 1, whiteness is much more than the color of one's skin; it is tied to one's identity expression and plays out in society in countless ways, especially in terms of social status. Since the late nineteenth century, most Jewish Americans have been Ashkenazi, arriving in the United States from Europe and Russia. Their skin color was commonly pale, which undoubtedly helped them to be perceived as white. Not all Jews "became white," of course. But Ashkenazi Jews did, and most American Jews are Ashkenazi. (This is one reason dominant Jewish narratives are Ashkenazi-centric.)

Becoming white played a significant role in the educational and professional advancement that Jews experienced over the last century. At the same time, privileges linked to upward social mobility were explicitly denied to other minorities, such as African Americans and Native Americans, and some Jews intentionally distanced themselves from such subordinated groups. Jewish ascendant mobility may also have been tied to the role Jews played in shaping prewar whiteness through Hollywood. The mid–twentieth century saw the rise of Jews in a number of other influential circles as well, including the intellectual, scholarly, and artistic.

For many, the perceived phenomenon of American Jews becoming white epitomizes one of the paths Jews in many places have taken—or been permitted to take—from modernity forward: assimilation into the broader non-Jewish milieu. It has also surely played a role in Jews' identification in terms of ethnicity rather than religion, an identification that reflects a similar shift away from religiously defined identities in the United States and Europe generally.

Assimilation in the United States is also reflected in the increase in Jewish Americans marrying non-Jewish Americans (see chapter 12). Such partnerships have played a role in the creation of new Jewish rituals, such as the "Hanukah Bush" (chapter 7) and Haggadot (Passover Seder prayer books) designed for interfaith families.

The highly publicized 2011 marriage of Marc Mezvinsky, a Jew, and Chelsea Clinton, a Southern Baptist, also illustrates this trend. The editor of the *Forward,* the American Jewish community's oldest newspaper, for example, noted that the wedding, co-officiated by Reverend William S. Shillady and Rabbi James Ponet, was "a milestone of sorts, a measure of social acceptance, a sign that we've arrived." (This opinion was not universal.)

Accommodating Americanness: Choosing Not to Rock the Boat or Working within the System?

Another reason American Jews have risen in power is due to the myriad ways they have worked within the dominant non-Jewish structure rather than in opposition to it. Take, for example, the certification of kosher products. In supermarkets and convenience stores in any major American city (and most minor ones), many of the food items are halakhically certified as kosher.

How do we know? Because such items are labeled with a *hekscher,* a symbol that is virtually undetectable to someone unaware of its existence. The most common *hekscher* is the "OU" (fig. 10.9), a certification given by the Union of Orthodox Jewish Congregations. In developing this system, Jewish Americans have been able to keep kosher while also eating "American" foods.

Another way Jews have worked within the American system rather than in opposition to it has been through the building of an *eruv* (lit., "mixing" or "blending," referring to a ritual enclosure). Many observant Jews follow the prohibition of carrying objects from a "private" domain into a "public" one on Shabbat (and other Jewish holidays). But according to halakhah, if a specific type of perimeter is built around an area, one may carry objects within that space. (In other words, extending a border around an entire neighborhood creates a large private domain, halakhically speaking.) Traditionally, an eruv is an actual wall, but in the United States a common way of building an eruv is to add string or a thin, unobtrusive rope to the telephone and electrical wiring that surrounds American neighborhoods, thus enclosing a larger communal space. This allows observant Jews, for example, to carry prayer books or push a baby stroller from home to synagogue on Shabbat. Like the hekscher, you wouldn't even know the eruv was there unless someone pointed it out.

The Jewish Narrative within the American Narrative

Finally, elements of dominant Jewish narratives have become integrated into the dominant American narrative—another illustration of Jews having "made it" in the United States. One important thread has been the telling of stories connected to the Shoah. Several mainstream Hollywood movies on the Jewish genocide have been box-office smashes, including some, such as *Schindler's List,* that went on to win numerous Oscars. Books such as *The Diary of Anne Frank,* by a teenage Jew living in Amsterdam during the Nazi occupation of the Netherlands, and Elie Wiesel's *Night,* an autobiographical depiction of Nazi death camps, have become required reading for many American high school students. (Wiesel also appeared on the *Oprah Winfrey Show* a number

FIGURE 10.9. Kosher ketchup. The Orthodox Union, or OU, is one of the institutions that certifies American food products as kosher. The circle with the letter U inside it is OU's *hekscher* symbol, representing their stamp of approval.

of times and discussed his experiences.) Art Spiegelman's graphic novel *Maus* achieved great acclaim, not only in the United States, where it won the Pulitzer Prize, but internationally. All of these forms of communicating the horrors of the Shoah have played a role in making the Jewish genocide part of a non-Jewish American consciousness.

American Jews: From David to Goliath and Back Again

Tough Jews and the Mob

In the first half of the twentieth century in the United States, Jews were not fighting a literal war, as they were in British-occupied Palestine. But they were fighting for a place at the table. One avenue for achieving this was to become gangsters. Some Jews reflect a certain pride in these "muscle men," though perhaps with mixed emotions, given that such figures committed crimes such as theft, assault, and murder. The most infamous group of gangsters involving Jews was the New York City–based group dubbed by the press "Murder Incorporated," responsible for between four hundred and a thousand contract killings in the first half of the twentieth century. Rich Cohen, author of the bestselling book *Tough Jews,* explains: "These were people who grew up in certain neighborhoods where [the mob] was one way to get ahead. These were very tough guys in a very tough world, in a time when Jews were being beaten up and even killed—and they weren't taking s—t from anybody."

Some argue that Cohen holds these gangsters up nostalgically as "success" stories and "model Jews"; if they "still thrived today," Cohen has said, "the Jewish community would be better off." Writer Jeffrey Goldberg understands this pride: "These gangsters were as tough as the Irish and as powerful as the Italian mob, and when I discovered this fact at age 12 or so, it thrilled me. This reaction is easy to understand: I was, at the time, facing the oppression of antisemitic schoolyard thugs, and in my revenge-fantasies, Bugsy Siegel and Gurrah Shapiro were lining up on my side, blackjacks in hand."

This pride, conflicted or otherwise, is reflected in other venues as well. A 2010 art exhibit at the Jewish Community Center of San Francisco, for example, *Wise Guys: Mobsters in the Mishpacha* (Family), presented famous crooks such as Benjamin "Bugsy" Siegel and Louis "Lepke" Buchalter not critically, but somewhat admiringly. It would be difficult to find an example of any other criminal group, minority or otherwise, being depicted in such laudatory fashion.

Certainly, some of this attention has to do with Americans' fascination with organized crime, as demonstrated in the popularity of movies such as *The Godfather* and *Goodfellas,* and top-rated television programs like *The Sopranos* and *Boardwalk Empire.* But perhaps something more is going on here in terms of Jewish self-perception regarding power, and the communal pride that emerges when Jews are depicted as fighters.

Superheroes and Power

Jewish "tough guys" and "fighters" challenge many stereotypes, standing in contrast to centuries of communal powerlessness. Some contend that Jews' desire for power inspired the creation of the first American superheroes. When Superman appeared in print for the fist time, in DC Comics' *Action Comics* #1 in 1938, writer Jerry Siegel and artist Joe Shuster, both Jews, had created a character that embodied superhuman power, something seemingly lacking within Jewish self-perceptions in 1930s America and Europe.

This "wish fulfillment" was perhaps even more explicit in Marvel Comics' superhero Captain America, co-created by two other Jews, Joe Simon and Jack Kirby,

around the same time (1941), a human with extraordinary strength who focuses on defeating the Nazi agent Red Skull. (Superman also began fighting the Nazis during the 1940s.) Other giants in the comics field include Stan Lee, the co-creator of such famous characters as Daredevil, the Fantastic Four, the Incredible Hulk, Ironman, Spiderman, Thor, and the X-Men, among others. (Not to mention the fact that Maxwell Gaines is commonly credited with creating the first comic book and Will Eisner is described by many as the grandfather of graphic novels altogether.)

American Jews: The United States and Israel

United States and Supporting Israel

One indicator of Jewish power today is the support the United States government has given the Jewish State. In fact, the United States has had a close relationship with Israel for decades. The American government, for example, was the first country to de facto recognize the Jewish State, some eleven minutes after Israel declared independence in May 1948; then there are the tens of times the United States has vetoed United Nations Security Council resolutions critical of Israel, or the enormous annual foreign aid given to Israel—among other things indicating the lengths to which the U.S. government will go to ensure Israel's strength.

Regarding foreign aid, for a number of years Israel has received more than $3 billion annually from the United States in economic and military assistance—20 percent of the total foreign aid given by the United States each year. Indeed, the State of Israel has received more aid annually from the United States than any other country since 1976 and, since World War II, has been the largest total recipient of U.S. aid in the world. This seems all the more lopsided given that Israelis constitute only a little over one-tenth of 1 percent of the world's population (eight million in 2013, versus seven billion globally). Linked to this aid, by most accounts, Israel's military is the strongest in the Middle East—or perhaps even one of the most powerful in the world.

There are many reasons for this strong alliance. Putting aside the common argument that the United States is proud to support Israel as the only liberal democracy in the Middle East (a claim that is sometimes critiqued based on the military occupation of the West Bank and Gaza), many contend that backing Israel serves the United States' geopolitical interests (i.e., supporting the most powerful country in the region gives the U.S. a strong foothold there). Americans also have a sentimental attachment to Israel, possibly due, as scholar Stephen Zunes notes, to understandings of the country "portrayed in the idealized and romanticized 1960 movie *Exodus,* starring a young Paul Newman."

American governmental support for Israel also helps the American economy. For example, specific parameters are attached to the annual $3 billion in aid that the United States gives Israel; much of the money has to be used to purchase military armament from American weapons manufacturers and to repay American banks the interest on previous loans given to Israel.

Then too, millions of Evangelical Christians have lobbied the American government to support Israel, though their reasons are more theological than anything else. Their argument commonly goes that support for Israel will lead to Jews' "returning" to the Holy Land, thus fulfilling a biblical prophecy about the "ingathering of the exiles," which will expedite the coming of the messiah, Jesus Christ.

The "Israel Lobby"

The strong U.S.-Israel alliance can also be explained by the decades-long political activism of a number of Jewish-led organizations. Just as the lobbying of Cuban Americans or Irish Americans has influenced U.S. government policy toward Cuba and Ireland, Jewish Americans have strong voices when it comes to America's relationship with Israel.

In their controversial book *The Israel Lobby,* scholars John Mearsheimer and Steve Walt argue that this influential bloc—the best-known member group of which is the American Israel Public Affairs Committee (AIPAC)— almost single-handedly influences American foreign policy regarding Israel. Other commentators, from across the political spectrum, while recognizing that the Israel Lobby in general and AIPAC in particular are powerful, challenge the idea that the tail (the Israel Lobby) is wagging the dog (the United States). Despite the influence such activist groups wield, many Jews nonetheless lament Israel's weaknesses and the ever-present possibility that it will be destroyed.

At times the Israel Lobby is called the "Jewish Lobby." Although organizations such as AIPAC are mostly made up of Jews, a number of non-Jewish lobbying groups support similar positions in terms of American foreign policy vis-à-vis the State of Israel. As mentioned, a number of powerful Evangelical Christian groups fall into this category, including Christians United for Israel (CUFI),

perhaps the largest among them. Take, for example, the following data compiled by the Pew Research Center: "When asked whether God gave Israel to the Jewish people, more Christians (55%) than Jews (40%) say yes. . . . And the share of white evangelicals saying that God gave Israel to the Jews (82%) is on par with the percentage of Orthodox Jews who believe this (84%)." (Yet whereas Christians make up 78.4 percent of the total population of the United States, Jews represent about 2 percent; see fig. 10.1.)

Israel as David (Not Goliath)

Israel's self-proclaimed "defenders" often reference proclamations made by such groups as Hamas and Hizbullah, or Middle Eastern leaders such as a recent Iranian president, regarding an intention to destroy the Jewish State. They also point out that the twenty-three member countries of the Arab League completely surround the State of Israel: David confronted by multiple Goliaths (fig. 10.10a). This biblical metaphor does not exist only within Jewish American and Jewish Israeli discourses; it is also repeated in editorials and articles in influential American newspapers such as the *New York Times* and the *Washington Post.*

As far back as 1967, and at key moments in the Israeli-Palestinian conflict such as during the First Intifada (which began in December 1987) and the Second Intifada (which began in October 2000), Israeli leaders have likened themselves to David, and their opponent—whether member-states in the Arab League or different Palestinian organizations—to Goliath. Sometimes this metaphor is voiced to call for renewed support for the Jewish State, the only truly "safe haven" for Jews (special topic 10.4). In turn, Palestinian leaders have also claimed to be David to Israel's Goliath (fig. 10.10b). Part of the fuel for these collective feelings of fear and insecurity are no doubt connected to ongoing violence taking place in Israel and the occupied West Bank and Gaza.

Power, Perception, and Self-Promotion

Ironically, some of the American Jews who are most vocal about Israel's powerlessness and the rise of antisemitism are also the ones most responsible for perpetuating the image of Jews having disproportionate power in the world—for with perceived power comes additional power. For example, every few years the Anti-Defamation League (ADL), a United States–based antisemitism watchdog group, sponsors some of its board members

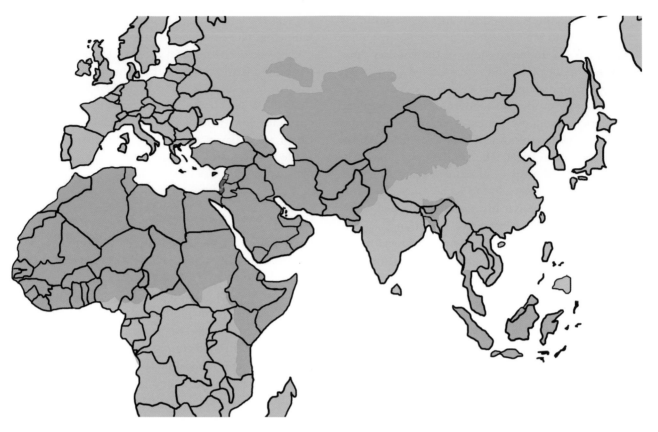

FIGURES 10.10A–B. David or Goliath? *Top:* The State of Israel in relation to the world's Muslim- and/or Arab-majority countries. Groups supporting the U.S. government's current political positions vis-à-vis the Jewish State often promote the narrative that the State of Israel, as David, is surrounded by multiple Goliaths. *Left:* A Palestinian boy throwing a rock at an Israeli tank, an image used to represent the Palestinians' David to Israel's Goliath.

and donors on an international trip led by its longtime executive director, Abraham Foxman (as of 2015).

A few years ago the group traveled to Italy, where they met with a number of influential individuals including the U.S. ambassador to the Vatican, the mayor of Rome, and the pope. On the day before their appointment with

the leader of the worldwide Catholic Church, a documentary filmmaker asked Foxman how he and his group were able to get meetings with such important people with the explicit purpose of combating antisemitism. Foxman responded:

SPECIAL TOPIC 10.4
THE JEWISH STATE: REPRESENTATION AND SECURITY

For many Jews, the State of Israel continues to play an invaluable role for the worldwide Jewish community in two central ways: as the ultimate representative of Jews and as the only place Jews can rely on as a safe haven.

Representation

A number of things reflect the belief in Israel as the worldwide representative of Jews. First, and most obvious, is the fact that Israel is the only Jewish-majority country in the world and the only country self-described as "the Jewish State," as is laid out in a number of places, including Israel's founding document, the Declaration of the Establishment of the State of Israel.

Second, many Israeli leaders have claimed this position. For example, in early 2015, following violent attacks carried out against Jews and non-Jews in Paris, Israeli prime minister Benjamin Netanyahu claimed that he had gone to France "not just as the prime minister of Israel but as representative of the entire Jewish people." Many Jewish groups in the United States challenged Netanyahu's declaration, which he made a handful of times thereafter in 2015.

Finally, it is common for Jews and the Jewish State to be conflated, by both Jews and non-Jews alike. Take, for example, the official state apologies delivered by the former presidents of Austria and Germany in 1994 and 1999, respectively, for the role their governments played in atrocities committed against Jews during World War II. Both leaders addressed members of the Israeli Parliament, the Knesset, as opposed to delivering their apology in their home country and addressing Jews worldwide (i.e., the State of Israel was not part of World War II, and in the 1990s no more than one third of Jews worldwide lived there).

Security

For many Jews, the State of Israel is the only place where Jews are guaranteed safety. Some consider Israel's existence to ensure there will not be a potential "second Holocaust," as the Jewish State would never allow it. Arguably, although more Jews are killed regularly for being Jewish in and around Israel than anywhere else (e.g., in active service in the Israeli military), such episodes are commonly perceived as the precise reason why Jews need a safe haven. The Law of Return continues to give many Jews comfort in terms of their safety (i.e., granting them citizenship based on their Jewish identity), if even in a theoretical sense, further concretizing the perception that Israel and its leaders represent Jews worldwide. A common contention is that whereas Arab-majority countries in the Middle East may fight Israel for land, Israel is always fighting for its very existence and for the existence of Jews.

It's their perception, the power of the Jewish community, which is one of those signs of the antisemitism, which is—it's a very thin line, you know. They believe . . . we're more powerful than we are. I've always said that Jews are not as powerful as Jews think we are, nor as powerful as our enemies think we are. We're somewhere in between. But they do believe, to some extent, that we can make a difference, in Washington, and we're not going to convince them otherwise. So, how do you fight this sinister, conspiratorial view of Jews without using it?

Foxman's response is perhaps counterintuitive. He admits to taking advantage of the stereotype that Jews manipulate world events—a perception rooted in such antisemitic texts as *Protocols of the Elders of Zion* (see chapter 9)—precisely as a means of fighting antisemitism.

Foxman is far from the first Jew to use the nonsensical belief that Jews control the world to his advantage. In raising support for a new Jewish country among both Jews and non-Jews at the end of the nineteenth century, Theodor Herzl amplified this myth, creating the fictional perception that modern political Zionists were profoundly influential despite their minuscule numbers. Around the same time, Nahum Goldmann, the founder of two internationally recognized Jewish organizations, the World Jewish Congress and the Conference of the Presidents of Major American Jewish Organizations, also played up the illusion of Jews' power, for what he felt was the express benefit of the Jewish community.

Twenty-First-Century Zionism: From Zionisms to Zionism

As mentioned earlier, the word *Zionism*—just like the signifier *Jew*—is often thrown around by both Jews and non-Jews as if it has a single meaning. In Israel, the dominant meaning of Zionism is informed by a wide array of understandings. But in the United States, Zionism is seldom presented in a nuanced way. Instead it is commonly discussed as an either/or proposition, as in: you are either

An Ancient Jewish Sect . . . in San Francisco?

When a friend asked me what time the community's prayer service began, my instinct was to answer, "*Shul* starts at 9:30 A.M., but my contact told me there wouldn't be a *minyan* until 10:00." Though I caught myself before saying *shul*, a Yiddish term for synagogue—an Ashkenazi-centric word I had been raised with that this group did not use—I stumbled over the second half of the sentence. My friend gently reminded me that the community didn't necessarily follow the rabbinic idea of a minyan, an edict in the Talmud requiring a quorum of ten adult males (or, in many contemporary communities, males and females) in order to recite specific prayers.

This was a new prayer service for me, and I planned to arrive a few minutes after ten in an attempt to be inconspicuous, figuring I could slip in unnoticed. (Unlike at many churches, it is not uncommon to arrive at a synagogue service a bit late.) But this turned out to be a silly plan. Not only was the synagogue building relatively small, but there were no more than a dozen people there when I arrived, and everyone knew one another. I was clearly an outsider.

At first glance, Congregation B'nai Israel seemed similar to any other synagogue I'd ever been to, with announcements about prayer services and communal gatherings, and the word *Shalom* displayed on a sign outside the main entrance. But as I entered the foyer, I started noticing differences. In the antechamber to the main prayer room were ten or so pairs of shoes in individually designated shelves. Having visited a number of Buddhist, Hindu, Muslim, and Sikh houses of worship, I didn't find removing one's footwear before entering a prayer space unusual. But I had never seen this done in a Jewish-identified space.

After putting my shoes on one of the shelves and grabbing a *siddur* (prayer book), I entered the building's central room, where a group of practitioners were already engaged in prayer, standing shoeless on overlapping prayer rugs. Listening to the community's prayers (mostly in Hebrew, almost exclusively taken directly from the Hebrew Bible) and watching them fully prostrate themselves when approaching the ark (the sacred closet or bureau that typically contains a community's Torah scrolls), I found the experience both oddly familiar and strange.

In fact, this group was extraordinary. They were Karaite Jews (see fig. 11.3). In existence for centuries, this now almost extinct Jewish sect has frequently been described as surfacing in opposition to Jews who accepted the authority of "the rabbis." Indeed, since their beginnings

some Jews have rejected them as heretics. But here I was—in 2011—in a Karaite synagogue in Daly City, a small town just south of San Francisco more famous for being the inspiration of a 1960s Billboard hit popularized by Pete Seeger, "Little Boxes," than for housing some of the last descendants of an ancient Jewish community.

Are There Borders to the Jewish Community?

On October 27, 1958, a little over a decade after the State of Israel was established, Prime Minister David Ben-Gurion sent a letter to some forty-five Jewish communal leaders around the world, asking them one of the most loaded questions for any group: Who should be counted as one of *us* and who should not? Specifically, he wanted to know how the new self-proclaimed Jewish State should define a "Jew." The Jewish State had been in existence for ten years, and it had permitted hundreds of thousands of immigrants to become citizens based simply on their being "Jewish." But it did not yet have a precise definition of what that meant.

This leads us to a critical question: If Jews are so diverse—culturally, ethnically, nationalistically, politically, racially, religiously—can *anyone* be Jewish? Does this community have any borders or boundaries? If so, what are they?

Border Characteristics

One way to understand a community's norms is to look at its margins. Defining what a community *is* necessarily includes a self-understanding of what it is *not*, implicitly and explicitly. Likewise, outliers, those on the margins, whether by choice or not, exist in a liminal space in relation to a community's dominant "truths." Sometimes communities are more candid—even rigidly so—about what they *are not* than about what they are. This does not mean that a group's fringe defines its narrative or vice versa, nor that that fringe and the dominant normative group are binary opposites. Some communities have multiple centers and margins simultaneously.

Definitions of social identities are not a mere intellectual exercise. They play a central role in shaping a people's status, which in turn affects how people interact with one another every day. For minorities such as Jews, definitions of identity have had life-and-death consequences (see chapter 9).

To deepen our understanding of the seemingly porous boundaries of twenty-first-century Jewishness, this chapter examines three "border characteristics," attributes of groups linked to the mainstream Jewish community that distinguish them from it and cause their Jewishness to be either questioned, suspected, or even rejected outright. Through this endeavor, we also explore the question of whether there are any boundaries at all to being a Jew. Border characteristics, de facto and in some cases de jure, separate "us" from "them," revealing ways that Jews separate themselves from the 99.8 percent of the world that is not Jewish.

These three border traits are: (1) claiming to be the *true* descendants of the biblical Israelites (i.e., authenticity); (2) rejection of rabbinic authority; and (3) denial that they are Jews although others say they are. Each characteristic is embodied in at least two "border communities" in existence today. To illustrate each characteristic, I introduce each group with a brief historical background, a description of its dominant narratives and how these conflict with the mainstream Jewish community, a summary of dominant scholarly opinions regarding the community's connection to normative Jews, and an exploration of how the group's Jewishness is understood by the Israeli government (Israel being the only nation-state that grants automatic citizenship to people based on their having a Jewish identity).

This framework will help us understand how these groups are connected to and why some are shunned by the mainstream Jewish community. They will also help us see the extent to which Jewish identities are dependent on self-description as much as on labeling by non-mainstream Jews and non-Jews.

The purpose of this chapter is not to clear up uncertainties regarding who should be counted as a Jew and who should not. If anything, its purpose is to make this answer more ambiguous.

(1) Authenticity: Who Are the Real Israelites?

Claims of authenticity are a common component of communal identity construction. One way that people attempt to prove the legitimacy of their identity is by laying out a familial connection, a so-called bloodline. For example, many in the contemporary Jewish community maintain that this group can trace itself back some three millennia, all the way to the biblical Israelites and Hebrews. A dominant Jewish narrative holds that those referred to in the Torah as *bnei yisrael* (the children of Israel) are the ancestors of today's Jews. (As mentioned in chapter 2, the biblical Jacob changed his name to Israel; and his twelve sons, from whom the Israelites descended, were also called the children of Israel.)

But as we have seen, we do not know definitively when Israelites shifted into Jews, nor do we know for sure if specific Israelite tribes are the antecedents of twenty-first-century Jews. In fact, Jews aren't the only contemporary community that claims to be the progeny of the Israelite tribes of the ancient Middle East. Aside from Jews, groups such as Afghani Pathans, British Israelites, the Church of Latter Day Saints of Jesus Christ (also known as adherents of Mormonism), and Rastafaris are but some of those claiming to be the *true* descendants of the biblical Israelites.

The Samaritans and the African Hebrew Israelites of Jerusalem—who, respectively, are based in Israel and the occupied West Bank (the latter area also commonly called Palestine) and in Israel—also make this assertion. Though none of these declarations can be proved one way or another, in contending that they are the real Israelites, Samaritans and African Hebrew Israelites of Jerusalem are simultaneously denying the authenticity, and even identity, of Jews. This is no small thing, especially because they are doing so in the biblical Land of Israel, the "Jewish homeland."

SAMARITANS: BACKGROUND

Aside from the "good Samaritan" of the Christian Bible, most people today have never heard of the Samaritans, let alone know that this ancient community still exists (fig. 11.1). According to their tradition, Samaritans have lived continuously in the Middle East for millennia, longer than any other group. They also claim to be "the true descendants of the biblical Israelites. . . . We are Israelites, not Jews." Whereas Jews commonly trace themselves back to the biblical tribe of Judah and other tribes it absorbed, Samaritans maintain that they are the descendants of tribes deriving from three of Jacob's other sons, Ephraim, Menashe, and Levi. In other words, both groups have complementary traditions; they have common ancestors (Abraham, Isaac, and Jacob); and each descends from different Israelite tribes.

Some scholars reject the Samaritans' claim, arguing that the Samaritans didn't emerge from Israelite tribes but rather first appeared in the eighth century BCE immediately following the Assyrian conquest of the biblical Land of Israel. This theory presupposes that a portion of those Israelites who survived the Assyrian destruction adapted rituals based on their situation, thereby creating a new community. Others build on a similar foundation, but with the variation that after their victory the Assyrians brought in a foreign group to colonize and repop-

On a side note: In the United States, Karaites have largely lived under the radar, and most American Jews don't even know they exist. The largest population of American Karaites, estimated in total at fewer than one thousand individuals, lives in the San Francisco Bay Area, which also has the country's—and Western Hemisphere's—only Karaite synagogue; there, they get along fine with the organized Jewish community. In fact, during the 1950s the Jewish Federation of San Francisco sponsored several Egyptian Karaite families to move to the area as legal refugees, thereby guaranteeing their asylum.

MESSIANIC JEWS: BACKGROUND AND IN RELATION TO JEWS TODAY

Without question, for virtually all conventional Jewish organizations the Messianic Jewish community is the most controversial of the communities discussed in this chapter. While a defining characteristic of Karaite Judaism is the rejection of rabbinic authority, Messianic Jews generally accept that authority—except, of course, regarding one issue in particular: whether Jesus should be accepted as the embodiment of God. In this sense, Messianic Jews are arguably more similar to Reform, Conservative, and Orthodox Jews in their working within a rabbinic paradigm, a system that Karaites reject outright.

Perhaps the only thing that most Jews—regardless of their affiliation (or lack thereof), no matter identified as Karaite or non-Karaite—can agree on with regard to the question "who is a Jew?" is that Messianic Jews are not *real* Jews and should not be accepted into the mainstream Jewish community. Some Jews go so far as to call them heretics, apostates, or even members of a cult; others simply ignore their existence altogether. And in contrast to the response toward other controversial groups, the Jewish institutional world has established a number of organizations with the sole intent of combating Messianic Jewish outreach toward conventional Jews.

In practice, the issue of Messianic Jewish rejection of rabbinic authority is a bit more complicated. Consider, for example, the traditional mainstream Jewish belief in the messiah. As I was conducting research on Messianic Jews, one ultra-Orthodox rabbi I approached expressed confusion over the term. "What's a Messianic Jew?" he asked. "Isn't it already part of the Jewish tradition to believe in the coming of the Messiah?" This was an especially poignant question, coming as it did from a rabbi who is part of the Lubavitch community of ultra-Orthodox Jews, more commonly known by the name Chabad.

As discussed in chapter 4, not only has belief in the coming of the messiah been a doctrine of Jewish tradition for at least two millennia, but over the last half century members of the Lubavitch community have vocalized their belief that their leader, Menachem Mendel Schneerson, *was* the messiah (and some still regard him as such).

But the label *Messianic Jew* does not refer to conventional Jews who believe in the idea of the messiah. Rather, Messianic Jews are those who identify as Jews and, in contrast to dominant Jewish belief, deem that Jesus is the messiah: that is, he came and will return. Perhaps a better descriptor of Messianic Jews is "Jesus-believing Jews," as suggested by scholar Dvir Abramovich.

Some of the reasons the majority of Jews reject Jesus include such rabbinic arguments as:

- Jesus did not fulfill the messianic prophecies conveyed in the Prophets;
- Jesus did not embody the personal qualifications of the messiah as described in the Talmud;
- biblical verses discussing the messiah that believers in Jesus say refer to Jesus are misinterpreted;
- and Jewish belief is based on national revelation, not revelation to a few individuals only.

Arguably, a belief in Jesus is the institutional Jewish community's red line, the virtual border that separates Jews from non-Jews. In this sense, Jews who accept Jesus as the messiah maintain a position contrary to rabbinic Judaism, since, from the Talmud through to today, rabbinic authorities have rejected Jesus.

A number of groups fall under the umbrella of Messianic Jews, including, but not limited to, Hebrew Christians, Jewish Christians, Messianic Christians, and Jews for Jesus, perhaps the best known (fig. 11.4). Some Messianic Jews identify as both Jews and Christians; others do not. Messianic Jews often observe conventional Jewish rituals, maintaining that they are following the practices of Jesus's disciples. For instance, in many cases

- they call their communal leaders "rabbi" and places of worship "synagogues";
- they have an ark containing a Torah scroll in their main prayer space;
- many of their congregants wear kippot (head coverings) and tallitot (religious prayer shawls);
- they attach *mezuzot* (small rectangular boxes containing parchments of biblical verses) to the doorways of their synagogues;

FIGURE 11.4. Jews for Jesus are perhaps the best-known group in the United States that falls under the larger umbrella of Messianic Jews. Part of their practice includes missionary work, actively pursuing potential converts.

- six-pointed stars are found in their prayer spaces;
- they do not celebrate Christian holidays, such as Easter or Christmas.

What sets them apart is that Messianic Jews accept the Christian Bible in addition to the Hebrew Bible (as opposed to saying that the New Testament replaced the "Old Testament"), and although most Messianic Jewish prayer services include traditional Hebrew liturgy, they refer to God as Jesus or *Yeshua*.

Estimates regarding Messianic Jews' worldwide population vary widely. Some maintain that the United States and Israel, the two countries with most of the world's practitioners, have, respectively, close to 200,000 and 6,000–15,000 devotees. (Recent estimates for the number of worldwide Messianic Jewish congregations also vary, between 65 and 153.) One problem in delineating precise numbers comes back to our original question: How do we define a Jew? Because Messianic Jews contend that they *are* Jews, many within their community do not distinguish themselves from non-Messianic Jews (and thus aren't considered in Messianic-Jew-only population counts).

As for the movement's origins, its devotees commonly date their community back to the time of Jesus, contending that their practices are the true, pure, and original form of Christian Judaism. Some add that their movement was marginalized during the first few generations after Jesus was crucified because of increased tensions among Jews who believed in Jesus, Jews who did not, and the larger non-Jewish Middle Eastern Roman world, ten-

sions that worsened in particular after the destruction of the Second Temple (see chapter 4).

While some scholars argue that the modern movement of Messianic Judaism emerged in the 1800s, most date it to twentieth-century America. As scholar J. Gordon Melton explains, "Messianic Judaism is a Protestant movement that emerged in the last half of the 20th century among believers who were ethnically Jewish but had adopted an Evangelical Christian faith. . . . By the 1960s, a new effort to create a culturally Jewish Protestant Christianity [had] emerged." Jews for Jesus, for example, began in the early 1970s. Some point to Israel's military success in the 1967 war, an event that some adherents interpreted as a sign of the redemption of the Land of Israel, as a watershed moment in the rise of Messianic Jewry.

As for how they are understood by the Israeli government, in 1989 the Israeli Supreme Court rejected a Messianic Jewish couple's application for citizenship under the Law of Return. In its hundred-page brief, the High Court argued that belief in Jesus as the messiah is the very issue that separates a Christian from a Jew, even for those who are born Jewish according to halakhah. Interestingly, most Jewish Israelis disagree with the High Court's position, maintaining that believing Jesus is the messiah is not incompatible with being a Jew. Similarly, a large proportion (34 percent) of Jewish Americans maintain that believing in Jesus as the messiah can be compatible with Judaism.

Doctrine itself aside, perhaps the two main reasons conventional Jews reject Messianic Jews are that, first, the latter group is known for missionizing toward non-Messianic Jews and, second, Messianic Jewish doctrine is linked to Christianity, a community that has historically had a precarious relationship with Jews. There is no doubt that dominant Jewish narratives regarding the historical proselytization and persecution of Jews by Christians play a role in this rejection. Added to Messianic Jews' challenges is their rejection by most Christians because they identify as Jews; whereas Jews label them Christians, Christians label them Jews.

(3) Outsiders: "We Are Not Jews (No Matter What You Think)!"

In his treatise *Anti-Semite and Jew,* Jean-Paul Sartre wrote that "the Jew is one whom other men consider a Jew: that is the simple truth from which we must start." Although Sartre's thesis has its shortcomings, those outside of a community certainly do play a role in defining that community. Identities are not defined by insiders alone. In fact, if a dominant group deems a subordinated people to have a particular identity, as the Nazis in Vichy France did regarding Karaites during World War II, labeling them Jews, it can be difficult, if not altogether impossible, to persuade them otherwise. This holds true even if the subordinated group adamantly denies the identity, as is the case with West Bank Samaritans and Kabbalah Centre devotees.

SAMARITANS

Although Samaritans—specifically those living in the occupied West Bank—don't call themselves Jews, Palestinians do. Just as the spoken Egyptian Arabic term for Karaites is *al-yahud al-qara'in* (Karaite Jews), the spoken Palestinian Arabic term for Samaritans is *al-yahud al-samarah* (Samaritan Jews). The Samaritans might be the only community in the world that is called Jewish despite their objections and historical data to the contrary.

The question of their identity is further complicated by the fact that some Samaritans living in the Nablus/Shechem region of the occupied West Bank identify as Palestinians, not as Jews or Israelis, a de facto decision the community generally made in the mid to late twentieth century in response to their ill treatment by the Israeli government. There are exceptions, of course: some Nablusi Samaritans do not identify as Palestinian (identifying as Samaritans only), and to make matters even more confusing, some Samaritans living in Holon, an Israeli city south of Tel Aviv, identify as Israeli and not as Palestinian.

THE KABBALAH CENTRE

In contrast to the Karaites, Samaritans, and African Hebrew Israelites of Jerusalem, members of the Kabbalah Centre—publicly, at least—profess *not* to have a connection to the Jewish or Israelite communities. In fact, their leaders and some of their most famous devotees deny even the weakest of relationships between the Centre and Judaism. Similarly, members of the Jewish community unaffiliated with the Kabbalah Centre rarely, if ever, claim the Centre to be part of the Jewish collective. Some Jews even charge the Centre with manipulating authentic Jewish expressions in order to profit financially. Such critics label the Centre's practices a form of "deception," "charlatanism," "commercialism," and even "brainwashing." One reason for this aversion is that the Kabbalah Centre is one of the largest organizations in the world promoting Jewish mystical practices.

There are a number of obvious linkages between the Centre and Jewish communal practices. For starters, the Centre's core sacred text, the *Zohar*—composed by one or more Jews, including the thirteenth-century Spanish Jew Moses De León—is central to the Jewish mystical tradition (chapter 6); the Centre's founder, his wife, and two of his sons identify as Orthodox Jews; and many of the Kabbalah Centre's communal rituals have been practiced in the Jewish community for centuries, such as the observance of Shabbat.

First established as the National Institute for Research in Kabbalah, the Kabbalah Centre was founded by Rabbi Philip Berg in 1965. Born Shraga Feivel Gruberger, Berg studied Jewish mysticism with a disciple of Yehudah Ashlag, a rabbi and Kabbalist who spent most of his life trying to popularize the *Zohar* among Jews living in Palestine and Israel from the 1920s through the 1950s despite never having more than a few students. Like his teachers before him, Berg received rabbinic ordination from an Orthodox seminary. (Two of his sons, Michael and Yehuda, who play central roles in the Centre's leadership, also received Orthodox rabbinic ordination.) But Berg modified Ashlag's teachings, with his most influential innovation being his decision to bring the message of Kabbalah to non-Jews.

From the 1980s onward, Berg and his wife, Karen, established Kabbalah Centres across North America. In the 1990s, they decided to make the Los Angeles Centre their world headquarters. During this period, Berg wrote numerous books on Kabbalah, gearing them toward a wider audience than the Jewish community alone. In this effort, he removed the terms *Jew* and *Judaism* alto-

FIGURE 11.5. Famous Kabbalah Centre devotee Madonna *(middle)* with Rabbi Yehuda Berg *(right)* and husband Guy Ritchie *(left)*.

gether from his writings; he also suggested that Kabbalistic texts such as the *Zohar* have historically existed independent of the Jewish community. From that time until around 2010, when he stopped teaching regularly in public, Berg presented the *Zohar* as a universal text without any connection to Judaism, despite historical evidence to the contrary.

Berg did not stop with merely separating the Zohar from its historical connection to the Jewish community. According to scholar Jody Myers, over time he presented traditional Jewish prayer services as if they were strictly Kabbalah Centre rituals, in particular those coinciding with Jewish holidays—whether observed once a year, such as Rosh Hashanah and Yom Kippur, or every week, like Shabbat. Myers maintains that Berg designated these practices as opportunities to meditate, as if the syncing of these particular prayer services with the Jewish religious calendar was coincidental. Needless to say, this gave his detractors more fodder.

American music legend Madonna, perhaps the best-known Centre devotee (fig. 11.5), has integrated Jewish

and Kabbalistic images into her music videos, and has had Hebrew letters tattooed on her body, such as the biblical name Esther. Yet as an outspoken supporter of the Centre, she has explicitly professed that there is no link between Kabbalah Centre practices and the Jewish tradition. Despite such claims, according to Karen Berg, "[Madonna] keeps a kosher home, she observes Shabbat, she [had her son] circumcised [and] had her husband circumcised." If accurate, what may seem like a case of cognitive dissonance to those outside the Centre seems to work for Madonna.

Paradoxically, despite the Centre's disassociation from many aspects of traditional Judaism and Jewish ethnicity, many of the Kabbalah Centre's devotees are, in fact, Jews. Karen Berg has even said that the Centre has been quite successful at reengaging Jews with the Jewish tradition: "The people who come in are Jewish. 90–99 percent are from backgrounds where they have nothing, they never learned anything Jewish, they were so turned off. . . . Now they marry Jewish, observe Shabbat, the whole works." Although the Centre claims its practices have no connection to Judaism, statements like these suggest that one of its goals is for its Jewish devotees to return to the practice of traditional Jewish rituals (as the Centre understands them to be observed), a variant on the phenomenon of *ba'alei teshuvah* (understood by some to mean born-again Jews).

Conclusion: Who Is a Jew and Who Is Not?

There are countless responses to the question, "Who is a Jew?" from those both inside and outside the Jewish community. Subcommunities have been part of this discussion in various ways: claiming to be Israelites or descendants thereof; applying for Israeli citizenship under the Law of Return; losing a member of their subgroup to a representative of a self-proclaimed militant group fighting against the State of Israel; claiming the authority to interpret Jewish law; claiming to follow a traditional belief (e.g., in the messiah); being labeled Jews by non-Jews; or by studying a core Jewish mystical text (the *Zohar*) and performing conventional Jewish rituals (e.g., observing Shabbat).

All three of the core border characteristics examined in this chapter—and the many other characteristics that fall within each—help shed light on potential boundaries between Jews and non-Jews in the twenty-first century. Although all Jewish identities are constructs, when groups with these border characteristics interact with mainstream Jews, the issue of identity emerges again and again.

Ultimately, the way one answers the question, "Who is a Jew?" speaks more to one's affiliation with and placement in relation to the Jewish community than any-thing else. But because identities are so central to human existence, conflicts between these border groups and conventional Jews are likely to continue. Conflicts are always related to identities in some fashion or other, and frequently intensify when a person's or group's identities are taken away, threatened, or violated.

"Professional Jews" (chapter 12) are usually more concerned with Jews marrying non-Jews than the existence of the border communities addressed in this chapter. Since 1990, more than 50 percent of Jewish Americans have married non-Jews, largely Christians, a phenomenon commonly referred to as intermarriage. In Northern California this statistic is as high as 70 percent. Although the trend of intermarriage isn't new, the rate at which it is happening is. Aside from being raised in interfaith households, Jewish Americans have also developed other hybrid identities, such as Jubus (Buddhist Jews).

Some people with multiple social identities refer to themselves as "half-Jews," despite there being nothing in halakhah supporting the idea that someone can be 50 percent Jewish. According to Jewish law, you are either Jewish or not. (Actor and activist Juliano Mer-Khamis, who was born to a Jewish Israeli mother and a Palestinian father, notably said that he was "100 percent Palestinian and 100 percent Jewish.") But most Jews are not committed to halakhah. And in terms of social identities, many Americans refer to themselves as racially and ethnically "mixed," but not necessarily as "half" of anything.

Chapter 12 examines the future of the Jewish community, focusing on, among other things, Jewish intermarriage and the profound role this is playing in shaping new Jewish identities.

TWELVE

Futures

Contents

Key Ideas

• For many, the future of the Jewish community is tangled up in questions regarding increases and decreases in the Jewish population, something that can only be assessed with a benchmark definition for "who counts as a Jew."

• Many "professional Jews" focus on delineating the best ways to shape Jewish identities, often seen as synonymous with the best ways to ensure "Jewish continuity." Some look to "Jewish education," others to "Israel education." Others focus on the rapid increase in the number of Jews marrying non-Jews (intermarriage).

• Over the last three decades, the Jewish institutional world in the United States has seen a number of shifts, whether reflecting changes in infrastructure (e.g., the reduction in importance of Jewish Federations) or the emergences of new and newly exposed Jewish subidentities (e.g., Environmental Jews, Queer Jews, and Multiracial and Multicultural Jews). In addition, many younger Jewish Americans self-identify

SPECIAL TOPIC 12.2
LIFE CYCLE EVENTS AND THE UNAFFILIATED

There are four basic transitional moments when lay or unaffiliated Jews often seek out support from "professional Jews": birth, adulthood, marriage, and death (i.e., life cycle events).

Birth

Many Jews perform a Brit Milah or Brit Bat for a newborn, a ceremony in which a baby is formally brought into the Jewish community (brit, covenant; milah, to seal or cut; bat, daughter.) Although the Brit Bat is a relatively recent practice and is not performed in many communities, the Brit Milah is a ritual described in the Torah, wherein a male child is circumcised, most often on his eighth day of life.

Adulthood

Many Jews also have a Bat Mitzvah or Bar Mitzvah, most often when a girl is twelve years old and a boy is thirteen years old. Although most Jews are not committed to halakhah (see chapter 8), upon reaching this age, traditionally speaking, a Jew is required to observe the mitzvot, or biblical directives, hence the name of this life cycle event. In some Jewish communities this ritual is very simple, entailing the teenager's recitation of a prayer during a Torah service, whereas in others, particularly in the United States, the event can be quite involved—sometimes more extravagant than some weddings. (Many think that Judith Kaplan, daughter of the renowned rabbi Mordecai Kaplan, had the first Bat Mitzvah in history, held in the United States in 1922, but in fact such ceremonies were performed in Italy already during the nineteenth century.) However enacted, such ceremonies mark the transition from childhood to adulthood.

Marriage and Death

The moments of transition marked by weddings and funerals often involve a number of centuries-old, intricate symbolic representations. A few of the characteristic marriage rituals involve a bride and groom standing under a four-cornered canopy (ḥuppah), the signing of a religious wedding contract (ketubah), and the shattering of a glass, all of which have multiple meanings. As for death, traditional practices include immediate burial of the body in a simple wooden coffin; a seven-day observance of shivah [lit., seven], in which friends and loved ones visit family members of the deceased in their home; and the recitation of a Jewish prayer called the Kaddish, which praises God.

Not all Jews perform rituals around these four life cycle transitions, of course, nor are all the practices described above observed by those who do. In addition, none of these events halakhically require a rabbi, and all of them can be performed without actually stepping foot in a synagogue. In situations when Jews in Israel or the United States want a rabbi to preside over a life cycle event but are unaffiliated with a specific synagogue, they sometimes hire a rabbi ad hoc.

"identified Jew" or "non-Jew." . . . If we want Jewish life to grow, and if we want our measurements of that growth to mean something, we will need to find a way to also emphasize the dynamic as well as the static dimensions.

In short, Kushner says, today's Jews need to figure out how to "do Jewish" on their own terms.

Perhaps it is just as Jewish communal leader Sidney Schwartz argues in *Jewish Megatrends:* younger Jews' identities are expressed more "covenantally" or "spiritually" than "tribally." They are more universal and less particular in terms of their worldview and what they mean by social action. In other words, if a Millennial Jew volunteers at a homeless shelter, even one explicitly affiliated with Christianity, it might be one of the multiple ways she expresses her Jewishness.

Another significant change, one that has obviously affected the Jewish community, is the epic role that technology now plays in our lives. Whether in terms of using computers, smartphones, or the Internet, Jews, just like everyone else in industrialized countries, have integrated new ways of interacting with the world into their daily routine. As scholar Dan Mendelsohn Aviv explains, the People of the Book have rapidly begun to become the people of social media, performing their Jewish identities virtually: "Despite these dire indications [such as the increasing intermarriage rate], younger Jews are engaging with Jewish identification, tradition and texts in a manner inconceivable to previous generations. They have taken their questions, God-wrestling, creative energy and desire to connect *online*. They meet and mate through online social networks. They exchange and

FIGURE 12.2. Over the last two decades a number of Jewish organizations have become popularized through social media. These are five such examples.

FIGURE 12.3. Environmental Jews. This student at Yavneh Day School (Los Gatos, CA), along with her schoolmates, is engaged in a program run by Urban Adamah, one of the many recent Jewish organizations engaged with hands-on environmental education in the San Francisco Bay Area (and beyond).

grapple with ideas through blogging, Facebook and Twitter. They share and remix the Jewish canon. . . . In short, they have created a Jewish community online that can engage any Jew with Wi-Fi who seeks engagement *anytime, anywhere and anyhow*" (fig. 12.2). In the Jewish institutional world, this phenomenon demands considerably more attention.

Environmental Jews

Another major trend is that Jews under forty are much more involved in social movements that increase awareness about and protection of the environment. Akin to their parents in relation to social movements of the 1960s and 1970s—such as the civil rights and women's liberation movements—since 2000 many Generation X and Millennial Jews have become involved in environmental activism. Jewish environmental educator Nati Passow, a Millennial who is a cofounder and executive director of the Jewish Farm School, succinctly summarizes the trend as follows: "Over the past several years, the Jewish environmental movement has become a vibrant force within the larger Jewish community, encouraging individuals and institutions to do everything from recycle, eat less meat, eat more meat (local and organic), plant gardens, create Green Teams, and eliminate disposable dishes."

Passow goes on to point out that whereas he is part of a younger group of Jewish environmental activists, previ-

ous generations had somewhat different intentions and methods. In past years, the American Jewish environmental movement "engaged individuals who were first and foremost sympathetic to the environmental cause and used the fledgling movement as an entry point into Judaism." Today's groups, in contrast—as Ellen Bernstein, the founder of Shomrei Adamah, one of the first national Jewish American environmentalist organizations, notes—attract younger Jews by embodying an ethos that orients toward environmentalism and Judaism as one and the same (fig. 12.3). (Nonetheless, the funding for current NGOs of this kind is given largely because of their ability to attract "unaffiliated" younger Jews.)

Educator Gabe Goldman has played a key role in establishing and shaping some of the most important Jewish environmental activists and organizations of the last three decades, something he continues to do today. Regarding how this newfound interest of younger Jews in environmental activism may affect the future, Goldman says:

> In the coming decades, this trend will likely not only continue but expand as new generations of American Jews struggle to define their Jewish identities. I believe this struggle will lead to the creation of new congregations of worshipers who celebrate Jewish life in the outdoors, as well as inside synagogue walls and pluralistic environmental organizations, that tear down traditional ideological barriers amongst Jewish religious sects. The

SPECIAL TOPIC 12.3
TOWARD QUEER JEWISH MAINSTREAMING

The 1969 Stonewall Uprising in New York City is largely credited as the tipping point for the modern American gay rights movement. A few years prior, in 1965, the Women of Reform Judaism passed a resolution calling for the decriminalization of homosexuality—the Reform movement's first official act in the direction of queer Jewish equality. Then in 1972, even as the Reform movement was taking a stance against the formation of Reform synagogues that identified as gay and lesbian (while also saying that gays and lesbians should be welcomed into synagogues), it recognized Beth Chayim Chadashim, founded in Los Angeles, as the first explicitly gay and lesbian synagogue in the United States, as a member-synagogue in their movement. The same year, the first gay Jewish group in the United States, Achvah Chutzpah, was founded in San Francisco, and the world's first queer Jewish organization, Keshet Ga'avah, was established in London. In 1973, a second synagogue inclusive of gays and lesbians, Congregation Beit Simchat Torah, was started in New York City.

In 1976, lesbian and gay Jews held a gathering in Washington, DC, which led to the First International Conference of Gay Jews in August of that year. In 1977, the conference was held in New York City, this time explicitly including lesbians as well. With additional conferences in Los Angeles (1978) and Israel (1979), the 1980 conference was held in San Francisco, at which time the World Congress of GLBT Jews was birthed (out of Keshet Ga'avah).

In terms of denominational positions, in 1977 the Reform movement publicly called for an end to legal discrimination against gays and lesbians in the United States; in 1982, it expressed support for gay and lesbian converts; in 1989, in a statement addressing the queer Jewish community, it declared that each one of their congregations "must be a place where loneliness and suffering and exile end"; in 1990, it passed a resolution officially accepting gay and lesbian rabbinical students into its seminaries; and in 1998 it officially sanctioned same-gender Jewish religious marriages.

In contrast, it was not until 1992 that the Conservative movement affirmed that LGBT Jews were welcome in their Conservative synagogues, youth groups, camps, and day schools, though they were not permitted to hold positions of lay leadership, let alone be rabbis. In 2006 the Jewish Theological Seminary in New York began accepting openly gay and lesbian rabbinical applicants.

Finally, the Orthodox community (including those identifying as part of "Open Orthodoxy") continues to maintain that homosexual behavior violates halakhah, despite Orthodox outliers such as Rabbi Steve Greenberg—an openly gay man with Orthodox ordination—who have pushed for greater inclusion of gays and lesbians.

Outside of these rabbinic enclaves, a handful of other Jewish American organizations have become more inclusive of queer Jews over the last forty years, such as the Chicago-based Jewish Family and Community Services, who acknowledged the need to include gays and lesbians in professional settings in 1976. Since the 1990s a number of United States–based NGOs that support and raise awareness about queer Jews have been established, such as Keshet (1996), the Institute for Judaism and Sexual Orientation at Hebrew Union College-Jewish Institute of Religion (2000), Jewish Mosaic: The National Center for Sexual and Gender Diversity (2003, which merged with Keshet in 2011), Nehirim: GLBT Culture and Spirituality (2004), and NUJLS: The National Union of Jewish Lesbian, Gay, Bisexual, Transgender, and Queer Students (which merged with Nehirim in 2010). Since 2000, a number of books and movies have given voice to the Jewish queer community, and academic studies have been conducted aimed at promoting inclusion of queer Jews in the larger Jewish community.

---

potential danger here is also the possibility that future generations of American Jews will become "niche Jews," whose view of, and relationship to, Judaism is contextualized narrowly, such as [through] environmentalism, and disconnected to the broader experience of Jewish life.

Queer Jews

Since 2000, there has been an increase in Jewish communal spaces embracing Jews who identify as lesbian, gay, bisexual, transgender, intersex, or other nonconforming gendered, sexed, and sexualized identities, referred to here as queer (special topic 0.2). As in other spheres of the Jewish community, this phenomenon arose in tandem with events outside the Jewish enclave. Much of this change began in the 1970s and 1980s, when a range of Jewish American organizations began to take public positions related to queer Jews and the new Jewish institutions they had established (special topic 12.3; fig. 12.4).

As of 2014, American Jews support civil rights for queer communities—in such contexts as the American mili-

FIGURE 12.4. Queer Jews. A rainbow, representing pride and diversity in terms of nonconforming gendered, sexed, and sexualized social identities (see special topic 0.2), merged with a *Magen David,* sometimes referred to as a Jewish star or Star of David (see chapter 7). The image was provided by Keshet, a group "working for the full equality and inclusion of lesbian, gay, bisexual, and transgender Jews in Jewish life."

tary, the Boy Scouts, and same-sex marriage—at rates higher than most other American communities. That said, more progress has been made in regard to lesbians and gays than those who identify as bisexual, transgender, or other nonconventional queer identities. And outside of larger cities, issues related to gender and sexuality are rarely a part of the Jewish American community's discourse. As in non-Jewish environments, when such issues do arise, they are often disregarded or seen as provocative.

Interestingly, the success of the queer rights movements has created new challenges for some queer Jews. In cities such as Atlanta, the membership of formerly gay-specific congregations is now approximately 50 percent nonqueer, and younger queers, many of whom have grown up in a climate of greater tolerance, are questioning the need for exclusively queer organizations. Same-sex marriage and adoption have changed the face of queer life in America as well.

One of the more important innovations regarding queer Jews is the creation of new blessings that celebrate gender and sexual diversity. A siddur (prayer book) published in 2009 by Congregation Sha'ar Zahav, a San Francisco–based synagogue founded in 1977, contains a number of such prayers, for example. One of the most noteworthy aspects of these blessings is that they are rooted in traditional rabbinic language and linguistic formulae, even though they honor ideas in relation to specific social identities largely absent from dominant rabbinic texts. Although these prayers are marginal to the standard liturgy used in conventional American synagogues, and not many American Jews are even aware of their existence, some believe that they will eventually be used more widely within non-Orthodox Jewish communities.

Multiethnic Jewish Communities

Over the last sixty years, in addition to marrying non-Jews, Jews from different ethnic subgroups have begun marrying one another at rates higher than ever before (fig. 12.5). Although we lack data on the statistical frequency of this phenomenon, by any account it is happening more—in the United States and Israel in particular—than ever before in history. Indeed, marrying a Jew from another subgroup would have been commonly considered "marrying out" in centuries past. Even intra-communal marriage among Ashkenazi Jews of varied backgrounds was often shunned prior to the twentieth century (see chapter 1).

The best data we have to illustrate this trend is from Israel, where intramarriage among Jews has been increasing since the state was founded in 1948. Attitudes regard-

FIGURES 12.5A–C. Multiethnic Jews engaged in programs run by Be'chol Lashon, an organization that "grows and strengthens the Jewish people through ethnic, cultural, and racial inclusiveness." *Top:* Rabbi Capers Funye lighting a Hanukkah menorah with Be'chol Lashon's multicultural community. *Middle:* Teenagers at Camp Be'chol Lashon, located in the San Francisco Bay Area. *Bottom:* A Be'chol Lashon program for a Jewish holiday, including Mexican fiesta flowers.

ing such marriages have become more accepting, especially among younger Jews. According to one study, between 1975 and 1990 not only did the rate of Jewish intramarriage noticeably increase, but marriage across Jewish subgroups was actually preferred. Members of subordinated Jewish subgroups (e.g., Jews of Mizraḥi descent) were also more open to the idea of marrying those from a dominant subgroup (e.g., Jews of Ashkenazi descent). However, when, for instance, a Yemenite Jewish Israeli woman has married an Ashkenazi Jewish Israeli man, the Yemenite identity within the relationship has tended to become marginalized. (Gender, of course, also plays an important role in such situations.) Notably, there is no trend currently toward dominant subgroups being more open to the idea of marrying into subordinated ones.

Although we don't have analogous evidence regarding the American Jewish community, one study suggests that there is in fact less tolerance for Jews from particular subordinated subgroups (e.g., African American Jews) marrying Ashkenazi Jews than there is for others (e.g., Latina Jews or Asian Jews). Only 17 percent of American Jews surveyed approved of a marriage of the first kind, whereas 51 percent supported the second. Yet the fact that such intramarriage is even possible is ahistorical. A century ago, such unions were virtually nonexistent.

In the United States, of course, biases reflect not just the Jewish American community but the American nation as a whole. Hesitancy expressed when a white Jew marries a black Jew, as opposed to a white Jew marrying a Latina or Asian Jew, derives, at least in part, from a deep-seated, historical prejudice in the United States toward African Americans.

Converting Non-Jews?

Some professional Jews have suggested that one of the best ways to grow the Jewish community is to convert more non-Jews to Judaism, that this is where resources should be invested. Professional Jews aligning against this position often cite rabbinic writings that say a potential convert should be turned away three times before a serious conversation about conversion can take place (though this tradition is but one of many).

Contrary to the popular notion that Jews have never been a group to engage in proselytism, during the Second Temple period, some scholars argue that missionary activity was a normal part of Jewish life. Scholar Salo Baron goes so far as to theorize that between 586 BCE and the first century CE the Palestine-based Jewish (and proto-Jewish) community grew in size from 150,000 to

8 million, something that would not have been possible without vigorous missionary activity (and a simultaneous "natural" increase in birth rates).

Some scholars point to the biblical Abraham as not only the "first Jew" (more accurately, perhaps the first Hebrew), but also, according to rabbinic interpretation, an active missionary. Others contend that Jewish missionary behavior declined only after the ascent of Christianity and the institution of laws that declared it illegal for Jews to engage in proselytism. Passages in the Christian Bible support the notion that Jews during the early Christian era actively sought to recruit converts. Still other scholars have said that historically Jews have turned to proselytism whenever the survival of the Jewish community was at stake.

Whatever the case, a number of twentieth-century Reform rabbis, in addition to a smaller number of Conservative ones, have called for a renewal of proselytism. Since the late 1990s, scholar Gary Tobin has also been an outspoken contemporary Jew calling for Jews to bring more non-Jews into the fold. Acknowledging the rise in intermarriage rates, Tobin has said that professional Jews should stop spending time lamenting this trend and instead proactively encourage more people to be Jewish. "We must abandon the paradigm that our children and grandchildren may become Gentiles and promote the thought that America is filled with millions of potential Jews." This position continues to be quite rare among Jews in 2015.

Toward Jewish Futures

Among academics, it is almost a given that texts addressing potential futures for the Jewish community cite a passage from a 1948 essay written by Jewish American Zionist Simon Rawidowicz, "Israel: The Ever-Dying People":

> The world makes many images of Israel, but Israel [the Jewish people] makes only one image of itself: that of being constantly on the verge of ceasing to be, of disappearing. The threat of doom, of an end that forecloses any new beginning hung over the people of Israel even before it gained its peoplehood, while it was taking its first steps on the stage of history. Indeed, it would often seem as if Israel's end preceded its very beginning. He who studies Jewish history will readily discover that there was hardly a generation in the Diaspora that did not consider itself the final link in Israel's chain.

Although this essay begins by underscoring the role the obsession with potential extinction plays in dominant Jewish narratives, Rawidowicz eventually takes us in a different direction. He contends, for example, that the first time in recorded history that a community called Israel is mentioned is in a text from thirteenth-century BCE Egypt, where it says that Israel would shortly thereafter become extinct. Yet these proto-Jews were not annihilated. As Rawidowicz notes, even non-Jews have falsely spoken about how Jews were fated to disappear. He ends his essay by underscoring Jews' perpetual state of dying, during which time, quite obviously, they have been living.

Whereas Rawidowicz looks to the past to support his thesis, futurists are not satisfied with analyzing what has already happened unless it is in pursuit of what has not yet happened. But some look to the past as a predictor of the future, in terms of the repetition of history. Many Jews understand the future of the Jewish community only in terms of the future of the State of Israel, and for a large number within this group the connection between the Shoah and the Jewish State is all too real.

Conclusions?

There's an old joke about a Jew stranded on a deserted island who builds two synagogues; when he is rescued, he is asked: "Why did you build two?" He responds, "One to belong to and a second I would never set foot in." There is a kernel of truth in this barb, but not because Jews are good at building institutions or because they are a cantankerous group. Rather, as far back as the Hebrew community, and through their subsequent rebirth as Israelites, Judeans, and, eventually, Jews, this group has never been uniform or consistent. There has never been *a* Jewish people, only peoples. Within the Jewish tent there have always been subtribes, subidentities, and subfactions. And yet, even though the Jewish community has never been homogeneous or monolithic, Jews and non-Jews frequently speak about "*the* Jews" as if they are a single, cohesive, interconnected group.

Perhaps the best way of looking at the potential futures of the Jewish community was proposed by Rabbi Marshall Meyer, one of the most influential Jewish leaders of the latter half of the twentieth century. When asked about a 1990 study that pointed to the rapid increase in the number of Jews marrying non-Jews in the United States, he said, "There has been deep concern with Jewish continuity and with the survival of the Jewish people. Let us begin by asking, survival *as what?*"

Jews have been incredibly successful at investing in their own communities, putting financial and social capital into figuring out how to ensure their continuity.

Yet much of the time, senior generations are using old or out-of-date models to attract younger Jews. As Jonathan Sacks, the former Chief Rabbi of Great Britain, observed, "The only people capable of threatening the future of the Jewish people are the Jewish people."

The twentieth-century Jewish genocide continues to shape Jewish worldviews. Sacks argues that feeding younger Jews a "diet of Holocaust education," especially given the rate at which Jews are choosing to leave the Jewish community, has proven unsuccessful as a framework in which to pass "Jewish identity to their children." Many older Jews, he says, are unable to remove their gaze from the atrocities of the past; in turn, this prevents them from looking forward.

As for the challenge of acculturation and assimilation, this phenomenon is not new to Jewish history. In fact, one of the clearest patterns found in Jewish communities across the globe for literally millennia has been Jews' integration of "non-Jewish" things into their community, including into everyday Jewish practices (see chapter 7).

If one goal for contemporary Jews is to give their descendants the space to perform their Jewish identities with freedom and support, enacted however differently from current ones, then it is imperative that there be new approaches to Jewish life. Some say that twenty-first-century Jews need to chart their own course, whether or not it deviates from the past. Such voices contend that younger Jews cannot be told that a connection to the State of Israel is required of them, for example. Instead, such ideas need to be presented as potential paths, as options. Such voices say that Generation X and Millennial Jews must be permitted to widen Jewish expression to include those perspectives that have been marginalized for much of Jewish history, such as those subgroups touched on in this book.

Ultimately, the future of this community cannot be predicted with certainty. Any attempt to do so would fail to reflect the factual messiness of Jewish identities. In my personal assessment, above all else the bulk of Jewish texts gravitate toward hope for Jews and non-Jews alike. Jews have the freedom to orient toward such a worldview or not. Only Jews will be able to take the decades-old mold of *the* Jew, reexamine it, acknowledge that within each Jew are multiple Jews—a seemingly endless number of subidentities—and allow them all to emerge.

As the renowned twentieth-century Yiddish writer and Nobel Laureate Isaac Bashevis Singer once explained (using a thick Russian accent):

> A man returned from Warsaw and told his friend, "I saw a Jew who *vas* poring over the Talmud day and night. I saw a Jew who *vas vaving* the red flag of communism. I saw a Jew who *vas* passing out leaflets to come see his new play on Spinoza."
>
> "So? *Vat's* so unusual about that?" his friend responded. "There are a lot of Jews in *Varsaw*."
>
> "But don't you understand, my friend?" the man yelled. "It *vas* all the same Jew!"

When speaking about what the future holds for a single Jew or all Jews, only one thing *is* certain. There are always going to be multiple understandings of Jews, Judaisms, and Jewish identities. This has always been and always will be. Perhaps once this fact is incorporated into the communities' dominant narratives, their futures will begin to arrive.

FIGURE CREDITS

0.1   Mary Kershisnik, based on "The Global Religious Landscape," Pew Research Center, December 18, 2012

0.2   © Arthur Sasse, Corbis

0.3   © "Creative Commons 'Kiss, DSC00040'," 2010, by www.beefybasses.com/VintageFenderBasses is licensed under CC BY 2.0/Cropped original

0.4   © "Creative Commons 'sarah-silverman-emmys-moustache'," 2009 by Maegan Tintari is licensed under CC BY 2.0/Cropped original

0.5   © Jim Britt

1.1   Wikimedia Commons/Public Domain

1.2   Wikimedia Commons/Public Domain

1.3   © Mary Kershisnik

1.4   © Dr. Shalva Weil, *Asian Jewish Life,* April 2014

1.5   Zoltan Kluger/Wikimedia Commons/Public Domain

1.6   © Nina Callaway, *The Kitchen,* April 15, 2008

2.1   Titian, *Adam and Eve,* c. 1550/Wikimedia Commons/Public Domain

2.2   © Jen Taylor Friedman, "Clone Minyan"

2.3   © Bruce Damonte, "As It Is Written: Project 304,805," on view October 8, 2009–March 29, 2011, Contemporary Jewish Museum, San Francisco, CA

2.4   © Aaron J. Hahn Tapper and Mary Kershisnik

3.1   © Aaron J. Hahn Tapper

3.2   Wikimedia Commons/Public Domain

3.3   © Mary Kershisnik, loosely based on Rachel Woods, "Lineage of Abraham and Israel," *About LDS Guide,* and Edward J. Brandt, "The Families of Abraham and Israel," *Ensign* (May 1973), 49, http://lds.about.com/library/bl/aids/aids2/israel_abraham_lineage2.pdf

3.4   © Mary Kershisnik, based on "Israel and Judah," Bible History Online, www.bible-history.com/maps/israel_judah_kings.html

3.5a   "The Temple at Elephantine, as it was in 1799," in Gaston Maspero, *History of Egypt: Chaldea, Syria, Babylonia, and Assyria,* vol. 5, pt. A, ed. A. H. Sayce, trans. A. L. McClure (London: The Grolier Society, 1903)

3.5b   Olaf Tausch, "Assuan Elephantine Chnumtempel 17"/Wikimedia Commons/Public Domain

4.1   © The Association for the True and Complete Redemption (poster)

4.2   Wikimedia Commons/Public Domain

4.3   Wikimedia Commons/Public Domain

4.4   © Ray Noland (formally known as CRO), "The Dream," www.gotellmama.org

5.1a   Joe Goldberg/Wikimedia Commons/Public Domain

5.1b   © Lehrhaus Judaica

5.2   © Babylonian Talmud, Vilna ed.

5.3   © Frédéric Brenner, "Faculty, Students, Rabbis, and Cantors," 1994, courtesy Howard Greenberg Gallery, New York

5.4   Oswalt Kreusel, "Kain and Abel," 1591/Wikimedia Commons/Public Domain

5.5   © Daniel J. Simons, 1999, www.dansimons.com, www.theinvisiblegorilla.com/videos.html

6.1   © Joshua Shamsi, "Tomb of David UMosher," Diarna Geo-Museum of North African and Middle Eastern Jewish Life, www.diarna.org

6.2	© President and Fellows of Harvard College, Imaging Dept.; Nicolas Ryckemans, "Elijah Carried to Heaven in a Chariot of Fire," Harvard Art Museums / Fogg Museum, Gift of Belinda L. Randall from the collection of John Witt Randal, R7702
6.3	© Mary Kershisnik, based on "The Ten Sefirot," in Arthur Green, *A Guide to the Zohar* (Stanford, CA: Stanford University Press, 2004), ix
6.4	© "Creative Commons 'Belz Purim 5766'," 2007, by Daniel575 is licensed under CC BY-SA 3.0
7.1	© ABC, screen shot
7.2	© "Creative Commons 'Hanukah Tree'," 2010, by Tojosan is licensed under CC BY-NC-SA 2.0
7.3	© Biblewalks.com, "Hammat Tiberias," Holy Land Sites Review
7.4a–c	© Aaron Hahn Tapper, 2002
7.5a	© "Jews in Mosul, Mesopotamia," Keystone-Mast Collection, UCR/California Museum of Photography, University of California, Riverside
7.5b	© "Family of Iraqi Chief Rabbi Hakham Ezra Dangoor in Baghdad, 1910," Jewish Museum, London
7.6	Sergei Mikhailovich Prokudin-Gorskii, "Jewish Children with their Teacher in Samarkand," c. 1910/Wikimedia Commons/Public Domain
7.7a	© Shmuel Yavne'eli, *Masa le-Teman: Bi-sheliḥut Ha-Misrad Ha-Eretz Yisraeli shel Ha-Histadrut Ha-Tsiyonit Bi-shenot 671–672, 1911–1912 (Journey to Yemen)* (Tel Aviv: Miflegot Poa'ley Eretz Yisrael, 1952), 80–81, 112–113
7.7b	Ba'asor Le'Israel, Masada Publishing, "Jewish Yemenite Bride," c. 1950s/Wikimedia Commons/Public Domain
7.8a	© Oren Ziv, Activestills.org, January 18, 2012
7.8b	© Lloyd Wolf, www.lloydwolf.com, "Olim—Immigrants to Israel," 2007
7.9a	© Ricki Rosen, *Tablet Magazine,* December 27, 2012
7.9b	© Yoraan Rafael Reuben, *Asian Jewish Life,* September 2012
7.10	© Mary Kershisnik, based on http://archive .silkroadproject.org/Portals/0/images/lg_ SilkRoadWallMap_color.jpg, and "Silk Road and Indian Ocean Traders: Connecting China and the Middle East," The Oriental Institute, University of Chicago, http://oi.uchicago.edu/sites/oi.uchicago .edu/files/uploads/managed/feature_blocks/ Silk%20Road_map.pdf
7.11a	© "The Kaifeng Synagogue," Jewish American Hall of Fame, based on "Kai Feng Synagogue," Beit Hatfutsot, Tel Aviv, Israel
7.11b	William Edgar Geil, "Chao Tzu-fang and family," c. 1910; courtesy of Stephanie Comfort and http:// jewishpostcardcollection.com
7.11c	© Jason Jia, Photographer, "Fully Jewish, Fully Chinese," December 14, 2012
8.1	© Mary Kershisnik, based on Asher Arian, Ayala Keissar-Sugarman, Dror Walter, Dahlia Scheindlin, Shaul Slepak, Tamar Hermann, and Raphael Ventura, "A Portrait of Israeli Jews: Beliefs, Observance, and Values of Israeli Jews, 2009," Guttman Center for Surveys of the Israel Democracy Institute (2012)
8.2	© "Creative Commons 'Lavater and Lessing Visit Moses Mendelssohn'," 1856, by The Magnes Collection of Jewish Art and Life is licensed under CC BY-NC-SA 2.0
8.3	© Cleveland Jewish History, "The Trefa Dinner"
8.4a	© "Creative Commons 'B'naiJacobOttumwaMechitza'," 2011, by Douglas Jones is licensed under CC0 1.0 Universal
8.4b	© "Creative Commons 'The men's and women's sides of the Western Wall'," 2012, by Fritzmb is licensed under CC BY-NC-ND 2.0
8.5	© I. George Bilyk, "On the Cutting Edge," in "In the Beginning," *The Jewish Exponent,* June 14, 2012
8.6a	© Kehilat Romemu, 2013
8.6b	© Charlie Steiner, still from video
8.7	© Aaron J. Hahn Tapper and Mary Kershisnik
9.1	"Nuremberg Laws," 1935, United States Holocaust Memorial Museum Collection/Wikimedia Commons/Public Domain
9.2a	"Inmates at Sachsenhasuen [death camp] Wearing Identifying Badges," December 19, 1938, U.S. National Archives and Records Administration/ Public Domain
9.2b	© "Jewish Badge," United States Holocaust Memorial Museum, courtesy of Fritz Gluckstein
9.3a	© Karen Gillerman-Harel
9.3b	© Stand with Us
9.4	Hartmann Schedel, c. 1493/Wikimedia Commons/ Public Domain
9.5	© DeVito/Verdi, Fast Company, and NCAI, "Native Americans Counter Racist Iconography with Racist Baseball Caps"
9.6a	© "Creative Commons 'Borat in Cologne'," 2006, by Michael Bulcik is licensed under CC BY 2.5
9.6b	"Der Stürmer Christmas," 1929/Public Domain
9.7	© "Creative Commons 'March of the Living 2005 in Auschwitz ("Arbeit macht frei")'," 2005, by Marek Peters, www.marek-peters.com, is licensed under GNU Free Documentation license 1.2

9.8	© Ed Stein, 2006	10.8	Wikimedia Commons/Public Domain
10.1	© Mary Kershisnik, based on "U.S. Religious Landscape Survey, Religious Affiliation: Diverse and Dynamic," The Pew Forum on Religion and Public Life, February 2008	10.9	© Heinz
		10.10a	© Mary Kershisnik
		10.10b	© Laurent Rebours, Associated Press, 2000
10.2	© "Creative Commons 'Postcard for Israeli Independence Day'" by Ze'ev Barkan courtesy of Hayim Shtayer, is licensed under CC BY-NC-ND 2.0	11.1	"The Samaritan Passover on Mount Gerizim," c. 1936, American Colony Photos, G. Eric and Edith Matson Photograph Collection
10.3a	© Franz Krausz, "Visit Palestine," Tourist Development Association of Palestine, c. 1936	11.2	© Cathrielah Baht Israel, "Shimon Peres with Ben Ammi"
10.3b	© Miskovits, "Toward a New Life: The Promised Land," c. 1935	11.3	© Ira Nowinski, "Boys and Men in Prayer in a Karaite Synagogue, Ashdod, Israel," 1985, Stanford University, Special Collections and University Archives
10.4	© "Costumes and Characters, etc., Group of Old Jews," Jerusalem, c. 1914, American Colony Photos, G. Eric and Edith Matson Photograph Collection		
		11.4	© "Creative Commons 'Jews for Jesus'" by d q is licensed under CC BY-NC-ND 2.0
10.5a	© Mary Kershisnik, based on "Israel Green Lines," Wikimedia Commons/Public Domain	11.5	© Richard Corkery, Getty Images, 2003
		12.1a–b	© Jack M. Barrack Hebrew Academy
10.5b	© Mary Kershisnik, based on "1947 UN Partition Plan-1949 Armistice Comparison," Wikimedia Commons/Public Domain and United Nations maps	12.2	© 70 Faces Media (Kveller and MyJewishLearning), © Spark Networks USA (Jdate), © Jewlicious, © Nextbook, Inc. (Jewcy)
10.6a	© Mary Kershisnik	12.3	© Yavneh Day School
10.6b	Wikimedia Commons/Public Domain	12.4	© Keshet, www.keshetonline.org
10.7	Wikimedia Commons/Public Domain	12.5a–c	© GlobalJews.org/Be'chol Lashon

INDEX

Page references followed by fig. *indicate an illustration.*

redemption through sin, 68

Redskins, Washington, 179, 180 *fig.*

Reform movement: American Jews' affiliation with, 166 *fig.*; Columbus Platform (1937), 149; emergence of, 93, 94; in England, 146; history of, 146–48; institutions/size/beliefs of, 160, 162, 164; on Jewish identity, 149–50; on Jewish laws, 93, 94; messianism of, 70; on mixed seating, 155; New Pittsburgh Platform (1999), 149; overview, 146; Pittsburgh Platform (1885), 70, 149, 151, 194; on queer issues, 149, 164, 240; rabbinic authority rejected by, 224; on revelation as continuous, 35; size of, 35, 224; Treifa Banquet hosted by, 152, 152 *fig.*, 153; in the United States, 148–50; in Western Europe, 147–48; women ordained as rabbis in, 44, 149, 156 *fig.*, 162; on Zionism, 194

refugees, MENA Jews as, 205

Rehoboam, 224

reincarnation. *See* souls and reincarnation

Reines, Isaac Jacob, 156

religion: and culture, 116–17; definition of, 158, 206; meanings of, 4, 141; vs. nationalism, 206–7. *See also specific religions*

remez interpretation. *See* PaRDeS

Rethinking World History (Hodgson), 15

Reuveni, David (or Ha-Re'uveni), 66

reward and punishment, 110

Ritchie, Guy, 229 *fig.*

rituals: animal sacrifice, 55, 130; cyclical, 38; dominant, 23; eating matzah ball soup, 23; lesser-known, 23–25; Lurianic, 106; and narratives, 23–26; an orange on the Seder plate, 25, 25 *fig.*; and sacredness, 48–49; after Second Temple's destruction, 55. *See also* Seder

Robinson, Jackie, narrative of, 17

Rokeach, Yissachar Dov, 108 *fig.*

Roma, 170

Romaniote Jews, 120, 128

Romans: Christianization of, 128; on circumcision, 52; Greek defeat by, 55, 118; Jews living under, 55–56; rebellion against, 64; siege of Masada by, 207–9, 208 *fig.*

Romemu (New York City), 158 *fig.*

Rosenzweig, Franz, 35, 56

Ross, Betsy, narrative of, 17

Ross, Tamar, 38

Roth, Joel, 82

Roth, Norman, 179

Roth, Philip, 216

RRC (Reconstructionist Rabbinical College), 149, 157, 161, 163, 165

ruaḥ, 104, 105

Ruth, book of, 102

Ryckemans, Nicolas: *Elijah Carried to Heaven in a Chariot of Fire*, 98–99, 99 *fig.*

Saadiah Gaon (Saadia ben Joseph Alfayumi), 43, 91, 126

Sabbath Prayer Book (Kaplan), 157

Sabbath Queen (Licha Dodi), 112

Sacks, Jonathan, 244

sacredness, 45; becoming sacred, 48–49; of Mount Sinai, 29–30; of temples, 51, 53. *See also* Zion

Sadducees, 143, 144–45, 224

Safed mysticism, 101, 105–7, 112

sages (*ḥakhamim*), 76

saints, 96–97, 106, 107

Salamon, Hagar, 129, 130

Salonika (Greece), 120

Samaias, 66

Samaritans: and contemporary Jews, 221–22; descent from Israelites claimed by, 219–21; identified as Jews, 228; intracommunal marriage by, 221; in Israel, 221–22, 228; as a Jewish sect, 221; vs. Judeans, 220–21; number of, 221; overview, 217, 219

Samaritan temple (Mount Gerizim, Wes Bank, Palestine), 54, 55, 143–44

Samuel, book of, 49, 62

Sand, Shlomo: *The Invention of the Jewish People*, 11

Sanhedrin, 91

Sanu, Yaqub, 128

Sarna, Jonathan, 155

Sartre, Jean-Paul, 139, 228

Sasso, Sandy Eisenberg, 156 *fig.*, 157, 163

Satmar Jews, 139

Scattered among the Nations, 26

Schachter-Shalomi, Zalman (Reb Zalman), 158 *fig.*, 159, 236

Schäfer, Peter, 99

Schechter, Solomon, 35, 153, 155

Schindler's List, 211

Schneerson, Menachem Mendel ("the Rebbe"), 60–62, 61 *fig.*, 66, 69, 97, 226

Scholem, Gershom: on evil, 110; family traditions of, 115; on Hasidism, 107–8; as a messiah, 66; on messianism, 68; on mysticism, 98, 99–100, 110, 111; on nothingness, 103; on Tzvi, 68 *fig.*; Zionism supported by, 195

Schwartz, Sidney, 238

Scientific Revolution, 145

Scroll of Esther, 124, 136

The Second Sex (de Beauvoir), 90

Second Temple (Jerusalem): building of, 53, 54; destruction of, 18, 55, 75, 76, 132; sacredness of, 53

Seder: Ashkenazi, 23; food served at, 23, 25, 25 *fig.*; *Haggadah* (*Pesaḥ* prayer book) used during, 13, 85; popularity of, 13; rituals of, 13, 23–25, 24–25 *figs.*, 27

"The Seeker" (Ramer), 86–87

Seeskin, Kenneth, 71

Sefer ha-Bahir (*Book of Illumination*; Isaac the Blind), 101, 110–11

sefirot, 103, 104 *fig.*, 105, 111

segregation of buses, 17

Seharane, 123–24

Seinfeld, Jerry, 179

self-flagellation, 106

Seltzer, Julie, 37 *fig.*

Sephardi Jews: vs. Ashkenazi, 21–22; Christian mistreatment of, 131–32 (*see also* Portuguese Inquisition; Spanish Inquisition); definition of, 22; diversity among, 131; emergence of, 131; from Greece, 120; group traumas experienced by, 175; lineage of, 22, 120; messianic beliefs of, 68; Moroccan, 22; under the Romans, 128–29; use of term, 22, 116, 131–32

Septuagint, 31

Serenus (Sari'a), 66

service/social justice volunteerism, 70–71

Seth, 42

sexuality and mysticism, 111

Shaar Hashamayim Synagogue (Thane, India), 133 *fig.*

Shabbat: Jewish businesses open on, 166; laws regarding, 94; and religiosity, 142; rituals regarding, 112; Saturday/Sunday observance of, 148

Shakespeare, William: *The Merchant of Venice*, 179

Shanwar Telis, 134

Sharett, Moshe, 196

shari'a, 91–92

Sharon, Ariel, 198, 200

Shas, 175

Shavuot, 38

Shazaar, Zalman, 192 *fig.*

Sheingold, Carl, 190

Shekhinah, 103, 107, 111–12

Sheol, 67

Shillady, William S., 210

Shiloh, 49

Shimon bar Yochai, 101, 102, 106, 107, 109

Shimon ben Yitzchak (Rashi), 102

Shlain, Tiffany: *The Tribe*, 25–26

Shlomo, 66

Shma prayer, 77, 81 *fig.*

Shoah (Holocaust): acceptance of American Jews after, 210; as antisemitism, 169, 177; and Ashkenazi Jews, 20; Austrian/German apologies for, 215; books/movies about, 211; collective Jewish memory of, 183–84; commemoration of, 172, 182; death camps of, 120, 170, 172, 172 *fig.*, 182–83, 183 *fig.*, 184, 211; death toll from, 170; denial of, 175–76; and diaspora vs. Zion, 57; discriminatory laws against Jews, 170–71, 171 *fig.*; education about, government-sanctioned, 175, 182–83, 244; as an experience not exclusive to Ashkenazi Jews, 175; Final Solution, 175; groups targeted by the Nazis, 170; and Israel's Declaration of Independence, 173–74, 174 *fig.*; learning of family members who died in, 169; and the "master race," 171; Nazis' definition/identification of Jews, 170–72, 171–72 *figs.*; "Never again," 183; and non-Ashkenazi Jews, 174–75; overview, 168, 170; relevance for all Jews, 173–75, 174 *fig.*; Salonikan Jews who perished during, 120; as unique, 172–73; use of term, 170; victim vs. survivor responses to, 181–82, 186

Shohat, Ella, 22, 176
Shomrei Adamah, 239
Shulḥan Arukh (Karo), 92, 105
Shuster, Joe, 212
Sibylline Oracles, 62
siddurim (Jewish prayer books), 42
Siegel, Benjamin ("Bugsy"), 212
Siegel, Daniel, 159
Siegel, Jerry, 212
Sigd, 131
Sikkuy, 204
Silk Road, 135, 136 *fig.*
Silverman, Sarah, 5 *fig.*, 179
Simeon ben Yohai, 42
Simmons, Gene, 4 *fig.*
Simon, Joe, 212
Simon, Paul, 7
Simons, Daniel, 87–88, 87 *fig.*
Sinai, Mount: dawn climb on, 29; overview, 8; pilgrimages to, 29; sacredness/symbolism of, 29–30; souls of all Jews at, 43, 44. *See also* Ten Commandments
"Sinai" (Feld), 86
Sinai Desert, 199 *fig.*
Sinai Temple (Westwood, CA), 159
Singer, Isaac Bashevis, 244
Sinti, 170
Six-Day War (1967), 198–99, 199 *fig.*, 200, 205, 227
613 *mitzvot* (biblical directives), 36–37, 68, 107. See also *mitzvot*; Ten Commandments
slaves, 130, 222
Smart, Ninian, 142
Smith, Anthony, 206
Smith, Jonathan Z., 48–49
smoking, 93
Smooha, Sammy, 176
socialism, 69–70
social media, 238–39, 239 *fig.*
Society for Humanistic Judaism, 157–58, 161
Society for the Advancement of Judaism, 156, 157, 161
Society of Reformed Israelites, 148
sōd interpretation. *See* PaRDeS
Solomon, King, 32, 49; and Ethiopian Jews, 129; Israelite kingdoms united under, 51; Land of Israel ruled by, 198; wives of, 233
Soloveitchik, Dov Baer, 194
Song of Songs, 30, 102
Soomekh, Saba, 124
The Sopranos, 212
souls and reincarnation, 103–5, 107
"Sovereign Self," 159
Soviet Union, 58
Spagnolo, Francesco, 157
Spain, 22, 56, 203
Spanish Inquisition, 22, 68, 131–32
Spiderman, 212
Spiegelman, Art: *Maus*, 211
Spinoza, Baruch, 33, 43; *Politico-Theological Treatise*, 145
Stand with Us, 174 *fig.*
Stanislawski, Michael, 207
The Starfish and the Spider (Brafman and Beckstrom), 47
Star of David (Jewish star), 118, 241 *fig.*
Steinsaltz, Adin, 88, 112
stereotypes. *See under* antisemitism

Stern, Avraham, 208
Stonewall Uprising (New York City, 1969), 240
storytelling, 13, 123. *See also* narratives
structural blindness or structural violence, 88
Stutman, Shira, 10
Suez Canal, 127
Sufism, 100
suicide, mass, 207–8
Sukkot (Feast of Tabernacles), 64 *fig.*, 80
superheroes, 212
Superman, 212
Supreme Court (Israel), 202, 221, 227
Supreme Court (United Kingdom), 6
Sussman, Lance, 149
Swarthmore College, 216
swastika, 118
synagogues: affiliation with, 159–61; first American, 20, 148; first gay and lesbian synagogue, 149; Humanist, 157; mixed seating in, 154, 154 *fig.*, 155; vs. the temple, 55, 148. *See also* First Temple; Second Temple
Synoptic Gospels, 144, 177–78
Syrian Jews, 121, 121 *fig.*, 132. *See also* Baghdadi Indian Jews
Szold, Henrietta, 195

Tabernacle, 49
Taglit-Birthright Israel (TBI) program, 235–36
Talmud: on the afterlife, 67; agaddah texts, 77–78, 82; authority of, 76, 77; Babylonian, 53–54, 75, 81 *fig.*, 135; on evil, 110; God's revelation on Mount Sinai and continued revelations, 34–35; *halakhah* texts, 77–78; "It is not in heaven," 83; Jerusalem/Palestinian, 75; on Jesus, 65; as male-centric, 88; on messiahs, 64; on the Mishnah, 77; mysticism's basis in, 98; organization/length of, 75; overview, 73, 75; questions vs. answers, focus on, 78–79; relevance of, 74–75; on the 613 directives, 36–37, 107; vs. Torah, 74–75; the Torah-Mishnah-Talmud relationship, 79–80, 81 *fig.*, 82–83; Vilna edition, 75, 81 *fig.*; on women, 88; on "your brother's bloods," 79–80. *See also* Gemara; Mishnah
Tanakh (Bible), 31
Tanna'im (rabbis of the Mishnah; also *tanna*), 76
Tawil-Souri, Helga, 204
Taylor, Charles, 2
TBI (Taglit-Birthright Israel) program, 235–36
tefillin, 35, 36 *fig.*, 82, 82 *fig.*
Tehran, Jews in, 124–25
temples, 54–55. *See also* First Temple; Second Temple
Ten Commandments (Ten Directives), 29, 36, 37, 46, 47 *fig.*, 86. See also *mitzvot*
Tendler, Moshe, 6
textbooks, American history, 18
Theudas, 66
Thkine Imrei Shifre, 111
Thon, Jacob, 195
Thor, 212
tikkun olam, 69, 71, 106, 112, 158 *fig.*
Tillich, Paul, 117
tisch, 108 *fig.*
Titian: *Adam and Eve*, 30, 30 *fig.*
Tobiad temple (Araq el-Emir, Jordan), 54, 55
Tobiah, 55
Tobin, Gary, 243
Torah (Five Books of Moses), 8, 28–44; on anointing, 62; and the "apple," 30; in Arabic, 91; ark storage of, 37; authority of, 160–61; basic storyline of, 35–36; books of, 31; canonization of, 32; centrality/importance of, 37–38; on chosenness (*see* chosenness, Jewish); components of, 31; in cyclical ritual based in cyclical narrative, 38; Documentary Hypothesis about, 33–34; on exile, 56; God as author of, 33, 37; God as male in, 29; God depicted in, 41–42; on good and evil, 110; historicity of vs. laws contained in, 32–33, 35; humans as authors of, 33–34; on intermarriage, 233; interpretations of, 10, 30, 35, 38–41, 43–44, 82; Jewish narratives in, 29; on lineage, 42; literary criticism of, 34; as male-centric, 38, 41–42, 87; on Mount Sinai, 29; as a mystical text, 98; Oral, 34–35,